Both One and Many

Perspectives in Process Studies Series

Process Studies refers to a transdisciplinary field of study inspired by thinkers like Alfred North Whitehead, Charles Hartshorne, John B. Cobb Jr., David Ray Griffin, and many others. It's a perspective that has influenced many people around the world. The process-relational perspective is a framework for conceiving reality according to the principles of deep relationality, harmony, intrinsic value, and change. The implications of taking these principles seriously are far-reaching. From cosmology and metaphysics to ecology, psychology, religion, and beyond, the Perspectives in Process Studies book series engages a wide range of topics from a process-relational lens, harmonizing fragmented disciplinary thinking in order to develop integrated and holistic modes of understanding.

Series Editor:
Wm. Andrew Schwartz

Both One and Many

Spiritual Philosophy beyond
Theism, Materialism, and Relativism

Edited by Oliver Griebel

Foreword by Andrew M. Davis

CASCADE *Books* · Eugene, Oregon

BOTH ONE AND MANY
Spiritual Philosophy beyond Theism, Materialism, and Relativism

Perspectives in Process Studies Series

Cascade Books
An Imprint of Wipf and Stock Publishers
199 W. 8th Ave., Suite 3
Eugene, OR 97401

www.wipfandstock.com

PAPERBACK ISBN: 978-1-6667-8164-9
HARDCOVER ISBN: 978-1-6667-8165-6
EBOOK ISBN: 978-1-6667-8166-3

Cataloguing-in-Publication data:

Names: Griebel, Oliver (1964–), editor; Davis, Andrew (1987–), foreword.

Title: Both one and many : spiritual philosophy beyond theism, materialism, and relativism / edited by Oliver Griebel ; foreword by Andrew Davis.

Description: Eugene, OR: Cascade Books, 2024. | Perspectives in Process Studies Series. | Includes bibliographical references.

Identifiers: ISBN 978-1-6667-8164-9 (paperback). | ISBN 978-1-6667-8165-6 (hardcover). | ISBN 978-1-6667-8166-3 (ebook).

Subjects: LSCH: Process theology. | Philosophical theology. | Panentheism. | Materialism. | Relativism.

Classification: BT40 B61 2024 (print). | BT40 (ebook).

VERSION NUMBER 04/29/24

In Memory of John Heron
(1928–2022)

The One-Many Reality is a non-separatist dualism, a dipolar unity.
There is the One, there are the Many,
that is the duality, the dipolarity.
They are in a state of mutual compenetration,
so the One is in the Many, the Many are in the One,
all of the Many are in each of the Many
and each of the Many is in all of the Many—
and that is the non-separatism, the unity.

—JOHN HERON

Contents

Illustrations

Series Foreword

Perspectives in Process Studies

The goal of this book series is to make accessible big ideas that are too often marginalized. By big ideas I mean ambitious, comprehensive, and fundamental questions about life, truth, meaning, and more. From cosmology and metaphysics to ecology, psychology, religion, and beyond, the Perspectives in Process Studies series has been developed to engage a wide range of topics from a process-relational lens, harmonizing fragmented disciplinary thinking in order to develop integrated and holistic modes of understanding.

Process Studies refers to a transdisciplinary field of study inspired by thinkers like Alfred North Whitehead, Charles Hartshorne, John B. Cobb Jr., David Ray Griffin, and many others. It's a perspective that has influenced many people around the world. The process-relational perspective is a framework for conceiving reality according to the principles of deep relationality, harmony, intrinsic value, and change. The implications of taking these principles seriously are far-reaching.

By recognizing that all things flow, the process perspective represents an alternative to static ontologies of being. Interdependent moments of experience replace independent substances as the final real things upon which the world is made. By extending subjectivity to all living entities, process thought deems the natural world intrinsically valuable. Therefore, the process perspective is fundamentally an ecological perspective. Process thought naturalizes the supernatural and normalizes the paranormal, contributing to the development of a new cultural paradigm that can account for the kinds of experiences regularly dismissed by many other worldviews.

Deeply appreciative of the natural sciences, process thought uniquely integrates science, religion, ethics, and aesthetics. It portrays the cosmos as an organic whole analyzable into internally related processes. In this way, process thought offers a constructive postmodern alternative to the mechanistic model that still influences much scientific work and is presupposed in much humanistic literature. Articulating a relational worldview for the common good, process perspectives create positive social change toward an ecological civilization.

Books in this series combine academic rigor with broad appeal and readability. My hope is that this series will be particularly useful for students, scholars, and armchair philosophers and theologians. However, I also hope that those interested in process thought but intimidated by Whitehead's technical jargon will find value here. Some texts will be more technical than others, but together these volumes will reflect the depth and breadth of diverse perspectives in process studies.

Wm. Andrew Schwartz,

Series Editor, Executive Director, Center for Process Studies, Assistant Professor of Process Studies & Comparative Theology, Claremont School of Theology

May 23, 2022

Foreword

O ur civilizational precarity is fundamentally philosophical in nature. It has to do with dysfunctional ideas and the ways in which these ideas find destructive expression in our lives, societies, and shared planetary ecology. There is an intimate connection between thought and life that we should not soon forget. This connection undergirds the entire philosophical tradition. As Alfred North Whitehead put it, "As we think, we live."

If one is to follow Whitehead in this, insight is gained when considering our current civilization, staggering as it is through the smoking ruins of modernity and postmodernity, and choking upon the lingering fumes of their dualistic and deconstructive modes of thought. Where do we go from here? What resources do we draw upon in forging a way forward? How do we reconstruct a better future in greater harmony with the nature and character of things as they really are? While we are afforded no simple answers to these questions, one thing is certain: We must change the way we think to change the way we live. This book is a collective effort to achieve these ends.

The problem of "the One and Many" is one of the oldest quandaries of philosophy and, in this book, it functions as a framework from which to develop what editor Oliver Griebel calls "many-one thinking." The relationship between the One and the Many is a key question of metaphysics and, for this reason, it is applicable to all domains of human life and striving, whether spirituality, ecology, politics, or religion. Many-one thinking seeks integrative and relational worldviews that reach beyond modern and postmodern thinking. Its style of thought is inherently interdisciplinary, and it draws from the best of transpersonal psychology, integral thought and process philosophy, of holistic thinking, spiritual practice, and various modes of cosmic evolutionary wonder.

This book showcases many-one thinking as a collaborative and diverse endeavor, unified, yet also steeped in multiplicity. Like the intersecting worldviews variously painted in its pages, one finds unity-in-diversity to be an abiding theme. Contributors range from creative academics to freelance writers and podcasters, some of them eco-spiritual grassroots enthusiasts; and chapters develop a host of questions, issues, and debates relevant to constructing a "metamodern" (what the Claremont process tradition calls a "constructive postmodern") world that is plural, participatory, spiritually open, and infused with values as traces of an immanent divinity, variously understood.

Ours remains a time of angst and opportunity. Reconstructing a future beyond the detriments of modernism and postmodernism may start with thought, but it can hardly stay there. The contributors to this book know this well. We require not simply knowledge, but wisdom; and where **know**ledge "knows," wis**d**om "does." As you explore the various possibilities found in these pages, may the inspiration of its ideas be expressed in the deification of your deeds. "As we think, we live."

Andrew M. Davis,

Program Director

The Center for Process Studies

May 26, 2023

Contributors

Bruce Alderman is associate director of the Blue Sky Leaders program at the California Institute of Integral Studies. His publications include the article "Integral In-Dwelling" (*Consciousness* 4.4 [2016] https://digitalcommons.ciis.edu/conscjournal/vol4/iss4/2), the book chapter "Sophia Speaks" (in Schwartz and Esbjörn-Hargens, eds., *Dancing with Sophia* [SUNY Press, 2019]), and the essay "Integral Religious Pluralism" (on the blog *Integral World* [https://www.integralworld.net/alderman2.html], 2019); and he co-hosts the podcast *The Integral Stage*.

Philip Clayton is Ingram Professor of Theology at the Claremont School of Theology and president of the Institute for Ecological Civilization (EcoCiv). His publications include *In Whom We Live and Move and Have Our Being* (coeditor [Eerdmans, 2004]), *Adventures in the Spirit* (Fortress, 2008), and *The Predicament of Belief* (Oxford University Press, 2011).

Elizabeth Debold wrote *The Mother-Daughter Revolution* (coauthor [Addison-Wesley, 1993]). She is on the editorial board of German-language *evolve magazin*.

Jorge N. Ferrer was professor of psychology at the California Institute of Integral Studies in San Francisco for many years. His publications include *Revisioning Transpersonal Theory* (SUNY Press, 2002), *The Participatory Turn* (coeditor [SUNY Press, 2008]), *Participation and the Mystery* (SUNY Press, 2017), and *Love and Freedom* (Rowman & Littlefield, 2022).

Oliver Griebel is a teacher, philosopher, and translator. He has published *Der ganzheitliche Gott* (BoD, 2014) and *Wir Vielen in dieser einen Welt* (Phänomen 2019), the German-language edition of the present anthology.

Tilmann Haberer is a Protestant pastor, pastoral counselor, and systems consultant. He coauthored (with Marion and Werner Tiki Küstenmacher) *Gott 9.0* (Gütersloher, 2010), in English as *God 9.0* (self-pub., 2016 [http://gott90.de/god-9.0-english/].).

John Heron (1928–2022) taught at the University of London for many years. In 1970, he founded the first center for humanistic and transpersonal psychology in Europe. His publications include *Feeling and Personhood* (Sage, 1992), *Sacred Science* (PCCS, 1998), and *Participatory Spirituality* (Lulu, 2006).

Steve McIntosh, an integral thinker, is president of the Institute for Cultural Evolution think tank. His publications include *Developmental Politics* (Paragon House, 2020), and *Conscious Leadership* (coauthor [Portfolio, 2020]). His philosophical books are *Integral Consciousness and the Future of Evolution* (Paragon House, 2007), *Evolution's Purpose* (SelectBooks, 2012), and *The Presence of the Infinite* (Quest, 2015).

Layman Pascal, an integral thinker, has coedited the anthology *Dispatches from a Time between Worlds* (Perspectiva, 2021), and cohosts the podcast *The Integral Stage*.

Thomas Steininger is a writer and journalist. He is editor of German-language *evolve magazin* and host of the podcast *Radio evolve*.

1

Opening Remarks by the Editor[1]

Oliver Griebel

The Philosophical, Ecological, and Spiritual Challenge

The challenge for today's philosophy is enormous. And even more so for spiritual and/or religious philosophy, which tries to hint at an Ultimate Reality of some kind and link it with a meaningful human life, not being a mere meaningless by-product of an ultimately pointless and uncaring universe. Is there a deeper meaning to the ecological bottleneck modern civilization is entering? What kind of attitude and activism and politics can we really adopt about it? Philosophy should also try to understand, try to think about possible ways out of the culture wars, which to a large extent are the revolt of still more traditional, often deeply religious cultures and milieus against our hypermodern civilization. Can a philosophy which has understood the lessons of modern life and the modern worldview, not only value but justify what matters to so many people, especially family and work and nation and religion, can it value and justify a sense of belonging and identity? Can we set humane limits (and how, economically and politically?!) to the obvious problems of human-unfriendly structures due to urban sprawl, consumerism, and what I would call cultural and intellectual *neglect*? Can we set limits to antisocial and antidemocratic mechanisms in modern technocivilization?

And, last but not least, can there be a spiritual and religious philosophy which is up-to-date, which accepts, indeed builds upon the results of modern science in terms of natural explanation and Big History? This is a problem for sure, since natural sciences, even without any materialist agenda involved, quite simply undermine many narratives of time-honored religion about humans, society, and nature, in many cases proving that nothing of

1. Translated and revised by the author.

1

that kind has ever happened. In his 2012 book *Evolutionaries*, Carter Phipps nicely gets to the heart of the problem, writing about a meeting with the keen and flamboyant thinker Howard Bloom:

> Unfortunately, as Bloom mentioned, as soon as you start invoking the word 'mystery', people tend to get nervous and think that the next thing you are going to do is start invoking supernatural forces and ancient omnipotent deities to explain it.[2]

Now, mystery (or a sense of wonder or of the sublime) are arguably the most *noncommittal* forms of spiritual or religious feelings. And it will prove to be challenging to modernize the very *committed* premodern claims which traditional religions made and still make about God, about what is natural and what supernatural. All great religions, Western and Eastern, were founded long before modernity, even before (or apart from) the hints of critically intellectual and liberal and emancipatory achievements in ancient Greek and Roman civilization. A modern reform thus would certainly have to radically change them, way beyond Martin Luther's Reformation for example. Of course, nobody wants to impose any kind of faith or creed on anybody, but if religion and spirituality are supposed to save modern civilization from self-destructing, they will have to be _not less than modern_, which presupposes that they will have integrated what being modern persons can teach us. This, after all, is one main idea of many-one thinking: integrating what seems to be opposing but really is complementing.

There are other main concerns, and one of them has to be addressed right from the start, because this book is very unusual in today's spiritual and religious literature, not only but especially in this respect: as an editor, I wanted to host two kinds of thinkers that are both many-one: who agree that there is the one ultimate unity of Being encompassing the stunning diversity of beings, and who also agree that this One is more than just matter or nature—that it's spirit—and yet who disagree about what this spirit ultimately is. Spirit is consciousness, this much seems clear to me, but what is consciousness? There is a parting of ways at this point, and it is crucial to understand it. Roughly, there are those for whom spirit, and therefore persons and God *per se* is what is aware of itself, what is self-knowing and self-reflecting; and there are those others for whom spirit, whether a divine spirit or a human mind, is "no-self," lacks selfhood, and *ultimately* isn't aware that it exists, and what it is. These alternatives, alas, not only contradict each other; they are plainly contrary. Whoever finds a way to mitigate this difference, please contact me so I can put you forward for the

---

2. Phipps, *Evolutionaries*, 112.

Templeton Prize. I doubt anyone will. Some think they can unite the two perspectives, but really they engage in some kind of inclusivism, telling the other side that, yes, spirit is in important respects *virtually* self-aware (or indeed, conversely, no-self), but that *just ultimately* it is not. This inclusion, which is a gentle form of reduction, is not forbidden or baneful in itself, I think; it's even a legitimate and honest thing to do . . . as long as we don't try to mask inclusion as a consensus (which it is not), because in the present case we say about other people that the God or the Divine they believe in ultimately is not as they believe it to be. Again, this difference of perspective is no problem, but let's be honest about it.

This deeper dive into philosophy right from the start is important, because otherwise you won't understand the choice of thinkers I made for this essay collection. And mind you, this difference between a no-self Divine and a God aware of him- or herself is not something merely academic or intellectual. It reflects a major difference between Western and Eastern religion (and the way they see personhood). Inside Western cultures and nations, it reflects a difference between people who call themselves religious (most often you recognize them because they are talking about "God") and those who call themselves spiritual (more often talking about "the Divine"). Note that according to a poll by the Public Religion Research Institute (PRRI), from the year 2017,[3] 18 percent of American adults identified as "spiritual but not religious." The formula seems to have been coined by Robert C. Fuller in his 2012 book *Spiritual, but not Religious: Understanding Unchurched America*.[4]

Furthermore, speaking of broader public discourse, the divine self or no-self division also still reflects the difference between (mostly university-based) theologians and (mostly freelance) spiritual thinkers, writers, and podcasters. Of course, as always there are gray zones in between the extremes, and bridge-builders (you can find some of them in this book), but the separation is there, plain to see. And indeed, there is a lived difference between the faith in the goodness and power, wisdom and justice of God, versus the mystical, especially meditative experience of participating in a Divine that not only transcends confessions, but is "void," meaning that it transcends anything, not just selfhood, but any of the above-mentioned "rather religious" qualities attributed to Ultimate Reality.

One of the purposes in making this anthology has been to house both "rather religious" and "rather spiritual" versions of many-one thinking, to

---

3. Raney et al., *Searching for Spirituality*.

4. The slogan was popularized by Fuller's book, but it was not he who invented it. For more detail, check out Wikipedia, s.v. "Spiritual but not religious."

call for acceptance of difference and to focus on common ground, which is the belief that the multitude of beings are all part of the one and only Being, which, whatever it may be, is not a purely physical universe or world formula, is no physical or otherwise ultimate "stuff," and is not just dead, insensate, inanimate matter. The approaches and styles of many-one thinking, even beyond the self-aware/no-self question, are quite diverse, and this is the main reason why this book is an anthology. In fact, I have to confess that it bores me to just set out my own views and in the process crudely sketch other options. I prefer letting them speak for themselves, showing off and contrasting them in concert with my own way to approach *die letzten Dinge*, ultimate things.

For those less familiar with literary and academic terms: an *anthology* is a collection of texts introducing into a subject matter or a way of thinking. This may sound somewhat intimidating, like something especially for an audience of experts, which is exactly what is *not* intended with this book. While it is true that most of the authors have studied or are teaching philosophy, psychology, or theology, the present collection comprises only two contributions in a stricter academic form (Bruce Alderman's and Jorge Ferrer's). Most of them are essays in the more relaxed sense the term is often used, that is, texts which aim to inform and critically compare; which can locate themselves in a broader context; which take position in a personal and engaged way; which consequently are not as sober stylistically as academic papers, either. And this opening chapter that you are reading is deliberately even less formal than the rest, in order to lower the inhibition or intimidation threshold still a bit more. This is important, since a worldview or spirituality that people outside academic circles cannot understand won't help with the rethinking and rebuilding that our civilization urgently needs. The texts collected in this book therefore try to make it as easy as possible for the reader, intellectually—albeit not easier. Philosophy is complex and diverse, as the world is, and it can't help challenging simplistic thinking habits and comfortable narrow preconceptions.

Many-One Thinking

This is also why the philosophical and spiritual stance which I call *many-one thinking* cannot lock itself up in one of the many academic ivory towers. Indeed, philosophy by its very meaning must not, for it isn't just one domain of science or humanities among others. Philosophy is about all things, about the world or cosmos or Being (or whatever you like to call it) *taken as a whole*. And many-one philosophy, as a holistic approach, can't help going for this wholeness again. Why "again"—has philosophy ever stopped seeking such wholeness? Both modern and postmodern philosophy largely have, and for decades. Whoever has read some modern, materialistic philosophy, or postmodern, relativistic philosophy, will have noticed that both of them have great problems even acknowledging the unity and coherence of everything, the world as a whole, "the One," as it is called in this book.

Postmodern thinking often dismisses this kind of ultimate coherence or wholeness as a conceptually impossible, likely patronizing, colonialist, totalitarian endeavor. But while this may be an argument against worldviews that see the universe as a fixed set or static order of things, it certainly is not a problem for "the One" of many-one thinking, *which is a dynamic and open wholeness and coherence.*

Modern materialism in turn, with its "theories of everything," which certainly isn't afraid itself of fixed sets or static orders of things, nevertheless mocks the world-as-a-whole whenever this notion is meant to really acknowledge everything, all kinds of entities and phenomena, not only the ones that natural sciences feel able to pin down and quantify, but also the ones that social and human sciences and indeed common sense would insist have to be seriously discussed, especially what living beings and persons are and what influences them.

We therefore need a holism reaching beyond both modernist and postmodernist thinking. However, not a holism in the one-sided sense some thinkers are using it, that is, reducing individuals to the wholeness they are part of. Many-one thinking says that the world or cosmos or Being is both *unifying*, through coherence and relationship and meaning and spirit, and at the same time essentially *plural*, home of distinct individuals that cannot be reduced to the cosmic and spiritual unity encompassing them.

Consequently, this book is not presenting *the* holistic way of thinking, but a diversity of thinkers sharing their views on the unity in which we all live. Any interesting philosophy is the fruit of a person who composes decades of experience and reflection and meditation on life and society, putting the notions that are the pieces of our basic worldview-language puzzle together in her or his very own, unmistakable way. And each of the many wonderful thinkers humanity has brought forth is very different from any other, is very individual (ironically even the very anti-individualist ones like French postmodern 1960s and '70s thinkers Michel Foucault—talking about "the death of Man"[5]—or Gilles Deleuze—replacing the individual with "the dividual"[6]). Or just think of the many spiritual authors who are

5. Foucault, *Order of Things.*
6. Deleuze, "Postscript."

selling their personal teachings as *the* impersonal divine revelation, when their influences, their personal moods and styles and approaches, their biases and weaknesses are so plain so see. Let us accept at last what distinguishes us as individuals, what divides us into (still diverse) opposing camps, and what even then still unites us.

The Delicate G-Word

Let us now go back a bit to the no-self-Divine or self-aware-God basic choice in spiritual-religious philosophy, also polarizing thinkers otherwise united by many-one ideas, with a "centrist" gray zone in between, which is made of the thinkers who hesitate or refuse to join one side, thinking they can dismiss the basic alternative, gloss over it, or mediate between the opposing camps. It is important to see that this difference between spiritual and religious thinkers has to do with the rather personal or nonpersonal way in which one experiences the One. Is it knowing you, understanding you, caring about you, *personally*? Or is it, for all its serenity and generosity and luminosity felt in meditation, so "void" that it ultimately even goes beyond the qualities of self-reflection, intentionality, sense-making, responsiveness, care . . . qualities precisely of the kind many think make persons "the image of God"? Spiritual-religious philosophy will remain as scattered into splinter groups as it is now—with groups bickering or belittling or playing down or mutually reducing or talking past one another or simply looking the other way—unless it seriously deals with and welcomes those who choose the other (opposing) basic view and unites around shared convictions and engagements.

So, in order to build a broad new philosophy current together beyond strict old-time religion, materialism, and relativism, I suggest, an encounter on par with spirituality and religion, an encounter with the Divine and God, has to take place. Yet, this won't be possible unless rather spiritual-minded people stop rallying with materialists, bashing their shared bogeyman-preconception of God. The so-called *theistic* concept of God, which separates the Divine from the world and beings and persons, is definitely outdated. But *panentheistic* and *cosmic-holistic* approaches, with their all-pervading and all-encompassing, not-less-than-personal God certainly are not. They are many-one. What indeed could be more natural than calling a self-aware wholeness or One . . . *God*? Unfortunately, in continental Europe, and even more so in the English-speaking world, whenever the word "God" is mentioned, many if not most people automatically understand "the Lord of the Scriptures," God, as Christian (and other monotheistic) confessions or theologies see "Him." Yet, the idea of a self-aware Spirit or Being or Coherence of the world need not justify itself by means of any special tradition, authority, or revelation anymore. It moves on from them anyway while trying to preserve their humane and cosmic and spiritual essence. Thus, the present essay collection tries to show that the Many-One *need not* be seen, but *can very well* be seen as the complementarity between everything there is, and the wholeness of it all, conceived as Spirit in the sense that *it is endowed with reflexivity, aware of itself—loosely speaking: knowing that it is, knowing what it is, knowing what it brings forth*. Not as a precondition, but as an option just as respectable spiritually as the void-Spirit, no-self alternative.

Now, many spiritual people today will challenge just this, telling you that you should not distinguish between the One and the Many, indeed that there can't be many distinct beings, ultimately, because this separates things and people and the Divine from one another, where in fact there is what's often called *nonduality*: not many, not two, strictly speaking not even one. Mind you that this is not the same thing as the *voidness* teachings, which deny that the Divine can have any quality, for otherwise it couldn't be ultimately encompassing. However, nonduality, which comes from Hindu theology, and voidness, which comes from Buddhist theology, have been amalgamated by quite a few Western spiritual thinkers. In this vein, the argument against a God aware of "himself" would be that s/he could not be all-encompassing because a self-aware God would be unable to encompass all that is un-self-aware. However this not so obvious at all; instead this idea may result from confusing (contradicting) dualism and (complementing) duality.

If we consider the Many and the One to be ultimately complementary, it is perfectly sound to suggest that the One can be aware of itself and the Many it encompasses, while the Many inside the One can be only more or less conscious and self-conscious, depending on what kind of beings they are, and what their relation to the One, to themselves, and among themselves is. This would mean that the Many-One is/are *both* aware *and* unaware of itself/themselves, rather than *neither* aware *nor* unaware.

The Bottleneck in Civilizational Evolution

This being said, suppose that one day people believing in a no-self Divine, and those believing in a self-aware God, accept that the other approach or faith is neither flawed nor pointless—aren't both of them idle anyway, being unworldly and . . . hopeless in the face of our failing modern civilization? Indeed, with our civilization's mad hubris that is heading heedlessly towards self-destruction, even still accelerating its kamikaze course, many people quite simply have lost the hope that there can be an encompassing One *of any kind* wherein humankind could find a meaningful place. Many are asking themselves: How could there possibly be a real meaning for us humans on this Earth—mistreated by ourselves!—inside an indifferent, pointless, merciless universe?

One possible answer, advocated by myself and others in this book, is: The cosmos is neither dead nor indifferent, and the very crisis of nature and culture we experience has its genuine meaning in the evolution of humankind. The moment of truth, the *kairos* we are facing is so enormous . . . it just makes sense. If there is some deeper meaning to our human existence and condition, then even the mere coexistence, mess, blockade, and conflict in which we and our countless fellow humans often live, must be an essential part of this meaning, even the way in which we collectively are acting and working against the biosphere we share, against our very future, makes sense. Indeed, the survival crisis of modern civilization forces us to face the fact that if we want to remain a humane civilization, we have to evolve, we just have to become much more conscious about our place on Earth and in the cosmos. Only by struggling to save nature and culture, only by struggling with and for ourselves, against the overexploiting, reckless, and ignorant beings we now are, you and me included, will we have a chance to get through the ecological and civilizational bottleneck that keeps narrowing as we keep on "humanspreading." It's been years, maybe decades since we have unbalanced nature (as it has been since the end of the last ice age about ten thousand years ago) to such an extent that we will have to prepare for many decades of permanent crisis. If we rise to this challenge, we will grow, and grow up with the crisis—nationally and internationally, humanely and socially, culturally and in terms of worldview, and even spiritually.

The idea of humankind *culturally and spiritually evolving*—not just biologically, but also in an evolution of social life and values, of politics and economy, of worldview and science—was a major concern of mine when I decided to try and set up a book project like this. For I believe that our civilization cannot be saved unless quite a few people especially in the Western world evolve beyond late-modern materialism, in terms of their worldview and self-conception, in terms of their conception of what a human being is, and in terms of their conception of how we in fact live and ought to live together. However, the notion of a human and cultural evolution, which in turn is part of a planetary and cosmic evolution, needs clarifying. "Evolution" in this broad and broadest context of an evolving Many-One on Earth and in the cosmos isn't supposed to mean a development or "unfolding" toward some foregone standard religion or enlightenment, toward a standard path to a "New Earth" or otherwise standard salvation. Experience from life, science, and history shows that healthily and freely evolving people tend to become in the process more conscious of the individuals they are, not less—while there may be spiritual forces at work which are making these same people's attitudes and intentions broadly converge. This should be kept in mind when authors in this anthology are speaking about human beings *evolving* culturally, spiritually, and in terms of how they see the world and live their lives.

The Three-Cultures War

One of the ideas I wanted to confess in myself in communion with others thinkers, through this book, is that an evolution of humankind beyond the world-dominating modernist civilization, an evolution that may help humane civilization survive on this planet, that may help us live together in a sustainable and solidary manner, and to become better persons for others and ourselves—such an evolution will have to be, if anything, an integration of cultures that now are indifferently coexisting in disdain towards or in hateful strife with one another. In the late '60s and early '70s the cultural and intellectual influence of (but also the divide between) tradition and modernity, and the so-called postmodern counterculture (what we may also call alternative or green culture) arising against both of them shaped my whole growing up.

I have always felt that we do need traditional values for cultures to learn and live and save and hand down a sense of where they came from and what they grew out of. And we need postmodern values in order to transform a rampant modern civilization into a sustainable one—a need which the family-church-and-nation (traditional) mindset even now blatantly fails to even understand. Yet in my lifetime, under the crushing rule of money and under increasing output and technocratic system constraints, the frictions and repulsions between what I'd like to call "the three cultures" have escalated (not least in the US) into a war of cultures that by now has begun to erode the very foundations of a healthy modern society whose economy and democracy are trying to work for all people.

"All people"—this cannot mean all humans who will ever live, but for sure it must include our children and grandchildren. For there is no way around it: the self-undermining culture-war dynamics keep us from tackling an even more fatal problem, the enormity of our war against nature, which is now becoming a catastrophe of geological dimensions, made possible and enhanced by technological progress and population growth. The war of cultures and the war against nature combined could destroy in a matter of decades modern middle-class nations, the humane standards they have achieved, and the natural resources upon which they have built their well-being, should we continue in the same style and at the same pace we've kept for the last sixty years. I have been sensing this since I was a youth in the late '70s, when books like the Club of Rome report, the Global 2000 study and the book *Das Ende der Vorsehung*[7] (meaning *The End of Providence*) by German eco-philosopher Carl Amery opened my eyes.

Overcoming modernism for me means *saving modernity from itself*, not destroying it. It's just the overwhelming, nearly totalitarian rule of modern economy and the materialistic worldview associated with it that must be overcome. The modern parts of our civilization which are valuable must finally be integrated with the traditional and alternative ones. There can be no going back to before modernity for us, but we cannot go on with our over-exploitation of nature either—given our technological means and impact, given the number of people on Earth, given also the extent of environmental damage already done. As I said, one aspect of many-one thinking certainly is the unity in diversity of traditional, modern, and green-alternative culture. The idea of integrating these even gave *integral* thinking its name (coined by philosopher Jean Gebser back in the 1940s). The hope behind it is to integrate the strengths of the three cultures while overcoming their respective self-destructive sides so that we can reach a new level of civilization which would be traditional, modern, and alternative at once—and more.

The Complementarity of the Universal and the Concrete/Historical

Very well . . . but what have philosophers, psychologists and theologians to contribute to this? Of course, there is no pure "philosophy of climate crisis" or "philosophy of mass extinction." However, there is a thinking which can help us learn from the crisis of culture and nature, help us see ourselves as many parts of the one humankind on the one planet Earth in the one cosmos. Philosophy in general is not only about ultimate principles, ideas, or concepts; it is also about our history and present—about modern life and the crisis of modernity we experience—about your and my personal life—about the multifaceted mixture of history, cultures, and persons we are and live in. The ideal or universal and the concrete or individual together form a polarity as well, I suggest.

And many-one thinking actually is a thinking in polarities, in complementing contrasts. *One* such contrast is the one between history and reality and life, on the one hand, and the order of things and ultimate reality on the other. These are like entangled arms, or two hands washing each other: one

7. Amery, *Ende.*

arm or one hand won't do. In many-one thinking, as I see it, complementarity, polarity, and duality are fundamental—and even ultimate. One pole is the many people and their individualities and biographies inside their many communities inside the history of humankind inside the many life-forms on our planet inside this evolving universe of stars and planets, the sprouting and branching of novelty and individuality inside the cosmos. The other pole is the cosmos as a frame and potential, its natural order, the coherence of its evolution emerging step by step, its meaning and spirit as a whole.

Surely not all people will be able to develop a many-one consciousness about the place of humankind in the world at large, and those who will be able to do so may not be as many as quickly, as humankind will need them. We can only hope that larger groups within many populations, especially among the elites who make decisions at larger scales (not merely in private or as consumers and citizens) and who influence public opinion, will rethink and change their ways and views, in order for us to tackle the disruptions as yet unavoidable on Earth and in its biosphere, and in order to implement the necessary adaptations to and transformations of our economical system and way of life, workplaces and infrastructure, democratic states and international cooperation. This changing of our views and ways will not lead to "the one" philosophy or religion; instead it will remain an open mindset, a broad frame of looking at the world and ourselves and (for some) also spirituality: the awareness of a humankind composed of many distinct individuals, families, milieus, and cultures, which at the same time are a community of fate on this one planet, in this one world.

The one world, *the one* universe, *the one* cosmos—is this One supposed not merely to *be* something, but also *do* something *with* us, maybe even *for* us, in a way remotely similar to what we would expect, say, from a caring parent? Does the One involve and engage your and my personhood and our lives and life-worlds inside the one world, offering us a "belonging"? Something like a home in this one world, and meaning in our lives? Might there even be some kind of healing or salvation coming from it? There are no obvious answers about what the spirit of the One and its power may be or cannot be, but the questions can't be avoided, and you will find quite a few explorations and hints about these in the present volume.

How I Came to "Think Many-One," and How an Anthology Came Out of It

Why, in fact, have I put together this collection of texts? Did I believe that this group of authors would be especially apt to address these issues and ask this kind of questions, in a many-one spirit? Actually yes. I somehow managed to convince almost every thinker whose writings had convinced me over the years to join the project (except Edgar Morin, the doyen of what he calls *complex thought*, whom I haven't even managed to contact, his French publisher not deigning to even answer an email of mine).

But this was only the last step in a long personal and philosophical path. Let me give you an idea of the roots and ripening of my own many-one ideas, for this may help you better understanding the book. In the mid-1990s I studied philosophy and logic, mostly analytic philosophy, the most modern-minded of all currents. As enthusiastic as I was about its conceptual rigor and its insisting that reasonable arguments be given, I was equally irritated and even revolted by the crude and brute materialism of this way of thinking. In fact, many analytic philosophers spent immense intellectual energy denying the human mind any freedom and power of its own (with respect to basic physical laws and matter as they define them) and denying spirit any reality beyond the human mind. What was hiding behind all this effort, quite obviously, was the wish not to leave open any gap, however small, through which anything whatsoever divine could keep or find any place inside modern thinking.

As unhappy as I was with this kind of materialism and atheism, I also was nearly as unhappy with the postmodern-alternative (as the name already implies) counterculture against tradition and modernity in which I grew up myself in the 1970s. The many-colored esotericism felt too simple and arbitrary to me, it did not even bother to live up, in an informed and critical way, to the facts we know today about the history of our planet and humankind, about the order of nature and life, about societies and cultures around the world, and about worldviews and religions. Moreover, while sharing the wish to fight traditional bondage and modern exploitation, I found it unrealistic to dream about the billions of people living in urbanized and technologically advanced civilization collectively "dropping out" and returning to nature in small, self-sustaining, and sustainable eco-communities.

Needless to say, the middle-class entrenching behind homestead and homeland and God, which I could so well observe in my own native Bavaria, wasn't a solution for me either, especially along with such a nature-adverse consumerism and shameless profiteering from an antisocial globalization. However, having grown up in a little village, I felt how important the rootedness in family and home, neighborhood and landscape, in common language, culture, and religion is.

Whoever wants to make democratic politics for humankind as a whole and for an environment in which we can live decently and humanely must take along, as it were, the traditional cultures and the milieus living and thinking traditionally. He or she must learn to accept that traditional-thinking people are just different from people in green-alternative professions or subcultures or mindsets, and different from the marginalized minorities they hold dear.

I was aware of this in the '90s already, but back then I could not have imagined the conservative and the alternative-minded converging culturally and politically the way they have today in some European countries, not least in Germany. Why is that? I believe that many people who think in a more traditional manner are beginning to understand just how pressing the ecological emergency is, and that the social and cultural and political neglect of "ordinary people" is threatening the quality of life for ordinary citizens and the power of Western middle classes to steer their nations politically.

As a philosophy student I tried to figure out some way to reconcile tradition, modernity, and alternative culture, not only in ecological and social respect, but also spiritually: Was it even possible to make a sound synthesis between God, a scientific worldview and postmodern mysticism? At university, there was no place for such a vision and ambition, anyway. After my master's thesis in 1997, I could not find a way to make a living and continue my studies, and this was the provisional end of the road for me as an academic philosopher, or at least as someone writing and speaking as a philosopher to the public and getting any attention.

In hindsight, I think that back then I also lacked life experience, the time it takes to mature as a philosopher. For it took me a number of years until I was able to take my next philosophical step, sketching my ideas in the book *Der ganzheitliche Gott* (The holistic God), in 2009. During the 2010s I discovered, one after another, philosophers who seemed to share my concerns about evolving our civilization and worldview. I discovered that others too had understood that overcoming the culture wars, this hateful and ignorant mutual blockade, was already becoming a matter of life and death for humane civilization: I explored integral philosophy and Spiral Dynamics, process theology and panentheism, transpersonal psychology and its continuation called participatory thinking, but also complex thought according to Edgar Morin—to name just the ones that most caught my attention over those years.

The civilizational-and-spiritual-evolution scenes I became familiar with are quite diverse. The scene in German-speaking countries is strongly influenced by the ideas of US thinker Ken Wilber (which he calls "Integral Theory"[8]); the French scene is much more dominated by adherents to Spiral

---

8. Wilber partly built on older approaches that already called themselves "integral,"

Dynamics ideas inspired by Clare Graves and his disciples Don Beck and Christopher Cowan, who were American thinkers too. In the United States themselves, the cultural-evolution scene is much more complex still. What I became aware of was that so far neither Wilber nor Beck nor most other spiritual writers[9] had managed or at least seriously tried to bring to bear this new Western school of personal-and-cultural-and-cosmic-evolution thought in all its *unity in diversity*. Rather, most spiritual thinkers seemed far too dogmatic and one-sided, with too much insider theory and too little practiced plurality.

I realized that there might be here a challenge for me to take on. Not the challenge to unite or lead in the sense of proposing an overarching theory pigeonholing all the other approaches, but the challenge of letting them approach things differently, and at the same time fostering the common values and the dialogue, eliciting the different little scenes, as it were, out of their shells. Surely this cannot be achieved by a single person or single book, the present anthology can only be a first attempt; yet it seems a natural format in order to practice the unity in diversity so many are merely preaching.

What for? Precisely for the necessary changing of our ways and views, as persons and as groups and cultures and societies and as the community of nations. It simply won't be enough to blog and podcast and publish a little here and there in minuscule groups, apart from what remains of the general public in our Western nations. When it comes to rethinking and rebuilding our nations in tight global cooperation, these "general publics" will become crucial; in democratic nations they will have to acknowledge and take responsibility for our most earnest situation and prospects, and they will have to vote for and take to the streets for and pay for and in many practical everyday-life ways contribute to the urgently needed system change. We are heading for disruption anyway, but if in our Western nations, middle-class-voter majorities don't form and assume responsible political action and also build true publics open for a thinking beyond culture wars, then we are bound for headless and helpless and hopeless decay.

Let me be clear: Even "general" publics and "majorities" of voters nowadays most often are minorities which in turn are partly orienting

---

notably by Gebser and Aurobindo, and there are other integral theories than Wilber's, for example Steve McIntosh's (some of it presented by himself in this anthology); therefore Integral Theory (Wilber) is not *the one and only proper and original* integral theory, a possible misappropriation problem which can be avoided by simply distinguishing the notion of *integral* in the larger sense, and "Integral" (with a big *I*), the name of Ken Wilber's specific integral theory.

9. Notable exceptions like Steve McIntosh, the podcaster team Layman Pascal and Bruce Alderman (coauthors in this anthology too), podcaster Jeff Salzman, or the late Terry Patten only confirm the rule.

themselves by even much smaller groups of elites, role models, multipliers, influential people. Whatever you like to call these, and whatever you think about the fact that people not always and only think for themselves—as things stand, there seem to be a limited number of us having the willingness and confidence and assurance and energy and influence to help the peoples of the world change the course of our gridlocked system. Something like 10 percent of the population? Individual changes in behavior won't be enough: many media people and politicians at all levels, many investors and managers and entrepreneurs, many NGO workers and activists will have to change their attitudes and work together. I am convinced that they can inspire and carry along majorities—the people.

We live in democracies, and if a relative majority of people doesn't take the helm and defend democracy, reckless rich people and resentful populist masses and determined fanatics will infiltrate, take over, and undermine democracy. Now we just can't experiment with this planet long enough until a majority of people will have learned from experience how and why groupthink and materialism defeat themselves on a global and historical scale. That's why I think that worldviews which advocate unity in diversity, cultural evolution and integration, will have to address the multicolored "10 percent" vanguard which can inspire and encourage and partly also guide and organize the peoples of the world.

Many-one philosophy and spirituality, including broader psychological and sociopolitical pictures about human beings, likely cannot reach most ordinary people, "the masses," being too intellectual, since we simply have not enough time left, ecologically. Instead, they must make themselves heard in what is left of a general educated public, be noticed and taken seriously by what is left of influential and serious mainstream media, at least in the Western world. At present, let us face it, we are far from gaining any such public attention for unity-in-diversity thinking. And this failure to yield public resonance has been going on for about twenty-five years, even with its most influential versions, which are Integral Theory and Spiral Dynamics. I felt it was time to try it in a different way, make this book, introducing many-one thinking through a quite diverse selection of thinkers, in order to show people there are ways beyond—not regressing back from—a modernity without much future.

Frankly, even when I invited my coauthors to join, I had my doubts if Western nations (I can't speak for other parts of the world) as they live and feel and see themselves, have a chance to change as much as quickly as needed. I don't even know if ecologically and politically we still have the time to make an impact with a new worldview synthesis going in the direction I sketched above. New paradigms, even those whose time has come, usually take a long time to spread.

But if you don't try, you can only fail. If you engage in any heartfelt concern and try to share it with others and they won't take you seriously and value the work you can give, then your very self-esteem is heavily affected. Anyone who believes he or she has something special to say or give, runs this risk. I felt this too, when I contacted the thinkers I liked and thought were many-one-minded, being myself a philosophical nobody. However, not to try wasn't an option. Indeed, I had a vision and believed in these other thinkers and had ideas of my own I thought were worthwhile . . and I have two children who one day may ask me, and probably will: What did you know? *When* did you know?[10]

So I decided to contact per email some of the persons who over the years had "caught my eye" as being special in terms of openness to other approaches, as critical and self-critical, and as advancing many-one think-ing in an original way. I sounded out a bit and eventually invited them to contribute an essay to an anthology. In the process, there have been two experiences which have become important impulses to the project.

The first one was making contact with the American philosopher and theologian Philip Clayton—around 2012—very open and friendly and re-spectful from the start, when I really was still intimidated by the complex project and the "big shots"—as compared to myself—involved. Second, in 2013, there was the truly special experience of discovering (through a ca-sual hint by a dear Facebook friend of mine, Timothy Saunders) the English transpersonal psychologist and philosopher John Heron, in whose book *Feeling and Personhood* I found, to my utter amazement, a version of the basic metaphysical many-one idea, published much earlier (in 1992) than the version I had advocated in my own 2009 book *Der ganzheitliche Gott*, which from my knowledge of the history of philosophy I had thought was novel: *the polarity and duality and entanglement of the cosmic-spiritual One (or Wholeness) with the Many (or Multitude) it encompasses.*

John Heron called this idea "the One-Many." And I was lucky to find all the other authors willing to accept something like this as a broad frame for our common concern, without them having to share in detail John Heron's (or my own) ideas about what this One-Many ultimately might be.

---

10. This question was asked, in a documentary I saw years ago, by US meteorolo-gist Paul Douglas, a most unlikely figure, a conservative-evangelical climate-crisis ad-monisher. In 2016, this brave and charming man published the book, coauthored with Mitch Hescox, *Caring for Creation: The Evangelical's Guide to Climate Change and a Healthy Environment.*

To emphasize that the scope of the idea is broader than John's approach, in this book it is normally referred to as "the Many-One."[11]

Initially, the plan was to publish the anthology in English first, for most of the coauthors are writing in English, and their target audience therefore quite naturally isn't the German-speaking cultural sphere. But it turned out that in the English-speaking publishing scene the divide between the "serious" university presses for academics and the "popular" publishing houses for intellectually not-so-ambitious literature may even be wider than in the German publishing landscape. Anthologies which aim to be accessible for the educated general public seem to be neither popular nor academic enough, as I had to learn. Not in the US or the UK, nor in Germany for that matter. Eventually the opportunity for a German edition presented itself in the person of one-man publishing house Tom Amarque and his Phänomen Verlag, who had already published Steve McIntosh's book *Integral Consciousness* in German, years earlier.

This was in 2019. Years later, I still had no idea whom to approach in order to publish the anthology in English. In 2022, I wanted to finally settle the problem by publishing the volume "on demand." In a last desperate try

---

11. For a long time I thought it was I myself who had coined this term. But, no, in fact it seems to be theologian Catherine Keller who first used the term "Manyone," in her 2003 book *Face of the Deep* . . . using "Manyone," mind you, not the hyphenated "the Many-One" of the present anthology, and using the term in a different sense. Many-One thinking, as I understand it, is in a stricter sense metaphysical: it is not much into biblical exegesis (except for Tilmann Haberer's contribution, to an extent); it is independent of the authority attributed to revelatory texts in general. And while it clearly goes beyond the scope of the present book to do justice to the theological and emancipatory intricacies of the *divine Manyone* (my italics) as Keller describes it, let me still try to give you a flavor of it, in order to get at the difference as well as at a certain relatedness compared to the *cosmic Many-One* that I am talking about. "Manyone" is Keller's explanation-interpretation of the puzzling plural of the first biblical name for God, which is *Elohim*, introduced in Gen 1:2, where his/her/their spirit or breath (*ruach*) is said to "hover upon the face of the waters." Indeed, in her Pre/Face to *Face of the Deep*, she writes that "[Chapter 10 of the book] . . . observes Elohim burst into a 'Manyone' of elementals and angels." (Keller, *Face of the Deep*, xx) And later on, still about the divine Manyone she writes: "Such a theology, neither monistic nor dualistic, prepares a pluralism not of many separate ones but of plurisingularities, of interdependent individuations, constantly coming, flowing, through one another." (Keller, *Face of the Deep*, 179). This is not quite what the present anthology tries to convey with the notion of the Many-One. Yet another observation of Keller's seems to indicate that there is an affinity all the same. Indeed, as she compares her Manyone with Whitehead's notorious dictum "The Many become One" (Whitehead, *Process and Reality*, 21), Keller also comments on another nearly as famous passage in Whitehead, *Process and Reality*, 348, which she quotes: "Only in relation to what we call creation can what we call Creator be signified, i.e. be imagined to exist. 'It is as true to say that God creates the world, as that the world creates God'" (Keller, *Face of the Deep*, 181).

I approached Andrew Davis, a young theologian whom Philip Clayton had kindly introduced me to years earlier, asking Andrew if maybe he had an idea. He gave me the advice to submit a proposal to Wipf and Stock Publishers. It was early December 2022 when I got the OK from them. Only a few days earlier, alas, I had got the message, again from Tim Saunders, that John Heron had just died, at age ninety-four.[12] I dedicate this book to him and his legacy, little known outside the transpersonal-psychology community, and least for his metaphysical ideas.

Introducing the Contributors in This Anthology

Let me now introduce the coauthors of this volume with their contributions. For all their unity in terms of civilizational, humane achievements, social justice and sharing, emancipation, individuation-participation, and ecological rebuilding, these are quite diverse among themselves, and there is the risk that the reader will fail to grasp what the essays can contribute by highlighting, each in its own way, the vision of a many-one worldview. Thus I will try and hint at how they cohere and complement one another through the way I have strung them together. The composition of an anthology is a delicate task. Which author appears in which position, and is anyone more appreciated or depreciated in the process? For me, several aspects have been most important: To what degree does a contribution introduce or deepen a many-one worldview? How accessible or challenging is the essay for philosophical laypeople? Is it an original contribution or a reprint from another publication?

It was important for me to put John Heron's essay first, and Philip Clayton's second. In my view, John's simply is the new classic articulation of many-one spirituality and philosophy. John gave us a new classic, but he is not the inventor. There have certainly been pioneers, like Whitehead, who in *Process and Reality* wrote: "The many become one, and are increased by one."[13] It is not this book's ambition to trace a history of the considerable number of philosophers and mystics, ancient and modern, who thought it was facile to reduce the Many to the One, or in a more modern and postmodern fashion, the One to the Many. To name but a few, Plotinus, Ramanuja, Aquinas, and Hartshorne, as well as numerous Christian Trinity

---

12. An overview of John Heron's work can be obtained on the website https://johnheron-archive.co.uk/books/.

13. See Whitehead, *Process and Reality*, 21. As an aside, although the present volume is published in Cascade's Perspectives in Process Studies series, it is not a process-philosophical book in any narrower sense. Even Philip Clayton is not really a disciple of Whitehead, Hartshorne, Cobb, or Griffin. However, the process perspective of each many-one approach that I know is strong and obvious.

theologians, have tried to value the relationship between the divine One and its many creatures . . . usually positing, however, that the Many ultimately depended upon the One, but not vice versa.

The idea of a radical *mutual* dependence of the One and the Many is something different. Whitehead has it, with a possible slight preponderance given to the Many. Still, to my knowledge, John Heron was the first thinker who metaphysically started with the very idea of an ultimate complementing *duality* (which is anything but an incongruous *dualism*!) between the One and the Many.

This sets a counterpoint with respect to the so-widespread spiritual approaches in the tradition of the Buddhist thinker-anti-thinker Nagarjuna, so-called *nondual* approaches. I say "anti-thinker" because Nagarjuna is a metaphysics deconstructor claiming that ultimate reality has nothing to it which can be conceived. His *shunyata* (voidness or, less metaphorically, lack of being-of-its-own) is a none-of-it-all, neither one nor two nor many, while Heron's One-Many is unity and duality and plurality, an all-at-once. To quote from Heron's contribution, "A One-Many Reality," which is an extract (chapter 9) from *Feeling and Personhood*:

> The end of the search does not put an end to expansive aspiration and attunement to the One. It does not finish off the distinct experiencer, only the separate experiencer: the disconnected differentiation of the ego, which is the outcome of illusion, is not to be confused with the unitive differentiation of the transfigured person, which is a mode of divine manifestation. Now if the end of the search does put an end to the distinct experiencer, then Mind is only One and not Many. If Mind is also Many, then its Oneness will include Many distinct experiencers.[14]

Philip Clayton certainly shares the idea that the Many cannot be reduced to the One. Yet this is not the main reason why I have chosen to put his—original—contribution, "Spiritual Evolution and Organic Participation," in the second place. One reason is that few thinkers are able to forge a bridge ranging as wide as Philip can, philosophically. The fact that he is so well-known and respected among philosophers worldwide has to do with his great experience and versatility and openness, marrying notably theology and natural philosophy and ecological thinking. What is important especially for this book is that Clayton was open enough to not just reel off some standard program, but to deliver an original contribution which truly is original: He not only brings in his work and thought so far, but also allows himself to be inspired by the other coauthors' evolutionary, participatory,

14. See below, Chapter 2, 35.

integral, and embodiment ideas. In doing so he draws a wonderful sketch of a many-one panentheism:

> A bad theology of the completed, all-determining God seriously weakens humanity's chances of turning around, ceasing our destruction of this planet's ecosystems, and beginning to build an ecological civilization. A theology of integrated physicality and interdependent becoming with the Divine, by contrast, spawns a genuine new way of being in the world, an organic coexistence with the cosmos and with the living systems around us.[15]

And then for something quite different . . . in its biographic style as well as in basic notions and theses. Layman Pascal, the youngest thinker in this anthology, in fact the only one born in the (in many respects new) age after the late 1960s cultural turning-point, is not a Christian-panentheistic thinker like Philip Clayton, nor is he a Christian-inspired integral thinker like Steve McIntosh, nor is he a Christian-nondual thinker like Tilmann Haberer, nor is he otherwise close to a self-aware-God position, as far as I can see. Actually, I put his essay, "What Do I Mean When I Say That I Love God?" in this place precisely to set a counterpoint. His philosophy of adjacency, which I would paraphrase as a "philosophy of the nearby and the nearly," isn't an attempt to save the idea and feeling of a God who in some robust sense is still a personal Divine; it's not an attempt to save God by overcoming traditional theistic ideas about the perfect, almighty, transcendent, and beyond-time Lord, attempts that Clayton, Haberer, McIntosh or I try to make. For Layman, as I understand him, the unity-in-diversity is always there, as a partial convergence and communion, yet *only ever almost* reached, and never for good. The One thus remains approximate, asymptotic:

> A God, for me, must be *nonessentialist*. "He" is not identical to himself. In fact, as the epitome of Being (which is incomplete, dynamic, and self-approximating), God is the very principle of self-approximation. He is an almost-ness that can outperform the definite, absolutized sense of certainty and identity with which previous epochs of mystics and philosophers have tried to define the superlative aspect of reality. I believe that a phenomenon does not have to be *total* in order to be maximal. It does not have to be perfectly completed in order to be optimally active.[16]

This way of approaching the Divine, to me, resonates a bit with Jorge Ferrer's idea of *the Mystery* (see below), the one Ultimate Reality that creates

---

15. See below, Chapter 3, 61.
16. See below, Chapter 4, 67.

beings, but at the same is many Ultimate Realities *cocreated by* beings. This, of course, raises questions about possible personal qualities of the Divine, which some would consider crucial and which are hard to mitigate, among which are consciousness of itself, making sense of and co-organizing (indeed *being* the coherence and meaning of) all there is, and not least relating to and caring for every single being *individually*.

Layman's and Jorge's positions, by the way, show that this anthology really is plural. I myself, editor and coauthor of this volume, for instance, would insist that the One has to be in some strong sense definite and unchanging, because otherwise the One billions of years ago would have to be different from the One today, neither of them therefore being really encompassing, quite obviously. So there are basic alternatives, and arguments for every choice, and that's a good thing. This regards the eternity of the One, its distinctness, its self-awareness, probably other qualities too.

After Layman's essay we have a very special jewel in this anthology for all those who want more references to postmodern and post-postmodern thinking European-style. In the original, German-language, edition of this anthology I had included Bruce Alderman's essay "Integral In-Dwelling," with its marvelous title expressing how persons and divine are intertwined or entangled. As Jorge Ferrer's essay is, so this one too is most challenging and sweeping and deep-delving. I fell in love with an invaluable line in it, which, by the way, could serve as a motto for this anthology: "We learn also to dwell among strangers, to be graciously hosted by differences that can be trusted to illumine what is neglected, undeveloped, or differently held in ourselves."[17]

However, from the reactions I got to the German edition, I came to the conclusion, heavy-heartedly, for I had translated "Integral In-Dwelling" myself with much lifeblood and sweat involved, that for a less academic public this essay simply was too difficult to access. So I convinced Bruce to include for the English edition a different essay of his, which is more accessible and shorter (making the anthology more *affordable* too), and which is still, believe me as a trained philosopher, sufficiently sophisticated: "Opening Space for Translineage Practice." Mind you that Alderman's contribution to this anthology dates from over a decade ago. His characteristic blend of influences has remained: a mixture of (among other sources) Ken Wilber's labyrinthine œuvre, transpersonal thinking (notably from Jorge Ferrer), Anglo-Saxon postmodern theology (for example, from Catherine Keller), French post-postmodern thinkers (like Bruno Latour and Jean-Luc Nancy), as well as post-postmodern thought currents known under labels like "new realism" or "speculative realism" (from Graham Harman and others). Still,

17. Alderman, "Integral In-Dwelling," 18.

Bruce's affiliation especially with Wilber's Integral Theory has loosened a bit over the years. For more recent formulations of his thinking, see https://jfku.academia.edu/BruceAlderman/.

I see "Opening Space for Translineage Practice" as composing two threads of thought, permitting myself to summarize it in the most broad-brush manner: one, the idea that spiritualities which are open and encompassing enough need not deal with one another in a reductionist or at least *one-sidedly inclusivist* manner, but can manage to treat each other as *mutually including* ("co-present") peers; and two, the very interesting idea in a many-one context that the Many (the multitude of any individual entity) "withdraw[s]" to any kind of reduction even to the One that encompasses them, even though all of them are expressions or gestures of the very same One . . . a "paradox" which may in fact be not paradoxical at all, but one of those complementing polarities crucial in many-one thinking. Bruce borrows here from ideas explored by thinkers like Levi Bryant (Object-Oriented Ontology), Jorge Ferrer, Graham Harman, Bruno Latour, and Jean-Luc Nancy. The following passage may give you a flavor of Bruce's way of thinking:

> Nancy's (2008) dis-enclosure, together with his being singular plural, invite us to think our multiplicity, to live and celebrate Being as a being-with that eludes tantalization or finalization, where every one is always more-than-one. In demanding acknowledgment of presence as co-presence, it calls us to recognize that each tradition is in some sense subject to that which exceeds it, and is already infiltrated by an otherness that indebts it to the open, both in terms of its relation to other traditions and to its own future.[18]

I found it useful to follow up Bruce's text with something less scholarly in form, instead more essayistic, and more this-worldly, Earthy, and from the natural sciences . . . It's my own contribution to this collection as a coauthor, titled "Human Beings on This Planet." In this text, I try to explore a little more broadly what Philip Clayton in his essay is also touching on: a many-one natural philosophy. I believe that whoever is taking modernity, modern life, and the modern worldview seriously must seriously deal with natural science, must not discard it or misrepresent it. What has to be challenged, however, is the materialistic interpretation, the atomism and geometrism and determinism, which routinely, standardly are being smuggled into modern science. My aim in writing this essay was to sketch

18. See below, Chapter 5, 117; Bruce is referring here to Jean-Luc Nancy's 2008 book *Dis-Enclosure: The Deconstruction of Christianity*.

a holistic and at the same time individualistic (or maybe better: individuating) reading of the same knowledge about nature, which explains more than materialism, instead of explaining away so much. It is key in such a natural philosophy to challenge the reduction of anything there is to "pure physics." Elementary interactions and particles have to be reinterpreted as elements of the natural order and evolution of the cosmos that—all in one—is physical, alive, culture and spirit.

My key argument is philosophical, but has a strictly scientific side: There is no intelligible worldview, scientific or otherwise, without information. Yet, information in all its forms—first thing—cannot be reduced or at least limited to purely physical entities, say, moving and transforming geometrical patterns. If you allow only for physical information in this sense, then most everyday, unproblematic, not least practical and scientific information, is being scrapped too. Second, even if such a kind of purely geometrical physics were consistent in itself, it still would not be coherent, leaving no place for genuine time, that is, for events, emergence, and evolution. Without time, however, something necessary for any human behavior and agency would be impossible: any kind of, say, "dealing with" and "processing of" information, upon which life, civilization, and indeed science itself clearly depend. The essay explores this argument in some detail. I close it with the words:

> Even the highest human achievements, the deepest abysses, the most wonderful revelations all range in the great coherence and framework of living in humankind on this planet in the one cosmos. This belief is not materialism, but it is a form of naturalism, not a supernaturalism. Tending to our natural lives and livelihoods, the families we come from, our cultural communities and our life together in states, as well as the global community of peoples: this is our origin, business, and task as humans. Let's not lose this ground under our feet, not spiritually, not socially, and not ecologically.[19]

My natural-philosophy essay, written for this anthology, is followed by Tilmann Haberer's likewise original, theological-and-beyond contribution "News from Antiquity: Integral Reflections on Two Central Doctrines of the Ancient Church." If Steve McIntosh, whose essay comes after Tilmann's, is an integral thinker inspired by Christianity, Tilmann is a Christian thinker inspired by integral ideas. He is a German Protestant pastor, to be exact. A good preacher who is able to make use of this talent in his writing will achieve texts as accessible as Tilmann Haberer's. His book *Gott*

---

19. See below, Chapter 6, 159.

9.0 (coauthored together with Marion and Werner Küstenmacher and available in English as *God 9.0*) is one of the few popularizing theological books that have given me something novel and deep and fresh. His contribution to the present anthology surprised me somewhat: early Christian dogmas interpreted as expressions of the Many inside the One. The early Christian bishops and theologians known as the church fathers, in a kind of tightrope act between Greek philosophy on the one side and Saint Paul and John the Evangelist on the other, brought forth the Trinitarian dogma about God being three persons all at once: the Father, the Son, and the Holy Spirit, as well as the christological dogma about Jesus being wholly God and wholly human, again all at once. Tilmann suggests that these dogmas, almost two thousand years later and most likely against the intention of their originators, can turn out to be integral and nondual truths, meaning that *each and every* human is also divine. He puts it this way:

> Indeed, it would be much easier for today's postmodern or post-postmodern/integral people to recognize that there are two natures in Christ if this were a statement about humankind itself. Then the significance of Jesus Christ would be founded not in the fact that he, as the only Son of God and unique God-human, had redeemed people from sin, death, and the devil, but rather in the fact that his followers recognized in him what is true for all of us. Resurrection could be interpreted as an individual and then also as a collective experience in which the disciples recognized what the true nature of Jesus was, and likewise their own true nature: that we are all immortal, eternal, divine—at least according to our deepest, innermost, true nature.[20]

Next comes the essay "Toward the Further Evolution of Spirituality," by Steve McIntosh, an extract from an already published book, chapter 7 from Steve's *The Presence of the Infinite*, which he adapted for the present volume. McIntosh is an integral thinker and also a panentheistic thinker, and this in itself is, say, uncommon. Today, only few thinkers who are spiritual thinkers rather than theologians or otherwise Christian apologists take the risk of championing a view where the Divine is maintaining a relationship of its own with each human person, and therefore must be *not-less-than-personal* (according to a formula I owe to Philip Clayton). With Steve McIntosh too, the One is seen as a Spirit encompassing everything and everyone, a spirit conscious of itself and who knows and loves each person as just this person. McIntosh doesn't try to understate the contrast between a God of this kind and the Divine of nondual (in this case again meaning *no-dualities*)

---

20. See below, Chapter 7, 176.

spirituality. Rather he sees a fruitful tension between the view of a personal God and a void Divine, an open dialectic which ought to be, as it were, upheld and withstood, and he predicts this tension will allow both nondualists and theists to grow spiritually, out of their current discord. He writes:

> Nevertheless, for those committed to a nondual path, the practice of experiencing the love that comes from the creative Source of the universe involves allowing for the truth that there is more to ultimate reality than a formless void or an impersonal oneness. Admittedly, coming to terms with the goodness, morality, and loving-kindness of ultimate reality may require reflection and contemplation on the part of nondualists, and reconciling this perfect love with the imperfection, suffering, and evil that remains in the finite universe is inevitably part of this task. But within the dialectical practices of evolutionary spirituality, integrating opposing forms of spiritual truth becomes desirable, achievable, and inevitable.[21]

The Many-One for Steve McIntosh means that while God as the caring infinity is incomparably more than each of us finite humans inside of him, he still is the deepest ground in everyone—the mystery of the Many-One entangled in one another, an idea which Bruce Alderman calls (mutual) "in-dwelling" or "with/in" or "co-presence."

The following contribution is Jorge Ferrer's paper "The One and the Many in Spirituality and Religion: A Participatory Vision," which is a combination and adaptation, suitably shortened so as to suit this anthology's frame, of his two essays "Participatory Spirituality and Transpersonal Theory" and "Religious Pluralism and the Future of Religion," both taken from the volume *Participation and the Mystery*. Whoever wants to get into Ferrer's thinking has to work her or his way through some of his academic and therefore challenging texts. It will be worth it, for Jorge has the courage to articulate consistent ideas about embodiment and enaction. The Many-One for him is so plural that there are many ultimate realities realized-cocreated-enacted by humans. He is even talking about a multiverse made out of many universes, each of them with its own Ultimate. Nevertheless, for him, there is a One behind these Many Ultimates, which, however, is not fully determined or determinable, something he often paraphrases as "the Mystery or Life or Creativity or Cosmos." He is taking a most far-reaching decision here, for if the One is so little determined, then it must be the All-Source rather than the All-Coherence of everything. Humankind and its individuals are bodily and cultural and intellectual expressions, "gestures,"

---

21. See below, Chapter 8, 210.

as it were, of this ungraspable mystery. Ferrer is well aware just how radical a decision he is taking here:

> Would not accepting their co-created nature undermine not only the claims of most traditions, but also the very ontological autonomy and integrity of the mystery itself? Response: Given the rich variety of incompatible spiritual ultimates and the aporias involved in any conciliatory strategy, I submit that it is only by promoting the cocreative role of human cognition to the very heart and summit of each spiritual universe that the ultimate unity of the mystery can be preserved—otherwise, an arguably equally unsatisfactory alternative emerges, forcing one to either reduce spiritual universes to fabrications of the human imagination or posit an indefinite number of isolated spiritual universes. By conceiving spiritual worlds *and* ultimates as the outcome of a process of participatory co-creation between human multidimensional cognition and an undetermined creative power, however, one rescues the ultimate unity of the mystery while simultaneously affirming its ontological richness and overcoming the reductionisms of culturallinguistic, psychological, and biologically naturalistic explanations of religion.[22]

This anthology opens with a thinker of dialogue and group work, the psychologist and facilitator John Heron. It also closes with, say, a more collective approach, with a spirituality practiced by people through talking to each other. This practice and interpretation is called "HigherWe," and it is presented by Thomas Steininger and Elizabeth Debold in their cowritten essay *"emergent dialogue"* (with a deliberately uncapitalized title). The idea of searching the spiritual impetus, say, and even the Divine itself in the plain interaction between people, who may struggle with one another, if only they care about each other too, this idea, I feel, resonates especially with Heron's or Alderman's work. Let me quote a key passage from *emergent dialogue* to give you a first impression of their way of thinking and practicing:

> So, the more each participant gives to the whole and leans in to the field with genuine curiosity, the more the whole awakens to itself and a shared intelligence begins to be expressed through the group. In this, the HigherWe emerges.
>
> The HigherWe is a decisive shift from individual consciousness; it creates a new identity of self-as-process within a larger, cosmic process. Something completely undivided opens up between the collective in the intersubjective that is self in a much

22. Ferrer, *Participation*, 228.

deeper sense than one's usual identity. Unlike individuated, personal subjectivity, the inner space of the intersubjective has no limits: the inner is the outer, the outer is the inner. In other words, when the individuals in the group have the repeated, almost uncanny experience of having their own thoughts and insights expressed by others in the group, the recognition of a shared interior experience develops. Each participant experiences being a focal point of the whole field in which Life is unfolding at the level of consciousness between human beings, rather than simply being part of a circle or a point on the circle. One begins to identify more with the process, relaxing into a deeper sense of self as limitless, non-separate, undivided unfolding. Simultaneously, because the HigherWe concerns collectives of human beings, the process is always dialogical: it is an unfolding of human culture and, ultimately, of the cosmos that has no end because there is always more to include and integrate. Through us and as us, in the emergence of the HigherWe, the Whole wakes up to the Whole.[23]

My own "Closing Remarks by the Editor" try to round off the anthology with some more sociohistorical context about the milieu and pedigree of many-one thinking, explaining why it is inviting postmodern-minded people to step beyond postmodernism with its hyperboles and abuses (out of the best intentions), inviting them, along with people having other mindsets, to become *post-postmodern*.

I would like to close these "Opening Remarks" with two thoughts which Thomas's and Elizabeth's essay neatly illustrate. Many-one thinking is not the teaching of some mastermind or guru or savior of humankind who persuaded himself or herself that she or he is able to transcend all other thinkers, or else is entitled to reinterpret and reduce other teachings to what he or she thinks is basic. Instead, many-one thinking is a shared thought project which no one oversees and about which no one knows where it may lead. In addition to the exchange between contemporaries willing to dialogue for the sake of the future of humankind, even despite differences notably about what the Divine and Ultimate may be, the broad many-one current is critically and self-critically borrowing from teachers and sages of the past.

Take care: There are spiritual authors self-infatuated enough to sell as "their" teaching what quite obviously has been inspired and adapted and sometimes copied from ancient thinkers—often without even naming these ancient sources, as if those modern writers were scooping only from their own spiritual experience or their own philosophical talent. And many

23. See below, Chapter 10, 249.

spiritual readers are refusing to engage in an intellectual, critical appraisal of past thinkers and their influence, so they are less aware of such a tearing out of context and misappropriation by today's best-selling writers. There is a collusion then between readers expecting an impossible degree of originality and revelation, and writers who for sales' sake are drifting into the dubious and misguiding, betraying the responsibility that comes with their influence on real people's minds and lives. With the overshooting and self-undermining crisis of late modernistic civilization, this responsibility now is more pressing than ever. Thomas Steininger and Elizabeth Debold give an example of meeting it, by naming intellectual and biographical influences and spiritual friends in German and US communities, and by letting collaborators in their project speak who usually do not "have a say," that is, who are not publishing or speaking or touting their work in front of a public.

Even now that more and more people dare to speak out in some internet forum or print-on-demand publication, and that fewer and fewer seem to be listening or reading, we are still sticking too much to what often seem to be overcome clichés about professors explaining to us the universe; about charismatic star authors; about world sages revealing to us the mind of God. What we need instead, I suggest, are thinkers and writers and seminar facilitators and bloggers and podcasters who are talking *to* each other and also respectfully discussing disagreement with each other, able to see one another in the shared intellectual and life-world and cosmic context, and facing the common challenge of saving a humane civilization on a livable planet. The awfully shrill and disintegrated marketplace of intellectuals and media and celebrities and communities rushing from one hype to another on the chase for fame and brand management and the quick dollar or euro is destroying the arena for a broad public which is mature and educated enough to help each other find their bearings in terms of values and politics and worldview. In order to be noticed inside this pandemonium with our many-one writings and teachings advocating the cultural and ecological and social and spiritual evolution and integration of humankind, we will have to somehow practice, if anything . . . unity in diversity.

Bibliography

Alderman, Bruce. "Integral In-Dwelling: A Prepositional Theology of Religions." *Consciousness: Ideas and Research for the Twenty-First Century* 4.4 (2016). https://digitalcommons.ciis.edu/conscjournal/vol4/iss4/2/.

Amery, Carl. *Das Ende der Vorsehung: Die gnadenlosen Folgen des Christentums*. Reinbek: Rowohlt, 1972.

Deleuze, Gilles. "Postscript on the Societies of Control." https://libcom.org/library/postscript-on-the-societies-of-control-gilles-deleuze/. Originally published in: *October* 59 (Winter 1992) 3–7.

Ferrer, Jorge N. *Participation and the Mystery: Transpersonal Essays in Psychology, Education, and Religion.* Albany: State University of New York Press, 2017.

Foucault, Michel. *The Order of Things: An Archaeology of the Human Sciences.* World of Man. New York: Pantheon, 1971.

Fuller, Robert C. *Spiritual, but not Religious: Understanding Unchurched America.* New York: Oxford University Press, 2001.

Heron, John. *Feeling and Personhood: Psychology in Another Key.* London: Sage, 1992.

Hescox, Mitch, and Paul Douglas. *Caring for Creation: The Evangelical's Guide to Climate Change and a Healthy Environment.* Minneapolis: Bethany House, 2016.

Keller, Catherine. *Face of the Deep: A Theology of Becoming.* London: Routledge, 2003.

Küstenmacher, Marion et al. *Gott 9.0: Wohin unsere Gesellschaft spirituell wachsen wird.* Gütersloher, 2010.

———, et al. *God 9.0:* Gröbenzell: self-published, 2016. http://gott9o.de/god-9.0-english/.

McIntosh, Steve. *Integrales Bewusstsein und die Zukunft der Evolution.* Hamburg: Phänomen, 2009.

———. *Integral Consciousness and the Future of Evolution: How the Integral Worldview Is Transforming Politics, Culture and Spirituality.* White Bear Lake, MN: Paragon House, 2007.

———. *The Presence of the Infinite: The Spiritual Experience of Beauty, Truth, and Goodness.* Wheaton, IL: Quest, 2015.

Nancy, Jean-Luc. *Dis-enclosure: The Deconstruction of Christianity.* Translated by Bettina Bergo et al. New York: Fordham University Press, 2008.

Patten, Terrence. *A New Republic of the Heart: An Ethos for Revolutionaries; A Guide to Inner Work for Holistic Change.* Berkeley: North Atlantic, 2018.

Phipps, Carter. *Evolutionaries: Unlocking the Spiritual and Cultural Potential of Science's Greatest Idea.* New York: Harper Perennial, 2012.

Raney, Art, et al. *Searching for Spirituality in the US: A New Look at the Spiritual but Not Religious.* Washington DC: Public Religion Research Institute, 2017. https://www.prri.org/research/religiosity-and-spirituality-in-america/.

Salzman, Jeff. *The Daily Evolver: A Developmental Take on the News* (podcast). https://www.dailyevolver.com/.

Whitehead, Alfred North. *Process and Reality.* Edited by David Ray Griffin and Donald W. Sherburne. Corrected ed. The Gifford Lectures 1927–1928. New York: Free Press, 1978.

Wikipedia, s.v. "Spiritual but not religious." https://en.wikipedia.org/wiki/Spiritual_but_not_religious/.

2

A One-Many Reality

JOHN HERON

I begin this chapter[1] with a summary statement of the metaphysical beliefs, expressed as a set of metaphors, upon which the theory of the person presented in this book[2] is based. I then give a recapitulation of my account of the person in the light of these beliefs. The remaining sections consider some oriental views from my metaphysical standpoint.

Metaphors for a One-Many Reality

It is a central tenet of this book that Reality is both One and Many, both being and becoming, both transcendent and immanent. There are some simple metaphors for the One-Many notion. There is the polarity of plane and point: a single plane is an infinitude of points. Another is the infinite sphere whose centre is anywhere and everywhere.

The basic spatial metaphor is that there is the infinitely large—the infinitude without; and the infinitely small—the infinitude within.[3] There is only one infinitude without; there are innumerable infinitudes within. Whatever the metaphor, you can't reduce one pole to the other, for the poles are fundamental, complementary, interdependent and interdefinable.

1. Heron refers here to chapter 9 of his book *Feeling and Personhood*, which constitutes his contribution to the present anthology. Whenever in this contribution he refers to a chapter, it is to a chapter of *Feeling and Personhood*, not of the present anthology.—Ed.

2. By "this book," he refers to *Feeling and Personhood*, which is retrievable and downloadable for free, in a photocopied but not retrodigitized version on https://johnheron-archive.co.uk/wp-content/uploads/2020/03/fandp.pdf/.—Ed.

3. See exercise 1 in the Exercises section annexed to this text.—Ed.

Another radical complementarity is that of involution and evolution, expressed in the metaphors of descent and ascent. There is a descent, an involution, an embedding of the One in the embryonic Many and an ascent, an evolution, a differentiated development of the Many in the One. The One is enfolded, not dissolved, in the Many; the Many progressively manifest, and do not disappear into, the One.

The metaphor of descent, the process of involution, is further elaborated by the metaphor of a down-hierarchy. From the One consciousness-as-such emanate the formative imaginal powers, the archetypes of creation, which radiate a manifold of energies and spaces. In these are the infinitudes within, the Many, in each of which an archetype is reflected as an entelechy, the ground of an up-hierarchy.

The up-hierarchy metaphor expands the metaphor of ascent. For the entelechy emerging from the infinitude immanent within each of the Many is a godseed, a formative potential. It upthrusts this potential in successive steps of the unfolding up-hierarchy, all of whose higher levels are latent in its lowest.

In terms of consciousness, the One-Many Reality is represented as the one mind with many differentiated centres of consciousness within it. Personhood is one such centre. There is no separation between this conscious locus and its setting in universal mind. Since its consciousness is not apart from this field, it can participate in all other centres too. Each of the inter-related many is unfolding within universal consciousness: a particular focus of development and a unique perspective within it.

The separateness of egoic states of being is an illusion to do with the subject-object split. Dismantling that illusion means that personal consciousness uncovers its true heritage—that it is both distinct within, and one with, universal mind. It is involved in a set of syncretistic, dialectical or, if you like, paradoxical categories. Everything is divine, and the divine transcends everything. Perceived particulars are both Many and One, distinct and identical. My individuation is exalted in the divine, and I lose my being in the divine. The divine is dynamic and static, a plenum and a vacuum, qualified and unqualified, personal and impersonal.[4]

Modern panentheism affirms the view that while all things are within the divine, the divine is not merely the whole of everything: it includes everything, is immanent in everything and transcends everything.[5] Paul Tillich's existential theology gives a special colouring to this view.[6] It pro-

---

4. Stace, *Mysticism.*

5. Hartshorne and Reese, *Philosophers.*

6. Tillich, *Systematic Theology.*

pounds an ecstatic and self-transcending naturalism. The divine is not a being among other beings, but being-itself, the creative source and ultimate meaning of all natural objects: it is found in the ecstatic character of this world as its transcendent depth and ground.

The being of the world participates in the underlying being of God. The divine, the unconditioned, is to be found only in, with and under the conditioned relationships of this life as their profound significance. God is the ground of our being as persons, our ultimate concern. God, being-itself, can be described symbolically as living, personal, spirit, love. It follows from all this that through our deep concern we participate in the divine being of the world and each other. And this is close to the account of feeling which I am advancing in this book.

The Person as One-Many

The One-Many Reality is reflected in the one-many structure of person-hood. There is one unique, distinct potential person who is actualized both serially and concurrently in all sorts of different manifest subpersons. At a certain period of life a person may be running concurrently the spontane-ous person, the compulsive person, the conventional person, the creative person, the self- creating person and the self-transfiguring person.

Of course, to say these are concurrent is not to say they are all on stage at exactly the same time; rather a person can move in and out of these dif-ferent ways of being one after the other during a day, a week or a month. The same person at the same general phase of their life can be conventional in one context, creative in another, compulsive in a third, and so on. We bring ourselves on bit by bit, in an improvisatory, piecemeal kind of way, now working at this, now sorting out that, slipping back here, and moving on with swift advance there.[7]

Within each of these main substates of personhood, there are sub-subpersons. The compulsive person lurches around between the distressed positions of oppressor, victim, rescuer and rebel. The conventional person moves from one stereotypic role to another, now man about the house, now young executive, now golf club member, now holidaymaker in Ibiza, now dutiful political supporter. The creative person may be innovative in several different fields: a social change agent in the winter, a writer and a painter in the spring and summer.

The self-creating person can, in their personal therapy, work with a wide array of different sets of subpersonalities, characterizing different

7. See exercise 1 in the Exercises section annexed to this text.—Ed.

semi-autonomous "energy patterns" or "operating potentials" in the psyche, getting them all into some kind of meaningful mutual adaptation. Stone and Winkelman[8] identify here the hurt child, the playful child, the magical child; the good and the bad mother or father; the critic; the perfectionist; the pleaser, and so on. John Rowan has written a useful book outlining past and present approaches to this way of working.[9]

The self-transfiguring person may be the priest or hierophant, the mystic, the occultist or magus, the seer, the oracle, the healer, the representative of this, that or the other power or presence, the cosmic joker, or the lost one in the dark night of the soul.

The theory of *skandhas*, which I put forward in chapter 5, brings in a whole new dimension of multiplicity, since it affirms that a person is born carrying other persons' unresolved behaviour patterns by virtue of some principle of affinity. If anything like this is true, then those concerned are all members one of another. The internal psychological multiplicity includes a corporate and collective one.

What I have called the entelechy—Rogers's selective and directional "actualizing tendency"[10]—which might be regarded as that principle of personhood which orchestrates and integrates the manifold of persons, subpersons and subsubpersons, itself appears as different kinds of guiding spokesperson—now affirming individuating, now participating, now proposing grounding, now reorganizing, now electing living, now learning.

In short, in a One-Many Reality, personhood is a dramatic multiplicity within a distinctive presence. And the paradox is that we find the uniqueness of that presence not by trying to restrict the multiplicity, but by celebrating its multifarious presentations.

Is There Anyone There?

Some western enthusiasts for transcendence of the subject-object split in a higher non-dual awareness of reality have written as if, by dissolving the viewpoint of a subject separated from an object, that is the end of a distinct, non-separable psyche. This view it is fair to say is primarily oriental and in its extreme form Buddhist, as I discussed in chapter 2, p. 38–39, although as we shall see later there are seeds of a very different account in Tibetan Buddhism.

8. Stone and Winkelman, *Embracing.*

9. Rowan, *Subpersonalities.*

10. Rogers, "Theory of Therapy."

One occidental version[11] describes Awareness, or non-dual experiencing, as meaning the end of any kind of experiencer; but the universe is still
all there as a diversity in unity, a seamless whole of distinct and mutually
interpenetrating particulars. It is just that it is no longer objective because
the subject has disappeared into absolute Mind, which is one with the universe it knows.

There is a hidden assumption, a metaphysical rigidity, in this account.
It allows diversity in unity, mutual interpenetration, only to the universe.
But this is an arbitrary restriction, and takes too quick a flight across the
water of experience. A less hasty account is that when separate subject and
separate object disappear, non-dual experiencing is revealed as an unitive
field in which there is mutual interpenetration between person and world,
distinct and non-separable. The end of the separate experiencer is simply the
beginning of the experiencer-within-Mind, who was really there all the time,
and who is of a qualitatively different order. The separation of seer from seen,
and both from the One, which was the illusory outlook of the ego, gives way
to the deeper and subtler realization that the differentiation of seer and seen
within an unitive transactional field *is* the Many in the One.[12]

One redoubt of those who believe that there is really no such thing
as an *experiencer* is the argument from transcendental subjectivity.[13] The
argument goes like this. Whenever you look for your self, you cannot see
it, because a subject cannot be an object for itself, just as an eye cannot see
itself. You may say you see this or that as your self, but as soon as you see
it, it has become object to a new and necessarily unseen subject. In other
words, there is a transcendental subjectivity which forever remains unseen,
whatever you say you see to be your self. The perceived cannot perceive. The
perceiver cannot be perceived.

The argument concludes as follows. You cannot see your self because
what is seeking and looking is *Brahman*, Mind itself. The seeker is the
sought. Knowing this is Awareness and puts an end to the search.

This view of the matter is presented as though the Awareness that God
is transcendental subjectivity is the final solution: the account with Reality is
settled, the experiencer disappears into experiencing. The gap between the
experiencer and God is absolutely closed simply because there is no longer
an experiencer so there is no gap. The journey is over, there is nowhere else
to go, no further step to take because there is no one there to buy the ticket.

11. Wilber, *Spectrum*.

12. See exercise 3 in the Exercises section annexed to this text.—Ed.

13. Wilber, *Spectrum*.

This closes the gap simplistically and without paradox. Transcendental subjectivity is an infinite regress: the subject forever transcends any account that can be given of it. But the infinity of the regress does not disappear because I know its divine origin. If I become aware of *Brahman* as transcendental subjectivity, it is not that my subjectivity disappears, but that I am aware of whence it issues. This does and does not close the gap. It initiates me into yet another version of the One-Many paradox: I know I am one with *Brahman* at the same as knowing that I am infinitely other. Hence the upsurge of numinous awe, glorification and a stream of praise.[14]

The end of the search does not put an end to expansive aspiration and attunement to the One. It does not finish off the distinct experiencer, only the separate experiencer: the disconnected differentiation of the ego, which is the outcome of illusion, is not to be confused with the unitive differentiation of the transfigured person, which is a mode of divine manifestation. Now if the end of the search does put an end to the distinct experiencer, then Mind is only One and not Many. If Mind is also Many, then its Oneness will include Many distinct experiencers.

Am I distinct within Awareness of Mind or not? If I am not, how did I become Aware, let alone report the occurrence? To know Mind as absolute subjectivity, that in which experiential subjectivity is grounded, does not mean the end of the latter but the start of its absolute transfiguration. There is only an end to its separatist, dualistic illusions, and to its search for a ground which it now knows. The dew drop does not slip into the shining sea and simply disappear for ever; rather it undergoes a total alchemical transformation. It interpenetrates the ocean without any loss of its remarkable distinctness.

Dipolar Unity

It is important not to be misled by the enthusiasm of the ancient texts for Oneness. There is a monopolar bias at work which really does not do justice, I believe, to the subtlety of the experiences being reported. As soon as the old mystics stepped into the domain of language and culture to write of their enlightenment (if and when it was that), they tended to fall foul of this kind of monopolar bias. Dipolar accounts of enlightenment are for the coming age; they involve a new level of sophistication in mystical reportage.

We must make a really rather obvious distinction between pernicious and non-pernicious dualities, or, if you like, between separatist, divisive dualities and unitive, complementary polarities. A couple bickering in a state

14. See exercise 4 in the Exercises section annexed to this text.—Ed.

of alienated hostility is an example of the former. Lovers in a profound unitive embrace, deeply and ecstatically at one with each other, is an example
of the latter. The subject-object, dualistic split of ordinary concept-laden
experience is an example of the former. The person-world unity of experience transfigured in the One-Many Reality is an example of the latter.

So that to say that something is dualistic is not *ipso facto* to say that it
is metaphysically pernicious. We need to know whether reference is being
made to a separatist dualism or a non-separate dipolarity. The One-Many
Reality is a non-separatist dualism, a dipolar unity. There is the One, there
are the Many, that is the duality, the dipolarity. They are in a state of mutual
compenetration, so the One is in the Many, the Many are in the One, all
of the Many are in each of the Many and each of the Many is in all of the
Many—and that is the non-separatism, the unity. And all this is Reality,
than which there is nothing other.

Blight from the East

It was from Asia that there first penetrated into Europe the world-denying
concept of the religious life, as Radhakrishnan[15] shows convincingly in his
Eastern Religions and Western Thought. Of course, every possible school of
religious thought has appeared in the East. But the most prominent regard
the multiplicity of the phenomenal world as an illusion grounded on ne-
science, want of discrimination, or ignorance. Release and deliverance from
it is the only goal, for the Real is the undifferentiated One. Variations of this
view are found in the Samkhya, the Vedanta and in Buddhism.[16] There is
here a general metaphysical negativity and monopolar bias: a flight from the
Many to the One, to God from the works of God.

"We owe to the East a conception of world denial which in its perverse
form undermines most seriously the creative powers of the spirit."[17] Guénon
in a classic study showed that the principles of the Vedanta strictly applied
mean that spirit is incapable of being expressively manifest in the human
realm in any convincing sense.[18] The oriental sages identified with the One
as a defence against coming to terms with the active creativity of the human
spirit as one of the Many, within the realm of the Many.

They wanted to persuade themselves they could disappear into Oneness and write off Manyness as illusion. They tried to jump from illusory,

15. Radhakrishnan, *Eastern*.
16. See Hyde, *Nameless Faith*.
17. Hyde, *Nameless Faith*, 46.
18. Guénon, *Man and His Becoming*.

dualistic ego-bound states of consciousness to a total identification with universal states of consciousness, irrespective of any stated position on the nature of the self. As a result they compulsively avoided the concept of personhood as a creative spiritual reality. And without a concept of personhood as that which can liberate itself from egoic illusions, and become *both* transfigured within a higher consciousness and manifestly expressive in the world, I do not think you can ever do justice to the Manyness within the One-Many Reality.

So we must ask whether the old mystics did always become universal. Did they necessarily enter Mind? Or is this sometimes an unnoticed and hopeful projection on our part? In chapter 10 I raise the issue that the ancient sages are people who suffered from two deficits: they had no working concept of repression at all; and they lived in cultures that had a minimal, undeveloped relation to the phenomenal world. In chapter 3 I gave reasons for supposing that their deeply repressed distress will have been relatively untouched by their meditative practices; and that its compulsive thrust will have remained, subtly distorting the whole spiritual enterprise.

Did they therefore, on occasion, displace themselves into strange mental states by sitting meditating in caves for long periods? Was it a case of compulsive transcendentalism being a castration equivalent, leading to the inner mental voice being pitched permanently an octave higher? There is a theodicean pathology in the life of the spirit that is very rarely raised by devotees of distant saints.

Lawrence Hyde is one of the few spiritually competent writers who has faced this issue squarely and fairly. In *The Nameless Faith* he wrote:

> There can be little doubt that in a large number of cases the exaltation attained by modern eastern yogis is nothing more than psychic in character, in spite of their own belief, and that of their disciples, that they have entered the sublime state of *Samadhi*. It almost looks, in fact, as if this illegitimate mode of escaping into the subjective is the oriental equivalent of our excessive concern in the West with the realm of objectivity.[19]

Asraya-paravrtti

There is, however, another side to the story from the East. Deep in the traditions of Tibetan Buddhism there are all the elements of a powerful doctrine of the self-transfiguring person. The starting point is *asraya-paravrtti*. This

19. Hyde, *Nameless Faith*, 49.

double-barrelled Sanskrit term means *foundation-change*. Govinda describes this as "a thorough transformation of our personality" that comes about through the mystical path.

For Govinda this transformation does not mean condemnation of ordinary experience, but building a bridge from it to timeless awareness. This is "a way which leads beyond this world not through contempt or negation, but through purification and sublimation of the conditions and qualities of our present existence."[20] It involves an alchemical process of transmuting the base metals of everyday consciousness into the "imperishable jewel of the adamantine mind." Hence ordinary states of being are changed into the states of bodhicitta, enlightenment consciousness. The ego-bound mind becomes cosmic awareness; awareness of the individual body becomes awareness of the universal body; selfish feeling becomes feeling for others, compassion, and a feeling of identity with everything; sense perception and discrimination become inner vision and spiritual discernment; ego-bound karma-creating volition is changed into the karma-free activity of the saint.

This is a path, a progression, it takes time in the ordinary sense. It culminates in the realization of the *Dharmakaya*, the universal principle of all consciousness. This, says Govinda,

> is a living force, which manifests itself in the individual and assumes the form of "personality." But it goes beyond the individual consciousness, as its origin is in the universal realm of the spirit, the *Dharma*-sphere. It assumes the character of "personality" by being realized in the human mind. If it were merely an abstract idea, it would have no influence on life, and if it were an unconscious life-force, it would have no forming influence on the mind.[21]

Govinda's idea of this "personality" is pretty minimal: he thinks of it as a "momentary form of appearance like a temporarily assumed mask."

Suzuki also takes the view, perhaps more robustly, that the concept of *Dharmakaya* implies the notion of personality: "The highest reality is not a mere abstraction, it is very much alive with sense and awareness and intelligence, and, above all, with love purged of human infirmities and defilements."[22] He says that even the *Dhyani-Buddhas*, transcendent presences encountered in meditative vision, have all the characteristics of personality. They are not merely personifications of abstract concepts but the transformation of a universal reality in the form of human experience.

20. Govinda, *Foundations*, 82.

21. Govinda, *Foundations*, 213.

22. Suzuki, *Essence*, 41.

What is behind all this is the traditional doctrine that every Buddha manifests himself on three planes of reality—the universal, the ideal and the individual—and has three corresponding bodies or principles: the *Dharmakaya*, in which all Enlightened Ones are the same; the *Sambhogakaya* which constitutes the spiritual or ideal character of a Buddha; and the *Nirmanakaya*, the human embodiment or individuality of an Enlightened One.

Seeded within this doctrine is the idea of the Enlightened One as a distinct cosmic presence. If you precede it with the account of *asraya-paravrtti* then you get a very early prototype of the mystic path as one in which the potentiality for distinct personhood within universal awareness is emerging from its cocoon of illusory egoic separateness.[23] And this, I believe, is what both Govinda and Suzuki are edging towards in their interpretation of the ancient ideas.

Still, we need more than a mere edging forward. We need a positive doctrine of the charismatic *person* who is attuned to the One and who is an active, creative presence in the diverse realms of the Many.

Exercises

1 The Infinitude Within

Meditate together for twenty minutes. Relax and become fully present. With closed eyes, become your heart and from everywhere on its periphery move in simultaneously towards the infinitude at its centre. As you draw closer to the centre from all sides, feel the spatial scale continuously magnifying so that you are expanding into the intensely intimate, ecstatic space of the immanent infinitude, which, at a certain point on the inward journey, glows into manifestation with the energy of bliss, like a jewel. Feel the mystery of your unity with the jewel. After the meditation, share your experiences.

2 Seven Chairs

Take thirty minutes each to explore your multiple personhood, using seven chairs. The focal chair is for your entelechy, your formative potential of personhood; the other six chairs are for your spontaneous person, your compulsive person, your conventional person, your creative person, your self-creative person and your self-transfiguring person. Make sure from chapter 3 that you have a good working grasp of these seven forms

---

23. See exercise 5 in the Exercises section annexed to this text.—Ed.

of personhood. Fix a large label on to each chair to show which person it belongs to. Start off in the focal chair and ask your six persons to share, as each is moved to do so, whether and how they are active in your current life. Move from chair to chair to give voice to each of the six. After all six have spoken, open up dialogue between them, seeing what they have to say to each other, and move from chair to chair as appropriate. Go to the focal chair whenever you feel the dialogue needs facilitation by your formative potential. If you want, arrange for your partner to keep the whole thing on the move with an occasional prompt about which chair to go to and what issue to take up. After both turns, give each other feedback, and discuss what the whole process yields.

3 Demystification

Explore together non-dual experiencing, in which subject and object remain distinct but non-separable, simply by looking at your own left hand held up with fingers extended and palm in front of and slightly to the left of your face. Now flex and extend the fingers to and fro, and feel that you are non-separable from the movement. Now stop the movement and feel that you are non-separable from the visual image of the hand—an image which your body-mind is deeply involved in generating. While focusing on the hand, attend to the visual images behind the hand and feel that you are non-separable from them since, as with the image of your hand, you are deeply involved in generating them. Discuss the experience. Did you become Mind, or enter a unified person-world transaction within Mind?

4 Meditation on Transcendental Subjectivity

Sit together in meditation and be aware of yourself as "I," as subject of the first person singular. Mentally intone the pronoun "I" as a focus for your sense of I-ness. Turn about in the very seat of your I-ness and attend to its Absolute Source, the universal I AM. As you turn about into this Origination, note the total dissolution of the separate sense of I-ness, of the egocentric focus. Note also, at the selfsame moment the egocentric chrysalis dissolves, your astonishing, exhilarating distinctness within the divine embrace. Share your experiences of this remarkable encounter.

5 Self-transfiguring Mime

Play Berlioz's *Harold in Italy* and as the music sounds take it in turns to express in mime, dance and movement your emergence from the cocoon of illusory egoistic separateness into distinct personhood within cosmic awareness. After both turns, share your experiences as artist and audience.

Bibliography

Govinda, Lama Anagarika. *Foundations of Tibetan Mysticism*. London: Rider, 1960.

Guénon, René. *Man and His Becoming according to the Vedanta*. London: Rider, 1928.

Hartshorne, Charles, and William L. Reese. *Philosophers Speak of God*. Chicago: University of Chicago Press, 1953.

Hyde, Lawrence. *The Nameless Faith*. London: Rider, 1949.

Radhakrishnan, Sarvepalli. *Eastern Religions and Western Thought*. London: Oxford University Press, 1939.

Rogers, Carl. "A Theory of Therapy, Personality, and Interpersonal Relationships, as developed in the Client-Centered Framework." In *Psychology: A Study of a Science, study 1, vol. 3: Formulations of the Person and the Social Context*, edited by Sigmund Koch, 184–256. New York: McGraw-Hill, 1959.

Rowan, John. *Subpersonalities: The People Inside Us*. London: Routledge, 1990.

Stace, Walter T. *Mysticism and Philosophy*. London: Macmillan, 1961.

Stone, Hal, and Sidra Winkelman. *Embracing Our Selves: The Voice Dialogue Manual*. Marina Del Rey, CA: Devorss, 1985.

Suzuki, D. T. *The Essence of Buddhism*. London: The Buddhist Society, 1947.

Tillich, Paul. *Systematic Theology*. 3 vols. Chicago: University of Chicago Press, 1951–1963.

Wilber, Ken. *The Spectrum of Consciousness*. Wheaton, IL: Theosophical Publishing House, 1977.

3

Spiritual Evolution and Organic Participation

Philip Clayton

Introduction

Religion, philosophy, and spirituality can be as much our enemies as our friends. After all, we are surrounded by violent religions, irrelevant philosophies, and trivial spiritualities. And yet, as we watch modernity self-destructing before our very eyes, and as the sense of urgency gnaws in the pit of our stomach, we know we have no choice but to return to the ancient questions in search of new answers. After all, superficial and self-serving answers to "the meaning of life" dominate today's marketplace of ideas. W. B. Yeats's words in "The Second Coming" are more true today than when he penned them a hundred years ago: "The best lack all conviction, while the worst / Are full of passionate intensity."

The contrast can feel almost unbearable: religion radicalized on the one side into a finely honed weapon of war, and trivialized on the other into a thinly veiled justification of the believer's comfortable consumerist world. The trouble is: in the history of humanity, religion has been *the* place where the languages of ultimacy were nurtured and developed. Our ancestors relied on accounts of the gods to compose sacred narratives about humanity's ultimate source and final destination. These sacred stories became the ground for the tribe's deepest identity, and from it the individual's highest responsibilities were derived. The most powerful calls to compassion and the greatest sacrifices for the sake of the group as a whole had their sources in religious ultimacy.

If religion no longer helps us to identify our higher selves, if it ceases to call us to compassion and to give us the language we need to explore who we ultimately are, then what will lift us above the numbing effects of the everyday? If we lack a worldview, a *Weltbild*, a *Weltanschauung*, then how can we weave together the insights that we gather into a meaningful tapestry? The Many in the One means coherence; the many without a unity means fragmentation.

What's most worrisome is that the collapse of a unifying language for the highest human values and grounding beliefs is coming at exactly the same time as we face an escalating global crisis. Today's human-induced disruption of the global climate is not like the wars of the past, where people stop dying when soldiers stop killing them; nor, even, is it like the threat of a global nuclear war, which either devastates the planet or is avoided. Climate change by contrast is like walking down an avalanche slope: there are some early steps where one can still turn back, and then there's a point of no return when it's no longer possible to escape devastating consequences. Unfortunately, as a species as a whole we look a lot more like a small child wandering foolishly along the top of the avalanche slope, lacking any awareness of how rapidly the dynamics of critical feedback loops spin out of control. Everything feels safe, everything looks like it always has . . . until it isn't. If the global scientific consensus is accurate—and science remains the best predictor of the future that humanity has—we have only a few years to pull back from our insane destruction of the ecosystems on which our species depends. Not to stop the disruption in time is to set in motion a global avalanche that will tear apart much of the planet's biosphere, with catastrophic effects that will last for hundreds, if not thousands of years.

It is not an exaggeration to say: humanity stands at the tipping point, and the entire biosphere now hangs in the balance. On the one hand, it's possible that we will learn once again to tell the story of the history of life as a process of biological and spiritual co-evolution in which all is interconnected and everything is thereby permeated with intrinsic value—a cosmology in which everything is sacred. Only a metaphysical worldview that grounds "the universe story" in ultimate meaning and value *in some way* will allow us to again participate organically in *All That Is*. Or, on the other hand, if we fail in our quest for unity and are unable to consistently act for the good of the whole, we may go down with the *Titanic*, the ship of modern civilization that we have built and are now steering at full throttle toward disaster.

It's a Personal Quest . . . for Each of Us

I have spent several decades researching, teaching, lecturing, and writing on the topics covered in this book. And yet I could not have written this chapter until recently—very recently, actually. I cannot draw you into the vision of oneness and diversity that emerges in the following pages without saying a word about why I am moving further and further from the classical accounts of God and world.

The provocative author Brian McLaren offers the briefest possible account of why people today must transition away from a classical Christian theology and a classical model of Christian institutions: "If you have a new world, you will need a new church. You have a new world."[1] Isn't it obvious that the same is true of classical accounts of God, and indeed of classical metaphysics as a whole?

We need a new metaphysical story. Most of us will agree on the main reason: the world has changed, and is changing, in unforeseen ways and at an extremely rapid pace. The Jewish philosopher Emil Fackenheim coined the term "epoch-making event" for changes that are so major that they inaugurate a new epoch in world history. He rightly described the *Shoa,* the Holocaust, as an event of such severity, and rightly so.

Ours is an age when these epoch-making transitions are piling up, one on top of the other, and ever more rapidly. Human-induced global climate change trumps all other injustices, since it will increasingly affect virtually every aspect of human life on this planet. If you read closely, you will see that in one sense this entire chapter is about ecology, even the metaphysical parts. But consider a few of the other issues we face: hundreds of new technologies that transform our lives in thousands of ways, from AI to drugs to weapons of mass destruction. The rapid withering of religion as we have known it. The abandonment of the "canon" of Western literature and the resulting transformation of classical higher education. The collapse of the clan or extended family group, and now breakdowns in the nuclear family. Economic globalization. The decrease in civic participation. Threats to democracy. The difficulty of finding communities of like-minded individuals with whom to participate in corporate life together. All of these factors together have made hopelessness the leading malaise of our age.

The first task of a leader today, I suggest, regardless of the field in which she offers leadership, is *to bring hope.* There are more than enough leaders who offer people false hope and false assurances, encouraging them to invest their time and money in causes that may make them feel good (and

1. McLaren, *Church,* 5.

that profit the leader) but will not actually make a difference. *To bring hope* also needs to be the standard for those who are leaders in the field of ideas, including in spirituality and metaphysics.

You will find this to be a more demanding standard than you might think. It requires one to modify existing answers again and again, looking for versions that really can bring hope. I hold these three goals to be worthy of our most serious attention: to work at helping postmodern men and women avoid harmful ways of speaking about ultimates such as God, to respond to the global crisis in productive ways, and to live out lives of compassion and relevance.

This chapter is an example. I must now say things for the first time that I could not have imagined saying even a few years ago. Systematic philosophers are rightly reticent to admit that we sometimes change our minds in big ways. But the standards I just formulated require this kind of honesty. As a *many-one* thinker (as Oliver Griebel likes to describe us) I have sometimes spoken of God as the unifying principle, often privileging the role of Mind or consciousness. Today, however, I begin with a different way of approaching the unifying principle:

Integrated Physicality

So we start with the diverse physicality of our everyday existence. Think of it as the first very general (metaphysical) recognition that we are embodied beings—seeing, touching, feeling, experiencing the world around us. By starting with physicality rather than physical*ism*, I avoid any claims that we are only physical, or that *only* physical things exist, or that physics is the measure of all things.

"Physicality" is not a technical philosophy term. That's good; let's retain its broader meanings and connotations. *The Merriam-Webster Dictionary* online defines it as "intensely physical orientation."[2] Even better is the *Cambridge Dictionary*'s definition: "the quality of being full of energy and force: *Durante dances with an impassioned physicality.*"[3]

Because "physicality" has not yet been domesticated by the philosophers, it's able to convey numerous different features of our existence: that we are embodied, that we have physical needs and desires, that we are animals who exist in interdependence with other animals and with this planet's

2. *Merriam-Webster*, s.v. "physicality (*n.*), https://www.merriam-webster.com/dictionary/physicality/.

3. *Cambridge Dictionary*, s.v. "physicality (*n.*), https://dictionary.cambridge.org/us/dictionary/english/physicality/.

biosphere, and that we experience the sensations and feelings of embodied creatures. Our conscious thoughts and experiences, whatever else they are, are caused by physical things external to our bodies, such as light and heat and the objects we touch, and by physical things that are parts of our bodies, such as neurons and hormones and neurotransmitters.

The adjective "integrated" adds two crucial pieces. First, because we know that we integrate multiple sensations and experiences and thoughts, we know that many different *types* of things and phenomena must exist. Physical*ism* is a reductive position—it reduces the many (types of appearances) to the one (the fundamental laws and constants of physics, and the matter/energy that obeys these laws). Physical*ity*, by contrast, is gloriously, exuberantly pluralistic. It says: we are embodied beings; just look at the incredible range of experiences that we have, the incredible richness of the reality around us! Physicality celebrates the many.

If the first meaning of "integrated" emphasizes the many, its second meaning raises the question of the One. But not as a metaphysical mandate, like physicalism. Instead, think of "integrated" in the sense of tying together—or at least *trying* to tie things together. "The One" now becomes a quest, not a metaphysical given with which one starts. The quest for integration is the quest for meaning.

This quest is easiest to understand in the first place as storytelling. A fictional story takes a bunch of events and tries to fit them together into a single interconnected narrative. We may like or not like the outcome; we may judge it as good or bad. Whatever our moral judgments, we discern the outcome as meaningful only when it takes a collection of pieces and integrates them into a whole—into a story.

Meaning-making in real life works in exactly the same way. Now, instead of fictional characters and situations, we have to work with actual persons and events, with the diffuse fragments of our own lives. A satisfying narrative is one that has an outcome that we can view as meaningful. We are always already involved in a quest for integration, in the (sometimes futile) task of tying together moments and experiences that don't quite all fit, like an imperfectly made puzzle with some pieces missing and others misshapen so that they don't fit where they're supposed to. The task is also open-ended; as the Greek historian Herodotus warned, "deem no man happy, until he passes the end of his life without suffering grief."[4]

---

4. This means linking the mental with the quest for meaning-making. Meaning-making is about telling a story. And actual stories *in vivo* are always open-ended—in part because of complexity (hence uncertainty) of natural systems, and in part because of the open-endedness and unpredictability of history.

The nineteenth-century philosopher Wilhelm Dilthey recognized that the incompleteness of the story does not only pertain to an individual life; it's true of *all* part-whole relations. An individual word gets its meaning only in the context of a sentence, a sentence in the context of a paragraph, and a paragraph in the context of the book; likewise, each individual event or moment of history receives its meaning finally only within the context of history as a whole.[5]

Integration as process and as quest—it's a beautiful and powerful idea, because it completely reframes the many-one question. We tend to picture the Many-One with static pictures, like a glass jar full of candies. Integrated physicality shifts us to temporal pictures, pictures of process and change. Our brains are never still; our bodies are always responding to external stimuli; cells are dying and being replaced. What was satisfying to the twelve-year-old no longer satisfies her when she's nineteen. Today's answers become tomorrow's questions.

Maybe that helps you see one of my worries about traditional languages of God. To start with God is almost by definition to start with the answer. Even philosophies that start with the Mind or the Soul are already promising their readers that they know the nature of that Ultimate Reality that provides meaning. By contrast, to begin with our physicality, with our raw embodiedness as perceiving-feeling-thinking beings, is to begin with the question.

The human starting point is much more like the famous raft metaphor from Otto Neurath.[6] We find ourselves, as we become conscious, floating on an ocean with no shore in sight, surrounded by flotsam and jetsam. Unsure what has happened, we began pulling together the pieces that are near at hand, strapping them together as best we can into a raft that we can rest on. Many of the pieces for telling meaningful stories about ourselves are already present around us; they come from our culture, our family, our education, and of course from our own experiences. On this account, then, the things related to our physicality as embodied beings are the givens we have to work with; and the process of storytelling becomes *the process of telling-ourselves-into-meaning*—the striving for integration, for unity.

In short, starting with integrated physicality is a way to emphasize that we are always persons in process, persons on a quest.[7] This starting point puts strong stress on always being incomplete in our being and thought.

5. Dilthey, *Gesammelte*, 7:233.

6. Neurath, *Erkenntnis*, 3:205–7. Cf. Cartwright et al., *Otto Neurath*.

7. Obviously "integrated" and "integral" are closely related. Here I consciously resist moving quickly to the latter term. "Integral," like "integer," has sometimes placed too much emphasis on "one." "Integrated," like "integration," puts the emphasis onto

On Integrating Pluralities into Unities

The visionary thinker John B. Cobb Jr. coined the term "deep pluralism." It's an interesting choice of words, since the "deep" implies that there are forms of pluralism that are shallow. The shallow pluralism that Cobb had in mind was the position of John Hick, according to which there is only one religious ultimate, the undifferentiated "Real"; all other statements about the divine represent projections onto the Real of our own personal and cultural constructions.[8] *Pace* Hick, Cobb defended the bold thesis that there actually exist multiple religious ultimates. He argued that there are three in particular: an ultimate with personal qualities (God, Brahman), an impersonal ultimate (world or cosmos), and creativity itself.[9]

There are actually multiple kinds of shallow pluralism on the market. One is the kind of relativism that we hear from our freshmen philosophy students. It's usually expressed in terms like, "My philosophy is that all philosophies are relative." College philosophy students express this stance as a virtue: it allows them to feel like they are advancing a position, and yet they do not need to judge anyone. (Some of their attempts are actually profound; think, for example, of the claim, "All that I know is that I know nothing else.") But if the goal is to advance a hypothesis that helps us to understand and interpret the world, they haven't really gotten off the starting line yet.

Cobb's view adds a beautiful complexity to talk of the One and the Many. For example, just think of how many different kinds of pluralisms there are: metaphysical pluralism (many different substances, or kinds of substances, exist), ontological pluralism (many different beings, or modes of being, exist), epistemological pluralism (different kinds of knowledge exist, that cannot be derived from each other), ethical pluralism (different kinds of things exist that are of intrinsic value). In fact, there are probably as many kinds of pluralism as there are pluralities.

It follows, though perhaps somewhat disturbingly, that *there will be multiple kinds of unity* as well. You find (or create) a unity by unifying the items in a given diversity. In the weakest cases, we say there is "some sort of unity" running through all the many parts, as when someone notes a family resemblance between the various members of an extended family. There are

---

making one—the *striving* for unity. This is a key theme for process thinkers in the tradition of Alfred North Whitehead. Whitehead's guiding principle was "The many become one, and are increased by one" (Whitehead, *Process*, 21). For Whitehead it's "the many" that come in first place.

8. Hick, *Interpretation*.

9. See Cobb's contributions in Griffin, ed., *Deep Religious Pluralism*. Although Griffin was the editor, the book's core concept, "deep religious pluralism," stems from Cobb.

temporal unities, when things become more unified over time; empirical unities; logical unities; and experiential unities. The strongest kind of unity is when differences dissolve and the many literally become one, without remainder or difference. When you look more closely at different theologies, or different metaphysical systems in the East and West, you find vastly different understandings of what "unity" means.[10]

In fact, I'm going to suggest, for *every* diversity, there is at least a potential unity. When we reflect on some collection of these unities, we want to know: Could they *also* fit together into some even broader unity? That leads, finally, to the largest metaphysical question of all: Is there a unity underlying all other unities—the One of which everything else is a part, the One in which absolutely everything that exists participates? What is that One, and what's the nature of *that* part-whole relation? How am I as a part related to the ultimately unifying One?

I hope, then, that as you work your way through this book on "unity in diversity," you will keep your eye on these questions. We can so easily get lost in the vastly different meanings of "unity." That's a good reason, in fact, for centering the remainder of this exploration on "integrating" (a verb) instead of "unity" (a noun). "Integrating" is a temporal word; it stands for the process of moving from the many (better: from *a* many) toward a unity. I interpret a term that some of my fellow authors use, "integral," through *integration*, understood as *the process of integrating*. Sadly, "unity" is too often interpreted in a static, logical way, as in classical Greek philosophy, or as in theologies of an unchanging God. Even theories of historical dynamics are sometimes presented in a timeless way, as if everything else changes but the theory itself stands above the fray, timeless and unchanging. Integral philosophies have not been completely immune to this temptation.

Link integration with the quest for meaning, as I have done above, and you can see why I am stressing the many kinds of unity: the unity of your insights at this moment, the unity of opinions between multiple people, the unity of one's experience over an entire lifetime, the unity of all moments of consciousness, and (for those who believe in it) an ultimate divine unity that relativizes or erases all differences between merely finite beings in order to arrive at the Ultimate One. What a different kind of unity that would be from a unity that exists "in" a diversity!

Now, perhaps, you understand why I insist on getting to these classical metaphysical questions, including the question of God, by means of

---

10. Perhaps the greatest debate among the Vedanta schools in Hinduism is the debate between the "nondualists" (Shankara and his followers) and the "qualified non-dualists" (Ramanuja and his followers). Few Western schools of metaphysics match the complexity of the insights and distinctions in this debate.

physicality. We are carried along in an all-pervasive process. *Panta rhei,* Heraclitus wrote; everything flows (or: all is flow). We can't speak of the outcome without speaking of—indeed, living through—the process itself. Words like "open-ended" and "incomplete" have not been popular among Western philosophers, especially in metaphysics. But they should be. If each individual really matters, *matters even in light of the ultimate,* then the process of our becoming must matter as well.

From Physicalism to Emergence

This next step builds naturally from the previous section. For, as it turns out, evolution is all about integrating pluralities into unities. We don't need to sharply separate out the evolution of the physical universe, the evolution of the biosphere, social and cultural evolution, and spiritual evolution.

In fact, to sharply distinguish them in these ways is to *dis*-integrate, not to integrate. A worldview that reduces everything to physics (physicalism) is a dis-integrating position. You can see the irony here: Physicalists promote their approach as a unifying position; in the 1950s it was called "the unity of science movement." But it is unifying in the way that colonialism is unifying. A colonial power "unifies" a country—but at the expense of subordinating local cultures and knowledges to the dominant power, or exterminating them altogether. We won't be able to grasp unity in diversity until we grasp the distinction between *integrating,* on the one hand, and a *unifying* that requires eliminating the distinctions between parts, on the other. Physicalism fits less in the former and more in the latter category. Technically, this term should mean "of or pertaining to physics." But it's far more often used to express the view that the physical world is *all* there is. There are no meta-physical realities—no God or Brahman or nonphysical ultimate reality.

Philosophers often call this a "deflationary" view. Francis Crick wins points for a particularly virulent deflation of our mental life:

The Astonishing Hypothesis is that "You," your joys and your sorrows, your memories and your ambitions, your sense of personal identity and free will, are in fact no more than the behavior of a vast assembly of nerve cells and their associated molecules. As Lewis Carroll's Alice might have phrased it: "You're nothing but a pack of neurons." This hypothesis is so alien to the ideas of most people today that it can truly be called astonishing.[11]

Astonishing, indeed.

11. Crick, *Astonishing,* 3–4.

The philosopher Daniel Dennett also famously argues that belief in a self is unnecessary. The neurosciences tell us what exists, and they are sufficient (he thinks) for explaining human actions and experiences. And then, of course, there's the problem that one can't locate the self:

> You enter the brain through the eye, march up the optic nerve, round and round the cortex, looking behind every neuron, and then, before you know it, you emerge into daylight on the spike of a motor nerve impulse, scratching your head and wondering where the self is.[12]

If I may put it bluntly, physicalism of this sort encompasses everything that's wrong with metaphysics. It does metaphysics in the mode of "all reality is just this," or "it's this but definitely not that." Francis Crick has just told you that you are "nothing but" a pack of neurons. Reality is objective *but not* subjective, value-free *but not* value-laden. Science is the ultimate arbiter of truth. (Incidentally, lest the reader think that this rejection of physicalism reflects religious prejudices, let me add that I am equally critical of supernaturalism, which can be dogmatic and exclusive in the *opposite* direction, as when theists claim that God is the only thing that really or truly exists, and all other things in the universe have a kind of secondary or derivative existence.)

It's crucial to recognize how emergent evolution leads in very different directions than physicalism. It promotes an *integrating* worldview. We can only do justice to the metaphysical debates of our day, and especially to the controversial term *God*, if we leave behind deflationary theories of the natural world and give the breadth and richness of physicality its full due.

Before we move on, let me quickly draw together what we've arrived at so far: *The worlds of the biosphere, social and cultural worlds, and the rich worlds of spirituality are emerging. The future of each of these worlds is not yet clear because they are not yet determined; each is in a process of radical becoming. Becoming, not stasis, is the nature of reality. Systems and modes of thought that seek to grasp this reality must themselves be in process. We need open systems of thought that respond organically to the ever-new data of emerging reality. We seek not to abolish the Many to get to the One, but to express meaningful emergent Unities in ways that honor the evolving, ever-changing Many.*

---

12. Dennett, *Elbow*, 75.

Biological and Cultural Evolution

I've urged that we start with integrated physicality, with embodiedness, because it encompasses all of our experience; it's a "yes, *all* of this" term, rather than a "nothing-but" sort of term. Now notice something else: human existence—indeed, the existence of all living things—on both the individual and the group level is about new things constantly emerging. Like the history of evolution itself, it's about novelty, unpredictability, and surprise.

Biological evolution is based on the principle of complexities that spawn complexities, in an ever-advancing spiral.[13] I've often written about the beauties of the biological sciences. More-or-less random variations in reproduction and ecosystems produce a huge variety of organisms ("phenotypes"), which multiply, or fail to do so, in their particular environments ("differential selection"). Single-celled organisms float in the water of a lake or ocean. Some evolve a little chemical motor, a flagellum, that can propel them toward nutrients . . . or toward toxins. Already by this point, agency and values have emerged. Which way the organism propels itself is a life-and-death decision. To move toward poison is the "wrong" decision, because it results in the death of the organism.

Gradually, organisms evolve better sensors of their environment and a rudimentary nervous system, so that they can "make good decisions" about where they hang out. Some organisms evolve to become land-based animals, and some develop primitive brains. Some of these animals-with-brains evolve to the point where they can "decide" which actions will probably help them and which will probably hurt them *before* actually carrying out the actions. Some of these species develop adaptive cultural practices (far more species than we once thought, actually) that they learn to pass on to their offspring, greatly increasing their ability to survive. Scholars of evolution now use the framework of "coevolution" to study the interplay of biological and cultural evolution.[14]

In one case, *Homo sapiens*, a species evolved with a far more complex brain than any of its competitors. It turned out to be a good investment (at least for *Homo sapiens*, if not for the rest of the biosphere!), and this species came to dominate its planet. We developed religions, and writing,

13. In Clayton, *In the Quest of Freedom*, I defend an "asymptotic" theory of freedom. The natural sciences show us a world with greater and greater unpredictability as complexity increases over evolutionary history. What happens is that the "error bar" for prediction—the range of the uncertainty about the outcome—increases exponentially as you move into more and more complex social systems.

14. A foundational text was William H. Durham's *Coevolution*. The authors working within the coevolutionary framework are now too numerous to list.

and massive civilizations, and arts, and most recently complex technologies. Our survival became less and less reliant on the biological evolution that got us here, and more and more reliant on our ability to mold the world. As humans gained global dominance, the rich ones transformed the face of the planet so that they could own and consume whatever they wanted, offering themselves whatever pleasures they desired. Eventually the masters of the planet forgot that they remain dependent on the ecosystems they inhabit. At this precise moment in our planet's history, we stand before the immanent collapse of many of those ecosystems. Yet our brains—or is it our spirits?—don't seem to have evolved quite far enough for us to recognize our mistake and return to the levels of consumption that our own science tells us are necessary for survival.

Integrated Physicality and the Mental

Within the coevolutionary paradigm, physical and mental experiences are fully acknowledged as real and as deeply integrated. What you are thinking and feeling as you read these words has everything to do with whether you ran five miles this morning, or didn't sleep last night, or whether you had three cups of coffee or three glasses of wine with your lunch, or (more radically) whether you have just had a stroke or an epileptic seizure or ingested psychedelic mushrooms.

Of course, the link works in both directions. If you are deep in despair, your immune system is probably weaker at fighting off a bacterial infection than if you are feeling optimistic. If you are absolutely determined to finish the marathon you are running, you are more likely to overcome your body's fatigue and reach your goal.

Balancing the mental and physical may be the most difficult task for many-one thought today. The tendency in professional philosophy is to overvalue the physical, as in the quotes from Crick and Dennett above. In reaction to that, some years ago I became one of the major advocates for "strong emergence."[15] In a certain sense this was the right course of action, given the hold of physicalism on many of my intended readers. But my critics have also recognized some of the dangers.[16] Strong emergence tends to privilege the mental over the physical, underemphasizing the pervasiveness of physicality in human existence.

15. I defended strong emergence in Clayton, *Mind and Emergence*; and in multiple books and articles since that time.

16. More recently, see Ritchie, *Divine Action*.

It also raises theological difficulties. If one's account of divine action is limited to God's influence on minds or souls, it begins to seem as if God cannot be doing anything else in the universe. In that case, God's influence would be limited to setting up the laws of physics at the moment of creation on the one hand, and to some kind of divine lure on human minds or souls on the other. That leaves about 13.71 billion years in which God is not involved with the created universe—a rather strange passivity, given that trillions and trillions of organisms have lived and evolved and died during that time. It is far less dualistic if one can affirm that there is some divine involvement "in, with, and under" every moment of emergent evolution in the cosmos. Against the intentions of strong emergentists—and against my own explicit goals in my writing—a kind of dualism threatens to arise. Moreover, in cases where women are associated with the body and men with mind, sexism becomes yet another an unintended consequence.

So in the new view that I am developing here, I am switching the emphasis. *Emergent evolution as a whole* should now be our guide, not just the emergence of mind. Integrated physicality helps correct for dualistic tendencies. For example, the paradigm of strong emergence tends to treat experiences of sensuality and sexuality as lower levels, and the *reflection* on such experiences as higher. From the standpoint of integrated physicality, the sexual bonding of a couple can integrate their concrete sensual experiences, their emotional connections, the thoughts and words they share, and the spirituality that they share. One does not need to subordinate physicality or de-emphasize touches in order to speak of love or find the spiritual meaning; the entire experience, in all of its dimensions equally, is part of a single integrated whole.

Likewise for mind and body more generally. Over hundreds of millions of years, living beings on this planet have gradually developed mentality. Only in the last thousands of years have civilizations arisen with written languages and complex cultural structures; the scientific age is only hundreds of years old; and the "age of information" has exploded only in the last few decades. In this cosmic process we come to know mind as an emergent. But if we don't continue to integrate it with the bodies and the ecosystems on which mind depends, we fail to understand ourselves as physical/mental beings. The ecological crisis is a direct result of this failure.

In short, one doesn't do justice to this story of emergence when one *starts with* Mind as the ultimate principle of unity, as if we could fully know the Mind of God. To comprehend unity in diversity, one has to discover mind as an emergent quality of physicality, not as the pre-existing root of all things.

Integrating Physicality and the Spiritual

It's immensely freeing to begin to think about spirituality in the context of integrated physicality. If "strong emergence" sets in motion this oppositional dynamic between the mental and the physical,[17] how much stronger are its effects when we begin to think about spirituality! In English, as in many Western languages, the etymology of "spirituality" suggests "of or pertaining to Spirit." No opposition is stronger in Western philosophy and theology than the opposition between Spirit and flesh, the Spirit and the body, the transcendent and the immanent, God and world.

It's time to challenge those oppositions. I suggest that we use the language of spirituality not merely for the moment in cosmic history when humans are the central focus—the brief time period since the world scriptures have been written and the great works of music and art have been composed—but throughout. Let's find value not only in the emerging mental worlds, but across the whole range of cosmic history. Let's learn to see the laws of physics as spiritual, as well as each type of thing that emerges: quantum energies, the first self-reproducing cell, the beaver's tail, the peacock's plumage, the spawning salmon, the opening bud of a flower, the sexual embrace, the fetus washed in amniotic fluid emerging from the birth canal.

This type of spirituality needs to be correlated with a worldview that "democratizes" mind or psyche, that recognizes its presence everywhere and not merely in an elite few souls. That worldview exists. Since the dawn of humanity it's been present in the beliefs and practices of indigenous peoples; it's also visible in many of the world's great religious traditions. It's *panpsychism*, the view that *psyche*—mind or consciousness or experience— is present in absolutely everything that exists. Nothing exists that is *purely* physical; all that is has some form of agency and creativity.

Professional philosophers have cast the spotlight on panpsychism in recent years, and sophisticated new versions are being developed and debated. Together with various other allies, I have defended "emergentist" or "proto-" panpsychism—expressions of panpsychism that retain a place for the process of transformative becoming that we have been tracing. Cosmic evolution offers complex examples of transitions from potential to actual mentality—in individual living beings; in groups, societies, and civilizations; and across the cosmic process as a whole.

The heart of this spiritual view of evolution is what I call *deep participation in unfolding unities*. We are physical-mental-spiritual

---

17. The evaluative connotations of "strong" and "weak" emergence inevitably convey that the more mental the better; and that in turn suggests (whether one intends it or not!) the principle "the more mental, the less physical."

unities-in-becoming. As individuals, in an important sense we do not yet exist; we are in our becoming. At the same time, we are always already embedded in relationships with others who find themselves in a similar process of becoming. Groups of unfolding individuals exist within communities and societies and cultures that are themselves becoming. The phrase "deep participation" expresses that we derive our very being through this process

Our being or essence is not like a container that holds our various qualities, which is sometimes how Aristotle thought of it.[18] Instead, our being lies in becoming.[19] That means that in this universe "unity" is an inherently temporal notion. Unities are not *given*; they are becoming.

Here physicality, emerging mentality, and spirituality meet. Spiritual evolution is already a part of this dynamic of becoming. The process of cosmic evolution must be understood from the beginning as a spiritual process. The alternative is to wait until a specific idea arises—say, belief in God—and then label that "spiritual." But to separate spirituality out in this way is to make integration impossible. Once such a duality between the "merely physical" and the "truly spiritual" is allowed to arise in this way, it can never be overcome. The despising of the body, the depreciation of our own sexuality, the valuing of rationality over intuition, all have their origins in this primordial imbalance.

You can see now why integrated physicality leads to a revolutionary transformation of spirituality, a spirituality beyond the dualism of "Spirit" and "matter." Consider just a few of the implications:

- "Spirituality = Spirit" suggests that spiritual practices must be designed to transcend the body so as to get to Spirit. But true spirituality is about integration—including the integration of body and soul or spirit.

- Many of the world's greatest spiritual traditions involve somatic practices. One thinks of yoga and tantra in the Hindu traditions, "sitting Zen" (*zazen*) in Zen Buddhism, and "davening" (rocking and praying aloud) in Jewish prayer. One prays and worships with one's entire body, one's entire physicality.

- Ayurveda in the Hindu tradition, traditional Chinese medicine, fasting in Islam and other traditions, and innumerable dietary practices in indigenous traditions represent ways that spiritual states are influenced

18. See Aristotle's notion of *hypokeimenon* or substrate. This notion, translated into Latin as *subiectum*, unfortunately became the first Western framework for a theory of subjectivity. In this chapter I am offering integrated physicality, as defined in these pages, as a more adequate framework.

19. Cf. Eberhard Jüngel's version of "being in becoming," developed under the influence of Karl Barth's doctrine of the Trinity.

by what people ingest. Psychedelic herbs, from peyote to sacred mushrooms to ayahuasca, have played and continue to play a crucial role in people's spiritual journeys. Too much is lost if one restricts spirituality to things that are caused by mind or spirit.

Central for Jews and Christians is the proclamation of the Shema, which begins "Hear, O Israel: The LORD our God, the LORD is one. Love the LORD your God with all your heart and with all your soul and with all your might" (Deut 6:4–5 ESV). The passage resonates with integration; we might say it's the call to work to unify one's physicality, mentality, and spirituality into a single process of becoming—the one in the many, the many in the one.

Integrated Physicality and the Divine

We come now to one of the most contentious intersections in our journey: can one still use the G-word? Does "God" necessarily mean the kind of timeless, nonphysical unity that I have resisted, or is there a way of understanding the Divine that adds depth to the image of unfolding unities-within-in-unities that has emerged in these pages? I close by exploring a concept of God radical enough to augment the spiritual-evolutionary worldview of our age and relevant enough to speak to the global ecological crisis.

The goal and telos of a process is in some sense present throughout the process—not as an actual finished product just waiting to be displayed, but *in potentia*, as a lure that draws attention to as-yet-unrealized possibilities, or as a dream that captures our imaginations and turns our attention in new directions. Many of the disputes today are fights over what that final goal is and how we should name it. The outcome of the ecological crisis, for example, may depend on whether we turn our thoughts and actions toward establishing a genuinely ecological civilization, or whether we continue to strive for the perfect consumer society with its pleasures and satisfactions.[20]

I believe this process of spiritual evolution toward deep integration and deep participation is not just in our minds, a construct of our hopes and fantasies. Instead, it is grounded in something deeper, something real, however difficult it may be to name it.

Across the world's religions, this ultimate Ground is given many different names: Brahman, Tao, codependent origination, Allah, Yahweh, God. The point of intersection of all these diverse terms becomes visible when we acknowledge that we are all *grounded* in something, no matter how difficult

---

20. This is a major emphasis of the nonprofit that I founded and lead, the Institute for Ecological Civilization (EcoCiv.org).

it is to name it. Almost all traditions affirm that the Ultimate Ground is one; it is the "all-oneness" (*All-Einheit*) or, as philosophers and mystics in the traditions of Plotinus and Spinoza have put it, the *hen kai pan*, the One and All. Almost all affirm that spiritual practices are necessary for us to perceive the Ground, and that when we do, we experience both compassion and the call to compassion.

The differences move to the forefront when one seeks to name the One, to identify its parts, and to outline the stages that lead to unity: the unity of the individual with herself, of community with community, of humans with the earth. The classical God of the Abrahamic faiths has fallen on hard times, and many seekers are turning to less dualistic views of the divine. Integral and process metaphysics have their birth here. Unfortunately, unresolved disputes have turned "integral" philosophies, which were intended to integrate, into a source of division, a *dis*-integration, for some readers. Still, the call to compassion and integration remains.

Continuing to seek the emerging Divine in the world and in ourselves radically changes the frame. As I tried to show in the previous section, spirituality understood in the context of a fully integrated physicality combines bodily and spiritual practices, creating unity rather than division within the person. Still, how we speak of spirituality and how we speak of the Divine are obviously linked: *you can't have an integrated spirituality and at the same time affirm a divided relationship between God and the world.*

That insight, I suggest, now becomes the main task for any theology that seeks to be adequate to our age. Talk of the divine is only helpful—that is, it's not the old God in sheep's clothing—if it can unite thought and practice. The Divine, understood in a fully integrated fashion, is a unifying and not a destructive term. Freed from the Angry Father, we recognize that we are always already contained *within* the Divine, and the Divine in us. (If you wish to avoid the term "panentheism" you can just think of this as the "double in.") Our spiritual task is then to recognize, internalize, and live out this truth—to practice our location, as it were. It is to learn to live as ones who flow with the Divine like fish in a current, or like one node within the living breathing network of life.

With both phrases in this chapter title—*Spiritual Evolution and Organic Participation*—I intend to counter dualisms that place Spirit (the mind or the male principle) in opposition to the earth, the body, and the female principle. There are not three separate forms of evolution: biological, mental, and spiritual; there is just the one reality of cosmic evolution, which is characterized by a continuous process of the emergence of ever-new properties and dynamics. Consequently, deep participation cannot lie only in the

Divine; it must also include full participation in the entire living, throbbing, growing biosphere around us and in us.

All these pieces really can fit together, I suggest . . . as long as we don't make God into a static unity. The components are already in our hands; we just have to have the courage to use them to conceive not only cosmic evolution but also the Divine itself. When we do, we begin to perceive God as a *becoming* unity, not a preexisting one. Like ourselves, parts of the Divine are already actual, and parts are still in the process of unfolding. (Whiteheadians like to speak of the two "poles" or dimensions of God, what he calls the *antecedent* and the *consequent* God.)

The process of the unfolding of the universe, and of all the individuals within it, is not finally to be separated from the process of the unfolding of God. Whitehead shows how deeply the two processes are connected:

The religious insight is the grasp of this truth: That the order of the world, the depth of reality of the world, the value of the world, in its whole and in its parts, the beauty of the world, the zest of life, the peace of life, and the mastery of evil, are all bound together—not accidentally, but by reason of this truth: that the universe exhibits a creativity with infinite freedom, and a realm of forms with infinite possibilities; but that this creativity and these forms are together impotent to achieve actuality apart from the completed ideal harmony, which is God.[21]

For Whitehead, the "ideal harmony, which is God" is precisely *not yet completed.* The *ideal* exists, or God exists *as* the ideal; and yet we find ourselves part of a pervasive process of cosmic spiritual evolution that aims in the direction of that ideal.

All this works only if divine unity is thought analogously to the other unities we have considered. All unities are partial; all are becoming; all remain dependent on the becoming unities that they include within themselves. The becoming of my self and my body are inseparable. Both are affected by my ongoing quest to learn, to integrate new experiences into my self-understanding, and to find meaning in an ever-changing world. God does not stand, impassible, above the fray. The divine becoming must be not unlike our own.

Why? Because the consequences of answering otherwise are catastrophic. To affirm a static God, a God of completed unity, is to affirm that the destination of the universe and of ourselves is already fixed. The so-called problem of evil inevitably arises, since God is now fully responsible for the outcome of all events, and thus for the level of suffering and evil

---

21. Whitehead, *Religion*, 115. Whitehead first presented the text at the end of Lecture Three of the series "Body and Spirit" in King's Chapel, Boston, in February 1926. For an online version of the text, see http://www.mountainman.com.au/whiteh_3.htm.

that we see around us. Our freedom disappears, because God must bring about the unity that "he" already represents, whether we wish it or not. Our range for agency becomes limited, for our power of agency to affect others is decimated when God is defined as the all-powerful one.

A fixed and static unity, a unity that already entails the final outcome of history, constrains and finally negates the process of cosmic becoming. In that case God is, as Wolfhart Pannenberg once argued, the all-determining reality (*die alles bestimmende Wirklichkeit*), and we are determined parts of his omnideterminism.

In these pages I have affirmed the Many, as well as the striving toward the Many becoming One. But this framework does not guarantee that a final unity will be achieved, or that ultimate divine unity pre-exists the entire process as such. If we are part of an open-ended process of becoming, then the divine unity is in becoming as well. And us? We too are parts of the same organic process, interdependent with the divine, co-creators of the world around us. We too are helping to determine the emerging unity in diversity.

Action in lieu of a Conclusion

Many authors write about the intellectual, spiritual, and political crises of our day: the crises of fundamentalism and violence, the crises of nihilism and meaninglessness. Yet no clock is ticking faster than the clock of global climate disruption, which threatens widespread economic and societal collapses within decades, if not sooner. The growing disharmony and disintegration (dis-integration) no longer affects the human species alone . . . as if it ever did. We are already taking hundreds of thousands of species with us, an escalating event that scientists are already calling the sixth mass extinction.

What we do to our ecosystems will return to haunt us, *until we learn to cultivate the world and ourselves, which means to evolve spiritually.* "Integration" is an empty word if it does not mean full organic participation in Gaia, the common principle of all life on this planet.

Jesus ended his most famous story, the parable of the good Samaritan, with the words, "Go, and do thou likewise" (Luke 10:37 KJV). People often cringe at the abstractness of terms like unity and diversity. However, abstract debates become important when they influence how we live in the world. To see ourselves as organic parts of an emergent evolutionary process . . . to recognize that we are not isolated individuals but parts of interdependent systems, and that our becoming contributes to, or blocks, the becoming of others . . . to know that the entire process is open-ended and that we are coconstituting the Divine as it is coconstituting us—each of these insights transforms our mode of being in the world.

In this sense, ecology and theology are inseparable. A bad theology of the completed, all-determining God seriously weakens humanity's chances of turning around, of ceasing our destruction of this planet's ecosystems, and of beginning to build an ecological civilization. A theology of integrated physicality and interdependent becoming with the Divine, by contrast, spawns a genuine new way of being in the world, an organic coexistence with the cosmos and with the living systems around us.

Bibliography

Cartwright, Nancy, et al., eds. *Otto Neurath: Philsophy between Science and Politics.* Cambridge: Cambridge University Press, 1996.

Clayton, Philip. *In Quest of Freedom: The Emergence of Spirit in the Natural World.* Edited by Michael G. Parker and Thomas M. Schmidt. Frankfurt Templeton Lectures 2006. Religion, Theologie und Naturwissenschaft 13. Göttingen: Vandenhoeck & Ruprecht, 2009.

———. *Mind and Emergence: From Quantum to Consciousness.* Oxford: Oxford University Press, 2004.

Crick, Francis. *The Astonishing Hypothesis: The Scientific Search for the Soul.* New York: Scribner, 1994.

Dennett, Daniel C. *Elbow Room: The Varieties of Free Will Worth Wanting.* Cambridge: MIT Press, 1984.

Durham, William H. *Coevolution: Genes, Culture, and Human Diversity.* Stanford: Stanford University Press, 1991.

Dilthey, Wilhelm. *Gesammelte Schriften.* 12 vols. Leipzig: Teubner, 1921–1936.

Griffin, David Ray, ed. *Deep Religious Pluralism.* Louisville: Westminster John Knox, 2005.

Hick, John. *An Interpretation of Religion.* Princeton: Princeton University Press, 1989.

Jungel, Eberhard. *The Doctrine of the Trinity: God's Being Is in Becoming.* Translated by Horton Harris. Monograph Supplements to the Scottish Journal of Theology 4. Grand Rapids: Eerdmans, 1976.

McLaren, Brian D. *The Church on the Other Side.* Grand Rapids: Zondervan, 2000.

Neurath, Otto. "Protokollsätze." *Erkenntnis* 3 (1932) 204–14.

Ritchie, Sarah Lane. *Divine Action and the Human Mind.* Current Issues in Theology. Cambridge: Cambridge University Press, 2019.

Whitehead, Alfred North. *Process and Reality.* Corrected ed. Edited by David Ray Griffin and Donald W. Sherburne. The Gifford Lectures 1927–1928. New York: Free Press, 1978.

———. *Religion in the Making.* Cambridge: Cambridge University Press, 2011.

4

What Do I Mean When I
Say That I Love God?

LAYMAN PASCAL

I.

That is a very good question. I suppose this query is another way of asking what I mean when I describe myself as a *theistic postmetaphysical
nondualist.* Those are obscure words but they collectively hint at my own
personal truth. In this essay, I will try to tell you what I really believe. It is a
risky challenge! It is especially difficult for me because I am deeply skeptical
about professed beliefs. I strongly doubt that most people know their own
values or can accurately communicate their worldviews. Beyond that difficulty, it also seems to me that authentic humans must have great humility
and flexibility toward our mental conclusions.

Yet, that certainly does not mean that I have no significant considerations about the architecture of reality. A great deal of my life has been
devoted to clarifying my inner picture of truth, and I would like to make
every effort to share my philosophical worldview and embed that in the
peculiar flavor and history of who I am as a person. This short essay will
tour through several interlinked facets of my vision in order to explore the
nature and consequences of my intellectual, emotional, and spiritual relationship to the sublime Many-One. Although we will need many nuanced
concepts and some challenging, abstract language, nonetheless these dozen
segments will be a deeply personal, even autobiographical, statement of how
and why I cannot help but worship Unity-in-Diversity even though I inhabit
a rational, pluralistic, and metamodern world.

II.

It is March in the year 2012.

I am sauntering happily down the sun-dappled sidewalks of Victoria, British Columbia, moving in the friendly shade of the ubiquitous cherry trees. Old churches and brick buildings on both sides. The smell of spring flowers and fresh bakeries. Uplifting, colorful graffiti by well-intentioned local street artists. My mood is excellent, my thoughts are delightfully arcane. While I pause to wait for the change of traffic lights, a smiling young man suddenly steps toward me with a strong intention.

He looks oddly out of place in this cosmopolitan paradise. His short-sleeved, white dress shirt is buttoned up to the neck. Dark, inexpensive dress pants. A midsized book under his arm. It is immediately obvious that he is a Mormon missionary from the Church of Jesus Christ of Latter Day Saints. I have dealt with them before. My heart winces subtly. The agents of official public monotheism are often *wearyingly* disappointing. Yet he is also just another human being like myself, so I smile at him and try to be very present.

"Can I talk with you about God?" he asks.

That is one of my most favorite topics, but I wonder whether there is any real chance of having a rewarding conversation with a predatory book-worshiper about the diaphanous numinosity of Being. Could he even hear my arguments? Would he react poorly to my belief that the historical reality of Jesus is both highly dubious and completely unnecessary for the spiritual and cultural functioning of healthy Christianity? Text-based desert monotheisms generally impress me as aberrative rather than normative examples of human religiousness. So I am wondering how much of myself I would need to stressfully conceal in order to have a civil and profitable conversation with this young salesman of religion.

I improvise an interesting possibility:

"I would love to speak with you," I say, "but I am deeply mistrustful of words and names. They are too superficial. How could I know whether or not we are both referring to the same *thing* when we use the word 'God'?"

Another good question.

Although I was raised in a New Age home which assumed God was infinitely everything, I also know that some religious sects specifically believe in God as a finite, super-powerful, ethnocentric entity. Any word that can conceal meanings that are as logically opposed as "infinite" and "finite" becomes almost a joke when it is deployed in public discussions. What does it matter if two people who do not know whether they are even discussing the same topic happen to agree or disagree?

"If you would be willing," I continued, "to put aside the word 'God' for now and, instead, simply *describe* what you are talking about—then I would eagerly engage in such a discussion." Happily, he agreed. As our talk unfolded, it became clear to me that, underneath the specifics of his organizational religious commitment, his personal interests revolved around the problem of the Many and the One.

There was, he said, a vast multitude of human beings but only One divinely embodied person (as specified in the Judeo-Roman legend of Jesus the Redeemer). Likewise, it seemed to him, a cult of atheistic materialism had taken over the world. This cult embraces the vast plurality of objects in our universe but rejects the primordial One who created and governed all that multiplicity. He passionately affirmed that a metaphysical unity stands over, above, and prior to the "illusion" of this world.

I found him to be very earnest and affable. Unfortunately, he lacked the requisite philosophical flexibility to make any sense out of my comments that "Manyness" and "Oneness" were inherently noncontradictory and deeply mutual concepts that are intrinsically implied by each other at even the most basic level of reality. We do not, I told him, even have the option of choosing one or the other. They are not thinkable as alternatives.

I said to him, "The separator is the connector."

I said, "Same-difference is a single concept."

My idiosyncratic attempts to describe a functional, not merely mystical, nonduality fell senselessly upon his deaf ears. Perhaps he had not read enough Heraclitus, Nagarjuna or Hakuin? And yet, I felt he intuitively understood that I was speaking about a God for whom I feel much faith and hope. In many ways, I sincerely worship this *generative, operational same-difference*. And how very close is that strange statement to this boy's claim that a One created the world and still makes it flow!

Yet a deep chasm separates his traditional, poetic language from my improvised conceptual description of transcendence. Perhaps it is no problem to say it either way. Many different kinds of statements can describe the same logical structures. However, I feel a bit sad if he does not—as I do—behold the Divinity between every two options, within the shifting gradient of an electromagnetic field, in the closeness of embodied lovers, and in every vision of a consilience approaching the artistic unification of many diverse elements. I personally see and feel a Divinity within those thresholds of proximity and convergence wherein we can no longer fully distinguish between the meanings of "separate" and "unified."

Human eyes and brains are dualistic. Each lens produces its own viewpoint, but there is still a special zone at which the parallax blurs into clarity and the dualism gives way to a vivid new depth of vision. The neuromechanics of sight are, for me, an analogy for how the vision of God can be deepened.

When the Many and the One are brought *just near enough* to each other, when neither concept can either escape or be canceled, then the parallax gives way to a new salience. In the incomparable nearness of the Many-One, there shines forth an invitation to an ever-new ecstasy that might redeem and reorient the world.

III.

If this all sounds very philosophical, that is good. In fact, I am a philosopher of some kind. What I mean by *philosopher* is not an institutional professional from an officially certified philosophy department but something more like a calling. I would describe a philosopher as a *difference worker* in the same sense that prostitutes are legally dignified as "sex workers."

It is the task of philosophy to develop the human spirit through a relentless and good-humored reconsideration of our common conceptual categories. Perhaps we have been making distinctions that are not actually real? Or maybe we have treated some matter as simple and homogeneous when it ought to be more authentically described as several quite different issues? These investigations are part of the compulsive task of the difference worker.

For example, I once suggested to an Anglican bishop that his outreach to atheists might be better served by broadening his understanding of the Many Names of God. What if, I said, the term "No God" was considered to be among the venerable and praiseworthy titles of the Deity? Then he could say, with a good conscience, that "No God" created the world and "No God" governs the events of our lives. All we had to do was to draw the boundaries of our differences slightly differently.

Of course the bishop balked, chuckled, and then outright dismissed my outlandish proposal, but for me the strangeness was an enticement rather than an obstacle. Essentially, I was suggesting *a/theism* rather than the typical contrast of Theism vs. Atheism. My duty as a philosopher was precisely to call the differences themselves into question. Is this mere semantics?

I bristle at that suggestion.

People are actually engaged in mere semantics when they attempt to dismiss something as "mere semantics." Just like they are engaged in philosophy when they try to draw a serious boundary that excludes "mere philosophy" from their notion of the reality of bodies and passions. There has been across history a reductive and hasty trend to eliminate the subtleties of thought. Nuances must not be trivialized. Many ultimate things make themselves available to us only through rare and subtle pathways. In Zen Buddhism, for example, the delicate logical and linguistic intricacies of Koan puzzles are understood as privileged vehicles for the arousing of wisdom and nondual illumination.

The master watched two students roll up their mats and put them away. Their performance was identical. He declared, "One of them has it but one of them does not."

What could be more plainly obvious than the fact that this fragment of Koan, shown above, promises a visceral enlightenment by guiding you through a nuanced thought structure designed to confront you with the force of a seductive Interbeing located between sameness and difference?

If you can lay hands upon the Interbeing here, then you may also find it thriving in every in-between, within each threshold, or in the double-ended space of every intimate relationality. God does not live "above" or "on the other side" of reality, nor is God simply identical to reality. Divinity haunts the terrain between those notions. Divinity occupies the margins, brings vitality to life in the tidal pools between the ocean and land, affords the phenomenological energy between two hands of the Tai Chi master, and opens the tangible eros between the lips of lovers.

That is what I mean when I say that I love God.

IV.

You have probably noticed that I referred to myself early on in this essay as postmetaphysical. I also scoffed at beliefs, exhibited deep skepticism about monotheists, and asserted that God does not occupy the "other side of reality." What does this all point toward?

In what sense am I *postmetaphysical* about Spirit?

The common assumption about postmetaphysics is that it asserts rational, scientific materialism in opposition to the classical history of superstition, myth, and intuitive cosmologies. No nonphysical entities! Just eliminate the whole invisible pantheon of the archaic imagination and remove all childish reification of abstractions. That is a beautiful challenge. It offers us a chance to start cleaning up our minds and stress-testing our habitual modes of thought. But for me, this sort of naive antimetaphysical thinking is still just the beginning.

I consider myself to be postmetaphysical in the Nietzschean sense. Nietzsche was a critic of unwarranted assumptions, mixed-up values, and ontological assertions among traditional, modern, and postmodern thinkers alike. Postmetaphysics is a much bigger thing than modern doubts about premodernists (or postmodern doubts about modernists). We must open up the half-intelligible root cellar of all our ideas, high and low. Unless you have seriously doubted whether or not "is" even exists, then you have not fully started to interrogate the world in a postmetaphysical fashion.

Yes, we should be skeptical about Gods, souls, and the substance of classical virtues. We should also be skeptical of truth, history, feelings, numbers, and even the concept of skepticism itself. We must be daring enough, and well-balanced enough, to complete the journey across this shifting terrain. If we succeed, though, where do we end up?

Let me tell you where I have ended up.

I would say that today my postmetaphysics has five main points: *Nonessentialism* (entities are self-approximations and not perfectly identical to themselves), *nonprimalism* (the highest things do not have to be the first things), *enactivism* (experiences are validated by processes rather than beliefs), *logical containment* (you cannot think of things outside of what you can think of), and *multiperspectivalism* (reality is not monological but rather a plurality of reality-tunnels that must be collectively taken into account).

That is the world for me. How does unity-in-diversity operate in this kind of postmetaphysical universe? How can God be described so as to pass through the gate of postmodernity, across the river of nihilism, and into the new metamodern or integrative cultural terrain that many good thinkers feel is both necessary and possible for a thriving human future? What kind of God is both real and lovable in the reality that I am describing?

Part of my philosophical work is to find conceptual interfaces between the constraints posed by my impression of transmodern reality and the deep, intuitive, mystical, and heart-awakening phenomena that our ancestors understood in connection with their notion of a Deity. I will therefore briefly cover these five points of my postmetaphysics.

A God, for me, must be *nonessentialist*. "He" is not identical to himself. In fact, as the epitome of Being (which is incomplete, dynamic, and self-approximating), God is the very principle of self-approximation. He is an almost-ness that can outperform the definite, absolutized sense of certainty and identity with which previous epochs of mystics and philosophers have tried to define the superlative aspect of reality.

I believe that a phenomenon does not have to be *total* in order to be maximal. It does not have to be perfectly completed in order to be optimally active. The centuries-old logic of mathematical calculus has demonstrated that we can work quite well with infinitesimals—regressing endlessly toward a horizon without ever reaching it. Armed with such powers of incompleteness, we have much stronger mathematics than mere algebra was able to provide.

Likewise, the principles of relativity and indeterminacy have given us a Physics that is vastly more precise and amazing than anything possessed in the science of our ancestors. Certain forms of incompleteness are more, not less, than completeness. I think of God in these terms. A constantly new idea. A divinity that shows itself in an endless movement of incomplete self-clarification that is analogous to the ever more precise and innumerable digits of pi. Pi is a single, functional ratio that recedes toward infinity without ever completing itself. It is the unity of a dynamic multiplicity that approximates itself without arriving at totality. God, likewise, is never pinned down and provides the never-pinned-down-ness of all things.

God is also *nonprimal.* "Her" virtues need not come first.

Our ancestors were not rational cosmologists with a strong objective theory of Time. They used the idea of the past as a tool to steer the present. Asserting that something has temporal primacy (i.e., comes first historically) was for them a way of honoring it—rather than a way of describing it accurately. The metaphysical God, they felt, must be the Creator in the same sense that a primitive Tribe may depend on the fantasy of their first chieftain and founder to whom they are endlessly indebted. Perhaps the popular notion of the Big Bang Singularity retains some of this archaic fetishization of firstness. An author must precede the book. The ironsmith comes before the swords that he forges.

Human-like agency is imagined as the senior principle of the world and therefore is enshrined with honor at the Beginning of All Things. This powerful way of feeling and organizing information is nonetheless profoundly preevolutionary. It treats values as fixed and constant over long periods of time. Today, we know that many of the best things emerged over vast epochs from out of other strange things with very different qualities. The original inventor-king did not make a perfect and constant unchanging order of the world. Not only has everything been constantly changing, but he himself is descended from the lowest rats, fungi, and viruses.

In modern labs, we have found that RNA "messenger molecules" existed long before DNA. Metaphorically speaking, the message certainly can come before the sender of the message. Perhaps the play then predates the playwright? Are authors added after the fact? Contemporary thinkers must wonder about such things. Strange loops, complexity, distributed agency, retroactive causality, mutation, great things descended from low things. The reality of today cannot simply inscribe our favorite things into the earliest history of the world.

And yet even in our postmetaphysical world, we still need a circumscribed set of seemingly metaphysical entities like logic gates, quantities, infinitesimal sequences, geometric consistency, computational rules, and so forth. We just do not need these things to be conceived, like angels or titans, as occupying a primal period of history. I believe they are better thought about as perpendicular to ordinary Time. Entering, or being folded into, every moment. Not coming first.

So too can God/Godliness continue to have a place of supreme significance in our hearts and our cosmology without being dubiously confined to the first moment of imaginal history. "She" is not the prime mover at the beginning of the sequence but an omnipresent contributor in much the same way that the logical syntax of mathematics is available at all moments and locations.

The contribution of minimal metaphysical implications to the ongoing operation of reality does not have a privileged primal location. Like many of the great classical philosophers, I locate the implicit form of God in the functions that permit logic to operate. The syntactic network of logical principles implied by the existence and operation of any viable physical universe presupposes that meaningful interactions, evaluations of validity, verification processes, and the negotiation between sameness and difference are already always possible.

"Something" provides a self-validating (tautological) protosyntactic cluster of anchoring principles that can enable universes to operate according to a set of laws of physics. Just as much as Descartes or Leibniz, I consider God not to be subject to casual human evaluation and verification but, rather, active as the root principle of evaluations and verifications of all kinds. This capacity, to ascribe value and accomplish validation, is itself maximally valuable and validated. It distributes those qualities to other comparisons. It empowers the operational possibility of any confirmation up to and including the maximum degree.

I have just said that God is real and lovable if logic works.

However, this does not require that maximal validation means the same as total validation. Nor does it suggest that such a force exists at a point in, or before, time. This integrated cluster (a many-one) of logical qualities has the same kind of existence as "or" and "and" or "not." And despite its omnipresent availability, it has neither a temporal priority nor spatial location.

Nor is it identical to any asserted cultural belief.

A postmetaphysical God is also *enactively* evoked by our contemplative practices, our neurochemical adjustments, cognitive and behavioral habits, etc. and then only secondly gets specified through the lens of our belief systems. The maximal (not absolute!) validity of $1+1=2$ does not exist as a result of hearing it asserted as a popular or authoritative fact. If we treat it as true because we have heard that it is true, then it is not *functionally* true.

A belief-assertion or belief-agreement can be sourced in different ways. If we source it in authority, habit, or group loyalty, then we are performatively confessing that it is not sourced through a rational or experiential appreciation of the facts of reality. Science, which was the first major wave of postmetaphysics, requires that we attempt to draw a boundary between these two types of beliefs. Postmetaphysical theism demands, at minimum, that we expect beliefs to be derived from procedures of experiential or rational verification. We become convinced, faithful, only by authentically going through our own process of meaning-making and confirmation. Otherwise it is merely a cultural assertion, and any cultural assertion can just as readily be denied. Modern and postmodern forms of critical thought have laudably struggled to tease apart functional truths from psychosocial agreements.

God is not real because you have heard about God. That is another way of saying that the God you have *heard about* is not real. Divinity is not a piece of public news. Your relationship to Deity is not like clicking "thumbs up" or "thumbs down" based on your degree of agreement with a social media post. My opinion is that we have a responsibility to distinguish belief from both social affirmation and the narrative claims of group membership. The God who is present as popular or authoritative hearsay, articulated as a simple "objective fact" was properly rejected by the emergence of modern rational and experimental culture. Yet, as many of our greatest scientists have privately attested, this does not remove the God with whom we can profitably participate and procedurally evoke through contemplative practices, shared meaning-making, and peak experiences.

Historically, human beings have tended to treat our own race (and the god of our race) as a pre-given, fixed, metaphysical fact whose primary function is to be agreed with, proclaimed, and attached to the special benefits of our local membership cults. Today this view is utterly untenable.

Our ethnicity itself is not simply given to us. It evolves as a social construction over long periods of time. It is more like a work of art than a physical fact. The fallacy of nativist, anti-immigrant politics is the belief there is a special, god-given quality associated with people who just happened to be born in a particular geographic region or within a particular pattern of ethnic descent. However, the reciprocal fallacy of the multiculturalists is that we should be neutrally open to all attitudes—rather than undertaking a special, challenging, and often exclusionary work of culturally forging a homogeneity of authentic citizens. Whether you immigrate from another country or out of a local womb, you cannot simply be embraced as a perfect, unchanging vessel of nonproblematic values and perspectives. Culture thrives or fails based on the health and intelligence of the institutions that are meant to create a trustworthy unity out of a multitude. Both the "right" and "left" positions are frequently stuck in outdated metaphysical assumptions about the essential nature of people's ethnicity and beliefs.

The same kind of thinking colors popular notions of God.

In order to have a socially useful form of the Unity-of-Diversity, we must understand it as a responsibility and creative cultivation. It is not magically given to people who are born in a particular group. You cannot get it just by verbally affirming it. And you are not "let off the hook" because you come from a different background. Cultural fragmentation, depression, and subjugation of society to private interests are inevitable unless we practice growing a One from our Many. That means we need to assimilate as much diversity as possible but not any more than we can assimilate. The Many-One, whether personal or cultural, is a reciprocal balance that cannot be engaged from any one "side" of an issue.

The emphasis therefore must be upon enacted practices, both individual and institutional. There is something holy, useful, and needed about civilization. It is a sacred thing. However, that sacred potency depends upon what we do and what we experience, not upon what we assert and affirm. It is no longer possible for the basic act of faith to be the confirmation of the peak "social imaginary" (God) characteristic of our local culture. An atheist can be more religious than a theist. Or a believer can be unfaithful. The issue is whether or not we are engaged in practices that enact the force of the shared numinous spirit which is possible within and among us. It makes no difference to agree that there is a unity of diversity. You have to find ways to *do* that unity.

In addition to being enactive, the postmetaphysical God is legitimately *multiperspectival*. To say He, She, or It about this Deity is not mere political correctness but an acknowledgment of the sheer diversity that the unity-of-diversity must unify. I have specialized in a type of philosophy called Integrative Metatheory. These models pay great attention to different valid lenses upon reality. We could, for example, discuss God as a first, second, or third person phenomenon. They all have their merits. God cannot, in a multiperspectival situation, be only a subjective, objective, or intersubjective entity. The postmetaphysical Divinity must be present equally in these different perspectival lenses and present even more completely when they are considered next to each other.

It should make no difference whether the Deity appears as a supreme Thing, Self, or Other any more than it should matter which cultural aesthetic or tradition is called upon to offer a description of the Deity's appearance. It should not even matter whether we like the word "God" or not. That kind of epistemological variation is appropriate and anticipated as part of this ontology. Basically, the structural and functional reality of the superlative relationship between Many and One presupposes *a high de-gree of self-consistency (one) that is unperturbed by a high degree of diversity (many)*. God is not located within one of the reality-tunnels; God enables all the reality-tunnels.

A flat model of the world might anciently have supposed that a single great totem pole or ladder symbolically ascends upward from the world toward the Peak Being. However, when we understand a spherical Earth is spiraling through cosmic space, we can see that "up" moves simultaneously in many opposed directions. Upward from the other side of the world is Downward from here, yet it does not cease to be consistently gauged by the same metrics of altitude.

That covers most of the postmetaphysical requirements that I place upon theism. Only one principle remains to be addressed:

V.

Logical containment has a special meaning in postmetaphysics. It is not absolute, but it still has the classical power to determine what is or is not "thinkable." In the epoch of quantum mechanics, we obviously need to synthesize a new hybrid of certainty and uncertainty. It was, after all, the introduction of rigorous indeterminacy and probability models that gave us the most precise physical information that our species has ever discovered. Incompleteness and approximation are an *advancement* in terms of the power and nuance of our understanding. They are more trustworthy than certainty.

I have called this a Metaphysics of Adjacency.

Notions of proximity, approximation, and "almost" become deep operational concepts whose value for truth and life exceeds the old promises of totality and completion. The simple identity of $1=1$ is vastly useful but also logically imperfect. It is $99.999\ldots$ percent true. Or, rather, we are never in a position to gauge whether its truth does or does not become total. A tiny parallax inevitably exists between the two sides of any equation. $1=1$ is "as true as it gets" but there remains a little wiggle room.

Gödel's theorem in mathematical logic shows us that even the most practical system of coherent computation can never perfectly enclose or justify itself. This, for me, is a big improvement. We move away from our armored fixation on essential identity toward an ambiguity that is not the opposite of clarity. To be "nearly identical" is the condition that has always given logical identities their power and which operates in the space between

One (pure identity) and Many (differences). I strongly advocate this kind of logic when considering the Many-One.

Unity and Diversity are *almost* the same thing. They share the "same difference" which blurs out at the threshold of their mutual functionality. And while we cannot say that the One is perfectly, implicitly contained by the Many, we also cannot say that it exists outside, above, or prior to the Multitude. We must therefore locate the Many-One in the specific condition of intensified proximity rather than imagining that One occupies some impossible "additional space." Logical containment forbids any space additional to reality.

This has tremendous importance when considering the relationship between metaphysical idealism and nihilism. Nietzsche famously denounced Christian popular metaphysics as "Platonism for the masses." He meant, among other things, that both the Folk and our scholars pretend to think what they cannot think. Nihilism, in our cognitive processes, takes the form of nonthoughts replacing thoughts.

Here is a nonthought: nothingness.

Here is another one: outside of reality.

And another: before time.

Trying to think of these things is good mental exercise. They show us the logical boundaries of thought. We are refined and strengthened, whether in reasoning or meditative exercise, by contemplating the edges of our cognition. It is good to enact this practice but bad to make it into the basis of a metaphysical assertion. Treating God as the one who started Time or exists outside of reality or created the universe from nothing tries to think of God as a nonthought.

Nietzsche, whom I love, was very concerned with the idea of living beings fantasizing that their possibility of highest value exists only after dying—in a world other than The World. He worried when individual persons hoped to improve themselves by becoming impersonal. And he especially criticized those theologians who placed Ultimate Value into an impossible thought. The Many-One is sabotaged when we act like the One both exists independently superior to the Many and also exists in a "place" where it cannot exist.

For me, nihilism does not describe a small handful of people who profess to believe in nothing. Rather it is a large number of people whose beliefs involve the metaphysics of an impossible world in which the Best Thing is unthinkable and essentially nonexistent.

In fact, perversely, if you think of God as an unthinkable power outside (beyond, above, or before) everything you find to be reasonable, then *you* are faithless—no matter what you sincerely claim to believe. God, for you, is *effectively unreasonable and nonexistent.*

So the postmetaphysical God is therefore *not* the creator of the world.

We may casually tolerate such traditional and potent poetic formulations of metaphorical truth about the divinity of creativity, but the very idea "creator of the world" seems to be one of those metaphysical concepts that are unnecessary and misleading. There is no position outside the world for a creator to occupy. We are all in this together.

Nothing outside, above, or before reality can be real. If you conceive God "dualistically" as being above, prior to, or beyond reality then you are treating the highest value as though it were absolutely nothing. Reality consists of all real things sharing the quality of realness. Anything real enough to be real is within reality and not a cause outside of reality—which would mean that it is not real. If God created Reality, then He is outside reality and is therefore not real enough to have created Reality.

That is a way of describing what I mean by postmetaphysical logical containment.

The *One* cannot be located outside the *Many*. The power of unified identity was never derived from its absolute difference to the relative truth of the multitude. Its power always came from relationality, approximation, almost-ness. That is good news. The One is not absolutely self-identical and distinct from the Many. It is blended into the Many because of the implicit logical connection that blurs them together. They cannot be thought about separately in a postmetaphysical universe. They can only be thought nondualistically.

VI.

The multiple is the inertia which can be retroactively discerned starting from the fact that the operation of the count-as-one must effectively operate for there to be Oneness.[1]

The quote above is from French philosopher Alain Badiou in his masterful volume *Being and Event.* It asserts that the presence of the One is not primordial but the result of a process—what I would call "one-ification." If you encounter the One, therefore, you must assume that one-ification has already occurred so that a multiplicity must have previously existed (and is still present as conceptual inertia) to provide the multitude that could

---

1. Badiou, *Being and Event,* 25.

be one-ified in the first place. Therefore, in some sense, the Many always precedes the One.

Here Badiou is arguing against Parmenides, the great Greek protophilosopher who taught that prior unity is the primary existential fact implied by the appearance of the plurality of beings. Thousands of years later, Arthur Schopenhauer made a similar claim about the Will—that it is necessarily One because it exists outside the realm of apparent division and the multiplicity of separate beings. Badiou disagrees. He believes the problem lies in mathematics. Ancient and classical philosophy closely linked their spirituality to their contemporary math, which was Euclidean, algebraic, and deeply anchored in the natural number line beginning with One. Today's contemporary math is sourced in Set Theory, which posits groups as the basic elements of reasoning. In this view, even a collection of one thing is actually a group containing itself AND "nothing else."

$1 = (1, \text{nothing else})$

So unity is always already a plurality.

I do not want to ignore the nuances of Badiou's thinking or pigeonhole his claims, but I immediately experienced his work as important and admirable in terms of rebalancing the relationship between Manyness and Oneness. The *unified identity* is not hiding behind or threatened by the presentation of diversity. It would be just as true to say that Oneness is concealing and obstructing the true, primal Manyness.

Both concepts are implied in the same breath. They are linked by a dynamic relationship of reciprocal structure. The One does not simply diverge into the Many any more than the Many simply converge into the One. A situation of simultaneous convergence-divergence describes the implicit mutual identity of unity-in-diversity.

Trying to decide whether One or Many is "primary" is a false decision. It cannot be decided any more than we could decide whether water molecules are made of hydrogen OR oxygen. The definition implies both. Can you think of many without thinking of "as opposed to one"? Does oneness have any meaning except by presupposing a comparative link to manyness?

A boundary, even a conceptual boundary, both divides and unites. Any comparison implies that the different elements being compared also share enough structure and syntax to be intelligibly compared in the context of a common reality. They must be *the same enough to be different*.

So my position is that One is not a thought. Many is not a thought. However, Many-One *is* a thought. When I speak of God, I am not proposing a Oneness that is opposed to the plurality of existence or even simply simultaneous with it. I am in love with "something" that cannot even be considered without deeply interlocking the meanings of both concepts.

VII.

Is such a God, in my opinion, created or discovered?

That is a most excellent question. Is the nondual Many-One already a fact about reality, or does it only exist when we performatively enact it? You have no idea how tragically rare it is for people to ask me such things! It is my habit to approach this problem by distinguishing three types of nonduality: *emergent, implicit, and analytical.*

Analytical nonduality is also what I call functional nonduality. It considers the ways that pluralities and unities are combined in the categories we use to analyze how the world functions. For example, the notion of the extended mind in contemporary cognitive science suggests that our relationships and our tools should be considered as part of our mind—parts of our memory, problem-solving, and evaluating systems. This is a way of analyzing a specific functional process that transcends conventional categories of Self and Other. You and your phone are not-two and not-one. Many operational examples of the Many-One or the Same-Difference are possible. They involve rewriting our categories to appreciate blurred distinctions in the way that systems behave. Another example is the way that unconscious intelligence processes and decision-making in human beings force us to unlearn the classical duality between "known" and "unknown" information.

In addition to remaking our analytic categories, there are also phenomena that can only be appropriately analyzed by attending to the fact of adjacency. Adjacency is a situation that is neither fully separate nor fused together. A compass, for example, performs its function when it is close enough to the magnetic attraction of the North Pole (i.e., the compass would not help you if you were in deep space) but not too close (it fails when you are actually *at* the North Pole). Analyzing this function means examining it in the context of nondual proximity, which is defined as being neither too distant nor too close, located neither as a dramatic identity nor as a dramatic separation.

Putting aside analytic nonduality, we come back to the other two kinds. We ask the question of whether nonduality is entirely implicit or emergent. Do we make Divinity, or was it there all along? It will not surprise you to hear that my answer is: both.

I place great emphasis on emergent nonduality. The integration or harmonization of a set of systems can produce effects that are greater than the sum of the parts. A surplus or excess dimension of coherence can be produced by the balanced cooperation of participants in dialogue, between genres of culture, or between facets of the nervous system (e.g., heart, mind, and body intelligences). The practices that cultivate this extra, "numinous" quality, coupled with the lifestyle of relating to this successful emergence, constitute human religious and spiritual existence in my opinion. We produce and work with a transcendental factor that orients our meaning-making, growth, inner wholeness, and interpersonal communion. And this numinous quality can be perceived as a deeper Self, a higher Entity, or a mysterious Energy. We can experience it through different lenses. This is what I call the integration-surplus model of spirit.

So we make God. But is that the end of the story? Is there any validity in a postmetaphysical reality to claims that the Divine is eternal, omnipresent, always-already existing? Perhaps.

Anecdote: It is late July of 2002. I am standing with a half dozen of my fellow Buddhist novices, inhaling the sea breeze among the trees of Ross Bay Cemetery. We are preparing for the Sunday morning meditation class at the nearby Sangha building. I am using specific mental details to help select an emotional state of calm, appreciative altruism. Some of my peers are worried about the inauthenticity of overriding their "natural feelings," but our master has been very clear on the need for intentional cultivation of harmonious feeling-states. These are typically states of "neurocardiac coherence" in which the electric signature of the neural activity in the chest synchronizes more closely with that of the skull. After a short introductory wisdom-talk, we sit in a semicircle facing our serene senior meditation master in his yellow-orange robes. His energetic presence and his archetypal example seem to help us each go more deeply into our own conscious trances. I do not know how much time has passed, but suddenly something shifts. My sense of identity falls out the back of my head, swoops around the outside of the room, and peers back at me, mischievously, from my master's eyes. The phenomenon is uncanny and delicious. I want to jump up and shout, "That's me—over there!!!" After a while it wears off. Transpersonal consciousness. Two separate bodies with one Self.

But what does it mean?

Is this Emergent Nonduality? Did my heart-mind coherence and generally balanced perception allow the "different objects" to be temporarily integrated into a surplus coherence?

Or is this Implicit Nonduality? That would mean that there was always only One Self. Either the whole human species, or possibly the whole cosmos, is a single subjectivity veiled by the illusion-generating habits of ordinary perception, which I had temporarily penetrated. This is the standard interpretation, used in the great mystical traditions, to describe these alternative states of consciousness. But ancient cultures and individual mystics are often not particularly concerned with the objective ontology of reality. A good argument can be made that this kind of speech (speech that affirms an exalted prior consciousness that has always transcended all different bodies and selves) is not scientific evidence at all but rather a poetic approach to honoring the importance of surplus integration states, which experientially exceed the limits of our brain's ability to reason, keep time, and make ordinary distinctions. I accept that challenge. I agree that most of every experiential encounter with "higher powers" is *created* through our actions and then *interpreted* through our biological, social, and psychological habits of perception. It is of supreme value, yes, but it is mostly something *new* emerging in that moment rather than the discovery of an ancient fact about objective reality.

However, I do believe there *is* a role for implicit nondualism.

Here's how I think about that:

The ability to generate coherent emergent properties, including a "numinous" surplus of coherence resulting from adequate integration of subsystems, is nonlocally available. Like the laws of physics, it can be accessed at all times and in all places. Our personal ability to generate higher states of perception, our collective ability to come together in spirit, and even the capacity of physical energy systems to periodically evolve into new emergent regimes of depth and complexity, are permitted by the informational architecture of reality. The underlying logical principles (of the computations that enable a universe to operate) provide a set of qualities and ratios that syntactically orient the events of successful integration, consilience, and convergence. It might be imagined as a holographically or fractally distributed attractor-pattern that provides the primitive template and "flavor" for *apotheosis*—moments of god-making.

Implicit nonduality is the signature that permits the ubiquitous potential for emergent nonduality. So, although I do not credit the eternal preexistence of either a cartoon God or a highly significant universal Self, I nonetheless presume the existence of a minimal, protosyntactic architecture that bears the traits of Divinity in their most negligible form while also making more significant versions of itself available through the constructive processes of life and behavior in the unfolding universe.

Postmonotheist culture inherits the idea of a single God who has ruled from the beginning. We are often confused by the more common ancient idea that Deity can be generated. Romans exalted the city of Rome and the man Caesar into gods. Aztecs spoke of the "place where gods are made." People, places, and things could be divinized in the ancient world, but the successful cultivation of Deity experience depends on many factors both practical and theoretical. Just as the science of physics negotiates between experimental data and mathematics, so too must the science of religion negotiate between instances of god-experience and the logical prerequisites for such experience.

A postmetaphysical, nondual theology must explore both these facets of unity-in-diversity. And not merely for the edification of philosophers. The dynamics of spiritual and religious experience have consequences for individual health, general meaning-making, and the capacity of societies to unite, in a balanced way, to mobilize on behalf of higher values.

VIII.

I denounced a cartoon God above, but I am not against religious mythology. However, I appreciate the mythic lens in a special way that highlights both its humanity and its connection to the nonduality of the Many-One. To understand my approach, consider how the generic modern word "Deity" evolved. Like many modern people, I was raised to imagine fantastical ancient populations worshiping a cartoon-like god *named* Zeus. So I was somewhat stunned later in life when I studied the etymology of the word— realizing that Zeus (Deus) was not a name. Not exactly, anyway. It was also their straightforward word for "The God" just as "Deity" is our word for the same thing.

This led me to wonder if pagan theology was not quite as pagan, exotic, and childishly superstitious as generations of Judeo-Christian and Islamic scholars (and their secular successors) had led us to believe. It seems likely that loyal monotheistic scholars would exhibit a semiconscious investment in exaggerating the psychological gap between *our* advanced religion and *their* primitive fantasies. This dualism bothered me.

Ancient peoples were simplistic in many ways, certainly, and they typically had a magnificent aesthetic tradition of personifying their Divine Principles into stories, images, and statues. Average people in the past may well have taken the "soap opera" narratives of the Gods very seriously. Yet this leaves out a great deal of important psychological and social information about how they experienced Deity and how they related to the conceptual principles embodied in their dramatic pantheons. Our typical modern framing of their beliefs tends to ignore its potential rational sophistication. This framing also risks being dehumanizing and divisive. Why? Because it erects an unnecessary cultural membrane between contemporary/conventional and foreign/exotic. *They* get to live in foolish fantasies while *we* are confined to disenchanted modernity. The same boundary creates two prisons.

We still do this in many translations of the Qur'an. Frequently, we translate all the words into English, German, or Spanish except that we leave the Arabic word for God (*Al-Lah*) oddly *untranslated*. While we may tell ourselves that we are being culturally sensitive, we nonetheless create a divisive situation in which it sounds like "they" worship a strange being named Allah instead of just worshiping our God.

We are apparently very sophisticated. *We* understand that War leads to Terror and Fear, but *those* primitive fools, with their strange beliefs, thought that the gods Phobos ("fear") and Deimos ("terror") were the twin children of the War God. Clearly, we are saying something very similar but in a manner that subtly infantilizes and excludes the Other.

I believe this has twin negative effects of (a) reinforcing artificial cultural division, (b) obscuring the degree to which our own contemporary colloquial terminology could, and perhaps should, be experienced as sacred.

This second problem is very interesting. Suppose that it was historically normal for human cultures to feel the existential potency and surplus meaningfulness associated with their colloquial, generic concepts such as War, Art, Love, Politics, Wealth, Wisdom, Death, and so on. Then perhaps contemporary people are malnourished human beings. We fail to feel the sacred resonances of our abstract physical, social, and psychological forces. Could it be that our cultural fragmentation, stagnation, and imbalance results in part from a failure to viscerally experience the transcendent features of our shared discourse? Are we taking the Gods' names in vain?

I listed two problems above. They are both deeply related to the issue of unity-in-diversity. The first problem involves the exaggerated division in human civilization, and the second issue relates to the cognitive unification of many elements of perception. Here's how that works:

Firstly, although it is important to respect real ethnogeographic, historical, and neurophysiological differences among human beings, that is not more important than honoring our shared universal humanity and the dignity of all persons. The ancient ethical imperative of humanism is today also coupled to the practical need for a shared transcultural mobilization against accumulating crises at the planetary scale. We need a sense of deep cooperation and spiritual resonance. That sense can be undermined by our habit of fetishizing the exotic, foreign, and "incomprehensible" nature of other people's sacred ideas. In order to balance the Many and One of human culture, we may need to be more responsible about allowing all their sacred words to be entered into our own colloquial, psychological, and philosophical language—rather than excluded as though they were the strange, glamorous names of legendary characters belonging to groups of people whom we can never really understand.

Secondly, human minds have a marvelous ability to abstract multitudes of examples into singular generalizations. Consider one of the few instances in which we actually translated the sacred colloquial phraseology of the Other into English. It was the situation of the pre-European religions of North America. Today we still speak of their faith in Raven, Coyote, Wind, and Great Spirit. This is so wonderfully visceral and straightforward that it continues to invite sensitive people from all cultures to make inner contact with that style of ecologically oriented shamanic spirituality. What kind of cognitive processes are involved in worshiping Raven? It involves the generalized abstraction of many personal and cultural experiences of particular ravens into a single (to coin my own word) *mythocolloquial* principle. Raven is the singular embodiment of the raven-ness perceived to be common to all the ravens. It is a way of thinking "the many" ravens as One Raven. It does not replace the many ravens with one "god of ravens," but rather it embraces all the instances in a common experiential fact.

Many-One.

IX.

Obviously, there are many interesting pathways that open when we switch over from viewing religion as a set of cosmological assertions and begin instead to view it as a set of practices to invoke and cultivate the transcendent quality of the Many-One in both personal and social affairs. One pathway that attracts me deeply is the redemption of sinfulness. Can the classical concepts of guilt, remorse, and sinful transgression be rehabilitated in a postmetaphysical context? I think so.

The "free will" of sinners can be a dangerous idea. Naive notions of autonomy allow us to dismiss the suffering of others and ignore the complex, systemic causes of human behavior. It is old-fashioned metaphysics to believe that we are each a singular "I" who has complete responsibility for all their own choices and outcomes. This is why metamodern philosophers, among whom I am sometimes counted, have a tendency to speak of the Dividual—rather than the individual.

Our psyche is a community of different selves, deeply embedded in our social and physical environments, and "subject" to frequent cognitive dissonance among our competing drives and perspectives. This plurality, however, does not mean that more unity is impossible. It means that we have to work at integrating our inner multitude—just as Freud, Jung, Gurdjieff, and Heidegger, among others, suggested. Authentic individuality may have an inner seed, but it does not become our real condition until we start to work with the inner contradictions that have been hidden under superficial social ideas about simple individuality and responsibility.

This possibility of an emergent, higher-order, inner Many-One requires two things. First, we must engage the metacognitive space that both views and exceeds our various thoughts and values. That is a work of mindfulness. And we must also voluntarily (it cannot be forced) lean into the friction and painful recognition of our inner disunity. Unless we can occupy the places of cognitive *dissonance*, we cannot begin to transform them into a higher cognitive *resonance*.

These two practices are the heart of a postmetaphysical notion of sin.

We are not per-defined as culpable, unified beings. Instead, we have to volunteer for the attempt to be integrated and responsible. Integrity is a creative option. The One of our psychological Many is something we need to cultivate.

Ongoing efforts toward higher-order, inner integration involve a deep willingness to encounter the contradictions between our ideas and actions—or between our different valid value systems. Feeling these torn intensities and trying to assume the position of responsibility for them is a work of "remorse." It is a constant voluntary encounter with the mismatch between what we hoped we were doing and what we actually are doing. The interpretation of responsibility, of taking blame for sin, allows us to practice being in the position of control relative to the errors and incongruities of our divided psyche. And for many people this rewarding effort is assisted by the fantasy that "God is watching"—i.e., that your inner chaos is, in principle, inspectable and amenable to a higher judgment.

Despite the many ways in which perverse cultural incentives and simplistic metaphysics have misused the concept of sin, it nonetheless remains possible to view it favorably as a form of the pragmatic, nondual postmetaphysics of unity-in-diversity. Thinking in terms of integrated pluralities can clarify the positive, rational utility of many otherwise discarded metaphysical concepts.

But aside from its practical resonances, how deep does the power of the Many-One go?

X.

On my Canadian birth certificate, it says "Cyam Pascal" but for years folks have been calling me Layman Pascal—so I have adopted that name. It was not a big leap. It has many of the same letters and, like most nicknames, it contains a subtle joke. In English, we say "layman's terms" when we hope to learn about a complex topic without the jargon of experts and academics. My friends told me that I usually spoke about complex topics in very colloquial terms but described ordinary things in an arcane, intellectual fashion—often requiring me to innovate my own terminology. However, my new name contained one other interesting reference:

Layman Pang was a famous character in Chinese Zen folklore. This fellow was a householder and family man who happened to have trained alongside the great Zen masters of his generation. Although he refused to take the official robes of a monk, he was nonetheless respected as an expert on Koan practice. The tales of Layman Pang typically concern his visits from Zen adepts and masters hoping to engage his insight into these famous non-dual contemplation tools. So my nickname also resonated with my growing, idiosyncratic and nonmonastic obsession with the deep logic of Koan-activated states of consciousness. What a profound pleasure it was (as still is) for me to sit in the snow with Hakuin's commentaries on the *Hundred Perfect Koans of Master* or the *Chan Whip that Drives Students to the Zen Barrier*!

As a young boy, I had a flippant curiosity about Zen. I casually puzzled out amusing answers to "The Sound of One Hand Clapping" in the same way that I entertained myself with mathematical paradoxes. Later, however, I came to appreciate the matter more deeply. Or at least more personally.

I realized that I had been culturally conditioned to think of Koans and paradoxes as challenges to "Western logic." The idea was that they proved the impossibility of achieving true wisdom through the use of analytic intelligence. Let that go. Allow the mind to slip into the silent stream of spaciousness between-and-behind mental activity. Put down all concepts and become the empty mind-essence. This is a very common assumption. I received it from all kinds of meditation teachers, New Age books, and popular Western translations of medieval Asian texts. It can definitely be a useful practice but I slowly began to view things differently.

In classical Zen texts by Koan masters, I started to see a pattern of complaints about "do-nothing Zennists" whose sitting practice merely emphasized relaxation, release, and empty self-watching. They seemed to be saying that it is inadequate to merely let go identifications and surrender your mental struggle. In fact, you need to make the mind work very hard in order to have the experience that the Koan puzzles are meant to evoke in our consciousness. To open the Kensho Eye did not mean to release logic but to work unusually rigorously to stay at the heart of the paradox of all logic in order to learn its special form and be transformed by its uncanny suggestiveness.

Focusing on the mind-essence, I realized, could have two very different meanings:

If your metaphysical assumption is that the mind-essence is the blank and spacious background of mental activity, then you will try to release yourself into that transparent mystery. However, you might also conclude that the essence of mind is the basic operation of distinction-making. Increasingly, I began to conclude that the root of cognition is that primitive act of comparison and evaluation. Thus I attributed my many great and small satori experiences to intensive engagement with the irreducible fact of a simultaneous same-difference that must be adjudicated.

The Master, having returned from his walk, told us definitively that the only place where omnipresence could possibly fit is in the small glade out behind the monastery.

The logic of such statements (my own in this case) offers intense access to a joint impossibility-and-necessity that can strongly affect consciousness if it is frequently repeated or persistently concentrated upon. I believe the resulting amplification of metacognition and self-awareness common among Koan students can be attributed to the fact that the basic process of adjudication of what is identical-or-not-identical is itself the root of cognition and perception. That is what the practice amplifies. This meant that I was beginning to interpret my Koan practice through the lens of the Metaphysics of Adjacency (MOA).

MOA is a description I created in order to help articulate the metaphysical presuppositions of postmetaphysical pluralism and integralism. What are the unique metaphysics required by all kinds of postmetaphysics? Like an idiot, I took this question seriously! After long pondering, it appeared to me that the key special feature (of any system in which multiple experiences of reality are *valid*, whether they contradict or complement each other) is that realities are ontologically "next to" each other in varying degrees. They resemble each other or distinguish themselves through an implied, pre-existing gradient of similarity-and-difference.

Relativism, quantum mechanics, and multiple perspectives are examples of people trying to appreciate reality as the variable proximity of different experiential viewpoints. Relationship. Approximation. Proximity. Parallax. These become primary thought tools when characterizing existence in a pluralistic or postpluralistic universe.

Adjacency.

My proposition here is that the One thing (common element) implied by the multitude of things is specifically the relationship-of-multiple-things-to-each-other. This one factor is distributed everywhere in the Manyness. You cannot even have a manyness without it because it *structures* the Manyness. The universal, structural precondition of multiplicity is the syntax-like relation between degrees of approximation among patterns. No pattern is either detectable or thinkable if it is absolutely different or absolutely identical to another pattern. To show up is to occupy the gradient of approximation between identity and nonidentity.

Same-Difference.

Collapsing identity and nonidentity into a single logical function is a powerful way of inspecting the most primitive and potent example of the same-difference, the basic version that enables cognition to operate. There are, of course, other beautiful aspects to Zen Koan practice, but this one is very significant. The effort you make to enter into the trap wherein you cannot move between options (because the possibility of evaluation between options is itself the one object of your visceral contemplation) is a frustrated motionlessness that melts into a thoughtlessly luminous movement in all directions. It is a fountain of radiant joy that can be discovered wherever you look.

XI.

Another important place to look for the Many-One, I believe, is the evocative imagery of the ancient Mesoamerican calendar. Aztecs and Maya invented elaborate mathematical and astronomical systems. They symbolized these in a calendar-like mandala in which the great circles of celestial time concentrate around a surprising "divine face" that appears in the center.

I do not perceive this as a flat image. Instead, I imagine it as the inner ceiling of a holy dome arching upward toward a strange, new intelligence who peers back down from the apex. It is an organized pattern of coherent convergence that reaches its zenith, folds back upon the system, and reveals a higher, emergent phenomenon sourced in the integration of multiple systems.

A New One Emerging from the Cosmic Many.

American philosopher Ken Wilber, among others, has suggested that reality is structured as an evolving growth hierarchy or "holarchy." Senior holons do not derive their status through dominating other members of a particular community in evolutionary competition but by operating as the next greater sphere of inclusive enfoldment. This "great nest" of enfoldment reaches from atoms to molecules to cells to organisms and beyond. A cosmos of holons. Each layer is a whole which combines many parts into a newly unified quality of depth that can, in turn, potentially evolve as part of yet another emergent, higher-order whole.

So that strange divine face peering down at me from the domed Aztec ceiling of Time looks like the view from within any holon that encounters its next integrative stage of inclusive, emergent identity. That face is the site of a docking procedure whereby one whole system (of many parts) orients itself within a greater, more inclusive whole system (of many parts).

Is that God peering back down at us?

My view is that the threshold itself displays what we could call the divine pattern. God is not the particular next level but always the shape of "every next level"—the threshold function of the unification of a multitude into a unity that is more than the sum of its parts.

Humans are inclined to think in exaggerated ways. We tend to imagine that a force needs to be absolutely infinite in order to overwhelm our consciousness. Yet, in the real world, people can drown in only a few inches of water. It does not have to be an already existing total infinity just to transcend your little mind, It only has to be a bit bigger than your current visceral experience of being in a world. Our concept of God may have always been simply "the next level" relative to whatever you think is real. Yet that basic shape, the configuration template of a *next, more inclusive integration*, may in fact be enabled by something timeless and omnipresent. At least as timeless and omnipresent as mathematical logic. Elsewhere in this essay, I have described what I consider to be the implicit nonduality of a Deity-like cluster of operations implied in the syntax of all possible realities. But an outstanding question remains:

How far up does this function go?

Is the entire universe integrated into a single wholeness-of-manyness?

The whole cosmos is not like any other single holon. It may not even be correct to call it a "whole." After all, it cannot have any next level outside of itself. There is nowhere else to go. Unlike every other known entity, the cosmos cannot eat or excrete anything outside of itself. Yet many mystics, and even many physicists, have been impressed with the feeling that the entire system is a mega-entity. Some have supposed it was always a singular cosmic being while others, like Teilhard de Chardin, have implied that it is growing toward becoming a unified, self-aware being.

The way that I excavate the linkage between thinking that (a) the All is One, and (b) the All is not One, is to consider the maximum scale of diversity (i.e., the set of all things) as *virtually* unified. We can say that it acts, under certain conditions, as if it has a common organizational threshold—without thereby committing ourselves to the nearly impossible assertion that the whole universe simply *is* a single metaphysical entity.

Here's how that could work:

As reality changes from moment to moment, it maintains an intelligible consistency. Many schools of physics have struggled to logically describe the manner in which the universe is updated, in each moment, at each iteration of the computation, with information it needs about what the rest of the universe is doing. Every actual change in the universe seems to fit so well with all the other changes that we are able to abstract the self-consistent laws of physics from examining these transformations.

This suggests to me that reality must include an ongoing self-reconfiguration in which the momenta of existing patterns are collectively integrated and fed back to the local states of the whole system. We would otherwise see glitches everywhere and physics would routinely fail.

The extremist tendency of human metaphysical thought would therefore suppose the existence of an instantaneous power to accomplish this distributed updating. A more cautious, postmetaphysical notion would simply state that this coherently informed self-reconfiguration needs to occur as fast as our ability to locally detect it. To paraphrase computer scientist Stephen Wolfram, we simply do not encounter the updated condition until we have also been updated.

Such an overall operation is very suggestive. It is *as if* there is a unified self-reflective and self-ordering nexus for the manyness of the universe. Our hasty instincts may wish to either dismiss or reify this idea into a solid God, but, speaking postmetaphysically, we can happily surrender ourselves to the as-if-ness.

A virtual wholeness of the cosmos is just fine. It can negotiate between the ontic plurality of real entities and . . . themselves. This ongoing circuit, from all local entities back to all local entities, can be stable and self-consistent without being fundamentally asserted as an additional super-entity— regardless of occasionally appearing as such to human beings.

It is simply not important to state definitively that one "super holon" is holographically distributed into the form of each local Many-One. The exact same pattern could simply indicate a significant consistency between the way that whole entities emerge from multiplicities and the way that all the parts of the universe maintain informational coherence.

I imagine it is difficult to tell whether I am being too rational or too mystical? I hope that is the case. Such in-between territory strikes me as extremely fertile. Now let us go one step further:

We should imagine this virtual feedback nexus (informing the universe about itself at a maximum rate) also produces an extra quality—a coherence that is more than the sum of the parts. A phenomenon analogous to the novelty and wholeness produced by the periodic evolutionary integration of local multitudes into local unities. Such an idea imagines something like a *holy spirit*. Surplus gestalt information that occurs at the virtual godhead point and spills over to offer a pervasively transcendent quality to all holons at all scales. That is almost plausible. You will not be surprised that I take solace in that "almost." I am walking a dangerous tightrope between science, skepticism, mysticism, philosophy, and faith, but I believe this tightrope *can* be traversed with a little improved skill at balancing and, perhaps, a dash of inspired daring.

This is my vision of theistic postmetaphysical nondualism. It haunts me and convinces my heart. It even seems to me that I have witnessed this "virtual divine reflux" coming toward me like an eternally half-born God, a Self that is myself but greater than myself, and that also can be some exquisitely daunting supernal energy.

Such a God is more than merely the (quite valid) idea of a second-person cognitive relationship with the great emptiness of Being. It is a superlative structural factor that clarifies the generic benevolent direction of evolutionary emergence as a specific aesthetic flavor and moral obligation.

A Deity of this sort has a will, a law, a directionality, that we serve more or less adequately. This is not just the neutral background of reality to which we must acclimatize ourselves. It is the virtual apex of convergent patterning spilling over itself, back into the logic of all local encounters, to provide the perpetual presence of your potential purposeful participation with all beings through an orientation toward the shared horizon of being.

XII.

It is the summer of 1998.

With my more experienced, first girlfriend, I take psilocybin mushrooms for the first time. As we wander in a lush cedar forest together, I marvel at the extraterrestrial insectoid forms of branches and roots. I am overwhelmed by the clear and sheer volume of a raven's beating wings passing overhead. Shamanism encroaches upon me from all directions. It seems to be the only practical response to this real world of pulsating, interacting life and vivid, transrational complexity. I remember very clearly the sheer delight that I felt when I bent down and brought up a handful of fertile forest soil, telling her, "The dirt . . . it isn't dirty. It's clean." Materiality, embodiment, and ecology are obviously not the opposite of divine purity. I saw that these were the very nature of the sacred.

A few hours later, the return of my normal brain chemistry was yet another cause for ecstatic delight. When the vision of infinity turned back into a single, simple rock in the yard, I realized again the error of imagining that impersonal, infinite abstraction was somehow superior to the lived, finite, and shared world.

"A rock can be anything," I told her, "A rock is everything, of course, but actually it is much better if it is just a rock! That's the right arrangement."

This *one* thing was the best way to be *many* things. Form is the form of the formless.

Reason is transrational.

Time is eternal.

Materialism is sacred.

Same-difference.

All of these seeming paradoxes and revaluations are united across a common syntactic bridge, an ambidextrous gradient of relational approximation that distinguishes what otherwise cannot be distinguished. The separator is the connector. But this is not all philosophy and Zen Koans. I learned that day in the forest that this is also deeply *indigenous*.

Traditional shamanism is not perfect. It has real limitations related to its ethnocentric rituals, mythic ideation, dubious drug use, zealotry, naive acceptance of visionary states, and archaic customs of social behavior that can include many abusive and prepersonal habits. However, everything I have been pointing toward in this chapter requires our future spirituality to be transhuman, ecological, embodied, transrational, improvisational, oriented toward healing and toward flow, and in service to the global village. Shamanic.

Something similar to archaic technologies of the sacred must become the privileged locus of human and spiritual maturation for a planetary civilization in which the many peoples share a basic human unity, and in which the many parts of ourselves are experientially integrated into more whole, more holistic, and more meaningful intensities of being-in-the-world. This spirituality cannot be located away from the material. We have a moral and practical obligation to organize ourselves around an inclusive, relational, developmental, and existential attitude that finds the highest within the lowest, the infinite within the finite, and that realizes its deepest goals in the space between seemingly contradictory realities.

God is in the dirt.

Now I am confessed. It has been an emotional ordeal for me to risk saying what I actually believe about the world. My view will probably not satisfy postmodernists, scientists, naive mystics, traditional religionists, or independent skeptics. Yet I feel like I am describing something that they all have in common. There is a place for all these forms and phases of humanity in a theistic postmetaphysical nondualism that embraces rationality, science, neuropsychology, evolution, mythology, linguistics, pluralism, nonabsolutism, deep relationality, spiritual praxis, and the need for a religion-like culture that operates at (at least) a metamodern level of sophistication with a deep rooting in the principles of embodiment, ecology, and subconscious intelligence that are implied by a new planetary shamanism. That is what I believe.

Amen.

Bibliography

Badiou, Alain. *Being and Event*. Translated by Oliver Feltham. London: Continuum, 2006.

Kido, Master. *Every End Exposed: The 100 Koans of Master Kido—With the Answers of Hakuin*. Translated by Yoel Hoffman. Berkeley, CA: Autumn, 1971.

Zhuhong. *The Chan Whip Anthology: A Companion to Zen Practice*. Translated by Jeffrey Broughton and Elise Yoko Watanabe. Oxford: Oxford University Press, 2014.

5

Opening Space for Translineage Practice

Some Ontological Speculations

BRUCE ALDERMAN

A n Integral spirituality invites multiple possible realizations:

1. The development of integrally informed schools of thought within existing religious traditions, which may encourage greater balance and scope of vision and practice than have been previously realized, while also providing opportunities for tradition(s) to reciprocally and uniquely inform, or even transform, Integral thought itself (an AQAL Christianity, and a Christianity-inflected Integral);

2. On the philosophical level, and in its role as a metasystem, the facilitation of robust and transformative interfaith dialogue among traditions through the provision of a shared metalanguage (an encounter among autonomous paths which may or may not involve actively "borrowing" from each other, or practicing across traditional boundaries);

3. The emergence of a new global, integral, or world spirituality as a complete path in itself;

and/or

4. The cultivation of a sensibility which would allow practitioners to skillfully embrace and navigate within multiple spiritual worldspaces simultaneously, as they learn to surf their vertiginous crests rather than being dashed by the waves of incommensurability (a translineage practice, or what Marc Gafni[1] calls "dual citizenship").

---

1. Gafni and Murphy, "Passport."

In a previous paper, "Kingdom Come," I discussed two of these possibilities (the emergence of a new Integral religion and the development of an Integral postmetaphysical model of interfaith relations). In this essay, I would like to focus on the fourth possibility: making some speculative gestures towards the Integral facilitation of a translineage religious orientation. Although I expect the thoughts I develop here would apply equally to several of the other scenarios listed above, I am electing to focus on translineage religious practice for two reasons. First, it is becoming an increasingly common option in postmodern spiritual culture (although, as Gafni[2] and others have noted, frequently at the expense of depth of vision or commitment, as spiritual consumers drift rootlessly from one practice and teacher to another). And second, for those who do pursue a translineage path seriously and with rigor, it may be the field where the incommensurability between faith traditions, with their potentially conflicting truth claims, soteriological ends, and conceptions of ultimate reality, may be felt most acutely and personally by practitioners.[3] While the first point suggests that such an inquiry is indeed timely and an emerging cultural need (as more individuals move into a worldcentric orientation), the second poses a challenge and invitation, particularly for those Integral practitioners who see shortcomings in a too-easy perennialist inclusivism and are seeking an approach which does justice to the plurality and precious particularity of the world's many wisdom traditions.

I identify the second point as a challenge because, until relatively recently, Integral Theory did, indeed, espouse a version of the perennial philosophy, and thus arguably also endorsed a form of universalist religious inclusivism. In this view, each of the world's many religious paths is seen as orienting more or less successfully or completely towards the same metaphysical ultimate and the same final realization (in potential if not in actual practice). As I argued in "Kingdom Come," however, and as I will further develop here, the postmetaphysical, enactive turn in Integral Theory represents a subtle but profound shift in orientation, one which, I maintain, invites and supports a nonrelativist, deep or integral pluralism, capable of nonreductively holding and honoring the rich multiplicity of humanity's many religious truths and worldviews. Specifically, I believe that the postmetaphysical

2. Gafni, "Evolutionary."

3. For an excellent discussion of this topic, I recommend an interview of Raimon Panikkar by Swami Abhishiktananda (Father Henri Le Saux): "Swami Abhishiktananda: An Interview with Raimon Panikkar," YouTube video, https://www.youtube.com/watch?v=SOMcDuHh31g/. In the interview, Panikkar lovingly and movingly describes the lifelong struggle of his good friend Father Henri Le Saux (aka Abhishiktananada) to concurrently walk his chosen Christian and Hindu paths faithfully and with integrity.

turn in Wilber's[4] work supports proceeding on postmetaphysical and meta-physical levels simultaneously. Postmetaphysically, the Integral approach embraces metaphysical pluralism, viewing metaphysical systems as enactive operators which play a role in the enactment of particular, ontologically rich worldspaces. And metaphysically, Integral Theory advocates the adoption of facilitative metaphysical models, such as the Three Faces of Spirit, which invite deepened appreciation and integration of the major perspectives on divine reality available in the world's major religious traditions.

There is work yet to do here, however. While Wilber[5] first introduced a postmetaphysical orientation more than a decade ago, in the footnotes of *Integral Psychology* and in a few scattered essays,[6] I believe we have yet to unearth or trace out some of the deep implications of this turn for In-tegral Theory as a whole. In particular, the ontological implications of this turn are, I believe, still unrecognized or underappreciated. Sean Esbjörn-Hargens[7] has recently made some very important, and pioneering, steps towards articulating an ontological model consonant with Integral Theory's (pluralist) epistemological commitments, and I offer this essay in the hope of further contributing to this effort. As I will discuss below, an implicit or explicit commitment to the metaphysics of the One—a monistic ontolo-gy—frequently has underlain, and supported, various problematic forms of religious inclusivism (whether traditional or perennial philosophical) and even, arguably, informs John Hick's model of religious pluralism.[8] So, if we are interested in developing an Integral approach capable of nonreductively accommodating and fostering multiple religious enactments, particularly in the context of a robust translineage spirituality, it is imperative that we ex-plore both the implicit ontological commitments of Integral Theory to date, and the promise of the emergent participatory and multiplistic-relational ontologies that are being forged in the crucible of interfaith and intercul-tural dialogue and engagement.

To this end, and for the purposes of this chapter, I would like to bring Integral Theory into conversation with several post-postmodern philoso-phers and theologians who I believe have much to contribute in this area. In particular, I intend a polyphonic performance—one in which a collec-tion of disparate voices, in parallel and contrapuntal movements, will help us to reflect on a suite of themes relevant to an Integral, translineage spiritual

4. Wilber, "Excerpt A"; Wilber, *Integral Spirituality.*

5. Wilber, *Integral Psychology.*

6. Wilber, "On the Nature"; Wilber, "Excerpt A."

7. Esbjörn-Hargens, "Ontology of Climate Change."

8. See Griffin, *Deep Religious Pluralism.*

practice. The major themes to be explored here include the post-postmodern rehabilitation of ontology; the relevance of the metaphysical reflections on the Many and the One for conceptualizing the integral relation of religious worlds and worldviews; participatory and postmetaphysical models of the enactment of spiritual realities; and several recent multiplistic, relational, and nondual ontologies which may give us the subtle conceptual resources necessary to hold multiple religious orientations concurrently. After I lay these perspectives out alongside each other, I will attempt to bring them in closer contrapuntal relation through the related concepts (introduced below) of generative (en)closure and dis-enclosure, in the interest of articulating an integral pluralist approach capable of honoring both the interdependence and precious particularity of each of our religious practice traditions.

Rehabilitating Ontology after Postmodernism

Whether in contemporary philosophy,[9] phenomenology,[10] religious studies,[11] or transpersonal or Integral studies,[12] an increasing number of theorists across multiple disciplines have been attempting to think beyond the ontic-shy, epistemological cul-de-sac of cultural and linguistic relativism that has marked much postmodern theorizing. As Ferrer notes in *The Participatory Turn*, the postmodern linguistic turn has been particularly enervating for the field of religious studies, as religious truth claims have come to be regarded as little more than language games. "Apart from certain confessional or theological works," Ferrer writes, "current academic thinking on religion displays an intense skepticism toward any metaphysical referent or transcendental signifier in religious discourse. Post-metaphysical thinking, in short, deprives religious truth of any ontological significance beyond language."[13] While the strategies for moving beyond the postmodern bind adopted by the thinkers listed above vary significantly, there is—remarkably—broad consensus across these disciplines that the positivist and postmodern bracketing, if not outright banishment, of serious discussion or speculation about ontological, extralinguistic, or nonempirical dimensions

9. Badiou, *Being and Event*; Bhaskar, *Realist Theory*; Bryant, *Democracy*; Deleuze, *Difference*; Harman, *Prince of Networks*; Harman, *Quadruple Object*; Latour, *Reassembling the Social*; Meillassoux, *After Finitude*; Nancy, *Being Singular Plural*.

10. Gendlin, "Implicit Precision."

11. Ferrer and Sherman, eds., *Participatory Turn*; Panikkar, *Cosmotheandric*; Griffin, *Deep Religious Pluralism*; Keller and Schneider, eds., *Polydoxy*.

12. Ferrer, *Revisioning*; Ferrer and Sherman eds., *Participatory Turn*; Esbjörn-Hargens, "Ontology of Climate Change"; Morrison, *SpinbitZ*; Roy, "Process Model."

13. Ferrer and Sherman, "Introduction," 24.

of reality is no longer necessary, and has become, particularly in its more stringent forms, limiting and counterproductive for the advancement of human knowledge and well-being.

Before I turn to the reflections of Ferrer and Keller on this issue, particularly as it relates to translineage spirituality, I would like to review several distinctions offered by Joel Morrison[14] that I have found to be clarifying: the polar distinctions between ontic and epistemic, and ontology and epistemology, respectively. These distinctions will be useful for us for the light they will shed on the current epistemological cul-de-sac of the postmodern linguistic turn, but also because they will help us to contextualize the Integral project—and this chapter—in relation to postmodern ontological skepticism and several recent philosophical movements which argue for the revaluation of ontological inquiry.

Figure 1: Ontic-Epistemic Polarity[15]

As the figure above illustrates, these terms can be applied self-referentially to each other—using the Taoist insight into the identity of opposites—to illuminate both the epistemic nature of ontology, and the ontic nature of epistemology.[16] The relation of these terms to each other can be most easily understood, as Morrison points out, by recalling "that 'ology' itself refers to a field of study, or knowledge, the real world of the epistemic, and that the 'ic' points out a real aspect or feature of reality [i.e., ontic]."[17] In other words, ont*ology* and epistem*ology* are relative forms of knowledge, or polar

14. Morrison, *SpinbitZ*.

15. See Morrison, *SpinbitZ*, 178.

16. Morrison, *SpinbitZ*.

17. Morrison, *SpinbitZ*, 552.

distinctions drawn within the domain of the epistemic, while the epistem*ic* and ont*ic* domains are polar aspects of the real, the former transcending and including the latter (since knowledge is both embodied and real, regardless of its domain of focus or its representational clarity or acumen).

These distinctions are relevant quite for Ferrer's participatory project (discussed in detail below). In particular, the recognition of the ontic nature of epistemology plays an important role in the pragmatist/participatory strategy he has identified as essential for moving beyond the linguistic turn in religious studies. As noted above, the current trend in religious studies to view religious categories and knowledge claims primarily as linguistic performances has come at a heavy ontological cost, at times fostering, as Ferrer puts it, "a linguistic idealism hardly distinguishable from nihilism."[18] To move past this, and to begin to reclaim the ontological integrity of religious knowledge, Ferrer follows pragmatists such as Peirce and Royce in viewing language itself as ontic—as a performance of the real.

Rather than conceiving semantics in terms of epistemology and demanding that our languages impossibly represent a wholly nonlinguistic reality, participatory thought considers that Peirce and Royce made the right move by attaching semiotics not primarily to epistemology but to ontology. Communicative acts and semiotic exchanges take place, first and foremost, in the sphere of the real, the ontological, the realm of signifying bodies and events upon which the subtlety of human cognition and language may supervene.[19]

Using Morrison's distinctions above, we might say that semiotic exchanges take place in the *ontic*, rather than the ontological, but Ferrer's meaning is clear: if semiosis goes all the way down, as Peirce maintains, as a feature of reality at all levels, then language becomes, not simply a representational mapping of the real world without any ontological depth of its own, but a living performance of, and thus also a means of transformative, participatory engagement with, that world in its ontic fullness. The map, as Morrison[20] stresses, is a *part* or *expression* of the territory, and as such, has the power to act creatively in and on it.

This point is directly relevant to the enactive core that informs both Wilber's and Ferrer's approaches, so I will return to a fuller discussion of it in the next major section of this chapter. For now, I would like to briefly use these distinctions to illuminate certain important issues and tensions within Wilber's Integral model, particularly with respect to the postmetaphysical

18. Ferrer and Sherman, "Introduction," 17.
19. Ferrer and Sherman, "Introduction," 17–18.
20. Morrison, *SpinbitZ*.

turn in his theory and its emphasis on the primacy of perspective. Taking the time to do this will, I hope, be instructive for two reasons: it will help Integrally contextualize the ontological focus in this chapter, and it may also help to clarify, and address, several recent criticisms of Integral Theory as appearing to endorse epistemic absolutism[21] or as committing the "epistemic fallacy"[22].

Wilber's quadrant map, as a map which identifies and contextualizes four of the major perspectives available to human beings (subjective, objective, intersubjective, and interobjective, has proven to be quite a powerful epistemological tool. Not only has it helped practitioners take broader, more integral approaches to the interrelated domains of their lives, it has helped identify and guard against various forms of quadrant absolutism (which occurs when one perspective or domain of knowledge is privileged above all others). To a great extent, it has accomplished this simply through clearly demonstrating the ubiquity, and equal importance, of each of these major perspectives. But while the Integral approach has been effective in identifying and countering various forms of absolutism *within* the epistemic domain, several critics maintain that it commits another error: it privileges the epistemic to the exclusion of the ontic, or else it conflates the two, and therefore commits another, more general form of absolutism, which Speculative Realist and Object Oriented philosophers would call the "epistemic fallacy."[23] Regarding this latter error, Bryant writes:

> A critique of the epistemic fallacy and how it operates in philosophy does not amount to the claim that epistemology or questions of the nature of inquiry and knowledge are a fallacy. What the epistemic fallacy identifies is the fallacy of reducing ontological questions to epistemological questions, or conflating questions of how we know with questions of what beings are. In short, the epistemic fallacy occurs wherever being is reduced to our access to being. Thus, for example, wherever beings are reduced to our impressions or sensations of being, wherever being is reduced to our talk about being, wherever being is reduced to discourses about being, wherever being is reduced to signs through which being is manifest, the epistemic fallacy has been committed.[24]

21. Morrison, *SpinbitZ*.
22. Bhaskar, *Realist Theory*; Roy, "Report."
23. Bhaskar, *Realist Theory*; Bryant, *Democracy*.
24. Bryant, *Democracy*, 60.

To clarify, then, we could distinguish between two forms of absolutism: *epistemological (or quadrant) absolutism*, which is the absolutizing or unjustifiable privileging of one perspective or knowledge domain over all others that Integral Theory has so powerfully addressed; and *epistemic absolutism*, which entails either the reduction of ontological questions to epistemological ones, or the banishment of ontological thinking altogether from accepted modes of discourse, as is found among more extreme proponents of the linguistic turn critiqued by Ferrer[25] above.

Does Integral Theory commit the epistemic fallacy? When Wilber writes, in *Integral Spirituality*, that each thing *is* a perspective before it is anything else,[26] this might appear to be the case. It suggests that the *being* of an object is identical with one's *mode of access* to it. But as Morrison[27] notes in a related discussion on the problem of epistemic absolutism, while Wilber does sometimes say that everything is a perspective before it is anything else, he frequently balances such statements with the (ontological) observations that everything is holonic, and that perspectives are always already embodied (in individuals and cultures). These statements should help mitigate concerns that Wilber is continuing the banishment of ontological thinking that Ferrer[28] and Bryant[29] critique among certain postmodern philosophers.

From an *epistemological* perspective, I believe it is indeed appropriate to argue that things are perspectives before they are anything else, including things such as holons or bodies. Known things presuppose means of knowing, or modes of access. But this is quite different from making an ontological claim. Ontologically, such a statement would seem to imply a universe of free-floating, disembodied perspectives—a very un-Integral "'I' without an 'It,'" as Morrison[30] puts it. If we do not, then, take the idea that everything is a perspective seriously as an *ontological* truth, we would seem to be left with two options: (1) abandon ontological talk altogether, or (2) take the metaphysical step of positing ontological givens apart from perspectives (such as holons, which ontically *embody* perspectives). While this move might make some postmetaphysically inclined Integralists uneasy, I believe it is both justifiable and necessary, particularly if we are interested in avoiding the epistemic fallacy. Can it be done without falling into the forms of metaphysical absolutism that postmetaphysics aims to avoid?

25. Ferrer, "Plurality of Religions."
26. Wilber, *Integral Spirituality*.
27. Morrison, *SpinbitZ*.
28. Ferrer, "Plurality of Religions."
29. Bryant, *Democracy*.
30. Morrison, *SpinbitZ*, 570.

I believe it can be. For, if, with Bryant[31] and the Object Oriented Ontologists, we can recognize the error and inadequacy of conflating the *being* of things with our *mode of access* to them; and if, in reflecting on Morrison's[32] distinctions above, we are able to acknowledge ontology and epistemology as *relative* fields of knowledge within the *real* domain of the epistemic, then we can take up ontological reflection again as a worthy, if admittedly speculative, endeavor. We can pose ontological questions—"What must be the case, what must I transcendentally deduce as given, for this world to be as it is and to function as it does?"—alongside the familiar epistemological questions that engage and exercise us as Integral practitioners, without concern that doing so necessarily entails indulgence in the forms of absolutizing thought that posmetaphysics aims to redress.[33]

Such, at least, is the spirit in which I am approaching this chapter. Acknowledging at the outset the speculative nature of this exercise, I hope nevertheless that such an inquiry into the ontology of a translineage religious orientation will be fruitful and generative of insight for fellow practitioners. Let us turn now to the next step in this journey.

The One and the Many

One of the central concerns of first philosophy, of fundamental ontology, is the question of the relation of the One and the Many. Which is primary, if any? Like a single note sounding again and again, this question has been posed across multiple cultures and times, and we have answered it multiply. The fact that the question is universal, but its solutions have been many, is suggestive: while this question is fundamental to human thought, its power may lie elsewhere than in the promise of a final answer, a final privileging of the Many or the One.

In eluding easy resolution, the question is generative: it calls us ever deeper into the mystery of being, of our being-together. How we hold it, then—how we engage with it, and what light we draw from it in our living, thinking, and practice—matters, for our responses to its solicitations, individually and collectively, play out in our relationships and institutions, both secular and sacred.

31. Bryant, *Democracy*.

32. Morrison, *SpinbitZ*.

33. See Wilber's discussion of involutionary givens in Wilber, "Excerpt A"; or the explication of onto-logics in Roy, "Process Model"; and in Roy and Trudel, "Leading"; or Morrison's discussion of formative protocols in Morrison, *SpinbitZ*.

In the next two sections of this chapter, I will consider several recent offerings, several new iterations, in the fractal unfolding of this call-and-response. Each of these voices is responding, in his or her own way, to problems posed by previous answers to the question of the Many and the One: whether the hegemonic and colonizing tendencies of monist ontologies, for instance, or the relativistic and nihilistic tendencies of pluralist ones. In this effort, each is attempting especially to think beyond deconstruction; to chart paths through and well past the postmodern resistance to presence and ontology; to pronounce the integrity of being anew.

These reflections will be relevant for translineage spiritual practitioners—amongst whom I count myself—for several reasons. Our view of the relation between the Many and the One, for instance, is entangled with our perception of our relation to the divine, and the divine's relation to the world. When we are born into or adopt a spiritual tradition, we typically inherit along with it an often quite complex set of ontological commitments. Significant, and sometimes quite disturbing or anguishing, tension or confusion can arise when we choose to embrace and practice across multiple traditions and find ourselves confronted with seemingly incommensurable depictions of the divine nature, or divergent valuations of the plurality of creation. Identifying the deep ontological presuppositions that inform our traditions' cosmological or theological positions will not be likely, in itself, to resolve the tension—but it can invite an unfolding inquiry into the heart of that tension that itself will be generative and transformative.

Similarly, when we practice across lineages, we may encounter resistance in one or both of the traditions to our doing so. I have been warned on more than one occasion against attempting to graft a sheep's head onto a yak's body! And there is good sense in this—to avoid watering down or distorting a tradition, or to avoid being dashed by waves of incommensurability—but if we have decided, against all sensible advice, to take a translineage path anyway, to inhabit different worlds concurrently, or to allow a new one to grow from their mingling, then we may be aided in our efforts by some of the reflections, the visionary models of being and knowing, explored herein.

Related to the above, and as I discussed at the beginning of the chapter, the common interreligious orientations of exclusivism, inclusivism, and pluralism may each be found to imply, and to presuppose, an ontology which reinforces its position and its modes of knowing and valuation. I do not believe there is a deterministic causal relation between one's ontology and one's view of other religions, but I *have* found that any particular articulation of an interreligious orientation will be found to imply certain ontological commitments, and thus ontological inquiry can be helpful in opening and transforming limiting perspectives. The "problem" of interreligious orientation is typically posed in the context of interfaith dialogue, of course, but it is clearly relevant for translineage practitioners. On an individual level, how do we hold and interface with our chosen traditions? How might such an inquiry help further differentiate and individuate them in our lives, as uniquely flowering, wild ecologies? And how might it deepen their inter-relations, their folds and imbrications?

We will explore several such possibilities in the coming pages.

Participatory Enaction

In a number of recent writings, Jorge Ferrer[34] has been advocating for a participatory model of spiritual enaction as a new paradigm for moving religious studies beyond the impasses of dominant trends in postmodern interreligious scholarship, which tend either to view religious worlds as fully cultural-linguistic constructions, or as partial or incomplete views of a single metaphysical reality. Rejecting both strategies as undermining of the integrity of religious worldviews, he recommends the adoption of a partici-patory, enactive model of spiritual knowing, and a pluralistic, ontologically "thick" orientation towards spiritual truths. Drawing on the enactive model of cognition developed by Francisco Varela and Humberto Maturana, and situating it within a participatory sensibility which has informed various premodern and modern philosophies, the participatory-enactive approach denies the Kantian dualism of framework and uninterpreted reality, instead regarding spiritual experiences and other events as ontologically rich enact-ments or emergences, indelibly shaped but not wholly determined by, or reducible to, our linguistic categories or cognitive frameworks.

In this view, spiritual worlds are *cocreated* realities, called forth out of the open, creatively responsive mystery of Being. This model is similar, in some regards, to Almaas's[35] notion of the Logoi of Teachings, according to which the various spiritual philosophies and traditions of the world—with their unique realms of experience and soteriological possibilities—are understood, not simply as human constructions, but as the unique flowers of our creative participation with Being. Here, Almaas seems to preserve a sense of spiritual paths as creative revelations, not only of Being, but by Being: what emerges is not entirely up to "us."

An enactive, and therefore participatory, cocreative, understanding also informs the latest phase of Wilber's work, of course. While Wilber-5 is often identified as the postmetaphysical phase of Integral Theory, this

---

34. Ferrer and Sherman, eds., *Participatory Turn*; and Ferrer, "Plurality of Religions."

35. Almaas, *Inner Journey Home.*

is a misleading designation if this is taken to indicate that Integral Theory is averse to ontological thinking or speculation, or that it considers all religious (or other) truth claims to be claims about language or "merely subjective" experience (a charge that Ferrer[36] has, inappropriately, leveled against Wilber's work). Wilber-5 involves, among other things, the integration of postmetaphysical and enactive orientations—where enactments are, indeed, ontologically "thick," body-and-world transforming acts or events. Where Wilber's approach differs from Ferrer's is primarily in his AQAL framing (and extension) of enaction: bringing more specificity and clarity to the various modes and stages of enaction available to human beings.

But to return, for the moment, to Ferrer's model: in positing that religious worlds are the "products" of human engagement and interaction with a creative spiritual power or mystery, Ferrer[37] aims thereby to preserve unity in the midst of the pluralistic profusion of religious worlds. Rather than seeing religious worlds and spiritual ultimates as pre-existing, isolated islands or entities—a metaphysical welter of wholly independent and un-related universes and beings—he asks us to view these worlds as relatively independent, emergent realities called forth by human engagement with an *undetermined* (meaning multiply determinable, not simply indeterminate) spiritual creativity, in and with which we all collectively participate.

While Ferrer argues for the necessary acknowledgment of the vital role of human cognition in the manifestation of spiritual realities—as they are described, experienced, and related to in our various religious traditions—it is important to frame it in such a way as to mitigate the latent potential for anthropocentrism that might be invited by such an orientation. One way of approaching this, which is already implicit in the enactive approach adopted by both Wilber and Ferrer, is to stress that, while spiritual worlds are, in part, human enactments, this does not entail the subordination of Being to human consciousness. In other words, Being is not simply a product of human beings: rather humans participatorily have their worlds only in and through and with the creativity of Being. Humans are wholly Being's doing, and humans are the doing of Being, but humans do not exhaust or define Being's creative effulgence.

Both Ferrer's[38] participatory and Wilber's[39] postmetaphysical models of enaction already go a long way towards establishing an epistemological and ontological "framework" for translineage practice. Each enables us to

36. Ferrer, "Participation, Metaphysics, and Enlightenment."

37. Ferrer, "Plurality of Religions."

38. Ferrer, "Plurality of Religions."

39. Wilber, *Integral Spirituality*.

understand our various traditions—with their particular practices, visions, beliefs, and so on—as unique means of spiritual enactment, or as I will say later, as "generative enclosures." From this perspective, and to play with the revaluation of the nature and enactive power of language discussed earlier: each is a unique way of pronouncing and invoking (a) reality (where the "a" in parentheses indicates that both Reality and "a reality" are being invoked at once). In the pages that follow, I will take several excursions, and introduce a few new terms, but in a sense my aim is not to introduce a fundamentally different vision than Wilber's. Rather, I consider these notes to be embellishments on the Integral postmetaphysical theme, where sometimes the counter-notes help to call new resonances from the underlying melody.

The Principle of Irreduction

In translineage practice, then, participatory enaction, or integral tetra-enaction, invites us to see spiritual realities, experiences, and soteriological possibilities, in enactive terms—as participatory cocreations. And *as* enactions, our spiritual realities and worlds are both continuous with the tradition(s) in which we practice, as well as *discontinuous*: each enaction is a new, creative emergence out of the mystery. This does not necessarily mark a break with tradition, however; rather, it sees tradition itself as embodying Being's newness, as the continuous/discontinuous flow/irruption of Being's creative power, as every "event," every actuality—chopping wood, carrying water—is.

To unpack this a bit, and to better trace out the implications of this notion for a translineage orientation to spiritual practice, I would like to briefly introduce a concept from Bruno Latour's philosophy which has been helpful to me in clarifying my own views on this topic. The view I will ultimately develop in this chapter is not a Latourian one, but as I hope to demonstrate, the concept has direct bearing on the notion of the dis/continuity of enaction—as well as the related ontological questions of the One and the Many, of Wholeness and Particularity—that I contend are relevant for developing a robust and supple translineage orientation.

The concept I would like to creatively employ is Latour's[40] principle of irreduction. In short, the principle states that 1) no object, no actor or event or actuality, is ultimately reducible to any other; and concurrently, that 2) it is nevertheless always *possible* to perform, or enact, such reductive analyses, with the knowledge that such reductions come at a cost and will always, by definition, entail a loss in the form of distortion or oversimplification.[41]

40. Latour, *Pasteurization*.
41. Harman, *Prince of Networks*.

Latour's central insight, in other words, is into the *irreducible particularity* of every actuality or actual occasion. Here is how he describes the first dawning of this insight:

> I knew nothing, then, of what I am writing now but simply repeated to myself: 'Nothing can be reduced to anything else, nothing can be deduced from anything else, everything may be allied to everything else.' This was like an exorcism that defeated demons one by one. It was a wintry sky, and a very blue. I no longer needed to prop it up with a cosmology, put it in a picture, render it in writing, measure it in a meteorological article, or place it on a Titan to prevent it falling on my head . . . It and me, them and us, we mutually defined ourselves. And for the first time in my life I saw things unreduced and set free.[42]

While Latour, to my knowledge, never makes such a connection, I hear in this poetic passage the same flavor of "suchness," the same celebration of the simple, causally liberated being of things, that saturates Zen poetry or art.

On philosophical and ethical levels, I see the recognition of irreducible particularity of actual occasions—of enacted realities—as an important way of safeguarding the integrity and even autonomy of emergent realities. It accomplishes this (1) by protecting objects or entities from philosophical undermining or overmining; and (2) by guarding against a lurking human will-to-power that might inform an enactive paradigm which is entertained without such recognition. I will address the first point in some depth before turning to the second.

To begin, undermining and overmining are philosophical strategies which seek to explain the appearance or manifestation of ordinary objects through metaphysical appeals to *more real* underlying or transcendent forms or processes.[43] Specifically, an undermining approach suggests, reductively, that objects are simply surface appearances, and that their true reality is located in their underlying atomic or molecular components, for instance, or in some deeper structure. By contrast, an overmining approach denies that individual objects or entities really exist, locating reality instead in transcendent processes, dynamic fields, laws, and so on. Both strategies effectively put ordinary objects or entities "under erasure," undermining their reality in favor of some preferred metaphysical strata of being. Latour's epiphany, then, represents a radical breaking with both of these (very

---

42. Harman, *Prince of Networks*, 13, quoting Latour, *Pasteurization*, 163.
43. Harman, *Quadruple Object*.

common) forms of "elsewhere philosophy," allowing him to see objects with a renewed innocence, "unreduced and set free."[44]

In Object Oriented Philosophy, particularly in Harman's post-Heideggerian framing of it, this Latourian irreducibility of things is understood in substantialist terms, with each particular object being defined by an utterly withdrawn, nonrelational core or substance. In this understanding, which Harman[45] develops out of Heidegger's reflections on the ontological status of "tool-beings" such as hammers, each emergent object retains an essential interiority cut off from all relation to any other object. In my own thought, however, while I appreciate and want to preserve this insight into the irreducible integrity of things, I would like to do so without appealing, as the Object Oriented Ontologists do, to wholly withdrawn substances or things-in-themselves. To this end, I have found another concept by Joel Morrison to be useful: his Principle of Nondual Rationalism, which holds that "infinite divisibility equals indivisibility." As Morrison puts it: "Infinite divisibility necessitates that there can be no fundamental or absolute division because there will always be a deeper level of divisibility, and hence, with infinite divisibility the absolute is fundamentally indivisible."[46]

To relate this to Latour's principle of irreduction, I propose a corollary principle, that infinite reducibility equals irreducibility. To put this succinctly: rather than viewing the irreducible particularity of things as related to Harman's withdrawn substance (island-like thing-in-itself-ness, wholly divorced from all relationship), we can, following Morrison's principle, discover it in the infinite potential for reducibility itself. There is support for the infinite scope of reducibility in Harman's object ontology:

> [Contrary to Heidegger's contention,] the hammer as a real tool-being is not located in the basement of the universe at all, since a layer of constituent pieces swarms beneath it, another layer beneath that one, and so forth. Instead of saying that the regress into constituent objects is indefinite, I would go so far as to call it infinite, in spite of the ban found in Kant's antinomies on ruling either for or against an infinite regress of pieces. After all, to be real means to have a multitude of qualities, both real and perceived. And given that an object must inherently be a unity, its multitude of qualities can only arise from the plurality of its pieces. Thus there is no object without pieces, and an infinite regress occurs. Despite the easy and widespread mockery of the infinite regress, there are only two alternatives, and

44. Harman, *Prince of Networks*.
45. Harman, *Prince of Networks*; Harman, *Quadruple Object*.
46. Morrison, *SpinbitZ*, 86.

both are even worse. Instead of the infinite regress we can have
a finite regress, in which one ultimate element is the material
of everything larger. Or we can have no regress at all, in which
there is no depth behind what appears to the human mind. Both
options have already been critiqued as undermining and overmining, respectively. And if the infinite regress is often mocked
as a theory of 'turtles all the way down,' the finite regress merely
worships a final Almighty Turtle, while the theory of no regress
champions a world resting on a turtle shell without a turtle.[47]

With the positing of infinite depth of objects or constitutive relations—
turtles all the way down, reminiscent of Wilber's holonic model—there is
clearly no final reduction possible. Where I possibly differ from Harman is
in my rejection of the need to posit a withdrawn substance, since I believe
Morrison's Principle of Nondual Rationalism can deliver the particularity
and integrity of objects that Harman is seeking. Infinite divisibility, as Morrison argues, amounts to its opposite: indivisibility in and as the absence of
any final divisibility; or as I contend, irreducibility in and as the absence of
any final reducibility.

My suggestion, in other words, is to hold reducibility and irreducibility at once. In this view, each particular object or entity, as a unique site of
bodying forth of the whole, is infinitely reducible, there being no end to the
possible constitutive relations or compositional elements we can trace out.
At the same time, each particular, in eluding any final reduction, is also at
once absolutely unique and wholly irreducible.

In an interreligious or translineage spiritual context, this notion has
at least two interesting implications: (1) It scuttles easy, perennial philosophical, cross-tradition equations of religious concepts or categories, since,
while such comparisons can be made—and can indeed be helpful and fruitful—the absolute particularity and integrity of spiritual realities ensures that
no such comparison will ever be adequate to capture the fullness of any
emergent reality; and (2) this resistance to ultimate reduction suggests, also,
that spiritual—or any other—realities cannot be ultimately or finally reduced to any other particular parts or processes, using any of the reductive
categories of choice, whether cultural or biological or psychological. Even
tetra-enaction, while a useful and powerful concept, cannot finally exhaust
or reductively account for the mystery of any particular emergent.

Thus, to relate this back to the concept of participatory enaction, and
the concern with the will-to-power that might be masked in an overly an-
thropocentric interpretation of it: the principle of irreduction, in the reading

---

47. Harman, *Quadruple Object*, 113.

I have offered here, dashes the pretension that humans, or human practices, can serve in themselves as ultimate explanatory causes of any particular reality, spiritual or not. We are participants, yes, but in a creative mystery that exceeds and eludes any such final reduction.

Lastly, to return to my observation at the beginning of this section that our spiritual enactions are both continuous and discontinuous: the continuity of our spiritual enactions lies in their infinite reducibility, the unending lines of constitutive or compositional relation we can trace out from each, unique bodying forth of the whole; and the discontinuity lies in the absolute particularity, the irreducibility of each emergent reality. In being what it is, irreducibly, everything is inviolable, an utter concreteness. If we like, we can view this as an extension—a further democratization—of Marc Gafni's notion of the Unique Self. Everything, every enaction, every bodying-forth, is, in the sense I have indicated above, a unique self.

This suggests, if we are attentive, a curious entangling of the Many and the One. To help unfold and develop this insight, I will turn now to explore several concepts that are emerging in the field of constructive theology.

Nondual Ontological Pluralism

In "Kingdom Come," I introduced several recent attempts to move theology beyond the shortcomings and aporias of modern and postmodern theories of interfaith relations, from Ferrer's participatory enaction, to S. Mark Heim's Trinitarian pluralistic inclusivism,[48] to Griffin's deep pluralism,[49] to Raimon Panikkar's radical pluralism.[50] To this list should be added the recent work of a group of authors who might be referred to, collectively, as the Polydox theologians. A recent, representative text for this movement in constructive theology, *Polydoxy*, presents a wide-ranging series of essays which center, to varying degrees, around three intertwined threads: multiplicity, unknowing or evolutionary open-endedness, and relation, each of which co-implicates the others. This triune set of perspectives lends itself readily to a Trinitarian analysis, and several authors take up that task, but the threads are held loosely enough to allow for other articulations as well.

In name, polydoxy is a theology of multiplicity, seeing in multiplicity, not an obscuration or a scattering or division of divinity, but divinity itself or divinity's affirmation—a divine manifold. In spirit, Polydoxy is a theology of relation. As Keller and Schneider write, "Relationality is the connective

48. Heim, *Salvations*.
49. Griffin, *Deep Religious Pluralism*.
50. Panikkar, "Pluralism of Truth."

tissue that makes multiplicity coherent, and it is the depth that makes our relations, all of them, strange and unknowable, even, or especially, in intimacy."[51] In practice, as the previous quote also suggests, Polydoxy is aligned, in part, with the traditions of apophasis and revelation—here, finding spiritual sustenance in the posture of unknowing, of ongoing openness to the surprises of relation and evolutionary emergence.

Rather than presenting a singular theological model or theory, such as we find in the works of Ferrer or Heim or Panikkar, *Polydoxy* enacts a mode of thinking—a holographically unfolding/enfolding logic which demonstrates "the fold, the pli, which distinguishes multi*pli*city from mere plurality. That enfolded and unfolding relationality suggests not a relation between many separate ones but between singularities, events of becoming folded together, intersecting, entangled as multiples. It is such connectivity that allows, indeed implies (im*pli*catio), the becoming coherence of polydoxy."[52]

How this shows up in the text is as a rich multiplex of divergent and convergent perspectives and themes, circling and crystallizing around the three, co-implicate attractors of multiplicity, unknowing, and relation. In this, the text—this performance—succeeds in its goal, which is to enact an *integral* field of difference without erasing multiplicity or subsuming it in a single narrative.

While *Polydoxy* is a professedly Christian theological exercise, I believe both its sophisticated mode of execution and its triune—one could say, nondual—onto-epistemology make the text relevant to anyone more broadly interested in the challenges of interfaith relations or an Integral, translineage spirituality. In particular, I find the themes of multiplicity, unknowing, and relation quite consonant with an Integral, evolutionary understanding; for me, these terms highlight, in fact, three of the implicit strengths of the Integral model: its embrace of epistemological and ontological pluralism, its evolutionary open-endedness, and its co-pronouncement of relation and difference (tetra-enaction). The use of these three terms by the Polydox authors to generates multiple compelling cases for a robust religious pluralism thus should be of interest to Integral practitioners interested in formulating models of interfaith relations and translineage practice.

I do not have space in this chapter to review the many offerings in this text, so I will focus for now on two perspectives that I believe are of special relevance: Roland Faber's notions of polyphilic indetermination and subtractive affirmation, and Jean-Luc Nancy's being-singular-plural.

51. Keller and Schneider, Introduction, 12.
52. Keller and Schneider, Introduction, 7.

The Indeterminacy of Light

To start, I will quote from Faber's essay "The Sense of Peace":

> In order to access multiplicity we need not violently destroy the abstractions on which the dualistic logic of the One and the Many is built, but we must non-violently *transform the function of the abstractions from serving the sub-stantialization of power.* Instead, these abstractions, insofar as they are implied by orthodoxy, must be transformed into a polydoxy that can release *their liberating potential for an experience, theory, and practice of multiplicity.*[53]

Faber's essay is a complex, polyvocal treatise thick with theological implications, to which I cannot begin to do justice here, but the above is suggestive of his broad trajectory: a nondual transformation of vision that fosters interreligious peace and liberates the potential for a "practice of multiplicity." This is facilitated, in part, through cultivation of an appreciation for multiplistic or "polyphilic" indeterminacy as a creative power which both fully affirms and exceeds the orthodox intuitions of tradition, and which allows practitioners to experience themselves at once as affirmatively and generatively "entangled" with other religions *and* as enveloped, as representatives of their particular traditions, in "a process of the renewal of unprecedented novelty that always is beyond any fixed identities of singular religions and their orthodoxies."[54] Concerning the former, Faber writes: "The para-doxa of a religion will inherently recognize its own poly-harmonious complexity against its own simplifications if it is not forced to leave its own [orthodox] intuition behind in order to attend an anonymous 'universal harmony,'" but if it can recognize the (interreligious) entanglement of its own unique beginnings in the world of experiences, conceptualizations, and communities."[55]

Whether intended or not, I read the above as a swipe at perennialist or identist models of pluralism, in which the affirmation and validation of plurality is purchased, ironically, through affiliation with, and subordination to, a generic oneness.

In Faber's account, we err if we identify divinity with either the One *or* the Many.[56] This is what he means by subtractive affirmation: the divine polyphilically affirms multiplicity, inwardly illumining the Many and the

53. Faber, "Sense," 48 (italics original).

54. Faber, "Sense," 49.

55. Faber, "Sense," 49.

56. Faber, "Sense of Peace."

One, but it eludes, or subtracts itself from, identification *as* multiplicity or the Many and the One. This active withdrawal, or kenosis, of the divine subverts the will-to-power (and the attendant violence) that flows from rigid identification with one or the other, and is curiously suggestive of David Grandy's evocative portrait of the ethical richness of light.[57] Light, he reminds us, facilitates intimacy with the expanse of being and with a vast multiplicity of others, immediately (un-mediatedly) presenting them to the eye, but *only by subtracting itself* from view. It is never light we see, but "things lighted." It is, borrowing Bortoft's term, like an *active absence* which facilitates presence; a paradoxical presencing and emptying which yields manifold relations; and a spiritual prosthesis, which, when donned, enables us to enact an affirming disidentification from the Many and the One.[58]

Faber's call, then—his recommendation for interfaith participants and trans-lineage practitioners—might be very simply put: *Think like light.*

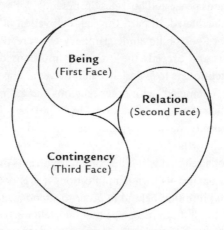

Figure 2: Integral Ontological Trinity (courtesy of the author)

Being Singular Plural

"A singular being," Jean-Luc Nancy says, "is a contradiction in terms."[59]

In the introduction to *Being Singular Plural*, Nancy, whose work informs the thinking of several of the Polydox authors, announces his intention to rethink ontology "by giving the 'singular plural of Being' as its

57. Grandy, "Otherness of Light."
58. Bortoft, *Wholeness of Nature.*
59. Nancy, *Being Singular Plural.*

foundation."[60] In juxtaposing the three terms, *being singular plural,* as he does, he means to communicate their absolute co-immediacy, without remainder, and without any suggestion of the priority of one over the other. Being-one is only ever being-with-many. What he wants to avoid, then, are the metaphysical models which posit the pre-existence of Being—where an original One is then dispersed into the Many, or an original Many is subsequently gathered up into One. For Nancy, there is no pre-existence, no originary state other than being singular plural, which itself, in every pluri-singular instance, is the origin.

Here is how Nancy puts it:

> Being singular plural means the essence of Being is only as co-essence. In turn, co-essence, or being-with (being-with-many), designates the essence of the co-, or even more so, the co- (the cum) itself in the position or guise of an essence. In fact, co-essentiality cannot consist in an assemblage of essences, where the essence of this assemblage as such remains to be determined. In relation to such an assemblage, the assembled essences would become [mere] accidents. Co-essentiality signifies the essential sharing of essentiality, sharing in the guise of assembling, as it were. This could also be put in the following way: if Being is being-with, then it is, in its being-with, the "with" that constitutes Being... Therefore, it is not the case that the "with" is an addition to some prior Being; instead, the "with" is at the heart of Being.[61]

In pronouncing "with" to be the essence of Being, in other words, Nancy distances himself from metaphysical narratives which posit a process of rupture or unification of originary being, but also from narratives which would posit a simple dialectical swinging between oneness and multiplicity. Being is immediately and nondually co-being, co-essence, singular plural.

In this understanding, one is always already more-than-one. A one without a second would be less than one, an improper or deficient one. As Morrison, following Buckminster Fuller, expresses this: "Unity [i.e., a unit, a singularity] is plural and at minimum two."[62]

In speaking (of) the singular plural of being, Nancy has found a way to give voice, as I hear him, to tetra-enaction as ever-present origin. But in speaking this way, he asks us to think the four quadrants at once, to *grok* their radical co-implication. There aren't individuals over here and

60. Nancy, *Being Singular Plural*, xv.

61. Nancy, *Being Singular Plural*, 30–31.

62. Morrison, *SpinbitZ*.

collectives over there. There is the being singular plural of every blooming object or occasion.

His view has bearing on, and nicely echoes, the comments I made earlier about things, or enactions, being irreducible instantiations of (indeterminate) wholeness:

> The singular is primarily each one and, therefore, also with and among all the others. The singular is a plural. It also undoubtedly offers the property of indivisibility, but it is not indivisible the way substance is indivisible. It is, instead, indivisible in each instant [au coup par coup], within the event of its singularization. It is indivisible like any instant is indivisible, which is to say that it is infinitely divisible, or punctually indivisible. Moreover, it is not indivisible like any particular is indivisible, but on the condition of pars pro toto: the singular is each time for the whole, in its place and in light of it.[63]

Nancy does not translate this "for the whole" in terms of *community*—for him, the term has been problematically reified, becoming more often than not an *eclipsing* whole—but he nevertheless finds, in the plural singular of our being-together, that the language of "it" slides ineluctably, and affirmatively, towards the language of "we."

In the plurisingularity and irreducible particularity of tetra-enaction, our respective faith traditions and practice lineages are thus, in their co-essentiality, collegially one (by one), one-with-another.

Generative Dis/Enclosure

I would like to gather several of the themes I have explored in this chapter together under the tabernacle provided by a pair of terms: *generative (en) closure* and *dis-enclosure*. The first term, generative (en)closure, is one I have been developing in the context of my reflections on ontology, embodiment, and Integral enaction. Its complementary term, dis-enclosure, is a Nancyan concept that I discovered while working on this chapter.

The relation of the term, generative (en)closure, to autopoietic theory should be clear: An autopoietic system, meaning a "self-making system," exhibits a definitive closure and circularity in its pattern of organization. While "(en)closure" can be read as a noun, signifying a fixed structure or a static condition, I prefer a more active or processual inflection: enclosure as the "act of enclosing." Here, the term is perhaps close to what Gendlin

63. Nancy, *Being Singular Plural*, 33.

means by body-constituting, in that both (en)closure and body-constituting are *generative*. As Gendlin writes,

> Body-constituting is a generative body-environment process (without the here-there split) . . . Everyone agrees that the body is made of environmental stuff, but it was assumed to be separate from the environment, merely perceiving and moving in it. But if we consider the body's formation as a body process, then the body is environmental interaction from the start. The body is identical with its environment in one body-constituting process.[64]

But body-constituting is generative not only in the formation and maintenance of the body; it is active as well in the ongoing differentiation of the environment and the generation of objects:

> Certain processes become differentiated; they occur just with certain parts of the environment. This generates specific environmental objects . . . The body is first constituted as environmental events and material, and some of this is always present in the environment. But some of it is intermittent; it disappears and reappears. For example, sugar, water, and light appear and are incorporated only sometimes. Then the body-constituting with these 'objects' becomes separated from the rest of the process (if the organism didn't die in their absence). Then the body has separate processes just for these parts of the environment. The moment they re-appear, just these processes resume. So we call these differentiated parts of the environment 'objects'. But to think this we need to say that when something implied doesn't occur, the body continues to imply it. Until something meets that implying ('carries it forward', we say), the body continues to imply what was implied and didn't occur. If part of what was implied did occur, then only the part that did not occur continues to be implied. This 'reiterated implying' is a basic concept. It explains how objects in the environment become differentiated.[65]

Gendlin's account is thus quite close to what I mean by generative (en)closure: this active enclosure, this enfolding and implication, is generative of other bodies and forms, i.e. enactive, in a single process of body-world flowering or co-constitution.

But the term (en)closure is suggestive of more than just the body, which is why I have introduced the term here. It evokes images of sheltering and sustaining structures—of tabernacles and dwellings and temples. What

64. Gendlin, "Implicit Precision," 147.
65. Gendlin, "Implicit Precision," 147.

kind of enclosure is a temple? What does it imply? The link here to Gendlin-
ian body-constitution is illuminating:

The body is a temple, and the temple is a body—a body which (ongoingly) implies a world.

We can similarly see cultures, traditions, teachings, communities of
believers in this light: (en)closures which, in and by their closure, are generative, enactive of difference. Holy days and retreats are generative (en)
closures in time.

To think these thoughts with those thinkers who have accompanied us
through this chapter:

With Ferrer, I see the generative (en)closures of our traditions,
churches, and lineages, whether singly or multiply held, each as uniquely
embodied means of participatory enaction—as creative expressions of our
invocational engagement with spiritual power or mystery. With Latour, I see
each generative (en)closure as the rounding of particularity, utterly and lib-
eratingly concrete, both irreducible and always-reducible or -relatable, and I
recognize that every difference makes a difference (and thus charges us with
an ethical imperative). With the Polydox theologians, I see in every generative (en)closure of body and tradition the folding and unfolding of the
relational *pli*, which situates us in multiplicity, and implicates us in the unknowing of our evolutionary becoming. With Faber, I affirm and creatively
reenact the formative intuitions implicit in the generative (en)closure(s) of
my tradition(s), while inverting and guarding against those closures which
would serve the (myopically identified) substantializations of the will-to-
power. With Nancy, I see in the generative (en)closure of any particular
tradition the singular plural of its being, the "with" that is constitutive of
its presence, where its singular presence is always already copresence, the
declaration of the impossibility (and the utter poverty) of the "Only One."
And with Wilber, the largely silent partner in this journey, I see generative
(en)closure as a holon—already plurisingular, the body of tetra-enaction—
which, *as* a holon, can never be mistaken for a (non-holonic) foundation or
ultimate, thus releasing it to the ongoing invitation of the divine's becoming.

Which brings us to the second term, *dis-enclosure*, since "release" implies the rupture or interruption of a certain closure. What is en-closed, of
course, must one day be un-enclosed. What is en-closed, as an en-folding,
is also always already an opening. Dis-enclosure is the marker of the generativity of death in the evolutionary unfolding of our being-together. The
gifts of death are many, as Michael Dowd reminds us:[66] it not only seeds and
clears the way for new form, as in the kenosis of a supernova; it is generatively

66. Dowd, *Thank God*.

enfolded into the very form(s) we take—in the daily dis/enclosure of cells which *is* our living.

As Nancy uses the term, dis-enclosure means both opening or empty-ing—the opening of a closed space, and the kenosis or auto-deconstruction of a worldview or a form.[67] While Nancy employs the term primarily in the context of an analysis of the modern deconstruction and secularization of Christian culture as the temporal fulfillment of Christianity's identification with the self-emptying God,[68] the term finds broader application in the writings of the Polydox theologians.[69] For the purposes of this chapter, I would like to focus in particular on Sharon Betcher's use of the term, which she recognizes as implicitly illuminating the field of the multiple, and which she relates to notions of emphatic vulnerability and intercorporeal generos-ity or obligation.[70]

Regarding the former, Betcher[71] argues that Nancy's dis-enclosure, in describing the auto-deconstruction of totalizing worldviews, implies or dis-closes a vision of multiplicity. For the end of totalization is a confrontation with Being's ungrasped excess, or Being's final ungraspability; the coming due of a particular world's IOU to the Kosmos.[72] In revealing and violating the closure of the given world, dis-enclosure discloses ex-istence as vulner-able worlds-in-becoming. As Nancy[73] might remind us, a world is always already a world-alongside-other-worlds. And dis-enclosure, as both an opening-*of* and an opening-*to*, is a confrontation and emptying of a world into a world, turning on the fulcrum of the plurisingular 'with' of Being.

Regarding the relation of dis-enclosure to empathy and generosity, Betcher suggests that trauma or suffering, as the dis-enclosure or rupture of the apparent sovereignty of the body or the self, is an opening which discloses our interdependence—our vulnerability to, and need for, others.[74] It is an opening which still offers a form of shelter, however, in that it may induct us into a life of care and mutual obligation. Citing several examples of individuals whose disability and chronic suffering had inspired them to new forms of engagement with the world, Betcher points beneath the endemic alienation and closure of the self-sufficient, postmodern ego to

---

67. Nancy, *Dis-Enclosure*.
68. Nancy, *Dis-Enclosure*.
69. Betcher, "Take My Yoga"; Rivera, "Glory."
70. Betcher, "Take My Yoga."
71. Betcher, "Take My Yoga."
72. Wilber, *Sex, Ecology, Spirituality*.
73. Nancy, *Being Singular Plural*.
74. Betcher, "Take My Yoga."

the intercorporeal entanglement of our bodies which announces itself in empathy and suffering.[75] It is in these prereflective responses that we come to an appreciation of (the need for, the co-implication of) manifold others in the very fold or enclosure of our being.

> Because "pluralism is not enough" (according to Keller), I suggest that the *pli* of Spirit, that "many-one," signals a fertile "fold" (i.e., *pli* or pleat) of difference within immanence itself so as to generate ligatures or obligations. The work of religion within this scene will be that of growing corporeal generosity into a social muscle. Consequently, [my recommended approach] develops the spiritual prosthesis of the practiced vow—the "yoke" or "yoga"—of corporeal generosity to creaturely need within the interreligious milieu of today's global cities.[76]

Keller identifies in this preconceptual being-given-over to others, this intercorporeal generosity, not a particular virtue but the *founding* of virtue: the subrepresentational condition of our very embodied and social interexistence. When gathered up into conscious living, however, intercorporeal generosity becomes grounds for a "yoga, or practice, of the open"—a practice of friendship growing from (recognition of) intercorporeal "ligatures of obligation" in which obligation itself is the "sphere of what I [the sovereign ego] did not constitute."[77]

> When one assumes the practice of a spiritual path setting out from the locus of this great open field, then one might experience the beggar or the CEO, like pain, to become one's spiritual teacher. Everything and everyone provides an opening to the practice of generosity, of sympathy at the cellular level. The yoga or obligation of neighbor-love is born of this, develops this generosity as a social muscle.[78]

This is not a practice of sovereignty, of self-making evolutionary subjects, then; it is a practice of vulnerability, of being a "patient of life."[79] But then again, these two are not-two. Dis-enclosure is, in other words, the contradictory vulnerability of each and every (en)closure as inviolable particular. Each particular, in its particularity, bleeds into the implicit—into the

75. Betcher, "Take My Yoga."
76. Betcher, "Take My Yoga," 60.
77. Betcher, "Take My Yoga," 70.
78. Betcher, "Take My Yoga," 69.
79. Betcher, "Take My Yoga," 68.

field of that which it did not constitute, but which it ongoingly implies in its rounded particularity.

Implications

How might we relate these thoughts on generative (en)closure and dis-enclosure to Integral translineage spiritual practice? I have not inquired with others, but I suspect that, for many of us in the Integral community, we have experienced a profound dis-enclosure in our spiritual lives: the self-emptying or deconstruction of our religions of origin. It is at once a rupture and a crisis of self-sufficiency—*There are so many other views out there! How can I have missed this? How can I continue to ignore it?*—and, perhaps, also an evolutionary step in our traditions themselves. What was special, and native, in the original sacred preserve, bleeds out and finds fulfillment in the concrete, in that "great open" manifold which exceeds and interrupts our boundaries. For Betcher, this violation of religious self-sufficiency, this irruption of vulnerability to otherness that illuminates our interdependency, tills the ground for the growth of a fertile interreligiosity—where, in the polyphonic field of the postmodern city, each tradition is called again to "remember itself as a practice,"[80] as a *way* of living well among ways of living well.

In practicing across traditional boundaries, in whatever translineage mélange we have gathered and cultivated, we are of course very likely transgressing the boundaries, breaking the "closure," of one or all of our chosen traditions, most of which have not—until recently—attempted to think outside the enclosure of their own self-sufficiency. As Integral interspiritual practitioners, can we find ways to both validate and defend the transgressive audacity of an interlineage practice, *and* to honor and preserve the integrity and precious particularity that each lineage rightly seeks to enforce?

In my reflections throughout this chapter, I have attempted to practice and communicate this by thinking both *dis-enclosure* and *generative (en)closure* at once, in the contradictory identity of the empty and the full, the many and the one. Nancy's dis-enclosure, together with his being singular plural, invite us to think our multiplicity, to live and celebrate Being as a being-with that eludes totalization or finalization, where every *one* is always more-than-one.[81] In demanding acknowledgment of presence as co-presence, it calls us to recognize that each tradition is in some sense subject to that which exceeds it, and is already infiltrated by an otherness that indebts it to the open, both in terms of its relation to other traditions

---

80. Betcher, "Take My Yoga," 60.
81. Nancy, *Dis-Enclosure*.

and to its own future. It reminds us, in other words, that each tradition is always already an interdependent arising and an evolutionary becoming. But a spirituality which only emphasizes openness or relation is in danger of sliding into lifeless diffusion or enervating relativism, and thus requires that we find ways to protect the uniqueness or integrity of our traditions. As I have argued above, I believe we find this not only in Nancy's[82] being singular plural, but in Latour's[83] principle of irreduction. Each relative tradition, in its radical and irreducible particularity, presents us with a unique and irreplaceable manifestation of the fullness of Being. When seen as generative (en)closures, each religious tradition becomes a unique tabernacle of Spirit capable of calling forth or enacting precious and inimitable spiritual fruits and soteriological horizons. Thus, while practitioners from multiple traditions may, indeed, describe similar spiritual states and experiences that transgress the boundaries of lineage, revealing a profound oneness in and through the many, the principles of irreduction and participatory enactment call us also to acknowledge and honor the irreducible and irreplaceable particularity of the spiritual visions and transformations afforded by each genuine practice tradition, not as limitations but as manifestations of the cocreative bounty of Spirit.

From one perspective—speaking for myself, and I imagine for others—translineage practice is not especially an issue or problem. It is simply what we are doing, as citizens of an emergent, transcultural society, and somehow it works itself out! But from another perspective, it is indeed a challenge, particularly if we want to travel deeply on our chosen paths, with integral and integrous attention to the demands of each, and to avoid the materialistic and frequently narcissistic default position of postmodern culture: the spiritual consumerism of the global marketplace. If we take this challenge seriously, if we are interested in pursuing an integral, translineage spirituality with rigor and humility, playfulness and finesse, then we are challenged to find new ways of thinking and praxis responsive to this task—where a trans-lineage orientation becomes a praxis-field itself.

My reflections in this chapter are admittedly open-ended and speculative, but I do not see this as a drawback: I believe speculation is what is called for in this domain. Speculation is not idle; it is generative and opening. It invites us to open what has been prematurely foreclosed—our taken-for-granted ontologies and epistemologies—and to begin to imagine being anew.

In my inquiry into my own translineage orientation, I have explored not only the visions of knowing and being implicit in my chosen traditions,

82. Nancy, *Being Singular Plural.*
83. Latour, *Pasteurization.*

but in Integral Theory as well. In its role as an epistemological metasystem, Integral Theory does not require commitment to any *particular* ontology—part of its role is, after all, to map the unfolding of various ontologies and epistemologies, the play of the Many and the One, over time and across cultures. But in practice, I believe it does have ontological commitments—in theory, to nonduality, which is a commitment I share. In language and presentation, however, Integral nonduality, sourced for years in a perennial philosophical orientation, tends at times to slide over into a privileging of the language of the One. For example, enlightenment—for all traditions—is defined equally as the experience of "oneness." Integral Theory itself, as a theory of everything, becomes the One Theory for all. And Spirit, defined and described as a transcendent and formless emptiness, elusive of any definition, nevertheless in its very abstract universality, may tilt us in our language and thinking, again, towards an implicit privileging of the logic and the metaphysics of the One.

In naming these tendencies, I am naming my own implication in each such move. This is, indeed, how I have often held and applied Integral Theory in my thought and speech as a translineage practitioner. But in naming these tendencies to slide habitually into some form of monism, I do not intend to indict the language or the logic of oneness; only its unconscious privileging, and its potential reduction of the Integral promise to a narrow inclusivism.

In the nondual and multiplistic approaches I have explored here, I hope to have introduced and given voice to a few additional modes of speaking and thinking which will serve as resources for Integral practitioners interested, as I am, in further unfolding and enacting this implicit promise, and in fostering a visionary light capable of nurturing the rare and wild fields of our growing translineage practices.

Bibliography

Abhishiktananda. *Swami Abhishiktananda: Essential Writings.* Selected with an introduction by Shirley Du Boulay. Modern Spiritual Masters Series. Maryknoll, NY: Orbis, 2006.

Alderman, Bruce. "Kingdom Come: Beyond Inclusivism and Pluralism, an Integral Post-Metaphysical Invitation." *Journal of Integral Theory and Practice* 6.3 (2011) 14–31.

Almaas, A. H. *The Inner Journey Home: Soul's Realization of the Unity of Reality.* Boston: Shambhala, 2004.

Badiou, Alain. *Being and Event.* New York: Continuum, 2005.

Betcher, Sharon V. "Take My Yoga Upon You: A Spiritual Plea for the Global City." In *Polydoxy: Theology of Multiplicity and Relation*, edited by Catherine Keller and Laurel Schneider, 57–80. New York: Routledge, 2011.

Bhaskar, Roy. *A Realist Theory of Science*. With a new introduction. Classical Texts in Critical Realism. London: Routledge, 2008.

Bortoft, Henri. *The Wholeness of Nature: Goethe's Way toward a Science of Conscious Participation in Nature*. Renewal in Science. Hudson, NY: Lindisfarne, 1996.

Bruteau, Beatrice. "Eucharistic Ecology and Ecological Spirituality." *Cross Currents* 40 (1991) 499–514.

Bryant, Levi R. *The Democracy of Objects*. Ann Arbor: MPublishing, 2011.

Deleuze, Gilles. *Difference and Repetition*. Translated by Paul Patton. New York: Columbia University Press, 1994.

Dowd, Michael. *Thank God for Evolution: How the Marriage of Science and Religion Will Transform Your Life and Our World*. New York: Viking, 2009.

Esbjörn-Hargens, Sean. "An Ontology of Climate Change: Integral Pluralism and the Enactment of Environmental Phenomena." *Journal of Integral Theory and Practice* 5.1 (2010) 183–201.

Faber, Roland. "The Sense of Peace: A Paradoxology of Divine Multiplicity." In *Polydoxy: Theology of Multiplicity and Relation*, edited by Catherine Keller and Laurel Schneider, 36–56. New York: Routledge, 2011.

Ferrer, Jorge N. "Participation, Metaphysics, and Enlightenment: Reflections on Ken Wilber's Recent Work." *Transpersonal Psychology Review* 14.2 (2011) 3–24.

———. "The Plurality of Religions and the Spirit of Pluralism: A Participatory Vision of the Future of Religion." *International Journal of Transpersonal Studies* 28.1 (2009) 139–51.

———. *Revisioning Transpersonal Theory: A Participatory Vision of Human Spirituality*. SUNY Series in Transpersonal and Humanistic Psychology. Albany: State University of New York Press, 2002.

Ferrer, Jorge N., and Jacob H. Sherman. "Introduction: The Participatory Turn in Spirituality, Mysticism and Religious Studies." In *The Participatory Turn: Spirituality, Mysticism, Religious Studies*, edited by Jorge N. Ferrer and Jacob H. Sherman, 1–77. Albany: State University of New York Press, 2008.

———, eds. *The Participatory Turn: Spirituality, Mysticism, Religious Studies*. Albany: State University of New York Press, 2008.

Gafni, Marc. "The Evolutionary Emergent of Unique Self: A New Chapter in Integral Theory." *Journal of Integral Theory and Practice* 6.1 (2011) 1–36.

Gafni, Marc, and Michael Murphy. "A Passport for Dual Citizenship with Michael Murphy and Marc Gafni [video]." 2011. http://www.ievolve.org/2011/08/a-passport-for-dualcitizenship-with-michael-murphy-marc-gafni/.

Gendlin, Eugene T. "Implicit Precision." In *Knowing without Thinking: Mind, Action, Cognition, and the Phenomenon of the Background*, edited by Zdravko Radman. 141–66. New Directions in Philosophy and Cognitive Science. Basingstoke, UK: Palgrave Macmillan, 2012.

Grandy, David. "The Otherness of Light: Einstein and Levinas." *Postmodern Culture* 12. 1 (2001). http://pmc.iath.virginia.edu/issue.901/12.1grandy.html/.

Griffin, David R. *Deep Religious Pluralism*. Louisville: Westminster John Knox, 2005.

Harman, Graham. *Prince of Networks: Bruno Latour and Metaphysics*. Anamnesis. Prahran, Vic.: Re.Press, 2009.

————. *The Quadruple Object*. Winchester, UK: Zero Books, 2011.

Heim, S. Mark. *The Depth of the Riches. Sacra Doctrina*. Grand Rapids: Eerdmans, 2001.

————. *Salvations: Truth and Difference in Religion*. Faith Meets Faith. Maryknoll, NY: Orbis, 1995.

Keller, Catherine, and Laurel Schneider. Introduction. In *Polydoxy: Theology of Multiplicity and Relation*, 1–15. New York: Routledge, 2011.

Keller, Catherine, and Laurel Schneider, eds. *Polydoxy: Theology of Multiplicity and Relation*. New York: Routledge, 2011.

Kleinberg-Levin, David Michael. *Before the Voice of Reason: Echoes of Responsibility in Merleau-Ponty's Ecology and Levinas's Ethics*. SUNY Series in Contemporary French Thought. Albany: State University of New York Press, 2009.

Latour, Bruno. *The Pasteurization of France*. Translated by Alan Sheridan and John Law. Cambridge: Harvard University Press, 1988.

————. *Reassembling the Social: An Introduction to Actor-Network-Theory*. Clarendon Lectures in Management Studies. Oxford: Oxford University Press, 2005.

Latour, Bruno, et al. *The Prince and the Wolf: Latour and Harman at the LSE*. Winchester, UK: Zero Books, 2011.

Levin, David Michael. *The Listening Self: Personal Growth, Social Change and the Closure of Metaphysics*. London: Routledge, 1989.

————. *The Opening of Vision: Nihilism and the Postmodern Situation*. New York: Routledge, 1988.

Maturana, Humberto R., and Francisco J. Varela. *The Tree of Knowledge: The Biological Roots of Human Understanding*. Boston: New Science Library, 1987.

Meillassoux, Quentin. *After Finitude: An Essay on the Necessity of Contingency*. Translated by Ray Brassier. London: Continuum, 2008.

Morrison, Joel D. *SpinbitZ: Interface Philosophy, Mathematics and Nondual Rational Empiricism*. Vol. 1. Self-published by the author. 2007. http://argos.vu/wp-content/uploads/2016/05/Morrison-Spin-BitzV1.pdf/.

Nancy, Jean-Luc. *Being Singular Plural*. Translated by Robert D. Richardson and Anne E. O'Byrne. Meridian, Crossing Aesthetics. Stanford: Stanford University Press, 2000.

————. *Dis-Enclosure: The Deconstruction of Christianity*. Translated by Bettina Bergo et al. New York: Fordham University Press, 2008.

Panikkar, Raimon. *The Cosmotheandric Experience*. Edited, with introduction, by Scott Eastham. Maryknoll, NY: Orbis, 1993.

————. *The Intrareligious Dialogue*. Rev. ed. New York: Paulist, 1999.

————. "The Pluralism of Truth." *World Faiths Insight* 26 (1990) 7–16. http://www.dhdi.free.fr/recherches/horizonsinterculturels/articles/panikkarpluralism.pdf/.

————. *The Trinity and the Religious Experience of Man*. Maryknoll, NY: Orbis, 1973.

Peirce, Charles Sanders. *Peirce on Signs: Writings on Semiotic*. Edited by James Hoopes. Chapel Hill: University of North Carolina Press, 1991.

Rivera, Mayra. "Glory: The First Passion of Theology?" In *Polydoxy: Theology of Multiplicity and Relation*, edited by Catherine Keller and Laurel Schneider, 167–85. New York: Routledge, 2011.

Roy, Bonnitta. "A Process Model of Integral Theory." *Integral Review* 3 (2006) 118–52. http://integral-review.org/back_issues/backissue3/index.htm/.

————. "Report from Critical Realism Integral Theory Symposium." 2011. http://integralpostmetaphysics.ning.com/forum/topics/report-from-critical-realism-integraltheory-symposium/.

Roy, Bonnitta, and Jean Trudel. "Leading the 21st Century: The Conception-Aware, Object-Oriented Organization." *Integral Leadership Review*, August 2011. http://integralleadershipreview.com/3199-leading-the-21st century-the-conception-aware-object-oriented-organization/.

Skolimowski, Henryk. *The Participatory Mind: A New Theory of Knowledge and of the Universe*. London: Arkana, 1994.

Thatamanil, John J. "God as Ground, Contingency, and Relation: Trinity, Polydoxy and Religious Diversity." In *Polydoxy: Theology of Multiplicity and Relation*, edited by Catherine Keller and Laurel Schneider, 238–57. New York: Routledge, 2011.

Varela, Francisco J., et al. *The Embodied Mind: Cognitive Science and Human Experience*. Cambridge: MIT Press, 1991.

Wilber, Ken. "Excerpt A: An Integral Age at the Leading Edge." 2002. https://integral-life-home.s3.amazonaws.com/Wilber-AnIntegralAgeAtTheLeadingEdge.pdf/.

———. *Integral Psychology: Consciousness, Spirit, Psychology, Therapy*. 1st paperback ed. Boston: Shambhala, 2000.

———. *Integral Spirituality: A Startling New Role for Religion in the Modern and Postmodern World*. Boston: Integral Books, 2006.

———. "On the Nature of a Post-Metaphysical Spirituality." 2001. https://web.archive.org/web/20060322225146/http://wilber.shambhala.com/html/misc/habermas/index.cfm/.

———. *Sex, Ecology, Spirituality: The Spirit of Evolution*. Boston: Shambhala, 1995.

6

Human Beings on This Planet[1]

OLIVER GRIEBEL

Not Making Our Minds Less Than They Are

P hilosophy is largely about how essential (or irrelevant) the human mind and human personhood altogether are, not just for ourselves, but in the world and ultimate reality itself, whatever these may be. Philosophy is about the meaning, impact, and freedom that the mental, the intellectual, and the spiritual may have beyond any one person, beyond humankind on Earth, as well as beyond other (possible) self-aware and world-viewing life-forms in general. Of course, the question about the reality of mind/spirit beyond us humans is also the question about "the Divine," "God," or however you like to call "it," "her" or "him." This is the question of whether there may be a spirit encompassing all there is, a spirit that could make the human spirit matter to the world as a whole . . . instead of ultimately mattering only to ourselves.

Opinions about the meaning of mind differ widely. Some dare the thesis that the world was only created in order to reunite humankind with God at the end of time. Others risk the barely less bold thesis that we are just an epiphenomenon of the universe and of life which by chance is aware of itself and able to reflect upon what the world is. If this were true, if mind and consciousness and sentience were mere epiphenomena, not causing anything, not grasping anything of ultimate meaning, then these would also be overwhelmingly unlikely and (in terms of evolution) superfluous accidents. One of the greatest contemporary philosophers (by the way not a religious or spiritual person) pointed this out in his 2012 book *Mind and Cosmos: Why the Materialist Neo-Darwinian Conception of Nature Is Almost Certainly False*:

1. Translated into English by the author.

123

Thomas Nagel

> We should seek a form of understanding that enables us to see ourselves and other conscious organisms as specific expressions simultaneously of the physical and the mental character of the universe.[2]

We achieve quite something in philosophy when, in thinking about such ultimate matters, we don't make ourselves *more* than we are—but not *less* either! The materialistic stance that a mental being like the human person lives in a world ultimately without mind or spirit, so that the human mind can't be said to really exist, seems absurd from a many-one perspective, where "the One," the world or cosmos or Being as a whole, complements "the Many," the beings and persons living inside of it. By "mind" and "spirit," I don't mean just what is highly cultural, intellectual, or spiritual; instead I am talking about the innocent fact that humans are conscious of the world, experiencing it, feeling it, imagining it, conceiving of it, acting on it.

In this essay, I will argue that as human beings we experience ourselves, experience ourselves in the world, and experience the world, *because as experiencing beings we are part and parcel of the world*. We must not be separated from it; our mind is a basic trait of the world, just like light or life are. It is not true that physical matter, however conceived, is the only thing really real, and that the "unreal" mind is an "image" of this material reality somehow "projected inside" a purely material brain, produced by it. Instead, life and mind themselves are as real as can be; they are the way the world experiences itself through beings. Life and mind are the "things" the world brings about which then in turn relate to the world. This can be expressed by saying that we *participate in the world*.

Not only shouldn't we make the mistake of thinking that we and our life and mind could be separated from "material reality": we must not either be separated from the animal sentience and consciousness out of which we once evolved to become persons, and which we still arise from as fetuses and babies. We are animals—*not just* animals, but animals *as well*! Concerning the human mind, this means, I suggest, that however highly evolved forms of spirit we may ever become able to envision and embody, there will always remain an animal foundation, experiencing its own body, experiencing other beings, one's offspring and relatives and life companions and friends and fellow humans—experiencing oneself as one feeds from one's environment, builds in it, and works in it. This is life experiencing itself, and even the higher forms of spirit created and discovered by humans, individually and collectively, in culture, religion, personal growth through personal experience, craft and technology, sciences and worldview, all of this, I believe,

anima

astral?

2. Nagel, *Mind and Cosmos*, 69.

grows out of the more basic life experiencing itself. Therefore, whenever we are trying to "abstract from" these roots beyond a reasonable measure, then spirit (in a general sense comprising the mental, the esthetical-cultural, the spiritual, and the intellectual) becomes idealized, unworldly, unnatural, lifeless, lofty, artificial.

What is a reasonable measure? Many spiritual people would like to restrict spirit to just the experiencing and celebrating of life. Yet, this kind of constriction of spirit to the natural in itself is just as unnatural as the opposite, "heady" extreme. One should not project onto all humankind and the whole world one's very own typically postmodern weariness about rationality, philosophy and science. The human mind and spirit cannot be limited to how you or I as individual humans, how our cultures and our biological species on Earth have historically, partly accidentally emerged and evolved. Our mind is reaching out to the world as a whole, as far as it can. The particular beauty of personhood lies in our ability to embody and express the cosmos, but a special tragedy lies in the limits set on us in this endeavor. Persons, by their mental gifts, can actively and creatively enter into a relationship with the whole cosmos, but also in arbitrary, selfish, and unhealthy ways.

Being partly autonomous, we do not accept quite a few things which are part of our very human condition, especially the fact that the world does not turn around us the way we would like it to, not any more than around any other being; the fact that we have to suffer, some of us suffer torments; the fact that our lives and what we love most and what matters to us will perish and be gone one day. Humans as mental beings are special also in this respect: they can be aware of pains and toils in their lives; be distressed and suffer from themselves; can feel lonely, exposed, and let down; can experience life and world as altogether futile and pointless; can doubt the coherence of it all and their place within it, despair about it, or fall apart by it. Our bodies, our lives, and our minds are so small compared to the whole that we should always strive not to "take it too personally," or too much as turning around our community or civilization. Nor should we try to express as individuals or groups more about the cosmos than we can really be and live.

Materialism has a somewhat converse problem: It totally misjudges the meaning and importance of life, experience, and spirit in the world. Materialism sees the world as "atomistic," that is, consisting of basic building blocks, particles of a stuff called "matter," functioning under mathematical laws which *per se* have nothing to do with life and sentience and mind. This atomism is not simply a *worldview* derived from research data; I contend that it is much more the social-political *self-view* modernist-minded people project onto nature and the world. It is the libertarian-technocratic hubris of the modern citizen, feeling unbound and unaccountable for humankind and their place on Earth and in the cosmos, pretending to be entitled and able to pragmatically dominate Earth and cosmos for the sake of their own interests and pleasure.

To this *atomism*, many-one thinking opposes *holism*: participation and individuation rather than particles and individualism. It is a thinking not starting from matter, but from the cosmos, a thinking where the human person and each distinct entity only exist inside the world as a whole, including elementary particles and quanta. From the many-one perspective fundamental particles like electrons and rays of light are not the sole basis for anything; they are not things ultimate in themselves: instead they must be seen as qualities and modi of the world's space and time, something like the finest interactions of the cosmic whole with its parts and the most tenuous universal rhythm of its evolving.

This is the point where people used to scientific thinking of the materialistic kind will ask: Why should ultimate reality consist of things as numerous and diverse and complex as matter, life, and mind, instead of just one kind of basic stuff or structure (particles, fields and the like)? Well, just because the world is not less complex. According to many-one thinking, simplicity can only be simplicity-in-complexity: The cosmos is the whole coherence which holds together things and aspects of all kinds, each distinct and different. The world just is not simpler, not more uniform. Materialism is willing (and keen) to sacrifice any bigger form and any big coherence. Herein lies its typically modernist arrogance and ignorance.

Our world is not an empty space filled with dead matter; rather it is a space for the many, an evolution of the many, and a timeless coherence of the many, all at once. And what we call life, sentience, mind, and culture must be part of and take part in the cosmic wholeness; it isn't "just in our heads" or "only in our language": it's not separate from matter and universe. Our minds are not locked inside our brains, looking out through the windows of our senses upon the world as it is "in itself"; instead we are the world as it is experiencing itself through parts of itself. One of the most distinguished German thinkers from the philosophical current called analytic philosophy, Franz von Kutschera, describes it this way:

> Polar dualism starts with the insight that reality never consists only of what we are observing, describing or explaining, but also comprises ourselves as subjects of this observing, as well as observation as our activity. We always are in a subject-object-relation, even when we are addressing only the objective part of this relation. [. . .] The physical world therefore has to be

understood as a world for subjects, and the mental world as a world of subjects experiencing and dealing with an objective, notably physical world.[3]

Kutschera is a man who in his youth studied physics, and as an analytic philosopher he is always concerned about empirical evidence and natural science and careful metaphysics. I am quoting him to prevent possible misconceptions that I might be taking here an unscientific, idealistic, or esoteric approach in this essay. In fact, I will try and challenge the materialistic worldview by a many-one worldview taking just as seriously the facts from physics, geosciences, biology, empirical social sciences, psychology, and so forth. Whatever you may have learned in school or at university about these I will try to take into account, and likewise most of the natural explanations about how things function . . . except for the materialistic ideology which often tricks its way into supposedly "pure" natural science. Rather than the materialistic building-blocks-and-modules approach, I will suggest a holistic and systemic one, based on the evolution of the universe and celestial bodies, life-forms, civilizations and persons the cosmos encompasses, based on the flux of substances and energy, and based on the use by living beings of information (especially through their genes and nervous systems).

Why Materialism Is Incongruous with Any Natural Concept of Information and Evolution

The notions of cosmic evolution and of natural information are crucial for a naturalistic worldview to count as many-one, and they are both incompatible with materialism. This is because materialism is *deterministic*, that is, seeing the universe as something which from its beginning until any future has to elapse in one precise way. Yet if anything ever happening were already fixed to the finest detail and farthest future, the beings and persons couldn't integrate information about their world into their life-form or biography, which however is crucial for any natural explanation.

Thus, when I say "information," I am not talking here just about matters of higher intellect or spirit or even the Divine; instead I am talking about the evolution and behavior of living beings in general, in a quite down-to-earth sense. To give you a first flavor of the argument, let me illustrate the idea of natural information I am advocating here by means of a thought experiment. Imagine your own life, humankind, life on Earth *in toto*, and the whole universe would "evolve backwards." In a materialistic

3. Kutschera, *Philosophie*, 212–13 (my translation).

worldview, this is a physically possible state of affairs and sequence of moments. What's worse: According to materialism, any natural evolution of
things "toward future" in fact is just another, perfectly equivalent description of the same "devolution" of things "towards the past." Indeed, time is
built into today's physical formulas in classical and relativistic and quantum
physics alike (reversible "quantum leaps" wouldn't do any better) in such a
way that "forward" time and "reverse" time are equivalent. Just like it doesn't
change anything about a film reel whether you play it forward or backward.
Each evolution, naturally "flowing" from past to future, then just seems to
be the flip side of an unnatural "devolution" coming from the future and
going toward the past. As a consequence there really wouldn't be any contingency or novelty, anything ever happening, emerging, or developing.

In other words, these formulas only allow for determinism. So what?
Isn't this maybe just an illusory problem, due to our illusory perception of
flowing time? Well, consider what such a "devolution" will look like. For instance, in a living being, the information about its life-form and environment
would not be organized and stored; instead you could see it emit information towards the things the information "should be" about. Corpses of beings
would resurrect and grow back into germ cells. Excrement would become
food. Waste heat would hit Earth from all directions, being transformed into
free energy, then radiated in the direction of the sun. These kinds of certainly
unscientific goings-on is the point of departure for my naturalist criticism of
materialism in this essay: that which is uncosmological, ungeological, and
unbiological time cannot be scientific time and thus can't be the last word
about physical time. If the usual "smooth" curbs of differential time functions
in today's physics force us to consider as a physical possibility for individuals and species in the history of our planet and universe the "un-storing,"
"un-processing" and "un-using" of information (as well as free energy in
the physical sense, and material resources for life), then these formulas can't
be the right way to describe the world, nor can the determinism which this
mathematics suggests.

In science, we can't help presupposing a very broad concept of information (much broader than computer information), since we can't seriously
doubt that the universe, Earth, life, and humankind will irreversibly develop
"forward" in time; we can't reduce any of these to something more basic and
different in essence. This entails a certain indeterminacy and autonomy of
living beings and persons, not an idealized but a robust one. And there's
more: For a natural-science concept of information, not only do we need
a world genuinely evolving, but we also need—and this is a central and
strong claim of mine—a natural order which is far more encompassing than
what mathematical structures, quantitative or geometrical or otherwise,

time

nature is more than numbers

can catch. For natural information refers to contexts and languages, to life-forms-in-environments and signs-in-cultures. A narrowing of this information to "matter-energy" or to other "purely physical" entities is unsound, arbitrary, and ideological. It is important to distinguish between forms and effects that can be locally delimited (say, "rather material" things) on the one hand, and on the other hand "things" that cannot be pinned down to some place or limited space in the cosmos: which are information and influences/factors which refer to open environments, to the yet-to-be-formed future, and partly to the world as a whole.

Information in a many-one sense, as I conceive it, is the participation of beings and persons in environment, community, and cosmos; it is not matter or some kind of "second matter" à la Daniel Dennett. Famously, Dennett has tried to reform materialism by materializing information as a sort of stuff made of information units, notably genes and "memes." This has to be seen in the context of the materialistic program of "closing the gaps" where the human mind might become spirit, reaching beyond the matter and physiology humans are made of, beyond their limited historical and cultural and personal contexts, instead reaching out for the universal, the timeless, the spiritual, maybe even for some kind of Divine. One major goal of materialism has always been to make all belief in any kind of Divine appear irrational. Yet, there are no reasons why the meaning of natural information should be limited to any stuff or situation or local region of space, or to any "concrete" context. It is therefore no surprise that Dennett was not amused at all about Thomas Nagel's book *Mind and Cosmos,* from which I quoted above, considering Nagel, I guess, a traitor in the noble fight against theism and other forms of obscurantism.

Now, please keep in mind that I don't mean to refute the natural and scientific worldview, instead I will defend natural and scientific thinking *against* its seeming guarantor, which is materialism with its determinism and atomism . . . but I will also try to defend it against excessively supernatural, at times antiscientific or pseudoscientific ideas about the place of mind and spirit in the world. Materialism makes us humans too little, and isolates us from the world. Many religions and spiritualities, conversely, seem to make us look bigger than a natural being can possibly be: ideally rational, morally competent and free, universally gifted with the deepest spiritual insight, ultimately preserved or restored by God.

Not Making Mind Too Big Either

Mind you: I am not denying there might be a sense in which humans, beyond their natural-being side, may also be spirit in such a radical sense;
however, this has to be investigated in the first place, more boldly than any
spiritual thought I am aware of ever has. Within a modern worldview, the
idea that there is an all-encompassing spirit or God who is omnipotent, caring about and taking care of each of us, and that "he himself" and our faith
and salvation are so altogether central to the world, this idea certainly cannot
be simply taken for granted. How can this fit with the humble and frail and
lost condition of so many if not most of us as beings on this planet, even
if we accept the variety and power and revelations of the human spirit to
be real? In an essay in his collection *Nach Gott*, Peter Sloterdijk writes, in a
similar vein: "Apparently, there is a multitude of creativities and reflexivities
in the world which can't be monopolized by a central divine instance. Earth
is a polyvalently intelligent place."[4] Obviously, Sloterdijk can only imagine
a Divinity that is "monopolizing" the mental and intellectual and spiritual
diversity present in the world. It seems to me, however, that the problem
here is not so much the Divine *per se*, but an anti-God-view which Sloterdijk
shares with many secular minds who are opposing traditional, autocratic,
otherworldly views of the Divine.

We therefore should take care to navigate carefully between the certainties of theology, Western and Eastern, and the certainties of anti-theology,
the materialistic and the postmodern (and the post-postmodern like Sloterdijk's). Many-one spirituality may find a way to not be crushed between
them, orienting by both a natural-planetary way of thinking and a cosmic-
spiritual one.

I believe that between the extremes of materialism and overspiritual-
izing, there is plenty room for this kind of both-and. This space is broad
enough for many approaches about how to see our participation in the
world. The approach I am taking in this essay is to found the reality and
importance of mind not on a special spiritual place or a special salvation
perspective we may or may not have in this world and existence, but instead
to try and start with the place of humans in our modern life here and now.
I am reflecting on the place our mind has in "nature" as natural philosophy
understands it, that is, in the evolving universe, on this planet, in its biosphere and in our bodies . . . the natural frame set to our human mind and
personhood.

4. Sloterdijk, *Nach Gott*, 21 (my translation).

About all this we, as modern humans, know vastly more than the ancient Greeks, Jews, Indians, or Chinese knew when they conceived their axial religions traditional and classical ideas about the human Mind and the all-encompassing Spirit. This forces us to critically evaluate their often idealizing and incredibly optimistic approaches to our personhood and place in the world.

Why do I say "optimistic"? Well, Earth and evolution are not tender at all with all life-forms, human and prehuman; nor are life-forms tender with one another. Although it is a proverb, "Eat or be eaten" is also a basic natural fact. Beings strive to feed themselves and to procreate through cosmic, life is robbery geological, evolutionary and ecological hardships and upheavals; they have to suffer, age, and die, and even most species sooner or later have to make their exit. Now, does the evolution of *Homo sapiens* on Earth look like the privileging or caring agency by an encompassing spirit? Humans have always had to struggle with the not-so-tender nature surrounding them, with germs and parasites, with injuries and the handicaps of old age. Our talent for signs and language, craft and technology was pushed by the struggle for survival during the ice ages, which also made us evolve physiologically and culturally. Moreover, our ever-branching-out (and cross-fertilizing) tree of genetic, ethnic-cultural, and linguistic variety cannot be separated from the bitter truth of humans isolating from each other, fighting, violating, killing, tormenting, humiliating and enslaving each other.

This seems to underpin a classic line of argument advanced by materialism: *Humankind is but a (rather unfortunate and miserable) by-product and accident of cosmic and planetary evolution; a result of its genes and neuron patterns and brainwaves, it is merely a highly evolved animal which by chance has developed some of the ultimately minor abilities of language and reason, craft and culture, being at most—as we can best see in post–World War II modernity—an egoistic market citizen who after all is only trying to act out his or her instincts, feelings, cultural dispositions, preferences, and interests (as far as they can be paid for or enforced). There quite obviously is no high spirit or divinity at work here, and therefore nothing is genuinely more than just matter and biology.* late modern malaise

This strikingly contrasts with the views about the human person that traditional believers or spiritual people or classical idealists hold: They see high culture, spirit, and divine action working everywhere; they see human beings as naturally making contact with God, high moral ideals, and deep insights; and they see the world ordered toward a good life and society, self-actualization and salvation. For them, all ultimately is or will ultimately become spirit.

Doesn't this blatantly contradict the facts of matter, Earth, human life and society, present and past? Or can these sharply opposed views be

somehow balanced out, avoiding the extremes? Ironically, these two warring camps share a premise that is by no means self-evident: Both presuppose that spirit can only be real, important, and effective in the world if
the world and human beings are created for morality, religion, intellectual
excellence, realization, and redemption, generally and clearly. But I believe
that we must first take a look at sentience and consciousness and spirit as we
encounter them in living beings—both in human beings and in other-than-
human beings—though they may not be as "perfect" we may like them to
be. Consciousness in this down-to-earth sense can be found everywhere on
this planet, and this is a fact by which we can counter materialism's spiritless
self-image, spiritless culture, spiritless economy, and spiritless worldview . .
a materialistic "anti-spirit" I would gladly grant everyone who likes it if the
rampant growth of our economy would not have become such a danger
to the future of our children and our humane civilization. To me, attack-
ing materialism means criticizing materialistic natural philosophy from a
natural-science perspective, and it also means explaining to materialisti-
cally thinking people how much they mentally reduce, fragment, and isolate
themselves, humanity, and life.

Why Practical Materialism Isn't an Argument
for a Materialist Worldview

By materialists I do not mean dogmatists and ideologues of a materialistic
doctrine, but what I will call *practical materialists*. Actually, such people
usually have no clear materialistic conviction, let alone theory. Their image
of what a person is, what they are, is more of an anti-philosophy, they simply
do not believe in a spirit that goes beyond the individual, or that is encompassing and timeless. There is nothing immoral or outrageous about this unbelief; practical materialists are often good people and fellow-humans. The
fact that they do not believe in a higher human spirit and an all-embracing
spirit of the cosmos has a lot to do with our modern way of life, our modern society of acquisition, consumption, and self-assertion. What occupies
and worries most of us most of the time in modern life (whether we really
stand behind it or are rather driven by it) also has a strong influence on
how we see ourselves, life, and the world. People's living conditions strongly
impact their values and worldview (which can also be an anti-worldview).
In Western societies, which are so heavily economy-oriented, many people
understandably do not see many peculiarly spiritual influences at work, and
consequently also feel little spirit in themselves, whether as philosophical
vision or religious awe or spiritual searching or a need for deeper meaning.

Consequently they will not believe in a higher spirit or deeper meaning in the world either.

This kind of perfectly normal modern disbelief is a problem for traditional worldviews because they have to assume that the divine spirit is accessible to all and that all can be open to it—except for those who are wicked by their own fault or have lost their way through their own failure. Today, however, we know of the world as an enormously complex, coherent, and functioning whole of natural laws, and we know of things that have arisen historically, which humans have not created, which they only roughly see through and certainly do not control, in which they are rather just cogs, with very limited possibilities for shaping circumstances, for increasing self-determination, or for taking autonomous moral action. Today we know too much about the world to blame human beings, in the traditional fashion, for their hardships in the world, for the dark sides of being a human, or for the impending failure of modern civilization. In order to come to a modern and at the same time cosmic-spiritual worldview, we would have to say goodbye to these kinds of traditional ideas: both the idea that we are to blame for the fact that things are going so unspiritually in the world, and the idea that the spirit which may encompass it is there to redeem us from the world . . . or indeed to redeem us from ourselves.

The very idea of a redemption of humans from themselves, from the supposed illusion of being a person of their own, a redemption into the one divine no-self—an idea that many Asian-inspired Western spiritualities believe in—this idea in fact may be something which is neither desirable nor possible. Spirit shows itself through people in so many different ways, but very few people are striving to overcome themselves, and if they are trying, even fewer manage to. What speaks for the fact that this might be or become different one day, or should be different at all?! Quite the contrary, the spiritual goal may not be to break away from the "illusion" of being a distinct person, but to break away from the error (in many ways) of being separated from the world as a person, or privileged over anyone else.

If we can learn to live with ourselves as humans as less pure or perfect spirits than we might wish and expect to be, then many modern-style practical materialists who have little need for, disposition to, or interest in highly spiritual things are no longer central to an argument for the materialist worldview. That is, materialism would have lost a main argument, since, besides the cruelty of nature and man, the missing or misguided spirit of the people is probably its best argument. The fact that materialistic modernity turns a great many people into materialists, in my view definitely isn't a material-causal phenomenon anyway; it is rather a social and psychological, cultural and ideological one. If living conditions change, and what these conditions do to our minds and days, then the prevailing materialist worldview and attitude towards life can also change quickly and profoundly, overcoming the materialistic zeitgeist.

And we have to overcome this worldview, for materialism as a world-dominating economic system and lifestyle is approaching its end, whether through self-destruction or through an ecological, solidarity-based rebuild. I think the failure of materialistic modernity has a meaning that clearly goes beyond the individual and even beyond humankind, and it is this: If we want to have a future as a humane civilization, then we have to learn that we are part of a whole, part of our human community on this planet in the one cosmos; we have to adapt to this true human condition of ours, care for it, and serve it. The survival crisis of modernity is a spiritual opportunity, a responsibility, and an insight into where we stand in the world. If we miss these and fail, it won't be a punishment. If we accept them, it won't be salvation. But the task of evolving in this emergency situation, ecologically and in solidarity—living into the experience of belonging to humanity and Earth and the cosmos—might very well become a worldview-altering moral and spiritual revelation for people who have always considered themselves irreligious.

My focus in this essay is not going to be the many teachings about individual salvation, the brotherhood of humans, a New Earth or an afterlife, although these questions (and attempts to answer them) do not lose their meaning if you choose a lifeworld-natural approach, as I do. There may indeed be things which go way beyond our ordinary life experiences in normal life and our ideas of natural laws, without therefore having to be supernatural. While I am convinced that there is a natural order that sets robust constraints to any wondrous events and radically self-transforming actions, still I am also sure that the signs and "contents" of the human mind play a role in nature going far beyond what the materialist building-block and billiard-ball thinking imagines to be "natural."

A Secular, Naturalistic, Ordinary-Life Approach Defying Materialism

I want to show how far materialism is from some of the most physical, natural, earthly, everyday, tangible things, and how much it even contradicts them in essential respects. Elementary particles as "stuff" making up the world, a block universe in which time "stands still," genes "determining" predispositions and development of the human body, or brain patterns "being" the human mind—all of this, I contend, is deeply unnatural, unphysical, and unscientific. I will suggest what I think is a much more natural view of the world: a holistic and evolutionary one that regards humans, life, and matter as delimited and autonomous only to some extent, and as parts of the cosmos always and everywhere.

From a many-one perspective, it is not possible to separate the hard facts of science and history (and economics) from the "softer" facts of mind and spirit, and dispose of these as unreal. Conversely, however, it isn't possible to dispose of the harder facts either. Postmodern relativism and constructivism has done and still does a lot of damage by making an anti-scientific stance socially acceptable, and today right-wing populists are in the process of dismissing the hard facts in our current crisis of culture and nature as something that left-wing scholars allegedly have invented for their own interests and power.

If we want to oppose this view, then we have to move away from relativism and towards a plurality that not only recognizes the unity of human-kind, but also the one natural order and the one cosmic spirit in which all human beings take part and to which all contribute, a coherence and spirit in which we are all arranged. Arranged?! Humans being part and parcel of an order of things that also sets spiritual and moral standards, a kind of cosmic authority . . . this of course is an idea that many postmodernist- or green-minded people can't be comfortable with. Haven't they deconstructed the old powers that be and their rule through force and religion, and the new powers that be with their rule through money and manipulation? Yes, and rightly so, yet I also believe it is becoming clear today that we have to put our very relativism in context, have to see ourselves inside a larger whole—in order to save humane civilization on this earth, of which we are children, and save it for our children.

My point of departure is not antispiritual; rather it *is secular,* and this is important. A great merit of modernity is the fact that we don't have to start with God or meditation when we try to say something about our lives and ourselves. The modern starting point is what we see when we look around: we see people who work to make their living; we see families and relationships between people; we see cities, landscapes, and infrastructure; we experience our ethnic communities with their languages and cultures, and how they regulate their coexistence as states; we see vegetation and ani-mals and agriculture; looking up we see outer space with the sun, the moon, and distant stars; we see what great writers and filmmakers and other artists, and what natural scientists, humanities scholars, and philosophers tell us about the life of people on Earth.

This kind of secular starting point is not something only modern scientists with their methods, experimental setups and training in techni-cal terms and mathematics can understand. A reduction of humans and the world to a "real reality" of elementary particles, gene codes, or brain patterns is not the secular endeavor I am talking about here. Of course, a modern worldview must be based on, among other things, what human biology, neuroscience, and basic physics have to tell us. But conversely, natural science must learn to see itself in the full breadth and complexity of our life as modern people in the biosphere on this planet; in our private lives as free, responsible citizens; in our shared culture; in our economic life; and in the way we organize politically. Never forget that modern natural science too is done by ordinary people in modern life on the surface of planet Earth.

So when materialists think that they can "scientifically prove" that there is a simple physical foundation in the light of which this complex modern lifeworld "actually does not exist," then they are demonstrating how unable they are to reflect on the bizarre and even absurd place their very own worldview assigns to themselves as persons. Indeed, this defies basic logic: "If my worldview is correct, then people are 'actually' not beings who have worldviews, thus my worldview does not exist either, and a nonexisting worldview certainly is wrong." In logic, this kind of self-defeat is called *reductio ad absurdum*. It simply doesn't work that way, and the fact that materialists relentlessly reboot this type of argument in ever-new versions is largely due to the modular, construction-kit thinking they just can't abandon, no matter what.

Many-one thinking is the opposite of such reductions. It is holistic and plural, and therefore has no problem with a complex modern era and civilization. The starting point is not any physical "building blocks" of reality or genetic "programs" of humans. Instead it is the planet with its geography and resources; the biosphere of living beings; human civilization and the people in it, including you and me in particular. In this lifeworld everything is real which is not merely mythical, fictional, or delusional.

Even as modern people we cannot simply get rid of all these deceptions of, limits to, or blinkers on our intellect, nor can we get out of our basic physical and biological frame. And why should we? The aim is not a complete and perfect understanding of the world anyway, but a less one-sided, more clear, more coherent one. There is no doubt that compared to humans in the Middle Ages, we can understand reality a lot better, if indeed we care to inform and educate ourselves. One important orientation is the whole range of topics, things, and facts about which we read in a sophisticated, critically intellectual newspaper such as the *Guardian*, *Die Zeit*, or *Le Monde*—although contributors to and editors of these organs are also quite often duped by materialistic propaganda.

It has been with the help of such a critically informed public sphere and self-critical openness to new insights that we have learned so much more about our place in the world since the beginning of modern times. A secular thinking in the tradition of the Enlightenment takes seriously everything that open-critical people can discover in terms of facts and factors, and this is not the same thing as the materialistic reductions à la mode. In fact, materialism is the degeneration of a thinking that once was progress, back then directed against medieval dogmatism and domination. It had set out to no longer allow important topics and facts to be narrowed down by traditional perspectives that only observe and allow what fits with their images of Man and God, myths and revelations. One must never forget what modernity has freed us from: the small-mindedness and prohibition of thinking, the censorship and persecution of those who think differently.

Modern people like us only are what we are due to this liberation. We have the liberty and the privilege to do something which during most of human history was way out of reach of all people: just look at things and compare them and judge for ourselves, or else look the other way and focus on our individual and domestic interests, sensitivities and purchase wishes. This "ordinary life" too is modern reality, hard facts happening right before our eyes, which, by the way, are very different from and much more than science that only experts and technocrats and professors can understand.

Mistaking natural science for a full-blown worldview has become a particularly great danger for the human spirit today. Many have given up trying to form and articulate a modern view of the world and the place of human persons in it. They capitulate to coming to grips with modern science philosophically, that is, to forming and grasping adequate intuitions about its basic concepts. They capitulate to gaining an overview of its foundations, and of all the fields of natural science that obviously must not be left out for a coherent and comprehensive and topical worldview. They capitulate to the hyperspecialized, overterminologized, technocratic science industry, and to the sheer mass of academics and their publications and statements in the media. Even scientists themselves largely capitulate, and in the fragmented, distorted and narrowed "scientific worldview" that materialistic scientists propose we no longer recognize ourselves (the way we do know ourselves!). Yet the experts are hard-core professionals that most of us cannot hold a candle to, rhetorically, even on issues where they lack ordinary common-sense judgment. In addition, modern materialism has a nimbus around it of practicality, logic, and inevitability. Whenever any supposedly backward-looking traditionalists or woo-woo enthusiasts speak up against the supposed overall competence of scientists, this just raises scientists' eyebrows.

The task is therefore to answer back in a scientifically and intellectually serious way to a "natural science" in which we humans, as we live and experience ourselves, do not figure; to contradict it with unproblematic observations of our natural world, with what defines us culturally and mentally, and with plainly visible everyday facts. In order to challenge materialism, one has to attack its self-contradictions, where it runs counter to the very foundations of modern science itself, where it undermines the very notion of modern personhood, a notion without which obviously science could not even exist.

natural science presupposes human personhood

Why the Human Condition and Modern Life, for All Their Mundane Traits, Don't Match the Materialistic Human Robot

The travesty here has become the program: the human person seen as a genetic, neurobiological, instinct-controlled robot. Materialists are usually also good advertising professionals and salespeople, so they only put on the table what is well received. They hide or cover up the more problematic consequences of their basic views. Back the 1950s they still were more honest. At the time, B. F. Skinner, with his behaviorist psychology, consistently operated according to the materialistic image of instinct-controlled human beings; according to Skinner, the human being is a stimulus-reaction machine whose mental life, if she has one, does not matter. The title of one of Skinner's books sums it up: *Beyond Freedom and Dignity.* With this stance, in my view, he hit rock bottom in the history of philosophy—since of course this is pure materialistic philosophy, no matter how hard it tries to disguise itself as empirical research. The tragic thing about Skinner is that he saw himself as a humanist, a liberator from authoritarian religion and politics. But with what he tried to do to personhood, this surely does not work.

At the time, this led other psychologists such as Abraham Maslow and Carl Rogers to counter behaviorism with a psychology that aptly calls itself *humanistic psychology.* (I already spoke about it in the Opening Remarks, because at the end of the 1960s *transpersonal psychology* emerged from it, by which most cultural-evolutionary philosophies are strongly influenced, from participatory thinking to integral thinking to Spiral Dynamics.)

The precise concern of humanistic psychologists was to preserve the patient's/client's human dignity by consistently taking as a starting point how she or he felt and saw and expressed himself or herself. It is typical of the operational blindness of materialistic psychology, of its inability to view itself critically, that it does not notice how absurd it is to treat a mental illness, indeed to define it, without starting from the patient's inner life, from the disturbances and suffering that she experiences in her emotional life, from her sense of reality, from her body awareness, from her self-image, from her waking consciousness, and from her ego-boundaries when interacting with others. These are all things that cannot simply be observed and "conditioned" on the patient: you have to talk with him about these, to relate to her in a way that comes from shared personhood, as a therapist meeting a fellow human.

Materialism has not preached its psychology of behaviorism much since the 1960s, because it became clear that it is badly received even by people who otherwise think in a materialistic way. It is also quite straightforward that such a robotic image of human beings even contradicts the (certainly not highly spiritual or idealized) image of personhood that even materialism needs for its ideas of economy, society, and the state: the idea of critically comparing consumers and responsible citizens who are able to act for their livelihood, household, family, and country. Robots cannot do anything like that—if we humans didn't manage to do this kind of things, then civilization altogether, not only modernity, would not be possible. Criminal law and contract law assume that adults are responsible, that they know what they are doing, that they understand when they are harming someone, that they can answer for their actions, that they recognize the value and rights and well-being of other people. No matter how neoliberal, libertarian or neopopulist an ideology is, they are all built on a basis of judgment, conscience and relative autonomy of action. None of them can reasonably incapacitate human beings (including themselves!) as robots, thereby releasing them from responsibility for themselves and others.

Thus a consistently materialistic image of wo/man cannot be maintained even under such tangible aspects as the medical-therapeutic, economic-social, and political-legal. No matter how merely practical and liberal and secular we want to see ourselves as human beings, we cannot see ourselves as completely automatic and mindless. Rather, we have to assume an inner life that is not just some "neuron pattern" or "representation" in the brain; we must presuppose an "inner" life naturally relating to the "outer" world, that really has something to do with ourselves as we know ourselves, with our life together, with the way we see the world, however personally colored this view of the world may be, however much in progress and however imprecise, however limited by immaturity, by all kinds of handicaps and challenges, adverse life conditions, and decay.

Materialism imagines a strict distinction between what the human being is as seen from the outside, objectively, "really," and what she is as seen from the inside, subjectively, "only seemingly." As we have seen, such a separation is incompatible with even the relatively moderate spiritual foundations of middle-class life. Many-one thought insists that things like character maturation and deeper interpersonal relationships, education and culture, worldview and all forms of the search for meaning and spirituality,

have to be taken into account for a modern scientific picture of human beings in the world. That's because these things clearly belong to our life in the
world, and there is no serious science that can generally exclude feelings, actions, ideas, and thoughts from a modern worldview, as mere appearances.
As I already said, there is of course illusion, fiction, delusion, and wishful
thinking, but all these weaknesses, disturbances, and games of our mind in
fact *presuppose* that the human mind experiences and understands lots of
things in a perfectly normal, limited yet unproblematic sense.

As I have tried to show, materialism, both in its worldview and especially in its concept of personhood, can easily and seriously be challenged,
and surprisingly in a commonsense manner, using nothing but highly plausible basic assumptions about us humans on Earth. The real challenge for
a many-one worldview does not lie in the distorted images of the human
being and the world she and he live in. The true challenge lies in giving *a
deeper, higher meaning* to the intellectual, moral, biological, spiritual, and
ecological *limitations* of humans, many of which we have discovered, or admitted to ourselves, only in modern times. If the human mind, if our efforts
as fellow humans, if our humane and social efforts, if our self-realizing and
intellectual and spiritual efforts, if all these actually matter to the world (and
not only to those of us who care about them!), then the mental traits we
possess and the feats we attempt should not be vain, negligible as compared
to the spiritual limitations that we have as short-lived beings formed by environment, culture, and family; as beings struggling to make the best of life
for ourselves and our loved ones; as managers of everyday routine; as strays
in our modern fictions, games, and pseudo-identities.

For me, this is the real challenge. Materialism as a worldview is self-
defeating, yet the fact that the human spirit is not always lived out in such a
powerful and convincing and worthy way in our ordinary lives also remains
a problem. We owe to modernity our awareness of the constraints and con-
tortions of our minds. The real pioneers of a modern image of personhood
are only secondarily the scientists and researchers who just in the nineteenth
and twentieth centuries really discovered us humans as natural beings on a
natural planet. In my opinion, it is the much more "realistic" novelists (and
screenwriters) who have explored the depths of our minds: people like Saul
Bellow, Charles Bukowski, Fyodor Dostoevsky, Michel Houellebecq, Kurt
Vonnegut, Carson McCullers, Arundhati Roy, and Émile Zola. They reveal
the inadequacies, the failure, and the misery of our personalities and of our
life together and against each other. They expose our delusions of grandeur;
our greed for fleeting kicks; our "seducibility" to charisma, sex appeal,
power, and beautiful appearances; our obsessions and fanaticisms; our dull
self-centeredness and clan fixation; what is unauthentic about us; and our

weak spot for illusory worlds. They have taken the traditional image of the inherently beautiful, divine soul created for the good life from its pedestal.

All of this comes largely from our natural and social condition as humans (our anthropology), from our physicality, and from our struggle with our environment and the earth—the struggle for survival and health, livelihood and security. Here I have to repeat what I emphasized earlier, in order to "rub it in": One cannot separate the harshness and violence between peoples, in professional life, on the street, or in the family, from the natural environment and history and Earth from which we come. All of these belong together. Today we know a great deal about how humans, their living conditions, their culture, and in some cases also how their experiences have developed—from chimpanzee relatives becoming Homo sapiens to Ice Age hunters to Bronze Age warriors to medieval serfs to the authoritarian petty bourgeois and postwar middle-class individualists. It has never been easy for people; a great number of them have always had to flounder and strive for a humble place in the world, often suffering badly, withering as persons, and dying early.

We are not to blame for the hardships and catastrophes of nature, for our often immoderate and mindless *appétits vitaux*, for our hereditary burdens and physical handicaps, for our immaturity and our deterioration through aging, for the fact that our intellect and our interests are quite narrow and self-centered. This is how the earth brought us forth, what our environment made us to become, and if there is an encompassing divine order of things, then it "didn't mind" us being and living this way. I cannot see anything that would suggest that we humans can simply get rid of the limits that are also set for our minds and intellects and spirits: the problems of growing up and coming of age, of getting old and dying, of making a living and having a livable life, of the arduous path of becoming civilized and educated, of violence, of the struggles for power, of ethnic conflicts, of scarce resources and ecological limits, of geological and cosmic disasters.

Interim Conclusion

I believe that by now I have gathered some important threads which I will need for the second part of this essay. I think that in an essay it is legitimate to encircle the topic in this way, meandering about, but never leaving the river basin, so to speak, taking the essay in this sense to be an orienting, pointed and also personal discussion (which for me belongs to any honest and realistic worldview). Today we already sense that there are no simple recipes and procedures that will lead to the one correct theory or the one complete system for seeing the many-one cosmos in all its complexity. Philosophy at best helps us to better understand the big questions at stake, and to distinguish them from "solutions" that are simplistic and one-sided and therefore worse than wrong: caricatures.

The first thread is to make the case against the doctrine of materialism, according to which the whole history of the world (mind you, from beginning to end!) is already fixed by completely predetermined paths of elementary particles or vibrations of elementary waves. This determinism and atomism is self-undermining, since in such a "block universe" there are no entities of the kind of . . . a materialist for instance. Indeed, if the world were a purely material world, then human beings would be purely material systems of particles and waves, and if such a purely physical system opened its mouth and emitted sequences of tones like "There is nothing but matter," then this could not be expressing an opinion about the world as a whole. There are no such things in a block universe.

Real humans, by contrast, in the real cosmos, can do this kind of thing certainly not only by virtue of any known or unknown physical laws; there also needs to be biological organization, bringing up, participation in a language community, and possibly participation in an all-encompassing spirit, the One. Even chimpanzees can't do this, and certainly simple living beings cannot; even less can "pure matter." By contrast, a materialist certainly can have ideas about the world, and be wrong about it. In this way, ironically, the mere existence of materialists shows that materialism is wrong.

This is good news for people who want spirituality to have its essential place, not only within humankind, but in the order of things, in the cosmos as a whole. Yet, notwithstanding our capacity (our gift) for constructing worldviews, what are we spiritually entitled to be given as suffering and longing beings on this planet? This is where the second thread comes in: the natural boundaries set for us by physics and biology, survival and economic activity on Earth, our struggles with one another, the cultural walls and the problems we have relating and responding to one another simply because we are such different persons and groups. This is not so good news for people who hope that the relationship between the human mind and the cosmic spirit will provide some sort of guarantee of peaceful prosperity, healing, self-realization, or salvation of any kind.

I think that the good news / bad news or cosmic optimism / cosmic pessimism or glorious personhood / deplorable humankind contrast, however, is not necessarily a problem in many-one thinking, since it is an evolutionary way of seeing the world, with inevitable natural tensions and dynamics being part of the picture. This approach sees the evolution of life-forms, cultures, personalities, and worldviews in the context of the still-becoming cosmos itself. This evolution does not stop on any plateau; it is an ongoing one, and a qualitative one at that. In the process, some humans and communities, today more than ever before, have the chance to more and more consciously participate in the world and become more themselves, something none of our ape ancestors and even maybe only a handful of our fifteenth-century ancestors were able to do. There is little perfection, greatness, or even resting on hard-earned achievements involved. Yet, for all our late-modern predicament and gloom and confusion, something is going on for the very first time on this planet, which has been around four thousand by a thousand by a thousand years! This is really special, in a historically objective way.

One inevitably is tempted to ascribe a meaning to this cosmic, planetary, and human evolution, such that some kind of salvation for humankind can eventually happen, be it a self-redemption through meditation, through reflection that we ourselves *are* the divine spirit, be it a world-historical process of salvation, a healing transformation of the world through the divine spirit. It turns out that it poses great problems to reconcile these radical ideas of humankind's release from suffering in a natural way with what the human mind accomplishes in the human body in human civilization in human life among other species on Earth. The becoming of the cosmos is always also a passing away, not only further development but also dwindling, decay, or destruction, the old being replaced or displaced by the new. Nothing on this planet appears to be made for eternity, especially not the Homo sapiens form of life, nor you or I as individual people having emerged from it. Nature on our Earth lavishly produces life, but it also wastes and wears it out on a large scale. Edgar Morin says:

> Reproduction (cell division, germs, sex, sperm and egg cells) is life's answer to the innumerable deadly dangers from the environment and to the inevitable disintegration of any organization. But just as the organization of the living, from the reproduction by germ or egg on, had to accept and prepare the death of the individual for the survival of the species. [. . .] The dialogical unity of the species and the individual not only corresponds to a mutual finality, where the goal of the species is the individual and the goal of the individual is the species; it also corresponds to the dialogical unity of two radical opponents: life and death.[5]

Right now we are experiencing one of the very rare large extinctions of species in the long history of the earth, caused by nothing other than our own overexploitation of nature. Such mismanagement by one form of

---

5. Morin, *Connaissance*, 76–77 (my translation).

life at the expense of so many others has probably never occurred in all the hundreds of millions of years of life on our planet. Is this a prelude to a transformation of the earth into an eternal paradise? Basically, the big question in this context is whether the dynamics between the cosmos and Earth and life as we know it from the history of planet Earth, a dynamics creating the new and destroying the old, if this dynamic can turn our planet into a "New Earth" carefully arranged around humanity in such a way that we can continue to thrive on it without ever perishing. Some also think that we can protect ourselves technologically and remodel ourselves in such a way that civilized humankind can also survive major ecological, geological, or cosmic catastrophes. I confess that none of this sounds to me like a many-one worldview that wants to feel, understand, and accept the place of humans on Earth and in the cosmos.

Thus my interim conclusion would be: There is nothing unnatural or unscientific about a big overall coherence and evolution of the cosmos, which is also reflected in the past and present evolution of life-forms, cultures, and individuals. However, this cosmic evolution always seems to be a blooming and a waning at the same time. Not only does timeless materialism appear unnatural, but so does the healing, salvation, or redemption of the species Homo sapiens *from* time, given evolution's vagaries and astronomic-geological disasters on this earth—at least this trajectory is hardly imaginable without fundamental changes in the natural order of things. Whether and how such supernatural interventions or spontaneous spirit-driven self-arrangements of things could emanate from the meaningful coherence and the inner evolving tendency of the cosmos itself, that should not be the subject here. I have the feeling that I can be of better use to the discussion by not discussing different ideas of salvation or how they might do justice to the history and present of people on Earth. Instead, I would like to investigate a little further how a many-one natural philosophy can stick closely and critically to natural research and the basic assumptions of modern natural science.

The starting point for my natural-philosophical criticism of materialism has been the grotesque image of a "world gone wrong," running backwards. It has become clear how many fundamental things in the world cannot "run backwards." In the sphere of "matter," included in what cannot run backwards are gravity, the flow and dispersion of (free) energy, and energy's usage for building something out of materials or for organizing things. In the sphere of life, what cannot run backwards are birth, growth, learning, aging and death—all of these being phenomena that have to do with information about the structure and remodeling of the body and behavior in the being's environment, especially the information coded in the genes and the nervous system. In cultural and technical domains, too, processes of collecting and storing, of also outputting and using information cannot "run backwards."

Towards the end of this essay I will say a few more things about how these cosmic-holistic and cosmic-temporal and cosmic-informational considerations relate to the great physical ideas of the twentieth century, which are quanta and Einstein's space-time. I want to say right away what I'm getting at: a worldview in which anything that exists, that is the case, that has impact, is co-determined by the wholeness of what there is. The equation material = real is wrong. There are particles, but they are not just there as primordial "stuff," existing of themselves, so to speak; instead they are particles of the cosmos, its finest structures and smallest effects, its developmental cadence. Life and consciousness, person and spirit, I claim, develop out of this fine structure of the cosmos, remain embedded in it, and live on it.

Natural Beings in a Both Physical and Spiritual Cosmos

Solar radiation consists of very simple and uniform waves which, with the help of relatively simple and uniform physics and chemistry, are used by the human body to develop and stay alive, to repair and to reproduce. But the information that a living body "means," especially the information in genes, in the nervous system, and in language, cannot be localized or limited in molecules and photons. A gene or a word has no meaning by itself. With genes, the "context" is what a living body does and can do within a species and its ecosystem and planetary environment with the help of the entire genome. This is not heavy speculation guided by wishful thinking; a great deal of recent research comes down to it, as the German biologist and teacher Axel Ziemke explains in his book *Alle Schöpfung ist Werk der Natur*:

> Just like epigenetics emphasizes the role of environmental influences on variability and inheritance in a completely new way, the importance of adaptability of individual development to environmental influences for an understanding of evolution came again into the focus of evolutionary developmental biology. The interrelationships between the organism and the environment are the subject matter of ecology. And so some researchers are already creating a new label for this new synthesis of developmental biology, evolutionary research, and ecology: "ecological

evolutionary developmental biology" or, as an abbreviation of
the corresponding English technical terms, eco-evo-devo.[6]

Biology itself is growing out of the straitjacket of materialism, it seems.

In the case of words, the context in which they have meaning is what
people do and can do with all of the language within their culture and human civilization. This information is not somehow inside physical bodies
and particles, nor is it inside systems composed of matter and radiation, nor
is it in their states or patterns. It is neither in a place, nor is it an object. And
it refers not only to things from physics but to the whole complex frame and
coherence of the micro-world, outer space, planet, biosphere, civilization
and people; it refers to the cosmos, where all kinds of natural substances and
events, types of things and forms of life, communities and individuals, have
their place—it refers to the cosmic wholeness of matter and information,
life and consciousness.

The cosmos gives the things and beings it encompasses part of their
meaning, gives them a place in the whole of what there is. Each thing is related to everything else, which is also one of the most common basic beliefs
among spiritual people. One imagines this cosmic "web" so dense that every
"pull" on any "thread" also sets in motion each other. But here we have to be
careful about what kind of beings we humans are, in what kind of environment on Earth. The universe is not organized and "inter-linked" in the same
way and intensity everywhere. In fact, outer space is pretty empty compared
to a celestial body as dense as Earth and as turbulent, geologically and me-
teorologically. Still Earth's mineral surface, the water, and the air are pretty
empty too, in terms of information and self-organization, as compared to
the matter condensed in a plant or an animal or a person.

Furthermore, every human being integrates a complex of ideas,
thoughts, attitudes, and actions into their living body, with its anatomy,
biomolecules, and metabolism, and its neuronal, sensory, genetic, and im-
munological information-processing, with its expressions of life, behavior,
self-perception, and inner life. As a condensation of matter, life, and spirit,
the human being is quite clearly delimited from his or her environment;
he or she moves fairly freely in it, and can behave relatively autonomously
and be "picky," which is also necessary for a living being in order to nourish
itself in order to survive and, collectively as a species, in order to reproduce.
Going beyond merely animal metabolism and behavior in this developing
flow-balance typical for living beings, humans also seek out stabilizing material, living and cultural and mental influences from their environment,
and they are astonishingly robust and adaptable to destabilizing influences.

6. Ziemke, *Alle Schöpfung*, 125 (my translation).

Thus humans are certainly not connected with the cosmos and all its parts in the sense that they are pulled along like puppets on an infinite number of strings. This picture of a total (indeed totalitarian) cosmic connection fails to recognize that a person is at the same time a "chunk of physics and chemistry," an organism, and a person, and as such is quite independent and active. The independence of a photon, if it has any, is something very different from the individuality of a person.

We are free to look for a place on Earth within our physical, geographical, ecological, social, cultural, psychological, economic and, in a narrower sense, spiritual possibilities and limits. Living beings, shaped by nature, are trying not only to preserve our own individual personhood but also to carry on the human form of life in the biosphere. The community of species on Earth is constantly evolving, and space for new generations is needed; therefore we just don't seem to be built to last. Seventy, eighty, ninety years of life are astonishing anyway for a being focusing in itself such a dense and rapid flow of matter, energy, and information.

As living beings and as a form of life, we strive to survive. Few people like the thought that they simply disappear; almost everyone would wish that something of them would be preserved, if only human civilization or the beautiful living nature on Earth (depending on what they are identifying with). But for a species to adapt to changes in the environment and the species community, the mortality of individuals is important; it does not take into account their wish to thrive and last, just as the sun or meteorites or the geology of the Earth can in no way be expected to conform to what is a catastrophe for this or that individual being or form of life. A many-one view of persons in the world tries to transcend the religious anthropocentrisms of old, where such natural occurrences are rewards or punishments for human behavior. Earth is simply the natural "stage" on which we are placed:

> Our responsibility is quite different when we affirm the panoramas and processes of evolution. At the same moment we also affirm that creation is not finished, that it is rather still in progress and that we are shaped by it as well as being contributors to it.[7]

Our natural and more specifically planetary limits are simply there, limitations for humankind as a species, as well as for you and me as individuals. Thus, how much of a spiritual being can we become? I am sure that we as loving, aesthetic, ideological and "worldviewing" beings can "incarnate" or "embody" something of the great cosmic whole, and this can be formative for our small human bodies, our tiny personalities, our little worlds. But

---

7. Amery, *Global Exit*, 133 (my translation).

how far can such a change go? Certainly the biology and physics of the human body set a narrower frame for "becoming spirit" and even more so for "supernatural powers" or some cosmic-salvation Big History (aka eschatology), which quite a few spiritual people hope for. The problem seems to be especially that our spiritual relationship to the cosmos affects less the body as an organism, and instead seems to impact much more our feeling, imagining, thinking, and behaving. Spirituality seems to remain about signs and consciousness in the broadest sense rather than about reorganizing spiritual living beings or life on Earth or even the history of Earth and the universe.

Personally, in my life, I have had very formative spiritual experiences, feeling like my mind was opening to the whole cosmos: in meditative immersion, in visions of the context and coherence of it all, in devotion to the natural course of things, in friendship, in experiencing nature and art. Still I see great obstacles, in myself just as in most people, to actually being spiritual beyond certain limits, given our natural heritage and grown personalities, as well as the many ways in which our biographies and everyday lives, our civilization and history contribute to quite firmly shaping us. I will come back once more to these delicate issues in the conclusion.

Anyway, the "material" obstacles which hinder spirit from being more formative in our lives don't imply at all that the hard facts about Earth and nature *alone* can be the foundation for a worldview for our time—and even less so the special observations and mathematical structures of physical research. Physicalism, as materialistic science is sometimes called, overrates in a grotesque way the extent to which the world is divisible and countable, measurable and modelable, as a set of isolated fundamental objects or purely geometric forms, as an ultimately dead universe. Conversely, there is, by modern standards, no serious worldview which does not account for all of the scientific research and knowledge we have managed to build up. Many-one natural philosophy has to encompass all aspects of culture and person and society, but also the whole breadth and depth of natural science, balancing out the former and the latter.

It's a bit analogous to the sustainable and solidary rebuild of modern civilization. We will have to push back against wasting and devastating and poisoning and democracy-undermining large-scale technology, but we will need all the helpful "big tech" and "small-tech" we can get, which in turn will be a mix of "high tech" and "low tech" at once. This will rely heavily on local competence and initiative and traditional methods and handicrafts, but must also be co-developed, coordinated, and protected by big-scale unities like nations and NGOs and private corporations and international agencies on a worldwide, humankind level.

A Block Universe versus an Evolving Cosmos

Similarly, many-one thinking has to deal with the physical "large-scale technologies," which are the great theories of quantum mechanics and relativity theory. What is materialistic about them, and where do they rather depict characteristics of the cosmos as a whole? We have to try and express more precisely where materialism becomes unnatural, which particularly is by declaring time to be unreal and mere appearance. There are points where this can be identified quite well. With this in mind, let me recap in short the problem of the "smooth" (continuous, differentiable) functions of time in modern mathematical physics that, if they described real time, would leave no room for the creation and evolution of anything new, no room for (partial) autonomy and creativity of living beings and people on Earth.

What is the problem with this seamless time, with particles and the objects composed by them traveling through space "as if on rails"? Well, if this were the way things are, then it wouldn't make any difference whether you say that an object moves through the world "forward" in time, or "backward." Indeed, just as every film can be played backwards, every continuous function (with a time coordinate t and a space coordinate s) has a strictly equivalent inverse function (with a time $-t$ and space $-s$). The picture of a "space-time continuum" or "block universe," where time lapses are "time-like distances," can quite accurately be thought of as a flip book. Each sheet is just an arrangement of pixels, and even if it looks like something is happening when you flip through the flip book, there really are only spatial relationships on the individual sheets and between the stapled sheets. Consciousness and life would definitely have no place in such a flip-book cosmos. Irreversible processes like the use of energy (solar energy and geothermal heat), or the use of information to organize molecules into an organism that is kept in a dynamic balance by the flow of matter and energy (metabolism), these cannot be laws of nature in deterministic physics. According to materialism, it's just as physically possible that the living person, human history, the biosphere, the evolution of species, the earth, and the solar system "re-envelop," instead of developing . . . that the sun sucks in radiation from space, that rivers flow out from the sea, that cars "un-rust," that complex animals "devolve" back to protozoa, and that old people rejuvenate into babies; that history beginning with the modern age becomes stone age and then ape age; or, indeed, that physics professors become kindergarten kids.

Unfortunately, I do not have the space in this essay to offer more than just a sketch of the role that matter (mass) and radiation (energy) may play if we take physical time to be a measure of rhythmical and cyclical events in an evolving cosmic whole—in contrast to the block universe or space-time picture, which is still the mindset of most researchers, textbook writers, popular science books, and fancy documentaries. In particular, there is no place here to do more than touch on the usual timeless reading of quantum theory. But saying nothing is impossible too, so a few paragraphs will have to suffice. However, I advise all readers who have not ever read anything about quantum theory to skip these.

Sparse Notes on What a Holistic and Evolutionary Quantum Theory Could Look Like

What is clear about quantum theory, to begin with, is it's not a theory of the smallest *particles*, but about what is called "action quanta," that is, about the smallest *effects* happening; that is, it's inherently a theory of time (*action*, in physics, means *energy x time*.) For example, anyone who has read Richard Feynman's very short and clear book *QED* knows that radiation quanta (like photons) are nothing like solid spheres on fixed paths through empty space, as materialistic naiveté imagines. Indeed light takes all the ways open to it, at once. Even a single quantum of light (a photon) emitted in one place always moves simultaneously through all openings and media (for example through slits or lenses) that it can penetrate and traverse; and at which point it "hits" depends on all of these routes, taken together! In addition, quantum effects do not always refer to phenomena that can in any way be imagined as particles; for instance they can also be sound quanta (phonons), bits of vibrations (!) that move through a larger object.

The determinism of quantum theory must therefore in no way be associated with an idea of solid matter "beads" or, worse, of "points," nor as traveling on fixed paths, since what is predetermined (and even this may be wrong) in quantum theory is only the *probability of measuring* a given quantum effect at a certain place on a measuring device. Where a quantum entity (or event) will actually be found will have to be checked each time; there just is no quantum theory about what causes the "collapse" of the quantum probability wave across the measuring device into individual observations, and what exactly will come out of them. Classical mathematical quantum theory does not say what dynamically happens at a measurement or more generally at an interaction of a quantum with large objects. Instead it postulates a *spontaneous and instantaneous* "collapse," which is neither a physical observation nor a description nor an explanation. Indeed, I doubt that something that "happens" for no reason and in no time, is a physical phenomenon at all. This gap alone indicates that something essential is missing from the theory, or is wrong in the whole approach.

It is a worrying fact that a serious attempt to not only bridge, but close this gap, to replace this probability-wave-collapse patchwork with a one-piece theory like Ilya Prigogine's from the 1990s, has basically simply been ignored, at most belittled by mainstream physicists. Prigogine had the idea that there are actually no exact locations and movements for the smallest effects called "quanta," a priori and microscopically; instead there are only probabilities of location and interaction at the smallest scale, which due to the enormous amount of resonances between the smallest interactions and their propensities average out to macroscopically form quite clear boundaries and shapes and organizational patterns, as much as we experience them; most of the "outliers" are dampened out, and only a few are amplified on a large scale. As Prigogine expressed it:

> Irreversibility and probabilities become objective properties. They are an expression of the fact that the physical world we observe cannot be reduced to individual trajectories [particle paths] or individual wave functions. If we . . . move on to an ensemble description [a description of the properties of large objects or sets of molecules], then there is no loss of information; rather, it allows us to incorporate many new properties.[8]

The Natural Philosopher Albert Einstein's Timeless "Space-Time"—and His Own Great Forgotten Idea Telling against It

In my view, the very materialistic approach of trying to "assemble" the world from particles instead of conceiving of particles as the smallest interactions between the actual foundations of things—namely the universe as a whole and the normal objects of our life on Earth—is misbegotten. I would now like to say a little more, again without going into too much detail, about Albert Einstein's attempt to geometrize the world, to spatialize time. And again I recommend to those who are completely alien to physics and especially the discussion about "space-time" to jump on to the paragraph beginning with the sentence "The story I related above about Einstein's block universe and Einstein's variable speed of light . . .," on page 154.

What is certainly true is that Einstein believed time to be a kind of curvature, that is, a geometrical property of a world which he believed was inherently timeless, a block universe made up of points that he called "space-time events" . . . a philosophically misleading move indeed, for whatever these space-time "events" are supposed to be, they are anything but

8. Prigogine, *Paradox*, 315 (my translation).

events, since *by definition* nothing ever *happens* in a block universe. Still, if the greatest physicist of all time sees it that way, who am I to contradict him?! As much a genius as he was, does this prove he was the creator of the natural philosophy ultimate in its assumptions? Now, they say that Einstein is like an oak tree on which the most clueless boars like to scratch their bottoms. Thus it might be advisable that, in order to be on the safe side, I get myself support from . . . Albert Einstein himself.

Indeed, after his special theory of relativity in 1905, Einstein worked obsessively to integrate mass and acceleration into this special theory in order to generalize it. In 1912, a few years before his general theory of relativity, Einstein had the idea of a *variable speed of light* that dispenses with space-time; that is, he tried to cope without his idea that gravity and mass and therefore ultimately material things are only curvatures in space-time, and that time is only one dimension contributing to the "paths" and "hills" making up the space-time "landscape." With the variable speed of light, on the other hand, time simply is not a geometrical variable; instead rays of light, in this picture, oscillate and spread more slowly in and around large and dense accumulations of matter, such as the sun. In this approach, rays and objects move and evolve for real, just more slowly wherever there is a lot of dense matter, than in the relatively empty space around it. Quite like in optics where light passes less quickly through glass or water than through air.

Einstein gave up on this promising and intuitively elegant approach for a reason which has nothing to do with the theoretical—indeed, he simply "miscalculated" in his formula, forgetting a factor that has to be taken into account for the variability of light waves in gravitational fields, an omission which, by the way, other physicists would correct only decades later. Einstein, in his day, got the formula wrong, and therefore got a wrong result for a well-known special observation that he wanted to explain by the theory he was trying to construct, and that classical physics could not explain: which is the delayed orbit of Mercury around the sun.

It is not overstating the facts to call Einstein's miscalculation *tragic*, for otherwise the timeless (and by extension mechanistic and spiritless) picture that materialism paints of the world would certainly not have become so overwhelmingly paradigmatic in twentieth-century modernity. Yet it's not just about miscalculating; timelessness also was something Einstein *wanted* to believe in, for two reasons. Firstly, he loved the timeless elegance of geometry; second, he hated the imperfection and messiness and transience of temporal things, not least socially and politically. Now while these are certainly reasons, in no way are they physical reasons proper. Still this kind of reasoning seems to have led Einstein, just a few years later, to the purely geometric space-time-mass-energy picture, the timeless block universe of general relativity.

What we have to put on record for our challenge of materialism is the fact that mathematically both of Einstein's approaches explain the deflection of light by gravity equally well, indeed are equivalent. As the physicist Alexander Unzicker points out in his 2015 book *Einsteins verlorener Schlüssel— Warum wir die beste Idee des 20. Jahrhunderts übersehen haben* (Einstein's Lost Key—Why We Overlooked the Best Idea of the Twentieth Century):

> However, the majority of physicists do not know this approach or at least do not believe in its completeness—it just looks too simple. [. . .] The Belgian physicist Jan Broekaert too, in an excellent article showing the general equivalence of the variable speed of light [i.e., the equivalence with the standard geometrical approach], has cited the best-known textbooks on general relativity, all of which talk about the variability of c [the physical abbreviation for the speed of light]. Mostly there is only missing the simple statement: Gravitation is nothing more than variable speed of light.[9]

Challenging the "spatialization" of the cosmos is essential for many-one thinking, which sees the world as an evolving wholeness, with plenty emerging novelty, and individuals whose self-organizing and self-creating autonomy is partly random. It is therefore interesting that Einstein's original, variable-speed-of-light approach to gravity, which doesn't reduce time to geometry or to a quality of outer space, also permits us to move from a materialistic perspective to a many-one perspective in another important respect. And that is the idea that *mass*, one of the most tangible physical properties besides *force*, could be an effect that the whole universe exerts on its parts. This is not, as one might suspect, a pseudoscientific, in fact esoteric idea . . . again, Einstein himself knew that his relativity could not explain the so-called inertial mass, that is, the fact that matter offers resistance to being set in motion.

Let me explain; this is easy to understand once you think about it. Things not only resist being lifted up (which is called "heavy mass," also known as gravity); even astronauts in weightlessness can feel when their spaceship accelerates, rotates, or decelerates. They are feeling the inertia of their bodies "in their guts." Now, Einstein wanted to get away from Newton's idea of explaining speed and acceleration relative to an absolute space

---

9. Unzicker, *Einsteins*, 158–59 (my translation). For more physical detail, see his papers: Unzicker, "Look at the Abandoned Contributions"; and Unzicker, "Mach's Principle."

"resting in itself," so to speak. And it intrigued him that inertial and heavy mass are equivalent, proportional (that is, for instance, that double weight means double inertia). This suggested they had the same origin. In order to replace Newton's idea of an absolute space by a *relative* one, Einstein would also have liked to implement physicist Ernst Mach's *relationalist* idea according to which things are inert because they are, so to speak, "held in place," by distant stars and galaxies, that is, by the rest of the universe.

However, Einstein didn't manage to work this idea into his general relativity. It was not until the 1950s that the idea of a variable speed of light was rediscovered by Dennis Sciama and Robert Dicke (independently of one another) and conceived in such a way that it connects varying speed of light and gravity. Working in the mid- to late 1950s, Dicke had a decisive advantage over Einstein in 1916—namely the fact that since the 1930s, data on the approximate size and density of the universe had become available, and reliable enough to allow one to estimate that the "retaining" influence of the universe should be of the same order of magnitude as the inertia that makes ourselves and the objects we know resist acceleration.

Again, I cannot go into more detail here, referring you to Unzicker's above-mentioned book and papers. However, what I just described may suffice to make my core natural-philosophy point, which is twofold. On the one hand, the example of the variable-speed-of-light idea shows that, contrary to what so many people think, modern physics *does not* inevitably lead to the picture of a block universe made up of points called "space-time events," a picture through which Albert Einstein actually helped shape and boost the materialistic worldview. Even with a physical quality *as paradigmatically mindless as mass is*, the evolution and impact of the whole cosmos come into play, a cosmos in interplay with its parts.

The story I related above about Einstein's block universe and Einstein's variable speed of light shows, in my opinion, that from a strictly physical perspective, nothing has been pre-established in favor of materialism. What does seem to speak for materialism—or rather: *who took sides against time back in the 1920s*—is a whole modern culture of scientists, with the sheer number and power of their tenures in universities and other research centers, with their academic staffs and students, with their specialist publications, and with their public influence, large-scale experiments, and supercomputers. Not only almost the entire community of physicists, but also probably a large majority of the other natural scientists in their wake, has opted against evolution proper and emergence and agency and spirit, often perhaps without much conviction or reflection, simply out of a feeling of lack of scientifically serious alternatives. Each of the approaches which could have helped underpin a physics of an evolving cosmos, including those by big and very big physicists like Dicke, Sciama, Dirac, Schrödinger, Prigogine, and originally Einstein himself—each of these nonstandard approaches was buried in the materialist mainstream tide, for decades. What could a handful of scattered visionaries, most of whom did not know about each other's efforts, achieve against thousands upon thousands of scientists who took a timeless, material, ultimately purely mathematical world for granted? If they were noticed at all (and all notice could not be avoided after Prigogine won the Nobel Prize in 1977), then they were dismissed with irritation and smugness.

It is telling, for example, that while I have been reading for decades the popular-science literature for an educated, nonspecialist audience, it was only through Unzicker, a physics teacher, and unsurprisingly a lateral entrant and lateral thinker, that I became aware of the frightening lack of plurality and self-critical thinking inside the physics community. Apparently not a single academic physicist was dissatisfied enough with timelessness and curious enough about alternatives throughout the long preceding decades, to gather the scattered threads that Unzicker, within few years, was able to find and (within the limits of his resources) to link, beginning with Einstein's not exactly secret idea from 1912 of a variable speed of light. Whatever you may think about the truth of the variable-speed-of-light approach, how is it possible that it was kept under wraps for so long? After all, science is about discussing serious alternative options, and this clearly is one. Well, basic assumptions learned at an early stage about the self-evident and the unthinkable, groupthink and icons, fear of career failure and ridicule: all of this has to be considered to explain this kind of hushing-up orthodoxy which one can hardly believe exists in modern natural science . . . but which apparently does.

And it is through the same kind of group and power dynamics, of what has to be and what must not be, that far-fetched mathematical structures that aren't in any stricter sense observable on natural objects, such as the big bang or black holes (thought of as singularities; that is, as infinities; that is, as physically meaningless entities), cosmic inflation, superstrings, dark mass, dark energy, or Higgs fields, could become parts of a standard physical model. In fact, these kinds of constructs make the most sense as attempts to preserve and protect absolutely a materialistic framework by means of eluding plain natural observation and explanation. One hardly dares to hope for it, but should daring nonconformist scientists ever be able to establish a physics against the gigantic materialist-minded science machine, which is so dedicated to atomistic, timeless, antispiritual building-block thinking, then a lot will have to be revisited which materialists had shelved in the heyday of materialistic science after World War II.

Overcoming the Building-Block and Module View of Nature

After these brief notes on what a natural philosophy of the many-one cosmos has to say about the timelessness of the great theories of quantum mechanics and general relativity, I would now like to try to integrate what we call the physical into the coexistence and interplay of things in our life-world, on Earth, and in the cosmos as a whole. In doing so, living beings and people in a planetary environment are particularly important, as is the living information encoded in the genome and the nervous system. This information cannot be "materialized" as isolated forms and local effects. To a large extent, it refers to natural coherences and resonances, to forms and expressions of life, to acts of culture and consciousness that are not material in any narrow sense. According to the cosmic-holistic understanding that I am trying to sketch here, any type of information, including physical and biological and mental and technical, ultimately relates to the cosmos as a whole; even elementary particles, living bodies, and the human mind do not exist by themselves, but only inside this wholeness. Individuals, effects, and domains in the cosmos are not nearly as independent and separated from each other as the modular thinking of materialism tries to make us believe.

It is important to re-emphasize here that when I am talking about information, no new substance is being added to the radiation of physics or the molecules of chemistry. Information is not another kind of stuff, or a replacement of the "purely physical" stuff; it complements matter. This can work out in a natural philosophy where matter and its dynamics are not determining everything in the world, exclusively. All human experience on Earth teaches us that information can flow through matter, can organize matter, can be stored in matter, can express itself in matter. This shows itself to be true not only in life and mind. For example, computers are only possible because their building materials and components are put together and run in such a way that the input of information causes exactly the output intended in the program, regardless of what exactly a certain electron or metal atom in a wire or circuit does through which information passes. The flowing information is in no way a property or product of the matter it flows through. Matter, as defined by physics, is something local, proximity-effecting, and determined. Information, on the other hand, can relate equally to the material fine structure of the world; to living beings in their terrestrial environment; to people in societies; to cultural, intellectual or worldview creations; or to the whole cosmos—indeed, to everything that taken together forms what I paraphrase by "the Many-One."

In order to make this more intuitive, let me give you a metaphor: What a house is cannot be explained by its building blocks, building materials, construction methods, technical installations, and furniture *alone*. A house is also about its (actual and possible) residents and their housing needs and family life and maintenance work. In the materialistic universe, the building blocks and the building site are simply there, even before the house is built. In the many-one cosmos there is nothing outside and before the house: it is constantly being expanded, it has its building ground inside itself, and in itself it also makes/lets emerge and evolve the whole variety of building materials, rooms and residents.

These two accounts of what a house and what the world is are so unlike because the materialistic philosophy of nature is so different from the cosmic-holistic one. Is it really true, for example, that in all dimensions, domains, and modes of being (such as life or personhood), nothing happens except for what could also be seen at the tiniest and simplest level of particles and radiation, fields and quanta, if only we could magnify them enough and observe them in all their bottom-level detail? From a cosmic-holistic point of view, this is odd. In this picture, the physical "stuff" such as photons, electrons, or protons has to be seen as relations between the cosmos and ordinary objects and individuals as we know them from our living environment.

For materialism there is a microlevel existing out of itself, indeed the only one that really exists, apart from which nothing actually has substance and effect. For many-one natural philosophy, on the other hand, there is no independent microlevel and micro-basis and micro-causation of the world: instead the one cosmos in itself is an evolving space that is the stuff and beat and medium of exchange for all its many individual parts and kinds of parts—and not just at the micro and cosmological levels, but at all scales, in all modes and forms of being, in all their variety and interplay. In this world-space there arise gas nebulae, stars, and galaxies; the geology and biosphere on planets such as Earth; ecosystems and sentient beings; cultures and the life and mind of persons, rising one after the other, and then joining in with one another. This kind of universe is the opposite of an empty, timeless, dead, spiritless space, ultimately just a mathematical structure made of geometries, vector spaces, symmetries, and the like; instead it is an evolving whole in which space, microphysics, and information, even where they are timeless, are not outside of time, and in which life and people and mind too are just as basic and ultimate as the finest structures of the cosmos that we call matter or quanta.

Conclusion: Natural Limits to Whatever Wondrous Things There May Be between Heaven and Earth

I would now like to conclude the admittedly very wide arc that I have tried to draw with a final reflection on the place of the supernatural in a natural cosmos. The relations between the One and the Many, between the cosmos and its parts, are alive in many ways; in terms of living consciousness and culture, they have a lot to do with dynamic signs and non-locatable information and "inner" experiencing, yet they must also be spatial and material, be expressed in tangible objects, visible forms, countable quantities, and measurable qualities. Only in this way can many-one natural philosophy be connected to modern natural science, and only in this way can it challenge materialism.

Much of what materialists would call unreal or supernatural is natural information about the whole cosmos and its different kinds of objects and beings and domains. Not every sign, not all information about signs, however, is natural information. A good deal of the information brought forth and fed and hosted by minds in dreams, myths, fantasies, and fictions refers to or represents what is real or possible in the cosmos in an only loose, fragmentary, or distorted way; it's illusion, an error, a self-conceit, sometimes also outright delusion. Nevertheless, I believe that "there are things between heaven and Earth" that elude our everyday ideas of normal cause and effect and information transfer and personal agency.

Even these kinds of (more or less) wondrous things can only happen within the framework of how the cosmos, Earth, and its living beings function, within the "rules" of evolution, biological organization, and metabolism, of self-preserving and passing. Natural types of things do not arise out of nowhere and (mostly) do not melt into thin air; they develop over long periods of time and leave behind remnants. Individual things arise from parents and preliminary stages and suitable substances; they use natural resources: energy (especially direct or stored solar energy) as well as the type of information they are able to experience, to embody, and to put into practice. Individuals have specific and personal powers, functions and abilities that leave them leeway, but also set them limits. The universe and its natural coherence, the earth and its ecology, our families and social and economic life, our genes and bodies and personalities: all of this "puts us in context," and I do not believe we or other beings or entities or presences can get clear of this cosmic framework. Even in our relative distinctness and autonomy we remain parts of the cosmos, made of and maintaining ourselves by what our sun and the atmosphere and the surface and crust of our planet offer; having to deal with these resources and our biophysical constitution and our fellow beings; coming from somewhere in our living environment and ending at some point and place. In my opinion, all of this "natural human condition" must also apply to phenomena beyond what we experience in ordinary life.

Even the highest human achievements, the deepest abysses, the most wonderful revelations all range in the great coherence and framework of living within humankind on this planet in the one cosmos. This belief is not materialism, but it is a form of naturalism, not a supernaturalism. Tending to our natural lives and livelihoods, the families we come from, our cultural communities and our life together in states, as well as the global community of peoples: this is our origin, business, and task as humans. Let's not lose this ground under our feet, not spiritually, not socially, and not ecologically. With this in mind, I would like to close with a word of hope and warning from one of the thinkers I love most, the late philosopher and physicist Carl Friedrich von Weizsäcker:

> Do we have concrete contents of hope? It is impossible to predict what is to come. But we see open ways. The way of science is open. What will holistic thinking teach us about human nature? [...] The way of ethics is open, for it is the way to learn to perceive others. The change in political awareness is underway. It is not impossible that we will have to learn from the greatest self-inflicted disasters. [...] The path to meditative experience is open. It is not the escape into an inner other-world; it leads back to the present, to reason.[10]

Bibliography

Amery, Carl. *Das Ende der Vorsehung.* Reinbek: Rowohlt, 1972.

———. *Global Exit.* Munich: Random House, 2004.

Bateson, Gregory, and Mary Catherine Bateson. *Angels Fear: Towards an Epistemology of the Sacred.* Advances in Systems Theory, Complexity, and the Human Sciences. Cresskill, NJ: Hampton, 2005.

Blau, Ulrich. *Grundparadoxien, grenzenlose Arithmetik, Mystik.* Philosophische Impulse 11. Heidelberg: Synchron, 2016.

Davies, Paul, and Niels Henrik Gregersen, eds. *Information and the Nature of Reality: From Physics to Metaphysics.* Canto Classics. Cambridge: Cambridge University Press, 2014.

Deacon, Terrence W. *The Symbolic Species: The Co-Evolution of Language and the Brain.* New York: Norton, 1998.

Diamond, Jared M. *Upheaval: How Nations Cope with Crisis and Change.* London: Lane, 2019.

Feynman, Richard P. *QED: The Strange Theory of Light and Matter.* New York: Penguin, 2007.

10. Weizsäcker, *Mensch*, 242 (my translation).

Griebel, Oliver. *Der ganzheitliche Gott*, Hamburg: BoD, 2014.

———. "Ken Wilber vs John Heron." 2016. http://www.integralworld.net/griebel2. html/.

———. "Nonduality—Non/duality—Many-One Duality." In "Integral Postmetaphysical Spirituality," ed. Tom Murray et al., special issue, *Integral Review* 15.1 (2019). https://integral-review.org/tag/griebel/.

Hawken, Paul, ed. *Drawdown: The Most Comprehensive Plan Ever Proposed to Reverse Global Warming*. New York: Penguin, 2018.

Heron, John. *Feeling and Personhood: Psychology in Another Key*. London: Sage, 1992.

Krause, Johannes, and Thomas Trappe. *A Short History of Humanity: How Migration Made Us Who We Are*. London: Allen, 2021.

Kutschera, Franz von. *Philosophie des Geistes*. Paderborn: mentis, 2009.

Morin, Edgar. *Connaissance, Ignorance, Mystère*. Paris: Fayard, 2017.

———. *Homeland Earth: A Manifesto for the New Millennium*. Advances in Systems Theory, Complexity, and the Human Sciences. Cresskill, NJ: Hampton, 1998.

Nagel, Thomas. *Mind and Cosmos: Why the Materialist Neo-Darwinian Conception of Nature Is Almost Certainly False*. New York: Oxford University Press, 2012.

Oyama, Susan. *The Ontogeny of Information: Developmental Systems and Evolution*. 2nd ed., revised and expanded. Durham: Duke University Press, 2000.

Peacocke, Arthur, and Philip Clayton, eds. *In Whom We Live and Move and Have Our Being: Panentheistic Reflections on God's Presence in a Scientific World*. Grand Rapids: Eerdmans, 2004.

Prigogine, Ilya. *The End of Certainty: Time, Chaos, and the New Laws of Nature*. In collaboration with Isabelle Stengers. New York: Free Press, 1997.

———. *Das Paradox der Zeit*. Munich: Piper, 1993.

Raworth, Kate. *Doughnut Economics: Seven Ways to Think Like a 21st-Century Economist*. London: Random House, 2018.

Reich, David: *Who We Are and How We Got Here: Ancient DNA and the New Science of the Human Past*. Oxford: Oxford University Press, 2018.

Skinner, B. F. *Beyond Freedom & Dignity*. Indianapolis: Hackett, 2002.

Sloterdijk, Peter. *Nach Gott*. Frankfurt: Suhrkamp, 2017.

Tarnas, Richard. *Passion of the Western Mind: Understanding the Ideas That Have Shaped Our World View*. 1st Ballantine Books ed. New York: Ballantine, 1993.

Thompson, Evan. *Waking, Dreaming, Being: Self and Consciousness in Neuroscience, Meditation, and Philosophy*. New York: Columbia University Press, 2014.

———. *Why I Am Not a Buddhist*. New Haven: Yale University Press, 2020.

Unzicker, Alexander. *Einsteins verlorener Schlüssel: Warum wir die beste Idee des 20. Jahrhunderts übersehen haben*. North Charleston, SC: CreateSpace, 2015.

———. "A Look at the Abandoned Contributions to Cosmology of Dirac, Sciama and Dicke." *Arxiv Physics* (blog) at Cornell University (submitted on 27 Aug 2007 [v1], last revised 16 Dec 2008). https://arxiv.org/abs/0708.3518/.

———. "Mach's Principle and a Variable Speed of Light." *Arxiv Physics* (blog) at Cornell University (submitted on 8 Nov 2005 [v1], last revised 6 Oct 2007). https://arxiv. org/abs/gr-qc/0511038/.

Weizsäcker, Carl Friedrich von. *Der Mensch in seiner Geschichte*. Munich: Hanser, 1991.

West-Eberhard, Mary Jane. *Developmental Plasticity and Evolution*. Oxford: Oxford University Press, 2003.

Ziemke, Axel. *Alle Schöpfung ist Werk der Natur*. Frankfurt: Info3, 2015.

7

News from Antiquity

*Integral Reflections on Two Central
Doctrines of the Ancient Church*[1]

TILMANN HABERER

Approach 1

S he was in her early or midthirties. Six years ago, she had met the love
of her life and had married him two years later. She was expecting their
second baby. Now, two days ago, her husband had received news that shat-
tered all plans, all hopes for a long and happy life, the entire future of the
young family: he had been diagnosed with a pancreatic tumor, in an advanced stage, inoperable. According to the doctors, he would only have a
few months to live.

With this devastating news, the woman came to the crisis and life
counseling center where I am working. One can hardly imagine the despair
that had befallen her. In an instant, her entire life was turned upside down,
her life horizon collapsed to this one phrase: pancreatic cancer. And then
she asked the question: "What is the point of all of this? What meaning does
this life have at all?"

How can I counsel this woman? How can I stand by her in her shock
and sorrow? Can I offer her a consolation sustainable beyond the day because it feeds on a spiritual source? It would be of little use in this situation
if I gave her any ready-made answers, no matter if I wanted to remind her
of the Christian conviction that Christ stood by her side, shared her suffering and was finally resurrected, which is why death has lost its horror; or
whether I pointed to the Buddhist view that our ego, our personality, indeed

---

1. Translated into English by the author.

the whole concrete life is only a ripple on the surface of the abyssal ocean of being, insignificant, in the next moment absorbed into the great, one, true, and pure being. Both answers would not take this woman seriously in her pain and shock. In the first case, her question about the meaning of life would be presented as already answered long ago, which would not be helpful because she needs a concrete answer for her concrete life, not a dogmatic platitude about something "valid in eternity." In the second case, the question of meaning would be dismissed as meaningless in itself. What she has experienced would, after all, be called not real. An only seemingly real Ego would experience only seemingly real despair. Her husband's illness was illusory, as were her husband, herself, and her children. Both answers are dogmatic in the bad sense (i.e., they ignore the concrete reality of life and offer no comfort).

If in such a situation there is any consolation at all, it can only consist in offering a space for this woman's pain, in showing compassionate presence, in listening to her silently at first and in appreciating her and her disastrous situation. Only gradually can further thoughts be brought into play, when shock, fear, anger, and pain have been acknowledged and the question of meaning arises again. This could then, indeed, be the place for a spiritually based interpretation, which I can carefully offer her, and here my own basic spiritual attitude is called for.

Approach 2

Spirituality is called for not only in the context of individual suffering, but also in the global, political realm. The crises and problems facing humanity in the first quarter of the twenty-first century—global warming, global migration and refugee movements, terrorism, species extinction, digitization with its unforeseeable consequences—cannot be addressed with blow-by-blow answers, with a reductionist and atomizing approach. Here what is needed is a holistic view that looks for deep connections; we need an inquiry into values, goals, and the meaning of our actions; we need the qualities of compassion, humility, and gratitude. In short, we need an attitude that can be described as spiritual.

This does not mean that only those who explicitly follow a spiritual or religious path can commit themselves to the preservation of our planet and life on it. Of course, one can do that on the grounds of a conscious, responsible secularism or humanism. But nowadays there are many people who regard themselves as spiritual or religious. What would the basic spiritual attitude have to look like, or, in other words, how would the basic spiritual attitude develop that could motivate and support these people to work for the life of all creatures?

In the search for both individual meaning and collective effort to preserve the planet as a livable home for all creatures, the religions would actually be good allies. For it is they who ask about the great whole, about the connection that sustains everything and from which everything emerges—actually, the ecological question par excellence. For a variety of reasons, some of them very good, religions are not given much credit in this social discourse. The Christian churches, particularly in Europe, have lost a great deal of credibility. In the Enlightenment era, they forfeited territory to scientists and intellectuals through their rigid adherence to premodern thought patterns; in the nineteenth century, they forfeited the trust of the working class through their close ties to state authorities and the bourgeoisie; and in the postmodern era, they have forfeited any claimed inclusiveness in terms of meaningfulness and the art of living. Indeed, much of what is said and done (or not done) in the churches seems to be part of the problem, not the solution. This is a great pity because it was all once meant to be different. The spiritual movement of the first Christian centuries, the solutions worked out and fought for in decades of philosophical-theological disputes, hold an amazing potential. I think it is worthwhile to raise this potential.

The Situation

Among the great errors of modernity is the idea that religion will soon die out. This statement will horrify some people because they associate religion with dogmatism, narrow-mindedness, rigorism, intolerance, and outdated ideas about man and the world, and they expect the extinction of religion to purify and liberate the human spirit. "Imagine a world without religion," Richard Dawkins wrote in his bestseller *The God Delusion*. He presents an image to the reader: the Manhattan skyline—including the Twin Towers of the World Trade Center. The message is clear: without the fanatical religiosity of the assassins, the towers would still be standing today, and the three thousand people killed in the attack on September 11, 2001, would still be alive.[2] With this highly emotionally charged symbolism, Dawkins illustrates his conviction that religion brings nothing but disaster to people and the world. And there are countless examples of how religion has oppressed and tortured people and generally made people feel miserable—and continues to do so.

2. Dawkins, *God Delusion*, 24–25.

Of course, one could also cite counterexamples without number. But this would all too easily lead into a fruitless exchange of blows between opponents and supporters of religion that misses the point. Whether we reckon religion to be good or not, it seems increasingly clear that humanity is indeed "incurably religious," as Nikolai Berdyaev put it. Or that religion is so much a part of being human that Homo sapiens is also *Homo religiosus*, as Reza Aslan points out in his recent book *God: A Human History*. According to Aslan, people come into the world with an intuitive knowledge "that they are embodied souls." In addition, they have an innate urge to suspect an agent behind any occurrence and to attribute human or at least human-like characteristics to this agent. Thus, the belief in a supernatural force—in spirits, demons, and eventually gods—comes into the world simultaneously with intelligence and the awakening consciousness of humans.[3]

It goes without saying that with this hypothesis no statement is made about the truth of certain religious teachings. It does not declare whether the religious intuition corresponds to a divine reality or whether it is a collective illusion concerning the whole (or large parts) of humankind. The thesis merely states that a basic religious orientation seems to be part of being human.

To a certain extent, this is also true for modern humans. Religiosity does not necessarily mean belief in a god or in several gods. To be religious means to relate to something greater than one's own humanity. This can be an idea, an ideology, a nation, anything that transcends humans and gives meaning and orientation to their life. Although, according to a recent survey, 38 percent of Germans (and as many as 73 percent of East Germans) do not believe in "a God,"[4] many of those who answered no nonetheless are most likely religious in a broader sense. Perhaps they believe in angels or in fate, perhaps they wear an amulet or knock on wood three times after having expressed a wish or a fear. Elementary religiosity in this broad sense can also be found everywhere in our modern society.

If the thesis is true that religion (or more precisely, religiosity) will not die out because it is inscribed, so to speak, in the source code of human consciousness, then it is important to promote a religiosity that is as "healthy" as possible: a religiosity that connects rather than divides, that is conducive to the life of the individual and to living together in the community, a religion that makes people strong and free and happy. We must begin to foster religiosity that does not require intellectual sacrifice but rather fits and corresponds to the consciousness of a modern and postmodern person.

---

3 Aslan, *God*, 19 (German ed.).

4. Statista Research Department, Glaube an Gott [Belief in God], May 30, 2011 (https://de.statista.com/statistik/daten/studie/169072/umfrage/glaube-an-gott-in-deutschland/).

Integral viewpoints, drawing on thinkers such as Jean Gebser, Sri Aurobindo, and Ken Wilber, assume that every human individual, as well as humanity as a whole, undergoes a development of consciousness, from the archaic, oceanic unity of the newborn through the magical, mythical, rational to postrational, integral consciousness. Such theories can also be applied to the development of religion. In our book *God 9.0: Where Christianity Could Grow Spiritually* I have shown (together with Marion and Tiki Küstenmacher) how religious consciousness unfolds and differentiates along the stages of development.

The Evolution of Consciousness. A Brief Outline

Archaic

The first individuals of the species Homo sapiens still lived in almost perfect unity with nature, of which they were a part; for them there was still no difference between the inner and outer world, just as a newborn cannot yet distinguish between itself and the environment.

Magical

This archaic period is followed by the magical, in which the connection to nature is still felt so strongly that people's behavior—such as incantations, dances, or totemic rituals—seem to have direct influence on natural phenomena. Everything in nature seems to be alive or animate; religious studies consequently speaks of animism.

Magical-Mythical

With the awakening of ego-consciousness, the numinous is perceived in the form of gods with distinct personalities; it is the magical-mythical time of the Homeric gods, the heroic sagas, and many of the Old Testament tales.

Traditional-Mythical

Small city-states and village communities grow to be kingdoms, and eventually great empires emerge like the Sumerian, Babylonian and Egyptian, ruled by kings with almost unlimited power. By analogy, God is now understood as the heavenly Father, who has his throne in heaven and pronounces and enforces his will through a heavenly hierarchy of angels. An earthly hierarchy mirrors this heavenly one, with the god-king at the top, aided by an army of officials in complex hierarchical orders; below them are the "people," likewise divided into freemen of various classes and serfs or slaves. The European variant of this traditional-mythical image of the world and God had its beginning in the Roman Empire and lasted until modernity. The structures of the Roman Church accurately reflect this traditional-mythical worldview, even today.

Modern/Rational

With the Renaissance, humanism, and the Enlightenment, modern rational consciousness arises. In the endeavor to understand the world, experimentation and observation take the place of the holy scriptures; authorities of all kinds now can be (and are) criticized. The American and French Revolutions are directed against traditional-mythical kingships and install (more or less sustainably) democratic structures. Natural science makes a creator God superfluous; man is dethroned several times: Nicolaus Copernicus moves the earth from the center of the universe and recognizes in it one planet among others; Charles Darwin replaces the idea that man was created by God as the "crown of creation" with the scientifically founded assumption that humans evolved from animal ancestors; Sigmund Freud proves that the proud ego is at best a lodger within the human personality, jammed between id and superego; and Friedrich Nietzsche proclaims modernity's battle cry: *God is dead! God remains dead! And we have killed him!*

Within Western culture, we currently still find ourselves largely in this situation of modernity. No wonder that half of the Germans do not believe in a God. But humanity is, as I said, "incurably religious," whereby the term "religion" encompasses much more than the classical religions. In this context we do better to speak of religiosity instead of religion.

Dead is the traditional-mythical God who sits enthroned in heaven, who watches over his people, who intervenes in the world from time to time as he pleases, who may arbitrarily suspend the laws of nature, and who judges people at the end of time, sending them to either eternal joy or eternal torment depending on their behavior. This God has had his day, for many. However, even in modern times there are still many people who—modern and enlightened as they may otherwise be—cling to the traditional-mythical image of God and even defend it aggressively.

But has religion died with the traditional-mythical, "interventionist" God? Certainly not. Humanity's incurable religiosity seeks other ways to manifest itself. This can be, as I said, through fandom of an ideology; through devotion to an -ism of any kind; through a fanatical adherence to an idea or a path, such as a diet; even militant atheism can take on appearances and traits of the phenomenon it opposes, thus satisfying the religious need.

Postmodern/Pluralistic

Modernity still determines our world to a large extent, yet increasingly is reaching its limits. Overemphasis on reason and neglect of other spheres of the human as well as of nonhuman nature have led to a world that many experience as cold and technical; the ruthless orientation toward profit has resulted in exploitation and destruction of nature. A countermovement is beginning, relativizing modern rationality with its binary logic and valuing other ways of cognition such as feeling or intuition more highly: the postmodern, pluralistic consciousness is emerging out of the modern, rational one. This also leads to a new preparedness for the spiritual dimension. The diction is not accidental: religiosity becomes spirituality; many postmodern people call themselves "spiritual, but not religious."

This distinction is typical of postmodernism. By religion it understands the constituted religion, in our latitudes mainly the Christian church(es). These include rituals and authorities, consecrated persons, laws, and regulations, church taxes, budgets, church representatives at political parties, broadcasting slots in public and private media, theological chairs at public universities, military chaplaincy, and (at least in Germany) denominational religious education as a regular school subject. The churches are rich and powerful, and due to all these attributes and privileges they are regarded as untrustworthy, ossified, unliving, not to say undead. These institutions, which are perceived as devoid of liveliness, strength, and spirit, are contrasted with spirituality as a living impulse. Spirituality is engagement, is feeling, is practice. Spirituality is inwardness, religion merely outward. Although drawing from religious traditions, spiritual people in this popular understanding do not want to be told what to believe, how to live, and how to practice. They often choose what best suits them from various religious or spiritual traditions. The most important spiritual sources here, besides Hinduism, Buddhism, and shamanism, are the mystical traditions of the West: Sufism and Christian mysticism. The traditional church forms—Sunday services, Bible evenings or prayer circles—are ridiculed, rejected, and discarded by these people who regard themselves as spiritual but not religious; church and Christianity (apart from a few exceptions, the mystics) are seen as outdated and done with.

Level-line Fallacy

Criticizing the churches is very justified in many respects. Nevertheless, I see the danger of throwing out the baby with the bathwater or, to put it more precisely: I see the danger of a level-line fallacy, as it already happened during the Enlightenment.

At that time, the church fought the great scientific discoveries of Copernicus, Kepler, Galileo, and others, because these discoveries contradicted the common understanding of the Bible, and objected to the modern view of the world, which took hold at the universities, in the studies and debating circles. Both the churches and the scientists made a momentous confusion, the aforementioned level-line fallacy. With the Copernican revolution and the scientific-experimental method, a new worldview (the modern one) suddenly opened up to the scientists; a new level of consciousness (the rational one) began to emerge. The church, which remained on the premodern, traditional, mythical level of consciousness, met the scientists with fierce resistance. This aroused the opinion among modern scientists that religion was premodern by its very nature and could not accept or even integrate the new findings at all. From then on, religion was considered antiquated and hostile to science. Conversely, the church retreated into the supposedly safe corral of traditional faith and insisted on its premodern positions. In other words, no one had the idea that there could be a modern version of religion. No one, or virtually no one, thought it possible that religion, too, could undergo an evolution from ancient and medieval ideas to a modern conception of the world and of God. The level of development at which the church people's consciousness was situated (the ancient-medieval, traditional-mythical understanding) was confused with the whole religious or spiritual line. Thus, the religious and the scientific world interpretations separated; they formed from now on hostile camps, fighting each other or ignoring each other, to the detriment of a healthy, holistic development of consciousness in Western society.

A similar trend could take place again today. Many of the postmodern, spiritual-but-not-religious people dismiss Christianity as a whole, calling it reactionary, outdated, no longer useful. As understandable as this attitude is for the most part, it misses the point. It may be that the churches act in large parts in boring, unvital/undead, and untrustworthy ways. It may be that living spirituality can be found everywhere else, but not in the Christian church. Nevertheless, I believe that an attitude that rejects Christianity as such again springs from the level-line fallacy. Even if it may seem difficult to imagine given the existing churches, like every spiritual phenomenon, Christianity can of course evolve and reach further levels of consciousness.

And this is also of urgent necessity. Western (Occidental) culture is decisively shaped by Judaism and Christianity; without the Judeo-Christian tradition, the Occident cannot be understood in depth at all. Thus, for example, the vision of a communist society formulated by Karl Marx can be understood only against the background of biblical, historical thinking, which assumes a beginning and an end to history—and which expects an age at the end of history in which all people will have what they need to live, in freedom and equality. Asian societies, with their more cyclical understanding of time, could never have developed such a notion, nor did they. Of course, Karl Marx did not consciously base his vision of a communist society on biblical ideas—he is known for fighting religion as "opium for the people"—but as the child of Jewish parents in nineteenth-century Germany, his whole thinking and feeling was naturally, although unconsciously, deeply rooted in Judeo-Christian thought, which was and is omnipresent in our culture like spiritual background noise.

Until today, this background noise of Judeo-Christian motives (besides Roman-legal ones) pervades Western culture, unconsciously to the vast majority of people and yet unmistakably in comparison with other cultures.

The Plan

If this is so, it would be of eminent importance to develop this Judeo-Christian thought in a healthy way. Especially in liturgy, but also in the popular conceptions of the Christian contents, much is still stuck on the traditional-mythical level of consciousness. At the same time, Christian theology in itself is much further along—as a university discipline it is completely at home in modern consciousness, and there is also already some postmodern, pluralistic thinking and acting in the ecclesiastical and theological context.

To me it seems important to develop Christian theological thinking even further into a post-postmodern, integral consciousness. Ken Wilber has the idea that it is precisely the high religions that need to drive the development of consciousness in their respective areas, because as the "guardians of tradition" they have sovereignty over the interpretation of the fundamental myths that shape society. This may seem more plausible in the USA, where Christianity is still much more rooted in society, than in secularized Europe, but in principle it seems to me that Wilber is right. If the churches would not only allow but actively develop and advance a post-postmodern, integral consciousness, they could set decisive impulses. They could serve as a "conveyor belt" and thus contribute to transporting the consciousness of society as a whole into further levels of awareness.

For example, it would be urgent for the churches to point out alternatives to the theistically understood God, the "Father in heaven," in their
proclamations. In the church proclamation, God—despite all the differences between teachers and preachers—is still predominantly the "supreme
being" who resides in a "beyond" and from there intervenes in people's lives
and in the world as a whole. This is the God of the traditional-mythical
space of consciousness, which modern, rational thinking has put an end
to. It is the God in whom the German theologian Dorothee Soelle said that
after Auschwitz one could no longer believe. Dorothee Soelle consequently
wrote a book titled, "Atheistically Believing in God."[5] Yes, it would be important to speak about an a-theistic, nontheistic God and to teach such a
God. A God who does not stand in opposition to the world but underlies it
as its depth and its mystery.

This God would no longer be someone to be afraid of. He would no
longer be the strict lawgiver, no longer the jealous lover who demanded
unconditional obedience or exclusive love. He would not be the inexorable,
just judge, who judges us after our death and—depending on the case—
invites us into eternal joy or casts us into eternal fire. This God would be
the primal ground and source of life, he would be creativity and Eros, he
would no longer be male at all, also not female or diverse, but beyond any
gender determination. He/she/it would meet us in every living being as well
as in the seemingly inanimate nature, but above all in the eyes of our fellow
humans. This would also correspond to what Jesus of Nazareth, according
to tradition, said: "Truly, I say to you, as you did it to one of the least of these
my brothers, you did it to me" (Matt 25:40 ESV).

As Utopian as this idea may seem, I would like to contribute to such
a development of consciousness in this essay. For this purpose, I will take
the central doctrinal contents of Christianity, the innermost core of Christian doctrine: the christological dogma (*Christ being true God and at the
same time true human*) and the Trinitarian dogma (*the one God existing
in three persons*). Interpreted integrally, these two complexes can develop
great intellectual and, hopefully, spiritual power. And perhaps, in the end, a
contribution to a healthier religion will emerge—a religiosity or spirituality
serving the whole, which is showing up in the many of individuals, and thus
can make people freer, more aware, and happier.

5 Soelle, *Atheistisch an Gott glauben.*

Dogmas?

A brief explanation is needed for the term dogma. For people who think and feel postmodern, the word is likely to be rather off-putting. For postmodernists, dogmas are authoritative doctrines coming along with the institution's full force, wanting to stop one's own thinking. They are part of a doctrine that one must submit to, that one must believe, even if one cannot agree with all of it intellectually or morally-ethically. There is some truth in this understanding. Dogmas belong to the traditional-mythical space of consciousness, in which authorities and hierarchies, revealed truths and binding doctrines are of great importance. Even if many who have arrived in postmodern consciousness can no longer imagine this; most people in the traditional-mythical realm need and want such authorities, such binding teachings, because they provide support and security. Of course, the system has enormous downsides. Whoever does not submit to the authority, whoever cultivates deviant thoughts, and whoever even expresses these deviant thoughts, must expect severe sanctions up to the death penalty— not to mention eternal damnation, which is a terrible, threatening reality for this realm of consciousness.

Why do I nevertheless refer to these ancient dogmas? Well, they are, in a sense, part of the operating system of Christianity and thus of the Western world. Only a few people are aware of them, but which computer user knows his Windows or her MacOS precisely? Operating systems, however, need an update from time to time. In the process, many essential components of the program are retained, while others are modernized, replaced, removed, and substituted with new, more functional ones. Obviously, the operating system of Christianity, as it is currently in use, is not quite up to date any longer. To function as a conveyor belt, it needs a refresh. But then, I am convinced, it can better perform its original function again.

The other question besides the why is the question of how: How do I refer to these old dogmas?

Dogmas in the original sense are doctrines agreed upon by a council, that is, an assembly of recognized theologians—often after long disputes and heated discussions. Once a dogma has been adopted, it carries great weight: it is the binding formulation of certain beliefs to which all who call themselves Christians must adhere. This is true for the traditional-mythical realm of consciousness, which has had a lasting influence on our culture and continues to do so today. But today, the dogmas of the ancient church cannot be considered undoubted, unquestionable truths that are "simply to be believed"—to stay with the metaphor: Today's operating system is more of an open-source program that can be adapted to the particular needs of the user. In other words, I see dogmas as a model that tries to describe a spiritual reality. I can use this model to interpret my own experience of reality, and I take it as an offer to set myself on a particular path of thought. Where the ancient thinkers seem not to go far enough, or if they are moving in a way, I cannot and do not want to follow, I take the liberty to add my own thoughts and to modify the model in such a way that it can speak into my postmodern and integral worldview, or better, in such a way that the model can enter into a dialogue with my postmodern and integral view. I try to do this with respect for tradition and with as much responsibility as possible. That is, I try not to make changes "to suit my taste," as traditionally oriented Christians might accuse me of doing. There is a big, important difference between arbitrariness and responsibility. When I expand or modify the dogmas, I do so because I believe these modifications to be essential in making the meaning and intent of the traditional statements acceptable and plausible to people today.

True God and True Human—the Christological Dogma

Jesus Christ is true God and at the same time true human is the core sentence of the christological dogma. The contradiction is obvious: God is commonly thought of as immortal, eternal, and omnipotent, whereas humans are mortal, finite, and of extremely limited power over themselves and the circumstances of their lives. How can someone be both mortal and immortal, eternal and finite, omnipotent and quite powerless at the same time? To understand how the Christian theologians of the first centuries came to formulate such a contradictory doctrine, we must look at the background, the history of ideas. Two motives play the decisive role: the belief that there is one God and the talk about the man Jesus' resurrection from the dead.

"Hear, O Israel!"

In the ancient Near East, the people of Israel were the first and only to believe that there is only one God. Although Greek philosophers thought about a single God (such as Aristotle's "unmoved mover"), religious monotheism was unique throughout the world of the time.[6] The formation of this belief is quite remarkable. Originally, the people of Israel probably worshiped other Canaanite gods in addition to the main god, Yahweh. Yet there were always

6. Akhenaten in Egypt (fourteenth century BC) and Zoroaster in Persia (sometime during the second or first millennia BC) attempted to install monotheistic religions, but both failed and did not establish a lasting monotheistic tradition.

efforts, especially on the part of the prophets, to enforce the sole worship of Yahweh among the people. However, even when sacrifices were made to other gods such as El, Baal, or Ishtar, which the prophets strongly criticized, Yahweh was considered "the God of Israel." After the Northern Kingdom of Israel was conquered by the Assyrians and made a tributary province in 722 BCE, the Babylonian king Nebuchadnezzar II conquered the Southern Kingdom with its capital Jerusalem in the year 587 BCE. The Israelite king and the entire upper class were taken into exile in Babylon. According to the religious-political logic of the time, Yahweh, the God of Israel, was thus also inferior to the Babylonian god Marduk. But an amazing theological volte-face occurred in the exile. The prophets had repeatedly threatened the royal house and the people of Israel with harsh punishments from Yahweh because they also worshiped other gods and disregarded elementary social regulations. A theologian or a theological school whose texts are handed down in the second part of the biblical book of Isaiah came up with the bold thought that their God was not inferior to the foreign god, but rather that Yahweh, the God of Israel, had used the powerful king Nebuchadnezzar as a tool to punish his unruly people Israel. Yahweh was therefore even more powerful than previously thought; indeed, Yahweh was the only God. There were no other gods besides him. Until then, monolatry had applied in Israel, that is, the existence of other gods was not denied, but only one god must be worshiped. Now, monotheism was born: the belief that there really was only this one God. Israel, or at least certain radical theological circles, held adamantly to this one-God belief. Israel's creed consists of two sentences: "Hear, O Israel: The LORD our God, the LORD is one. You shall love the LORD your God with all your heart and with all your soul and with all your might" (Deut 6:5 ESV) Belief in the one God establishes the identity of the people of Israel and is at the very heart of the Jewish religion.

"The Lord is Risen!"

At the time of the Roman emperor Tiberius, a certain Jesus of Nazareth was traveling through the Roman province of Palestine, preaching and healing people. This was nothing unusual. Nor was it unusual that the itinerant preacher was called the "Messiah" by his followers—the one who would liberate the land from the Roman occupiers. There were dozens of messiahs, preachers, and rebel leaders roaming the country in those troubled times. Finally, neither was it at all unusual that the Roman authorities, always eager to eliminate potential troublemakers, arrested this Jesus and executed him after a short trial. Like many, many others, he ended up on a cross, the usual instrument for executing agitators and rebels.

What was very unusual, however, was the behavior of his followers. Shortly after their leader's execution, they began to talk about Jesus no longer being dead, saying that he was resurrected, that he was alive—but not as a roused or reanimated corpse, but in a new, divine way. What exactly happened to the disciples so that they came to make such statements cannot be reconstructed. But it must have been an experience of such vehemence that not even persecution, torture, and the threat of death dissuaded them from their assertions. According to a very early confession text quoted by the Christian missionary Paul in his first letter to the church in Corinth (written around the year 55 CE, i.e., twenty to twenty-five years after the death of Jesus), several individuals, but also groups of up to five hundred people, saw the risen Lord. It is particularly striking that according to the Gospels the first people to encounter the risen Lord were women. Given the male-dominated culture of the time, *something* must indeed have happened for the accounts of Jesus' life and death to report this significant detail—already in the list of eyewitnesses cited by Paul, women are deleted. What kind of phenomenon this something was, as I have said, cannot be reconstructed.

The followers of the executed and, according to their conviction, resurrected man began to collect stories about their master and to write down his sayings. Whatever may have awakened in them the belief that he had risen, it also shaped and reshaped the narratives about Jesus. Many stories look at Jesus through a "post-Easter" lens; that is, they already see in the itinerant preacher the one who will later rise from the dead. For example, there is a story according to which Jesus, while praying alone with his three closest confidants, is suddenly "transfigured": he appears as a figure of light, and a heavenly voice calls him the Son of God (Matt 17:1–9; Mark 9:2–9; Luke 9:28–36). In the Jewish context, this does not mean "kinship" but is a functional designation—thus in Ps 2 the king is called the "Son" of God. Strict monotheism could not have allowed a Jew to call a man "consubstantial" with God. But the transfiguration story shows that Jesus was at least ascribed a very special, intimate closeness to God.

Through the missionary activities of Paul, who was a Jew but nevertheless a citizen of the Roman Empire and had enjoyed a Greco-Roman education, the confession of the risen Messiah—in Greek: Christos—came into the Hellenistic realm. For Greeks, ascribing divine nature to a human being was not a big problem. They understood the stories of the resurrection and the title "Son of God" in such a way that in Jesus God himself had come to humankind. Already Paul could formulate that Christ was "in the form of God," even that he had "equality with God" (Phil 2:6 ESV). But at the same time, these first Greek-speaking and Greek-thinking Christians had also adopted the strict monotheism of the Jewish faith—after all, Jesus himself was also a Jew. And here a dilemma arose. How can a human being represent God himself, when God is unique and superior to all human beings?

Two Natures

This dilemma moved young Christianity for the next three hundred years. To summarize very briefly a long process of reflection and discussion, there were in principle two groups—those who considered Jesus divine, and those who saw him as human—as a special human being, but basically as a human being like you and me. At some point, however, in the course of bitter disputes, theologians came up with the bold idea of thinking both together in the person of Jesus Christ: divine and human. In Jesus Christ, so the new thesis proclaimed, two "natures" are united, a human one and a divine one, and these two natures are not mixed with each other; neither is one transformed into the other. At the same time, the two natures are not separate and do not divide. The logical paradox in these statements was deliberately not resolved by theologians of that time; they left the statements side by side. At the Council of Chalcedon in 451, this doctrine of "the two natures of Christ" was declared binding as the only valid teaching about Christ.

The discussion, by the way, was not conducted by academic theologians in ivory towers. The issue of the nature of Christ also preoccupied people of the street. There are reports of brawls in the marketplace of Byzantium that ignited over the question of the two natures of Christ. For regular people, the question was also anything but academic. According to the conviction of the time, eternal salvation depended on the correct understanding of faith: the debates were always about the certainty of salvation—that is, the certainty of being accepted by God after death. The wrong belief would lead to stewing in hell. That is why the debates were so heated.

One for All or Example for All?

The discussion was always about the one historical man Jesus from Nazareth, in whom God had "incarnated" in a unique way. All other people were merely human, without a second, divine nature. One can find it astonishing that there was no discussion about the question of whether humans themselves might carry these two natures—that is, whether all people, you and I, are human and divine at the same time. After all, the creation myths of Genesis speak of humanity as being animated by God's breath and created "in our [God's] image, after our likeness." And after all, Jesus urged his dis- ciples to address God as "Father in heaven," just as Jesus himself called God his Father. Paul wrote in Galatians, "For in Christ Jesus you are all sons of God, through faith" (3:26 ESV). and the first Epistle of John, written around 100 CE formulates that "We should be called children of God; and so we are" (3:1 ESV).

On the other hand, Christ is called the "only begotten," that is, the one and only Son of God. Today, however, one could justifiably ask what the dif- ference between "the Son" and "the sons/children" of God is supposed to be.

Indeed, it would be much easier for today's postmodern or post-post- modern/integral people to recognize that there are two natures in Christ if this were a statement about humankind itself. Then the significance of Jesus Christ would be founded not in the fact that he, as the only Son of God and unique God-human, had redeemed people from sin, death, and the devil, but rather in the fact that his followers recognized in him what is true for all of us. Resurrection could be interpreted as an individual and then also as a collective experience in which the disciples recognized what the true nature of Jesus was, and likewise their own true nature: that we are all immortal, eternal, divine—at least according to our deepest, innermost, true nature. This divine nature is concealed, of course, by our personality, the character armor that we have woven and spun around ourselves since our first breath or even before, and which hardens and solidifies more and more in the course of our lives—unless we work very consciously to dissolve it again, through therapy, mindfulness practice, meditation, and self-reflection. Jesus would then have been a person whose character armor was so permeable, who was so vulnerable, transparent, and sincere that those around him saw the divine light shimmering, as it were, through all the cracks.

However, this idea, which may well be plausible to a postmodern, pluralistic-minded person, does not correspond to Christian doctrine in the traditional sense. The traditional-mythical religiosity puts very great emphasis on the infinite distance, the fundamental, categorical difference between God and human. But as a postmodern person, one can certainly ask about the reasons, about the cognitive interest that lies behind rejecting the idea that all human beings are just as divine as Christ, that they have two natures in themselves, just as he does.

Certainty of Salvation

As already indicated above, I see the first and most important reason for this attitude in the issue of certainty of salvation. We today can hardly comprehend the role this topic must have played in earlier centuries. The fear of being eternally lost and having to spend an indefinite time in a place of torment—or even only in a place of shadows, lifeless, without emotions, without movement or development—motivated people in a way hardly imaginable for postmodern consciousness. The crucial thing was to be on the "right side." That's why there was such bitter fighting over seemingly minor details; that's why there were persecutions, church splits, and wars. Eternal salvation or eternal condemnation depended solely on God, the incorruptible judge who ultimately judged people, and he did so not only according to their deeds but also according to their faith.

Religiosity is inscribed in the source code of human consciousness, but what concrete form and shape it takes depends on how people understand themselves and how their society is structured. In agrarian societies, the worship of fertility gods and goddesses suggested itself; in a monarchy, in which the king was absolute ruler over the lives of his subjects, God was imagined as a heavenly patriarch and great king. His Majesty was extremely sensitive and easily offended; any blasphemy, any slight offense to the divine majesty, was severely punished by this God. So, it was crucial to address God correctly and to have the right conception of him. Since God, unlike the human king, even knew the thoughts and the secret impulses of the heart, one also had to believe in him "correctly" in order not to incur his wrath. However, no matter how hard people tried, they could never succeed in being completely without sin—that is, in never offending the majesty of God. Therefore, one had to hope for God's forgiveness or acquire this divine forgiveness according to the existing rules.

This is where Christ comes in. Very early on, for example in a confession text from 1 Corinthians, it is said "that Christ died for our sins" (15:3 ESV). Jesus Christ is also "the Lamb of God" (John 1:36 ESV), and for people of that time it was as clear as day that this lamb was a sacrificial animal with which the wrath of God was averted. However, such a sacrifice for all mankind, or at least for all Christians, had to be so great and all-encompassing that an ordinary mortal man could never offer it. That is why Christ, the Redeemer, had to be a human being, but on the other hand he had to be absolutely superior to human beings: he had to be located completely in the sphere of the divine—unlike the other, "sinful" human beings—and that distinguishes him fundamentally from all other humans. To this day, devout, traditionally-mythically oriented Christians reject as blasphemous and deeply sinful the idea that ordinary mortal human beings could, like Jesus Christ, be of divine nature. Yes, "wanting to be like God" is considered the original sin par excellence.

The Golden Shadow

Concern for eternal salvation is thus one of the reasons why the divine nature is traditionally confined to Christ alone. A second reason probably lies in humanity's fear of their own greatness, or in their timidity in seeing in themselves what is plainly good, eternal, and powerful, for this is, as already mentioned, hidden under the thick layers of our character. In psychology, we sometimes speak of the "golden shadow," which means that most people have within them strong and good dispositions that they themselves do not recognize. Just as they repress their weak and destructive sides into the shadows, so most people do not have access to some of their strengths. To put it another way, their divinity lies deeply hidden in the "golden shadow." This also makes a lot of sense, because if a person with an immature personality claims to be equal to God and claims God-like power, it can easily end disastrously. Hitler, Stalin, and Pol Pot are horrific historical examples, and the movie *Bruce Almighty* shows a humorous variation of this intellectual game.[7]

Whoever wants to open up to the idea that the doctrine of the two natures does not apply only to the historically unique God-human Jesus Christ but is a blueprint for all human beings must also keep in mind that we humans are highly ambivalent: We are characterized by fear, egocentricity, self-overestimation and greed as well as by confidence, selflessness, and love. To claim that we have in us a divine nature is indeed quite a statement of faith—to really feel or see this nature will be quite rare. It is with us as, according to an old legend, Eurydice was with Orpheus: right at his back; but the moment he turned to see her and embrace her, she was gone. It is good to know about our divine nature, but we ought to handle this knowledge with extreme caution and restraint.

Submissive Spirit

Finally, a third reason for bestowing two natures upon only Jesus Christ is that in authoritarian regimes, typical of the traditional-mythic level of consciousness, it is politically opportune to keep the subjects dependent. Regularly, therefore, groups that assert humanity's inherent divinity are persecuted and exterminated. For a person who is aware of an inherent divinity may no longer be so easily bullied or even oppressed as one who considers himself exclusively weak, sinful, and in need of redemption. Both an authoritarian church, as it began to emerge from the second century on, and an authoritarian political system cannot have interest in its subjects

7. See Shadyac, dir., *Bruce Almighty.*

being too self-confident. They are supposed to be ignorant "sheep" who must be led and guided by "shepherds." Whoever assumes a divine nature in themselves, possibly gets the idea that they also have the authority to think independently. In short, the thought "I am related to God by my nature," if not "I am one with God," empowers human to freedom and independence from external authorities. This will not be welcome to most rulers. Thus, in the Western, Judeo-Christian-Islamic cultural area, the idea that humanity is one with God persisted for the most part only underground, in "heretical" circles, among mystics. And not a few of them had to pay dearly for this experience of being one with God—or better: for talking about this experience. A famous Islamic mystic, Mansur al-Hallaj, was executed for saying "I am the (divine) truth"; likewise, Shams-e Tabrizi, the friend and teacher of the probably most famous Sufi poet, Jalaluddin Rumi, was probably murdered for similarly unorthodox views. Many Christian mystics were also condemned and imprisoned for their statements, many were forced to recant, and more than a few were executed.

After Theism

If we look at the above reasons under today's postmodern conditions, they dissolve like snow in the sun. We live—thank God!—In a liberal democracy (and hopefully it will remain so, despite all populist, antidemocratic temptations). Freedom, self-responsibility, and independence from external authorities are no longer seen as signs of rebellion that should be suppressed, but as important goals in education and social life. Even if there may still be ministers in churches and other institutions who want to keep their "sheeple" as immature as possible in order to be able to control them better, the time of these sinister masters has expired. And even if the prevailing theology and church doctrine still emphasize the heavenwide difference between God and humans, many Christians are increasingly coming to realize that they are not far from God at all, but rather that "In him we live and move and have our being" (Acts 17:28 ESV), as the Bible already says.

A posttheistic God is not one to be afraid of. He will not get "angry" if you call him by the wrong name. He will also not send anyone to eternal damnation, because eternal damnation does not even exist. It is true that a person can fail in their life: they can fail in the task of bringing to fruition the potential inherent in them; they can fail in social, moral, or self-imposed goals and aspirations. Yes, this is true. But just as there is no hot place called hell anywhere beneath the surface of the earth, so there is no eternal damnation imposed by a God whom we would have annoyed by our behavior or unbelief. God is the reason and source of life; God will also take life to himself again; he/she/it will shelter us in the bosom of the life we came from. Eternal damnation is the result of the fear fantasies of people who lived in quite different circumstances than those we live with today, and the outgrowth of a consciousness marked by dualisms, of either-or and above-under.

And finally, the golden shadow, the fear of our own greatness, is certainly still present in the vast majority of people. Just as the dark shadow (parts are repressed into it that we could not bear at the present time) has its right, the golden shadow, as mentioned above, has its right, too. After all, today we live in a time and on a level of consciousness in which we can recognize these relations and work on them. The discovery of the unconscious by Freud and Jung and the development of psychotherapy have given us tools to work on both the dark shadow and the golden shadow. Integrating their shadow completely is something that very few people will ever be able to do. But realizing the mechanisms that keep us neurotic, dependent, and immature is possible—and so is a gradual improvement of our psychological state. Many postmodern people count this work among their most important, even noblest tasks. We no longer want to look at people in terms of what they lack, in terms of what is weak, sick, and immature about them. We look at people in terms of their resources. Of course, weaknesses, fears, and dependencies must not be ignored; on the contrary. It is important to face them, to realize and explore them. But they are seen as a challenge, as an opportunity for maturation and growth.

The paradox that people are separate from God and at the same time one with God—and, vice versa, that God per se is one but is present in the many—is accepted and shared by more and more people today. The influence of Eastern religions may play a certain role here, but the realization of this paradox also corresponds to experience of many people. Freed from the old thought taboos, they dare to name their experiences and stand by them.

The Paradox

Of course, it remains a paradox. The paradox that in Jesus Christ a divine and a human nature are united has been valid Christian doctrine for one and a half millennia. In earlier, premodern times this was a truth that humans could not comprehend with their minds and therefore had to "simply believe." In modern times, the doctrine of the two natures of Christ had a hard time because it seemed contradictory in itself and therefore had to be rejected by the logical mind. A good hundred years ago, however, the modern worldview began to change fundamentally. Taking the nature of light as an example, modern and state-of-the-art physics came to findings that seem to diametrically contradict binary logic. The so-called double-slit experiment shows that we need to describe a photon (or also mass particles like protons and even molecules) in two ways. Depending on the way of looking at it or the way of measuring it, a photon is either a particle (i.e., it has a certain and determinable mass, it is material in this sense), or it is an immaterial wave (which spreads spherically in all directions in space). Logically these two appearances of light are not to be reconciled, only mathematically and experimentally. This paradox, in association with other observations and calculations that seem contradictory in themselves, has led postmodern and integral thinkers to become comfortable with the paradox. They increasingly recognize that the nature of reality depends crucially on the perspective it is viewed from. The post-postmodern, integral point of view not only endures paradox; it loves it, because it has recognized that reality often cannot be described in any other way than precisely through paradoxical statements.

Thus, integral consciousness also gains a new access to some central elements of the teachings of Jesus from Nazareth, as they are handed down in the Gospels. As the core sentence of his proclamation, the Gospel of Mark mentions the cry "The kingdom of God is at hand" (1:15 ESV). The Greek expression translated as "the kingdom of God is at hand" is linguistically ambiguous. Rather it should be translated as "the kingdom of God has come near," which can mean both that the kingdom of God is dawning or is imminent and that it has already arrived. It is already here, and it is not yet here. Many exegetes regard this iridescence between already and not yet as essential for the message of Jesus. Another word of Jesus is rendered by the English Standard Version as "the kingdom of God is in the midst of you" (Luke 17:21), which is often understood intersubjectively, as "within the group." Linguistically, however, the Greek original can just as well be understood intrasubjectively, that is, internally: "The kingdom of God is inside, within you" or simply "in you."

This is one of the many New Testament references supporting the interpretation that humans are divine in their innermost being. Then human—every human being—would be identical with the One: eternal, everywhere, all-connected. On the other hand, of course, every human being is concrete and earthly, limited, localizable in space and time, isolated and mortal. One viewpoint cannot be played off against the other; both apply, depending on the way we look ourselves—in the same way that light is particle or a wave depending on the experimental arrangement.

An essential element of this theory forms the statement that the whole individual is divine and human at the same time. So, it is not that in the human being there is something divine, a divine spark or core; there is also no talk about an immortal soul, which would dwell in the human being. In this, the model differs from many esoteric or gnostic systems, each of which assumes that in the material shell of a concrete human person there is a divine part that must be liberated or developed, with the concrete human being representing an obstacle that must be overcome. The doctrine of two natures related to the human being as such emphasizes the exact opposite. The concrete, material nature of human is of just the same value as the eternal, divine nature. The task is not to overcome matter and leave it behind in order to ascend to supposedly divine spheres. Rather, it is our task, the dignity and essence of our "human nature," to live this concrete, bodily existence as intensively and consistently as possible and to fill it with love.

The One, the Great Whole, Being itself, traditionally referred to by the word "God," unfolds in the many concrete beings. They all share in the same being, and yet they are different beings. The One Being cannot be conceived without the many beings; conversely, the many beings are not conceivable without the One Being.

Traditional Christian doctrine formulates this idea in such a way that "the Word became flesh" (John 1:14 ESV). The "Word" we are talking about is a rendering of the Greek logos, which precisely means not only "word," but also "plan" or "reason"—and in the Hellenistic context of the time also the world's reason, the great context in which everything is connected. This logos is first equated with God in the Prologue of John's Gospel: "In the beginning was the Word, and the Word was with God, and the Word was God" (1:1 ESV), before it then says: "And the Word became flesh" (1:14 ESV), that is, it took on mortal, concrete, limited form. In traditional theology, as I said, this was related solely to the one man Jesus from Nazareth. If one understands Jesus as an exemplary model for humankind, this would mean that the divine word's reason, thus God himself, becomes flesh, incarnates, in every human being, possibly in the whole of creation. Thereby the present reality—the social, political, and ecological questions—gain in relevance and importance. They can no longer be played off against the "spiritual" or ignored ascetically. Whoever takes God seriously, whoever seeks the One, will find God or the One in the many, in the concrete, limited, unique reality.

Three in One

The idea that humanity has a share in the One, or better, paradoxically *is* the One, within Christian theology can also be verified with the second great old church dogma: the doctrine of the Trinity or Tri-Unity'of God. This doctrine states, in brief: God does not rest in himself in self-sufficient bliss. God is relationship, communication—in fact from his/her innermost, true being. To reverse a popular pun: The All-One is not alone, but dynamic communication in itself, a dance, a You and You and You.

The doctrine of the Trinity of God has an even worse reputation in modernity and postmodernity than the doctrine of two natures of Christ. Again, in premodern times it was said, basically, that what theologians have worked out and formulated in this area is not logical (one cannot understand it); one therefore must just believe it. It is obvious that enlightened reason cannot be satisfied with such a conclusion. Thus, in the present, the doctrine of the Trinity has also been abandoned by many Christians in favor of the doctrine of the good Rabbi Jesus who preached love and peace, so that following him entails an ethical but certainly not a cognitive imposition. In this view, the Hellenistic intellectual Paul then turned the simple, down-to-earth preacher of humanness into Christ, the God-being, and thus falsified the original teaching of Jesus. In addition, "the bishops" then invented highly complicated teachings, probably to keep the church people immature and dependent and thus submissive—at least this is what a popular and widespread modern myth wants.

From a modern point of view, the doctrine of the Trinity is indeed difficult or even impossible to accept in its contradictory nature. But postmodernism, which criticizes the binary, reductionist logic of modernity and tends to seek access to the paradoxical, the nonrational, also has difficulty with the doctrine of the Trinity, albeit for different reasons. A major concern of postmodern Christians is interreligious dialogue, and the doctrine of the Trinity is perceived as an obstacle in the dialogue with the strictly monotheistic kin religions, Judaism and Islam. Jews and Muslims often accuse Christians of betraying monotheism by believing in three gods. For them, the doctrine of the Trinity of God is a barely concealed form of polytheism.

Indeed, the talk of "Father, Son, and Holy Spirit" suggests a polytheistic understanding. "Trinity" is then understood as if there were three in agreement. The Christian imagery promotes this misunderstanding. There are countless images in which God the Father appears enthroned in the clouds as an old man with a long beard; in front of or next to him is Jesus in a loincloth with a crown of thorns and stigmata, and above both is the Holy Spirit as a dove from which rays of light emanate to the Father and the

Son, suggesting the connection of the three "persons." Sometimes Mary, the mother of Jesus, is also in the picture, who as "Mother of God" extends the trinity to a "quaternity." This does not correspond to the official doctrine, but for many devout Catholics this is how the true image of God looks—as, by the way, it did for the Swiss Protestant pastor's son, Carl Gustav Jung.

How these three "persons" should then form one Godhead is difficult to imagine. The reason for this difficulty lies, in my opinion, in an incorrect understanding of the word "person." Without diving deep into the complicated philological and theological contexts here, let us say this much: When the early Christian theologians used the term "person," they did not mean, as we modern and postmodern people do, a certain, distinct individual or a conscious subject responsible for their thoughts and actions. Rather, they used the term to refer to a way of existing, a way of coming into contact—from the human point of view: a way of experiencing God. In this sense, the One God makes himself tangible in three ways: as the Creator and Sustainer of the world (Father), as the man Jesus of Nazareth, the Christ (Son), and as the presence of God in the world and among human beings (Spirit). Christian theology has elaborated and finely chiseled this doctrine in detail. For example, one of the tenets of the doctrine of the Trinity is *Opera ad intra sunt divisa, opera ad extra sunt indivisa*—in English: "The works within are distinguished; the works without are not." This somewhat cryptic formulation is underlain by the following thought: the distinction into Father, Son, and Spirit concerns only the inner being of God. But when people experience God—whether through creation, through faith in Jesus Christ, or through the community experienced as instituted by the Spirit—in that experience they always encounter the "whole" God, never a "part" of God. For there is only one God; Christian doctrine holds to this as unconditionally as Jewish and Islamic doctrine. God, the ultimate reality, is One, undivided, without any other—and in three "persons" (i.e., in diversity, differentiated, manifold). In God himself, in the ultimate reality, is diversity, is communication and relationship, from the beginning and from the ground up.

Excursus: Ken Wilber and the Three Faces of God

In his book *Integral Spirituality*, Ken Wilber introduces the idea of the "three faces of God" or also "Spirit in the first, second, and third person"—whereby "person" is meant quite differently here, namely in the grammatical sense. With Wilber, the first person stands for the inner perspective, the "I," the second person for the counterpart, the "You," and the third person for that which is neither I nor You, the "He/She/It" (singular) and also the "They" (plural). This idea is captivating because it unites the different perspectives on God and mediates between the more Eastern and the more Western images of God. The third person of God: that is, the great chain of being, everything we see and experience in the world—the life impulse, the creative Eros of evolution, what is traditionally called the creation and so also called the creator, the power behind the creation. The second person stands for the God "vis-à-vis," as predominantly experienced and described in the western religions: the God who is radically different from his creation, who is approachable as a You, and who challenges us ethically. Finally, the first person stands for the God we can experience in the innermost part of our soul, at the bottom of our heart—the great "I am," the God of the mystics, the Buddha nature, or the Atman-Brahman unity.

I regard this thought as ingenious. Thus, it is possible to systematize the different religious approaches to God, the diverse ways of experience. The "God within me" no longer has to be played off against the "God vis-à-vis." God as the power I can turn to in prayer no longer needs to be defended against the God I find in mystical experience at the deepest bottom of my soul as my actual, deepest, and truest self.

It is tempting for Christian theologians to draw a parallel here between Wilber's theory and the Trinity of God. For example, Paul R. Smith in his book *Integral Christianity*[8] describes the Trinitarian God according to Wilber's model. For Smith, Spirit in the third person (or the third face of God) corresponds to the first person of the Trinity, the Father and Creator. Spirit in the second person would be the second person of the Trinity, Jesus, the Christ. And Spirit in the first person would correspond to the third person of the Christian Trinity, the Spirit.

This sounds charming, and the different approaches to God are well described. The idea of the three faces of God is enriching and enlightening also for the Christian understanding of God. But according to my understanding, the doctrine of the Trinity is about something slightly different.

The One, the Other, and the Third

Let us imagine the first person of God, the "Father," the "Creator of visible and invisible things," for once not with the image of the old man on a cloud. Let us imagine the "Father" nontheistically, freed from any anthropomorphic conception. Then we come to the primordial ground, to the source of all that is and of all that is yet to become. God is then Being itself. That which underlies everything, from which everything emerges. The loving

8. Smith, *Integral Christianity*; in even greater detail: Smith, *Is Your God?*

will and power that holds all that is in existence, in every nanosecond. The depth, the mystery of the world. It is a dimension—and much more than just a dimension—that lies and works "in, with, and under" the cosmos. The "unknown God" (Acts 17:23) of whom Paul speaks in Athens—"He is actually not far from each one of us, for in him we live and move and have our being" (17:27–28 ESV)—it is this God that I can find in the depth of my existence, but he/she/it encounters me also in the tree outside my window, in mountains and rivers and sun and planets and in the black holes at the other end of the universe. And this God encounters me in my counterpart, in every human being. In this respect, God, the Father, is in the Wilberian sense Spirit in the first as well as in the second and third person. This God is present always and everywhere, and whoever has eyes to see will perceive him in everything within and around. It is like a tilting picture, the so-called Necker cube. This figure can be seen as the grid drawing of a cube. The amazing thing is that you can see the cube from the top right—then the top right square is the back side. Or you can see the cube as if from the lower left, in which case it forms the front, facing the viewer. The square positioned at the bottom left becomes from one view the front or from another view the back. The picture is the same in both cases; our very perception makes the difference (scientifically speaking, the bistable perception). Both cubes are "there" at the same time, but we can only perceive one at a time. When perception "tilts," nothing changes except our perspective or focus. In this sense, we can say of God that he/she/it is present always and everywhere and at the same time "there" for us only when we perceive him/her/it. In this sense, God's transcendence is nothing necessarily different per se: God is not self-sufficient, secluded, or enthroned in a "beyond"; rather God (him/her/it) is the "inside" of the cosmos on whose "outside" our life takes place.

Now the second person of the Trinity comes in, the "Son." Let us recall: It is said of Jesus Christ that he is God and human at the same time. In him a divine and a human nature are united, and these two natures are "unmixed, unchanged, unseparated, and undivided." These four terms were declared binding at the Council of Chalcedon in 451 CE. That is, one cannot divide the divine and human natures into two "parts" of the person of Jesus Christ, nor are they fused into one, nor does the divine nature somehow transform into the human or vice versa. Both belong together integrally; one is never without the other. Again, the Necker cube could serve as an illustration—or let us think once more of the double-slit experiment that demonstrates the dual nature of light (particle/wave).

But this means that in God himself the human nature is contained as an essential component—"unseparated and undivided." The earthly Jesus, who was conceived, born, nursed, and swaddled; who learned to speak and walk and later took on a craft; who wandered the land, discussed, argued, laughed, loved, and raged; who ate and drank; who knew hunger and thirst; who slept and lay awake sleepless; who was sick; who certainly fell in love; who was loved and adored, betrayed and sold; who died miserably after a short life—this Jesus, this human life, is so interwoven with God's being that Christians cannot think of God without thinking simultaneously of this human life.

The majority of the theologians of the early church, whose convictions prevailed at the councils, were keen to emphasize that Christ was not created, but "begotten" and "born of the Father forever"—whatever one might imagine by that. This was done, of course, to emphasize that Christ, as the second person of the Trinity, is wholly divine. At the same time, however, he has a human nature, and according to this human nature he was born of a human woman named Mary. The idea seems to have been that through "supernatural" begetting by the Holy Spirit, Christ's uncreated human nature was placed in Mary, carried out by her, and born.

The interest in the divinity of Christ expressed in this strange conception is clear. But what if today we are guided by quite different interests because we see God differently than people did fifteen hundred years ago? If we no longer see God as the severe patriarch whose honor is offended by our sin and who must therefore be reconciled by a human sacrifice, but if we now see God as the source, the creative ground of all that is, the elemental force of love, which cannot be offended at all because it expresses itself in all that we are, do, and feel, then there is no need to emphasize the great, abysmal difference between God and the human. Then, in my view rather the following question arises: If we already speak of the "human nature" of Christ, which is "contained" in God, then is it not obvious to speak of human nature "in itself"; that is, to speak of what unites you and me and the man Jesus from Nazareth, which is common to us all—in which we all share? If human nature "in itself" is suspended in God, then we human beings, you and I and all who live and have ever lived and will live, are also suspended in God, in God's heart, in God's deepest, truest Being. Here we come full circle to what we have already found above on the basis of the doctrine of two natures.

But it goes even further. What actually is the "human nature"? What is it that, on the one hand, is common to all human beings, and on the other hand, distinguishes human beings from all other creatures? And where does it begin in the evolution from animal to human? Today, in the twenty-first century, we cannot think about human apart from the findings of modernity: the theory of evolution, for example; biology; genetics; and so on. At what point can we speak of humans? Did Homo erectus have "human nature"?

Did Neanderthals? Did Cro-Magnon creatures? Was there really one living being or better one pair of living beings between apes and ourselves, whose descendants were the first humans, while their parents still belonged to the animal kingdom? Anyone who has studied the evolution of life and humanity just a little bit knows that these questions cannot be answered. Humans are not as unique as they have long believed. Chimpanzees, ravens, and even some fish use tools; that is, they act in a planned and deliberate way, they have an idea of the goal of their actions—that is, of something that is not yet there. Elephants and whales mourn their dead relatives; they have differentiated and deep emotions. Rats seem to have empathy; that is, they can put themselves in the emotional position of conspecifics. Even rhesus monkeys recognize themselves in a mirror. That is, they have some idea of themselves, a kind of self-awareness. The border between us humans and our animal relatives seems to become more and more permeable with detailed research. The genome of a human is at least 95 percent identical to that of a chimpanzee; some analyses place the overlap at 99.4 percent. The fact that the difference between the genome of a human male and that of a human female is between 2 and 4 percent prompted the website rp-online. de to publish the somewhat lurid headline: "Men resemble apes more than women." And we, the supposed crown of creation, have 50 percent of the genetic material in common with a banana. Where does human nature begin, where does it end?

And finally, our body, without which human nature is inconceivable, consists entirely of matter, of "dead" material. Does "human nature" therefore also refer to carbon, hydrogen, calcium, selenium, and iodine?

Thus, from the theological formulation that human nature is integrated in God through the second person of the Trinity, it is in fact only a small step to the assumption that the whole creation is included in God. This step, as I said, the early church theologians did not take, and probably deliberately did not take, because the infinite distance between God and humanity was so important to them for the reasons discussed above. But should a fifth-century thinking taboo be binding for a person who feels post-postmodern and who thinks integrally? Do we not have the right and even the duty to continue to advance these approaches if we experience them as continuative? Theology, like any science, has always evolved—and so it must in order to remain a science. I am convinced that today we are facing another great evolutionary step—one that does away with talk of the absolute separation between God and the human, because we have recognized that Creator and creation are two sides of the same coin, two perspectives on the "tipping picture" of reality.

Theologically, the old formulation arose that in the second person of the Trinity all of creation, that is, the present, the concrete, the finite is suspended in God. If we have called the "Father" the inside of the cosmos, the "Son" would be accordingly the outside. Father and Son would be like the front and back of a coin: It is always the same coin, no matter whether we see heads or tails.

For such a view or at least for preliminary forms of it, evidence can be found even in the Bible. In the Prologue to the Gospel of John it says: "All things were made through him [the Logos/Word, i.e., Christ], and without him was not any thing made that was made" (1:3 ESV). The so-called Colossians Hymn confesses: by Christ "all things were created, in heaven and on earth, visible and invisible, whether thrones or dominions or rulers or authorities—all things were created through him and for him" (1:16 ESV). Statements like these establish the idea of the "Cosmic Christ," which is advocated, for example, by Matthew Fox or by Richard Rohr. Thus, Richard Rohr can say that the incarnation, the becoming-flesh of God or of the Logos, did not take place two thousand years ago in Palestine, but a few billion years ago: "The Christ is born the moment God decides to show himself, the moment God decides to materialize. Modern science would call that the big bang. The big bang is the birth of the Christ, 14.5 billion years ago."[9]

All that exists is from God; indeed: all that exists *is* God. At the same time, God does not merely merge into the world; our train of thought does not allow for pure pantheism. The world and all that exists is (in) God, but God is more than all that exists. This is also an idea that can be derived from the doctrine of the Trinity: The world corresponds precisely to only one of the two natures of the second person of the Trinity. According to the principle of *opera ad extra sunt indivisa*, God shows himself whole in all that is. But according to the other principle, *opera ad intra sunt divisa*, it can be assumed that God is not completely absorbed in all that is.

To all that is, after all, also belongs the imperfect, the suffering. This is the original meaning of the cross as a central Christian symbol. It stands for the fact that Christ, and in and with Christ, God himself, knows and has experienced human suffering from within, literally in his own body. This symbol, like much of the Christian tradition, has been misunderstood and misused many times. Thousands upon thousands have experienced the symbol of the cross not as a sign of God's liberating presence even in suffering, but as a sign of oppression and hostility to life. Under the sign of the cross, Central and South America were proselytized with fire and sword;

9. Rohr, "Cosmic Christ" (interview). Rohr misstates the time somewhat. According to the findings of astrophysics, the big bang occurred about 13.82 billion years ago.

under the cross, countless people—especially women—were told that life was a "vale of tears," that suffering and renunciation were the way to God and to the "real" life that could only be found in heaven, in an "afterlife" after death. To reiterate, this is a terrible misunderstanding. Rather, the cross is a sign that God, the fullness of reality, Being itself, is present always and everywhere. Not only in the "true, the good, and the beautiful," but also in suffering, in the ugly, in the bad, even in the evil. And therefore, nothing anyone may experience is in vain—no sigh, no laughter, and no cry, no breath and no heartbeat.

A God who suffers with and in his creation is, in my opinion, also the only way to endure the theodicy question. This question of why a good God can allow suffering in the world is, after all, the ultimate questioning of the theistic God himself. The assumption that God suffers in and with the world does not answer that question (it cannot be answered), but it does put the question in a different context. God is now no longer an omnipotent ruler distributing joy and suffering as he sees fit, but God is a cosmic whole that contains and includes within himself the perfect and the imperfect.

The Divine Breath

One could think that God is sufficiently described with what has been said so far. What else should there be besides the inside and the outside? Where does the third person, the Spirit, come from? It is difficult to grasp. In the Bible, several images are used: wind, the dove, tongues of fire, a power from God. Accordingly, it is noticeable that in the pictorial representations of the Trinity, the Spirit is not usually represented as a person[10]—usually it is as a dove hovering over the Father and the Son whereas in representations of the Pentecost event (the "outpouring of the Holy Spirit"), according to Acts, chapter 2, fiery tongues are placed on the heads of the disciples. The Greek and also the Hebrew word translated into English as "spirit" actually means wind or breath: breath—"moving air." According to the early church doctrine of the Trinity, the Spirit is something like God's breath that "goes out" from God. It is also considered a "person" but has a distinctly different character. It can be described as a force or energy (Greek: *dynamis*). There were hardly any disputes about the Spirit except for the so-called Filioque dispute, which, however, was essentially about the relationship between

10. A famous exception is the icon of Andrei Rublev, which on the one hand shows the visit of the three angels to Abraham and Sarah, but on the other hand is to be understood as a representation of the Trinity. Cf. Rohr, *Divine Dance*, 20–25.

Father and Son and not so much about the "essence" of the Spirit.[11] The Spirit simply seems to have been there when the relationship between Father and Son was clarified.[12]

Let us take up the image of the two-sided coin again: Father and Son are like the front and back of a coin. The Holy Spirit would then be that which is "between" Father and Son—that which separates and at the same time connects the two: in a sense the coin itself. Here is another image for this idea: The Spirit is the "bond of love" connecting Father and Son. The church father Augustine of Hippo (354–430 CE) put it this way: The Father is the lover, the Son is the beloved, the Spirit is the process of love. The medieval theologian Richard of St. Victor also understands the Father as the lover and the Son as the beloved, but for Richard the Spirit is the "co-loved." Love is not limited to blissful togetherness, but also wants and needs to relate to something third in order to be complete. If it were only about God being *good*, one "person" would suffice. If we see God as *love* (1 John 4:16), God must be two. A monad, a being completely blessed in itself alone, cannot love—it is completely independent and needs no counterpart. Whereas love as a process already presupposes two "persons," it still needs a third so that joy can also come to love. When a lover and a beloved rejoice together over a third something, then love is complete; many couples experience this when they have a child, but it can also be the shared joy of a good meal, a touching movie, or a delightful human encounter.

I find this view very charming. It expresses once more that God is relationship in himself. God does not rest in blissful seclusion in his Beyond, but is from his innermost being relationship, relatedness, love and community.

There is not much more to say about the Holy Spirit, the third person of the Trinity, at least as far as this reflection on an integral Christian understanding of God is concerned. In the context of reflection on church and community, on human being and acting in the world, one could elaborate a lot more, but this is not the place for that.

11. While Western theologians taught that the Spirit proceeds from the Father *and the Son* (Latin: *filioque*), Eastern theologians insisted that it was the Father alone who sends the Spirit. The dispute over this question was so fundamental that it resulted in the Great Schism in 1054—the division between the Western, Roman Church and the Eastern, Byzantine Church.

12. For the whole section, cf. Moltmann, *Trinity and Kingdom*.

Conclusion

What does this reflection contribute to the task set at the beginning? It is by no means my intention to present Christianity (again) as the "better" or even "true" religion by trying to place it in a post-postmodern space of consciousness. Postmodernism has thoroughly done away with such estimations, which is a good thing. It is rather about *one* possible mental approach to the indescribable and incomprehensible Godhead, even as this mental effort is only one way among others. God cannot be forced into concepts; only we humans, as thinking beings, need models of thought in order to understand reality. Contemplation, prayer, and common celebration are other, at least equally legitimate ways to approach the Godhead, the deepest Ground of Being.

This mental effort should then form a contribution for refreshing the horizon of values and meaning of our society, which is still basically shaped by Judeo-Christian ideas. For far too long, the traditional-mythical understanding of the world and God has shaped and determined the Western world with its separating, distinguishing, segregating approach: here the sinners, there the righteous; here the true doctrine, there the heresy; here the good, there the bad. Even if science and technology have long since been based on the modern worldview, even if postmodernism is making ever wider circles socially, yet it seems to me that in the dregs of culture this traditional-mythical thing still resides. Fear of change, xenophobia, and ignorance of the current environmental crisis and climate catastrophe can still cloak themselves in Christian garb and adorn themselves with the name "Christian." Criticism of religion, agnosticism, and practiced atheism within the population have so far not lessened the prevalence of the traditional-mythical vision of Christianity. This vision may have in fact grown in strength thanks to the above-mentioned level-line fallacy. My thesis is that this (mostly unconsciously) Christian-influenced sediment can only be loosened if underlying Christian doctrine changes, only if (to use language from earlier in this chapter) the frequencies of the religious background noise change and the old melodies are given new, integral harmonies.

For the Christian churches, this could bring drastic changes if they dare to blow the dust off their fundamental teachings and understand them in a new postmodern or integral way. What if the churches finally focused all their energy on how life on this earth can be sustained and can continue to flourish rather than on who is admitted to communion, to the priesthood, to the circle of "true believers," and who is excluded from it? What if as Christians we decide to no longer ask whether someone has the right qualifications and meets all the conditions to belong but instead open our doors in a truly welcoming way to all who need a roof over their heads, a warm bowl of soup, or a friendly word?

Such a change is likely to take some time and cannot be accomplished by individuals—and yet individuals must do theirs part, each in their own place, leading the way and blazing new trails. The new consciousness grows like grass roots that start from different places to form a network that will eventually change the surface of the earth.

In the depth of our existence we are one: one with all human beings and one with the whole of nonhuman creation; yes: one with God. We are not separate from everything, but deeply connected, because everything is connected to everything else. And this realization of the connectedness of everything to everything else is not "pagan" esotericism or excited New Age fuss. It is not an import from a foreign religion. Rather it comes directly from the heart of my own Christian tradition! Yet this is a Christianity that does not see itself primarily as a religion of salvation but puts the connectedness of everything with everything else at the center; this Christianity can look differently at the world, stand differently in the world, and hopefully also act differently in the world. If God is to be found in all living beings and even in all things, we must treat things and especially living beings with esteem and respect, not to say with awe. If I see God in the war refugee, in the fellow human being with a deviating political attitude, and also in the animal in the meat factory or experimental laboratory, and at the same time in myself, perhaps some behavior that has up to now seemed natural to me will become questionable. My value horizon will gain new coordinates; my conscience sharpens.

This does not yet result in concrete instructions for action—neither for accompanying people in a crisis nor for the manifold problems created by humanity that challenge us today. However, a spiritual attitude in which compassion is paired with humility and gratitude is, as mentioned at the beginning, a good starting position for finding solutions.

I am firmly convinced that Christians can dive deeper into this attitude if they better understand the core statements of their own teachings again. And I hope that they will join in this with many other people from a wide variety of religious, spiritual, and humanistic traditions. The world needs such a partnership.

Bibliography

Aslan, Reza. *God: A Human History*. New York: Random House, 2017.
Dawkins, Richard. *The God Delusion*. Boston: Houghton Mifflin, 2006.

Küstenmacher, Marion, et al. *God 9.0: Where Christianity Could Grow Spiritually.* Gröbenzell: self-published, 2016.

Moltmann, Jürgen. *The Trinity and the Kingdom: The Doctrine of God.* Translated by Margaret Kohl. San Francisco: Harper & Row, 1981.

Shadyak, Tom, dir. *Bruce Almighty.* Written by Steve Koren et al. Starring Jim Carrey et al. Universal Pictures and Spyglass Entertainment present a Shdy Acres Pit Bull production. 2003. Streaming on Netflix.com/.

Smith, Paul R. *Integral Christianity: The Spirit's Call to Evolve.* Saint Paul, MN: Paragon House, 2011.

———. *Is Your God Big Enough? Close Enough? You Enough? Jesus and the Three Faces of God.* Saint Paul, MN: Paragon House, 2017.

Rohr, Richard. "Cosmic Christ." Interview on *The Catholic Corner* (Youtube channel), posted January 19, 2011. https://www.youtube.com/watch?v=4LYQQO5uFtA/.

———. *The Divine Dance: The Trinity and Your Transformation.* New Kensington, PA: Whitaker House, 2016.

Soelle, Dorothee. *Atheistisch an Gott glauben: Beiträge zur Theologie.* Olten, Switzerland: Walter, 1968.

8

Toward the Further Evolution
of Spirituality

STEVE MCINTOSH

Some Context for this Essay

As I'm sure we all agree, as of this writing we face a planetary emergency. Mitigating global warming and working to prevent a climate catastrophe is therefore the duty of all responsible writers and thinkers. And over the last years my work has been primarily focused on overcoming the political problems in the United States that are stymieing meaningful action on climate change. However, as explained in detail in my book on developmental politics,[1] the problems of the Western world are spiritual as well as political, and there is significant overlap between these seemingly divergent fields. In fact, I feel strongly that the political evolution we need is ultimately tied to our spiritual evolution.

While spiritual evolution unfolds in many ways and advances along numerous lines, I believe the theological line of development is more important than most people realize. Practically all forms of spiritual experience and spiritual practice are linked with spiritual teachings of some kind. And all spiritual teachings, no matter how transconceptual they may aspire to be, are nevertheless underpinned by some form of theology. Working to evolve our philosophical theology will therefore redound to the evolution of our spiritual experiences and practices, which will ultimately contribute to the cultural evolution we need to overcome our planetary emergency.

My contribution to this anthology will therefore focus on "the further evolution of spirituality," which happens to be the title of chapter 7 of my 2015 book *The Presence of the Infinite: The Spiritual Experience of Beauty,*

1. McIntosh, *Developmental Politics.*

195

Truth, and Goodness. What follows is thus an adapted version of this chapter. Although the text stands fairly well on its own, before turning to its specific text, allow me to briefly summarize the arguments made earlier in *The Presence of the Infinite.*

In this book I argue that there are three broad categories of spirituality in the developed world, with a fourth category now beginning to emerge. I label these three existing categories (1) traditional religious spirituality, (2) secular spirituality, and (3) progressive spirituality. The fourth, emerging category is labeled evolutionary spirituality. Although evolutionary spirituality builds on and includes insights from the previous three categories, it goes beyond these existing types of spirituality by recognizing the spiritual teachings of evolution.

The spiritual teachings of evolution are discerned by interpreting the discoveries of cosmological, biological, and psychosocial science through the lens of integral philosophy. As I argue, these teachings reveal certain *necessary truths* which we do well to account for at the integral level of theological understanding (also known as the "evolutionary" or "postpostmodern" level). The necessary truths revealed by the spiritual teachings of evolution include a spiritually real evolving soul, a relatively free human will, a spiritually real finite universe, and the necessity of recognizing ultimate reality's self-awareness.

Due to space limitations I cannot recount my arguments for why these spiritual truths are indeed necessary in light of the spiritual teachings of evolution. And I acknowledge that some of the sophisticated readers of this anthology may deny or dispute these purported truths. But perhaps readers who are skeptical of ideas such as the self-awareness of ultimate reality may temporarily bracket their objections in order to consider my thinking in chapter 7, if only for the sake of argument.

Relating these necessary truths to our understanding of spiritual experience, I argue in chapter 6 of the book that a close examination of the historical world body of spiritual teachings, practices, and experiences reveals two broad areas, which I identify as "nondual" and "theistic" forms of spirituality. These two broad areas are like "attractor basins" of spiritual experience. And at the heart of each is an encounter with ultimate reality. Within nondual spirituality this encounter with ultimacy is known as the unitive experience, or *satori.* The unitive experience is most often described as total oneness or sublime emptiness. By contrast, within theistic forms of spirituality ultimacy is most frequently experienced as the *love of God.* Unlike nondual experiences of ultimacy, wherein a person feels absorbed in oneness, God-centered experiences of ultimacy are irreducibly relational— a person feels known and loved by the source of reality.

I argue further in *The Presence of the Infinite* that these two broad areas of spiritual teachings, practice, and experience are complementary, and their relationship is best understood as an interdependent polarity. An exploration of how the two poles of this interdependent polarity can serve to "true each other up" is the subject of chapter 7. This chapter focuses on the potential for a synthesis of nondual and theistic spirituality, which evolutionary spirituality is attempting to achieve.

In the present essay, an adaptation of chapter 7 of *The Presence of the Infinite* for this anthology, we consider the evolutionary implications of the interdependent polarity of nonduality and theism. These interdependent forms of spiritual experience, spiritual practice, and spiritual teachings can be found in every major world religion and in contemporary forms of progressive spirituality as well. And if it is true that this polarity is permanently recurring, and that both of these great spiritual traditions are ultimately interdependent, then working appropriately with this polar system can provide the key to our further spiritual evolution. That is, interdependent value polarities act as engines of evolution by serving as "wombs of synthesis," and by providing the fertile ground of tension from which new forms of emergence often spring.

Our focus here will therefore be on the potential for a new level of integration between nondual and theistic truth teachings and practices. First we consider the importance of concepts of ultimate reality and why all forms of spirituality inevitably rely on such conceptions. Then we consider previous attempts by both nondualist and theistic authors to fashion a working synthesis of these two fundamental spiritual poles. Next we examine the idea that the practice of each of these poles in its fullness ultimately requires reference to its opposing pole, leading to a consideration of the cultural conditions that will be required to foster the emergence of such a transcendent synthesis. The chapter concludes with a brief exploration of the more developed understanding of ultimate reality beginning to appear through the emergence of evolutionary spirituality.

In Search of an Evolutionary Synthesis of Nondual and Theistic Truth

Evolutionary spirituality's synthetic ambitions necessarily focus on the teachings of truth about ultimate reality found at the heart of these contrasting forms of spirituality. These respective notions of ultimacy transcend mere belief or idle cosmological speculation in the way they are each grounded in direct spiritual experience of either undifferentiated unity or the love of God.

Some nondualists may object to this focus on alternative truth teachings about ultimate reality by contending that such a framing is biased toward theism from its very start. Potential objectors may claim that nondual spirituality is concerned much more with practice than with concepts of ultimate reality. And I agree that it would be a mistake to try to interpret one form of spirituality by using the concepts and symbols of a completely different or competing form. However, despite all claims to the contrary, progressive nondualism clearly employs concepts of ultimate reality in the course of its work in the world. Indeed, nondual spirituality teaches that the realization of unqualified oneness or formless emptiness is the goal of enlightenment and thus the ultimate reason for the practices it recommends.

Even practitioners who evince little interest in conceptual teachings are nevertheless relying on such teachings by participating in the spiritual agreement structures that serve as the foundation of their practices. Stated differently, every significant form of spirituality uses its understanding of the truth about ultimate reality as the cornerstone of its worldview. And in the same way that one can use the foundations of a building without giving much thought to its structure or function, practitioners of progressive spirituality may be similarly unaware of how every spiritual path inevitably uses a specific set of truth teachings as its indispensable foundation.

In fact, at the center of practically every spiritual teaching is a concept or symbol of what is ultimately real. Ideas and ideals about ultimate reality thus serve as the source, or headwaters, for the watershed of values a given form of spirituality brings to society. Consider these examples: Thinking that ultimate reality is a stern judge may lead to both social order and oppression. Thinking that ultimate reality is merely physical energy and matter may lead to both scientific progress and nihilism. Thinking that ultimate reality is a formless void may lead to both peaceful equanimity and ambivalence toward progress. And approaching ultimate reality through a sophisticated conception that integrates absolute unified oneness with an unconditionally loving Creator may lead to both increasing social solidarity and a hunger for further spiritual evolution.

It is important to reiterate that teachings of spiritual truth and spiritual experience are tied together. So the evolution of spiritual teachings results in the evolution of our ability to experience spirit, which in turn expands our hold on spiritual truth. And as I am arguing, teachings of spiritual truth are almost always bound up with concepts of ultimate reality. So even as we discount the spiritual value of mere concepts, we must also recognize that it is through such concepts that the spiritual value of truth itself enters into our minds and thus into our work in the world. Therefore, because concepts of ultimate reality are central to every form of spirituality, the task of further evolving our spirituality inevitably entails the further development of our concepts of ultimacy.

Simply put, the goodness of any form of spirituality (in terms of its service value and leadership potential) goes hand in hand with the quality of its truth teachings regarding the nature of spirit. It is thus my contention that the spiritual leadership our society needs can be found through the re-alization of the enlarged understanding of ultimate reality that will emerge from a synthesis of nondual and theistic truth teachings.

Previous Moves toward Synthesis

We can identify a number of notable spiritual teachers who have previously explored such a potential synthesis. As early as the twelfth century the Hin-du sage Ramanuja taught a qualified version of nondualism, which was es-sentially panentheistic. Ramanuja, however, effectively rejected Shankara's prior teachings of the absolute undifferentiated oneness of ultimate reality. And although Ramanuja's teachings garnered a large following, his conflicts with the followers of Shankara were never resolved, and he failed to produce an agreeable synthesis that could unite the opposing schools of Hinduism.

More recent attempts to fashion a synthesis of theistic and nondual truth teachings within Hinduism can be seen in the work of Sri Aurobindo, who taught a sophisticated form of nondual panentheism. Yet, like Ra-manuja's before him, Aurobindo's teachings were rejected by the Advaitan followers of Shankara, as exemplified by Ramana Maharshi's repudiation of Aurobindo's evolutionary premises.[2]

Similarly, within Buddhism many of Thich Nhat Hanh's teachings can be recognized as partially synthetic in character, especially his teaching on free will. And his promotion of "Engaged Buddhism" has many affinities with evolutionary spirituality's focus on perfecting the universe through evolution. But he too has been criticized from within his own tradition for trying to smuggle non-Buddhist notions of a human soul into Buddhism.[3] But regardless of such criticisms, Thich Nhat Hanh's sophisticated spiritual teachings are aligned with the synthetic ambitions of evolutionary spiritual-ity, and he must thus be recognized as an important ally in this project.

Also starting from the nondual side of the polarity but moving toward a more synthetic position is philosopher Ken Wilber's recent writing about

2. See Godman, *Power*.
3. See Dodge, "Thich Nhat Hanh's Imaginary Soul."

the "three faces of spirit."[4] Through this teaching, Wilber has tried to better integrate theistic notions of God into his nondual conception of ultimate reality by incorporating the devotional practices of Bhakti yoga. According to Wilber, a truly integral spiritual practice should include the recognition of a "second-person" aspect of spirit that can result in an authentic "I-thou" relation between humans and spiritual reality. Wilber's recent efforts to more fully acknowledge and include theistic conceptions of ultimacy within his work have been welcomed by integral theists, and I too applaud this addition to his position. His teaching about spirit's three faces contributes to evolutionary spirituality's attempts to integrate and synthesize nondual and theistic conceptions of ultimate reality.

From my perspective, however, Wilber's notion of "God in the second person" does not adequately express or connect with the spiritual experience of the personal love of the Creator that is the foundation of the theistic pole. Although his teaching about ultimate reality continues to evolve, he has not modified or corrected his long-held position that "nondual realization is the single ultimate summit of spiritual growth" and that "theistic traditions rank lower than nondual ones."[5] Therefore, because his overall writing reflects a strong preference for nonduality over theism, and because his published explorations of "the second face of spirit" have been very minimal, Wilber's teaching in this area will need further development before it constitutes an authentic synthesis.

By contrast, another relatively recent example of an attempted synthesis that starts instead from the theistic side and moves toward the nondual can be found in the writings of German theologian Hans Küng. According to Küng, the development of a synthetic "Eastern-Western understanding of God" requires that Western religions respond to "the challenge of the East" and vice versa.

Küng contends that Eastern religious-truth teachings challenge the West to demonstrate:

> More respect in the face of the Ineffable, more reverence before
> the Mystery, in brief more awe in the presence of that Absolute

4. Wilber explains his "three faces of spirit" teaching as follows: Spirit in the *first person* is defined as the "great I"; spirit in the *third person* is defined as the "great It," or existence itself; and spirit in the *second person* is defined as the "great You or Thou" and as "something-that-is-always-greater-than-me," whose main purpose is described as providing a reason for personal surrender. Discussing the appropriate response to spirit in the second person, Wilber writes: "In the face of a God who is All Love, I can have only one response: to find God in this moment, I must love until it hurts, love until infinity, love until there is no me left anywhere" (Wilber, *Integral Spirituality*, 159).

5. These quotations are from Ferrer, "Participation."

that Jews, Christians, and Muslims call the one true God. The concept of the "void" could then be adopted in a Christian sense, as an expression of the ineffability of God. . . . His essence cannot even be fully disclosed from the standpoint of *being*: God is nothing of what is. He is no being, he transcends all beings. . . . Human thought here enters a realm where all positive statements (e.g., "God is good") prove inadequate. In order to be true, they must be immediately negated ("God is not good"—in a finite, human way) so as finally to be translated into the infinite: "God is ineffably, immeasurably, infinitely good, absolute goodness."[6]

Regarding the "Western challenge to the East," Küng calls for Hindus and Buddhists to better appreciate how "the Ultimate is not something indifferent to us. . . . The Absolute can be heard and spoken to, . . . it is a mysteriously communicative and responsive *Thou*."[7] As a panentheist myself, I find Küng's attempted synthesis appealing. But although he brings the theistic and nondual poles closer together, his analysis effectively leaves the poles lying side by side in an unintegrated relationship. His attempted synthesis has accordingly failed to satisfy nondualists, as demonstrated by the critique made by Kyoto school philosopher Masao Abe, who dismissed Küng's synthetic argument as "a misunderstanding."[8]

A variety of other spiritual teachers and academic thinkers could also be recognized for their explorations of a synthetic understanding of the theistic-nondual polarity. As examples, process theologian John Cobb, Benedictine monk Bede Griffiths, and religious philosophers Ninian Smart, John Hick, Raimon Panikkar, John Robinson, and Stuart Hackett have all produced noteworthy work in this area. Overall, I think all of these attempts at synthesis are commendable, and I am not sure I can do any better. However, I hope this brief discussion of some of these previous moves toward integration provides a sufficient background for the following exploration of my own approach to a potential synthesis of theistic and nondual spirituality.

Practicing Each Pole with Reference to the Other

If, as I contend, there really is an authentic, existential, indestructible dialectical polarity not only in the overall body of the world's spiritual teachings but also in the inner landscape of human spiritual experience itself, then this fact presents a golden opportunity. As a result of the freshly emerging

6. Küng, *Christianity*, 397.

7. Küng, *Christianity*, 398.

8. See Abe's response to Küng in Ives, ed., *Divine Emptiness*, 240–41.

insights of evolutionary spirituality it is now becoming possible to bring the impending synthesis of theism and nonduality further into being. Now that we are beginning to see this polarity more clearly than ever before, we can more effectively harness the power of this evolutionary structure to deepen our realization of both poles of spiritual experience through a process that better integrates the wisdom of each pole with its opposite.

The way each pole can serve to "true up" the other can be understood by reference to Taoism's well-respected yin-yang symbol. As shown in figure 1, at the heart or center of the black side is a small circle of white, and vice versa. And to the extent this symbol illustrates a principle of all existential polarities, it can be seen as pointing to the truth that practicing either pole in its fullness ultimately requires use of the other pole.[9] In other words, in their quest to know God and do God's will, theists would do well to reckon with the truths of nonduality—the truths of formless oneness and the truths of emptiness. Likewise, in their journey toward enlightenment, nondualists would do well to let the personal love of God shine into their hearts and feel the everlasting affection of our universe's Creator. Simply put, getting to the heart of each of these essential forms of spirituality means partially embracing its opposing yet complementary pole.

Figure 1: Yin-Yang Symbol (courtesy of the author)

Prior to the emergence of evolutionary spirituality, it may have been easy to conclude that the best approach to spiritual development was to find

9. While the yin-yang symbol provides a useful illustration here, notwithstanding the perfect symmetry shown in this symbol, the nondual and theistic poles need not be literally understood as balanced equals. Nor am I suggesting that either pole represents the perfect heart or center of its opposite, as in the symbol. But the principle of interdependent mutual enactment, as illustrated by this familiar yin and the yang, is relevant nonetheless.

a tradition or spiritual path that seemed to resonate best and then practice that path in its fullness. Stated otherwise, if Buddhism was one's chosen path, then one should go as deeply into this tradition as practicable and embrace its teachings as one's own truth. However, as evolutionary spirituality has emerged, moving further away from traditionalism and revealing an enlarged understanding of spiritual experience and the nature of ultimate reality, spiritual-path exclusivism, even at the postmodern level of development, becomes less tenable.

This is not to suggest that we should approach spiritual truth cafeteria style. Indeed, such a superficial approach can be seen as a shortcoming of progressive spirituality's relativistic pluralism. Rather, what I am suggesting is that at the integral level of cultural evolution, practicing either theism or nondualism seriously and with rigor—going to the heart of one's chosen path—means acknowledging a place for the white dot within the black wave and vice versa. In other words, now that we are coming to discover this existential polarity within both spiritual experience and spiritual truth, we can no longer be satisfied with either strict nondualism or strict theism.

While we can certainly remain focused primarily on one of the poles, and while we can continue to have loyalty to our chosen path (as discussed below), insular traditionalism is no longer viable at the integral level. To contend that the most advanced truth teachings of the pole that opposes our path are simply wrong or deluded or "lower" is to remain at the traditional level. Yet to contend that the two poles are essentially the same, or to ignore the contradictions and claim that they are simply a matter of different preferences, is to remain at the level of postmodern progressive spirituality. Thus, at the integral level of development we have to reckon with this indestructible polarity in a way that engages the tension of the poles in the quest for higher levels of spiritual emergence.

However, this practice of working with both poles to further the enactment of each in our experience requires more than simply acknowledging the truth of both. It is not just a matter of seeing the importance of each pole for the other intellectually. The kind of practice now being made possible through evolutionary spirituality involves the *active use of the inherent contradiction energy*—the existential challenge—that each pole poses to the other. What this may look like in the personal life of each practitioner is explored in the subsections that follow.

Nonduality's Apophatic Character

As discussed at length *The Presence of the Infinite*,[10] the rise of progressive spirituality over the last forty years has resulted in a still-partial yet ongoing merger of Western Buddhism and Advaita Vedanta Hinduism. This means that contemporary nondualism is itself largely a synthesis of these two great Asian traditions. And this shows how one level of synthetic emergence can lead to and make possible a next and even-higher level of synthesis. In other words, we can now use the recent synthesis of Buddhism and Hinduism to move toward the integration of nonduality and theism overall. But to do this we must appreciate how this first-level synthesis of Buddhism and Hinduism follows a primarily *apophatic* path to spiritual truth. Apophatic spiritual teachings approach truth through a negation or denial of what the truth is not. This idea was elegantly expressed by Meister Eckhart, who wrote, "Only the hand that erases can write the true thing."[11]

Nonduality's apophatic theme is found in Advaita Vedanta in its famous dictum *neti neti* (not this, not that), as well as in its exaltation of Brahman "without attributes" as the ultimate reality. This theme of negation can also be clearly recognized in Buddhism's focus on emptiness and its doctrine of no-self. Both of these spiritual traditions, of course, include abundant examples of positive and affirmative teachings, but most teachers of nonduality regularly employ the technique of negation to emphasize emptiness and dispel notions that "being" is an eternal "substance." Indeed, the word *nondual* itself is thoroughly apophatic.

Nonduality's focus on negation is explained by Buddhist philosopher David Loy, who writes that in Buddhism, "Sunyata [emptiness] not only refers to the absence of a self but becomes the most fundamental 'characteristic' of reality. In function it is the category which corresponds most closely to the Vedantic concept of Brahman, serving as the standard by which the reality of phenomena is negated. . . . 'Essentially, there is only one thing . . . *not even one*.'"[12] In his attempt to reconcile Buddhism and Advaita Vedanta within an overarching and unified theology of nonduality, Loy observes that Buddhism's emphasis on no-self and Advaita's emphasis on all-self are two extremes that "in trying to eliminate duality, result in much the same description of nonduality—just as one may travel east or west around the world to arrive in the same place."[13]

10. See McIntosh, *Presence*, chapters 2, 5, and 6.

11. Meister Eckhart, quoted in Holmes, *History*, 151.

12. Quoted in Loy, *Nonduality*, 7.

13. Loy, *Nonduality*, 203.

Contemporary nondual spirituality is not a complete fusion of Western Buddhism and Advaita Vedanta Hinduism; it is only a partial amalgamation of these two paths within a progressive cultural context. But even though much of the distinctive character of these two great traditions is preserved in the current cultural agreement of nondual spirituality, the merger nevertheless shows more clearly than ever before the apophatic character of the nondual pole of spiritual experience. And as we explore below, recognition of this negating function of nondual teachings is a key to their practice within the context of theism.

Nonduality and Emptiness

To the extent that nonduality is understood in the Advaita Vedanta sense as absolute oneness, it contrasts nicely with theism by holding up a polar opposite to the idea of a distinct and transcendent Creator. In other words, in this context the two poles are presenting opposing notions of an ultimate reality. But when nonduality is understood in the Buddhist sense as emptiness, it does not always refer to an ultimate or absolute reality. According to some teachers, the truth of emptiness empties itself of all totalizing or universalizing notions of ultimacy. And some may conclude that this interpretation of emptiness undermines my arguments for the existential polarity of theism and nonduality from the start. However, I do not think this is the case. Indeed, I think the recognition of some kind of ultimate reality (even if it is conceived of more as an *ultimate process* than as an ultimate thing) is an evolutionary necessity for all forms of spirituality at the integral level of realization. The totality exists necessarily.

The spiritual experience of the infinite itself confirms the infinite's ultimacy, so my contention that the theistic and nondual poles are both fundamentally concerned with an authentic ultimate reality is not just theological speculation—spirit's ultimacy is confirmed by its very experience. Further, the idea of spirit's transcendental quality requires the recognition of ultimacy of one sort or another, and it cannot be forgotten that the concept of a transcendent ultimate is a cornerstone of panentheism in all its forms. While some Buddhist teachers of emptiness may feel obliged to deny the existence of an affirmative Absolute to be consistent with the apophatic implications of emptiness, many end up reclaiming spirit's transcendental and ultimate quality through other means. Buddhist teachers have evoked the idea of an ultimate reality through a variety of alternative concepts, including the dharmakaya, nirvana, suchness, and even emptiness itself. Indeed, Buddhism's two truths doctrine clearly includes the concept of ultimacy by recognizing relative and absolute truth.[14] And while these doctrines might be interpreted so as to avoid acknowledging ultimacy, posttraditional nondual spirituality generally has little problem with the idea of an ultimate reality.

Notwithstanding the subtleties of these doctrinal distinctions, the significance of emptiness for nonduality cannot be underestimated. So the important task of discerning how theism's teachings of a transcendent Creator and nonduality's teachings of emptiness can be synthesized, or at least better harmonized, begins with an analysis such as this: Perhaps within human nature there exists what might be called an "original side" and a "whole side." The whole side lacks self-nature; it is co-arising with all other things and beings and is thus an undifferentiated aspect of the one unified reality—it partakes of nondual oneness while remaining impermanent. On this whole side of our nature we are empty of a separate existence—our true being is "interbeing," as Thich Nhat Hanh calls it. Our whole side thus shares the same identity of no-self (or all-self) that is the essence of nonduality.

The original side, by contrast, is the seat of our *individual personality*; it is the locus of our evolving soul and the ground of our free will. Indeed, our personal originality is confirmed by our direct experience of being one of a kind. And this personal originality can also be confirmed by our friends and associates, who know there is no one else exactly like us. Further, our originality and relative freedom as agents of evolution are evident in our ability to be creative. Recognizing the original side of our nature thus allows us to affirm our authentic status as sons and daughters of a living God—real beings in our own right who can love and be loved as individuals.

There are, of course, many models of the self. And this description of the whole side and the original side of human nature is not intended as a comprehensive theory of the human self/no-self.[15] Yet even as we hold this idea loosely, we may still ask, how can both be true at the same time without rupturing the unity of truth or otherwise defying logic? I think the answer, with respect to our human nature and with respect to ultimate reality overall, is that every existential polarity is itself a shadow of some higher unity that cannot be fully realized at our current level of evolution. And realizing this truth helps us recognize all such dialectical polarities as openings for further development—systems of transcendence and engines of evolution.

These two poles of human nature—whole-side emptiness and original-side fullness—tend to serve as the ground for the respective forms of spirituality with which they are associated. One side emphasizes our lack of

14. See the discussion of the two truths doctrine in McIntosh, *Presence*, 172; see also Hans Küng's discussion in Küng, *Christianity*, 388–89.

15. See the discussion of the self and the evolving soul in chapter 6 of McIntosh, *Presence*, 174–75.

self-nature, and the other emphasizes our individual agency and creativity. While most practitioners gravitate toward one pole or the other, some hover above both without committing to either. Still others may be pulled from their native pole toward the opposite pole in the course of their development. But to use the full potential of this existential polarity as a system of development, as I contend, our practice must seek synthesis. Yet it is important to reiterate that working toward such a synthesis inevitably entails a back-and-forth operation wherein contradicting affirmations are each held to be true alternatively through a recursive process that dynamically reincludes each by turns. So in this process we cannot expect to find a final stationary position, or a place of ideational rest. Nor can any single snapshot of this moving-back-and-forth process capture it or define its ultimate truth.

Nevertheless, bringing the truths of this existential polarity to bear so as to better understand our essential spiritual nature helps show how relevant these truths can be for our personal spiritual growth. As an example, I will give a brief account of my own attempts to practice emptiness in a panentheistic context.

Nondualism for Theists

I have come a long way in my relationship to nondual spirituality. When I first encountered it forty years ago, I didn't really understand it. Later, as I became more familiar with it, I rejected it and was even slightly bothered by it. But now I am coming to accept it as "true but partial," which has helped me appreciate how it is essential for a deeper realization of my own panentheistic spiritual path. And recently, through the practice of evolutionary spirituality, I have been working with it in a way that surpasses my previous approach of simply holding it in my mind as an incongruent truth I must nevertheless accept. This "truth practice" involves going beyond tentative philosophical reconciliation by using the truth of nonduality to actually advance my knowledge and experience of God.

In this practice, the apophatic nature of nonduality serves as a humbling critique of all my beliefs, reminding me never to be satisfied with the spiritual knowledge I have attained. The deep truths of nonduality help me appreciate how almost all teachings of spiritual truth, no matter how dazzling, are finite constructs that are merely rungs on a ladder, which I will eventually step over in my ascent. Stated differently, nondual spiritual truth helps chasten theistic spiritual truth by relentlessly pointing to the finite content of almost all positive spiritual propositions. Nonduality constantly reminds me that my human ego-self, my mind, and the phenomenal universe are only partially real. This finite realm of time is like a womb wherein I am still unborn—my spiritual reality is far from complete. My experience of this finite life is thus like a shell in which the "chick" of my soul is developing. But once the chick is hatched, the shell will be of little use.

By teaching me to hold my spiritual convictions lightly and not take myself too seriously, nondual truth helps "rinse the glass" of my mind, washing away any constructs and concepts that have lost their dynamism or vitality. These attempts to include the apophatic truths of nonduality in my understanding of what is spiritually real have helped me to continually start fresh with God, approaching our Creator with a "beginner's mind" free of expectations or preconceptions.

Even at the evolutionary level, theistic spirituality is in constant need of restraint to prevent the house of conceptual cards it often builds from distracting our attention from the unmediated experience of the infinite. This restraining is at least one way the integration of nonduality's apophatic teachings can help all those who seek to know God by continuously reminding us to remain circumspect in the face of the aspects of ultimate reality that will always remain an unknowable mystery to humans.

Conversely, not only does the truth of nonduality chasten and restrain my understanding of God, but it also expands and enriches my conception of our Creator's personal qualities. How the nondual pole helps to enact and vivify the theistic pole can be seen in nondual depictions of ultimate reality as essentially formless or empty. By fully expressing the completely formless character of the nondual pole, the teaching of emptiness serves to illuminate the full expression of the opposing theistic pole. In other words, when the nondual pole is understood in its extreme sense as the void, or as Absolute Nothingness (as Kitaro Nishida called it), the thoroughgoing absence behind this conception simultaneously provides a kind of inverse teaching that reveals God as an unconditionally loving parent, which (as discussed below) represents the contrasting expression of the theistic pole in its fullness. Simply put, the extremity of each pole helps enact the fullness of its opposing pole by symmetrical comparison.

By contrast, some teachers, perhaps sensing the partiality of either pole by itself, have moved toward the middle in their conception of ultimate reality in an effort to avoid either Absolute Nothingness on one side or a personal God on the other. This can be seen for example in nondual depictions of sunyata as interbeing, or in nominally theistic depictions of God as an impersonal creative force or as merely a "self-organizing tendency." While these attempts to partially depolarize ultimate reality are not all wrong, they do tend to mute the expression of each pole in its abundance. However, when I allow myself to embrace the depths of the nondual teaching that ultimate reality is void-like and thus feel the sinking sense of cosmic vertigo this produces, then I am better able to feel the contrasting fullness of God's everlasting love for me as an individual, which is nonduality's complementary antipode.

Beyond this subjective level of truth practice, integrating nonduality into my panentheistic path has also borne fruit at the intersubjective, or cultural, level. Reckoning with the teachings of nonduality has led to a deeper affinity with my friends and associates who are nondualists. By working with the theistic and nondual polarity—by attempting to discern the black dot in the white wave—I have become more curious about and less resistant to teachings that seem to negate my most closely held convictions. Again, this is not relativism; I am not giving up on God or concluding that God is essentially nondual. But I am finding a deeper level of sympathy for my fellow religionists—even for those who think my convictions are deluded.

The Love of God for Nondualists

Although I do not identify myself as a Christian, in my experience the high-water mark of theism remains the life and teachings of Jesus of Nazareth. Jesus's teaching even transcends Christianity in the way it speaks of eternal truths that are relevant for every spiritual practitioner. And at the heart of Jesus's message was the revelation of our Creator's unconditional parental affection for each creature. Jesus taught that God's "fatherly" love for each of us enacts a universal family—the "brotherhood of man"—that naturally follows from the fact that we each share the same universal Father/Mother. This is what makes Jesus's teachings so deeply moral. Ultimate reality's parental love creates both the reason and the duty to love one another, to "love our neighbor as our self." However, the teaching that the source of the universe cares about us as persons—that God knows us and loves us as individuals—discloses an aspect of ultimate reality that is undeveloped in nondualism. And this is the *goodness* of the Absolute—not just its excellence or even perfection, but its *caring morality*, which is really the highest kind of goodness. Nondualists may point to compassion as a cornerstone of their creed, but this essentially *personal quality* of compassion cannot find its source in an ultimate reality that is understood either as lacking personal qualities or as being completely *unqualified.*

For nondualists, acknowledging that, somehow, the universe is loving does not mean becoming Christian or even theistic. Although like Buddhism and Hinduism, Christianity is a beautiful religion for the most part, one need not accept its teachings as a whole to benefit from the practice of feeling God's love. Even though I am not a Christian, I have been greatly inspired by Jesus, so I know from my own experience that one can receive the spiritual benefits of Jesus's message without assenting to the doctrines of Christianity.

Nevertheless, for those committed to a nondual path, the practice of experiencing the love that comes from the creative Source of the universe involves allowing for the truth that there is more to ultimate reality than a formless void or an impersonal oneness. Admittedly, coming to terms with the goodness, morality, and loving-kindness of ultimate reality may require reflection and contemplation on the part of nondualists, and reconciling this perfect love with the imperfection, suffering, and evil that remains in the finite universe is inevitably part of this task. But within the dialectical practices of evolutionary spirituality, integrating opposing forms of spiritual truth becomes desirable, achievable, and inevitable.

Regarding the existence of suffering and evil in a "universe that cares," there have been numerous philosophical attempts to reconcile this seeming contradiction, with my favorite being that the potential for evil is the shadow of free will. But I think the best response to this concern is more spiritual than philosophical. And this spiritual response is found in the faith conviction that *all things ultimately work together for good*. This proposition of faith, however, can only be completely true if there is an afterlife in which innocent suffering can be redeemed. Indeed, from this perspective our earthly suffering might be seen as the inventory of our comparative joy in the future. Perhaps the greatest affliction a person could suffer would be to go through life without ever having been afflicted. Yet this is not meant to imply that evil or suffering should be tolerated; the ongoing presence of these horrors creates an urgent obligation to work for a better world. Nevertheless, faith in ultimate reality's essential goodness helps keep the pathologies of our world in perspective.

On the subjective level, the practice of receiving the love of God also involves loving our Creator in return. This practice may include acknowledging God's presence, being thankful, or even worshiping God in a posttraditional manner. In the same way that "spirit experiences us as we experience spirit," the more we love God the more we establish the channels of faith through which we can increasingly experience God's love for us. As Blaise Pascal wrote, "Human things must be known to be loved, but Divine things must be loved to be known."[16]

Further, on the intersubjective or cultural level, the practice of experiencing the love of God in a nondual context may also result in greater

16. Blaise Pascal, quoted in: *The University Record*, 112.

sympathy for the theistic foundations of Western civilization. And this sympathy may in turn help lessen some of the antimodernist and antitraditional sentiments that tie many progressive spiritual practitioners to the postmodern level of cultural evolution.

However, given my limited experience with nonduality, it is undoubtedly best that the further explication of this practice of experiencing the love of God in the context of a nondual spiritual path be left to those already committed to nondualism. I thus invite my nondualist sisters and brothers to give this a try and then share their experience with the rest of us. One need not accept any specific theological beliefs to experience this love. But actively denying our Creator's existence may tend to fog the glass through which such love shines.

The Enduring Value of Loyalty

Even so, it is important to add that the evolutionary practice of attempting to integrate these opposing poles of spiritual experience does not require us to become uprooted from either the culture or the teachings of the spirituality we identify with most closely. In the process of attempting to synthesize the poles, we must avoid the mistake of simply substituting one pole for the other.

An example of this can be seen on the theistic side where a number of progressive Christian teachers have recently become strong advocates of nondual spirituality, partially forsaking the core teachings of their own tradition in the process. Many of these nondual Christians contend that "Jesus was a nondual teacher." While we can certainly identify a few Christian mystics who were in fact nondual teachers, such as Meister Eckhart, Jesus's emphasis on the love of God and the growth of the soul clearly contradicts many nondual doctrines. In the Bible Jesus does occasionally refer to truths that can be interpreted as nondual. And his teachings as I understand them instruct us to follow the truth wherever it may lead, even into the truths of nonduality. But when nondual Christian teachers ignore the contradictions and the dialectical tension by claiming that one pole is simply the other, they misunderstand both theism and nonduality.

This observation begins to illustrate the point, discussed further in the next section, that we cannot effectively synthesize or integrate these existential poles by simply abandoning one of them. "Suicide is no way of cementing a relationship." Therefore, on the one hand, we must avoid overidentifying with a given form of spirituality to the exclusion of all others because this inevitably limits our growth and results in unnecessary conflict. But on the other hand, a certain amount of loyalty and identity must be invested in our chosen spiritual path if we are to receive its full benefits. That is, if we expect our spirituality to benefit us, we have to be willing to benefit it by advancing its teachings and practices in a way that contributes to our larger pluralistic spiritual culture.

With the rise of evolutionary spirituality, however, we can now begin to have it both ways. We can continue to identify ourselves (albeit somewhat loosely) as Buddhists or Christians or as followers of almost any kind of spirituality, while at the same time avoiding both absolutism and relativism in our quest for ever-deeper experiences of spirit.

Gardening for Synthetic Emergence

The spiritual teachings of evolution make clear that historically significant events of evolutionary emergence cannot be engineered or otherwise produced formulaically by human efforts alone. The work of promoting emergence is better compared to gardening than to building. According to this understanding of emergence, the best way to nurture the rise of a more evolved form of spirituality is to work to create conditions that will foster the emergence of an authentic synthesis, and then trust that a new form of life will eventually sprout up. Based on what we have discussed, I believe these prerequisite conditions for synthetic emergence include the following five elements of cultural understanding or agreement:

1. A sophisticated and respectful appreciation of the nondual pole of spiritual experience and the forms of spirituality that hold nonduality to be the ultimate reality.

2. A renewed appreciation of the panentheistic forms of spirituality that have brought forward a vision of a loving Creator that overcomes the limitations of traditional theistic religion.

3. A clearer collective recognition of the dialectical polarity between the nondual and theistic poles and how these essential modes of spiritual experience simultaneously conflict with and also complement each other.

4. A willingness to use the evolutionary method of dialectical epistemology (which Wilber calls "vision-logic") to perform the ongoing back-and-forth work of debate and reconciliation—the inevitable wrestling with tensions and contradictions through which a deeper understanding may appear.

5. A resolute intention to integrate nonduality's insights regarding the apophatic nature of the Absolute, theism's contrasting insights regarding the personal nature of the Absolute, science's stupendous discoveries of the empirical facts of evolution, and the confirming evidence of direct spiritual experience itself.

Although progressive spiritual culture may still be far from realizing these elements of cultural understanding, the work of developing these agreements involves teaching and practicing the exciting new truths of evolutionary spirituality. And this work can be done on many fronts and in many contexts.

Of course, the natural tendency is to approach this gardening for synthesis at a superficial level by declaring that it is just a matter of both/and thinking. We may be tempted to conclude that theism and nonduality are simply different sides of the same coin and that the contradictions they seem to present stem from the limits of finite human comprehension—that they are both true despite the disagreements and that's that. But according to the method of dialectical epistemology, such a conclusion would amount to a "compromise fallacy."[17] In other words, ignoring the conflicts or settling for the acceptance of paradox as a final answer would only provide a kind of false rest.

Rather than trying to make a polite pluralistic peace between these contrasting poles, the practice of evolutionary spirituality involves seeing how the dialectical currents of history are now bringing back the truth of our loving Creator—but bringing it back at a higher level that transcends the relatively immature and mythic conceptions of God found in traditional forms of spirituality.

Those privileged to participate in the birth of evolutionary spirituality can see that we live in a time of movement not equipoise. Emergence is on the march, and we do well not to try to quash this dynamic movement of history by clinging to progressive spirituality's habit of superficially declaring both/and in the face of most conflicts. Therefore, working toward such a higher synthesis involves a partial *negation of the negation*; one that reaffirms the timeless truths now being rediscovered by evolutionary spirituality, despite the challenges such truths imply.

However, nondualists need not feel threatened by such a renewed affirmation of the theistic pole. Nondualists who have an integral or

17. See McIntosh, *Presence*, 68, quoting Charles Johnston: "A compromise fallacy confuses integration with some additive middle ground. Rather than revealing the rich spectrum of colors that lies beyond black and white, they lead us to conclude that reality simply shows varying shades of grey."

evolutionary perspective understand how existential polarities mutually
enact one another, even if by dialectical turns. So they can be assured that
the reaffirmation of the theistic pole in the context of the emergence of evolutionary spirituality will eventually lead to an even deeper realization of the
nondual pole of spiritual experience.

Further, as affirmed by the first element of cultural understanding
listed above, evolutionary spirituality validates and confirms that nonduality is an authentic and important mode of spiritual experience. Therefore,
the full potential of evolutionary spirituality can be realized only through an
approach that includes practices leading to nondual experience—practices
that produce "a change in the very texture of life itself."[18]

The flowering of nondual spirituality within postmodern progressive
culture is an important historical development, without which the emergence of evolutionary spirituality would not be possible. And the fulfillment
of evolutionary spirituality's promise of more inclusive spiritual leadership
for our society requires that the continuously developing gifts of nondual
spirituality be honored and included within evolutionary spirituality's
emerging cultural agreement.

Glimmers of Integration

As I have argued, the experiential polarity I am labeling "nonduality and
theism" is an indelible feature of the fabric of our finite reality that will never
be completely resolved or rendered into a static thesis or a tidy belief system.
Although both nondual and theistic spirituality will inevitably be transfigured in the course of future history, the existential polarity from which their
differences arise is a permanent feature of human spiritual experience.

Progress, however, is still possible. Humanity's understanding of what
is ultimately real has clearly evolved over the course of our history. And
this evolutionary progress has been possible because humans can make authentic contact with ultimate reality. Because that which is ultimate is both
the center and circumference of reality, and because it lives within us as the
foundational essence of who we really are, we can experience it directly. Our
deepest experiences of spirit thus provide limited yet nevertheless veridical
testimony to the nature of the Absolute. However, while most spiritual paths
claim to provide authentic access to ultimate reality, their descriptions of
the nature of the Absolute vary widely. So is this simply a matter of the
proverbial blind men feeling different parts of the elephant? Of course. But

18. Blackstone et al., "Dialogues on Nonduality."

now, through the insights of evolutionary spirituality we are beginning to get a clearer picture of the elephant as a whole.

We can now glimpse the Absolute with new clarity because (1) it is only recently that we have gained access to the wisdom teachings of the ages within a global context; (2) it is only recently that we have come to understand spiritual experience in the context of integral philosophy; and (3) it is only recently that we have had access to the dialectical epistemology made available by the integral perspective. The use of this dialectical way of knowing can now help us grow beyond the unintegrated and unchallenged plethora of spiritual teachings that constitute progressive spirituality's "anything goes" pluralism. In other words, evolutionary spirituality reveals a clearer picture of ultimate reality because it can better evaluate diverse spiritual teachings and can thus perceive such teachings more accurately and integrate them more effectively.

Yet at the same time, most of the challenges to achieving a higher level of integration remain. As examples, is it possible to hold the teachings of no-self and emptiness as ultimately true in the face of our experience of free will and creative progress? Is it possible to work toward the evolutionary perfection of self, culture, and nature in the context of the teachings that desire is the cause of suffering? Is it possible to maintain the conviction of undifferentiated oneness in the light of a transcendent and immanent loving Creator? Even though our emerging understanding of the dialectical nature of humanity's experience of ultimate reality helps us transcend the limitations of progressive spirituality, cognitive dissonance remains. But at the very least, coming to know the substance of these differences is part of the spiritual education required for practitioners of evolutionary spirituality.

However, even as we acknowledge the persistence of these challenges, by deepening the practice of each pole by engaging its opposite as described above, we might be able to dimly discern the future state of development of this synthesis.

Speculating on a Future Synthesis

Although the spiritual experiences imparted by nondualism and theism both provide partial access to ultimate reality, my intuition tells me that this reality is more than a polarity. While it may manifest as a polarity in the finite realm of time, it must be more than this. Yet as we have seen, to conceive of it as simply oneness is to effectively side with one of the poles (confusing oneness with wholeness). But conceiving of it alternatively as simply twoness is not satisfactory either. So rather than falling back on earlier arguments from both sides that contend one pole is ultimate and the other penultimate, or rather than settling for a conception of a polar ultimate reality, we might entertain the notion that the Absolute is not merely dipolar, but is actually *tripolar*. In contrast to the familiar yin-yang polarity shown in figure 1, this triune relationship is suggested by figure 2, the "diagram of the supreme ultimate" of Lai Zhide, who introduced the original yin-yang symbol into Chinese philosophy in the sixteenth century.[19]

Figure 2 shows how two opposing poles can enact a third central element through their integration. This symbol thus depicts a unified trinity of three interactive elements. Although speculative, this analysis suggests that perhaps ultimate reality has a triune structure or essence consisting of a loving Creator, an unqualified Absolute, and a third binding element that is at once both and neither. Although this idea is largely beyond experience and is merely a conceptual theological conjecture, it is bolstered by both reason and faith.

Figure 2: The Taijitu of Lai Zhide: "Diagram of the Supreme Ultimate" (Wikipedia, s.v. "Lai Zhide" [https://en.wikipedia.org/wiki/Lai_Zhide#/media/File:Taijitu_Lai_Zhide.png/])

This evolutionary theological hypothesis—that ultimate reality is a *tri-unity*, or "the three, that are two, that are one"—could at least help us avoid the inelegant notion of plural ultimates. While the idea of a trinity may sound too Christian for some, we can observe that triadic concepts of deity can be found in many ancient religions from both the East and West. And we should also not ignore the fact that the three primary values—the beautiful, the true, and the good—form a unified triadic system in themselves, which certainly suggests their connection to some kind of triune

19. See Wikipedia, s.v. "Lai Zhide."

source within the nature of the ultimate. In fact, even the dialectical process of evolution itself demonstrates a kind of three-ness in the way it overcomes polarity in its ongoing advance into the new.

While the synthetic cultural progress promised by evolutionary spirituality will certainly require more than mere theological speculation about the trinity of divinity, it seems to me that further contemplation of the nature of ultimate reality will be a necessary part of this historical process. And as we come to increasingly understand that in the human experience of spirit we are literally encountering the presence of the infinite in the finite, we may begin to reinterpret and even play with traditional symbols, as shown in the fractal depiction of the yin-yang symbol illustrated by figure 3.

Figure 3: Fractal Yin-Yang Symbol

This synthetic process of emergence will of course take time, like all forms of evolution. Indeed, it is only just now that we are beginning to see the polarity of nondual and theistic spiritual experience with the requisite clarity needed to recognize this polarity's potential to give rise to a higher synthesis. So here at the inception of this emergence we cannot expect a mature expression of the synthesis that we are only beginning to sense may actually be possible.

Moreover, and notwithstanding the above, I trust it is clear that I am not capable of framing an evolutionary synthesis of nonduality and theism by myself. Faced with the awesome spiritual truth of these polar veils of ultimate reality, I am like a candle trying to illuminate the sun. Further, my loyalties to a panentheistic vision of a loving Creator, together with my limited experience of the nondual pole, render me unable to frame a satisfactory or otherwise workable synthesis. So the best I can do is suggest the prerequisites for emergence as set out above and then join with other evolutionaries in the work of helping to bring about these cultural conditions.

The achievement of an authentic evolutionary synthesis of nonduality and theism will require many religionists and spiritual practitioners working on it over decades, so that the glacial polish that occurs as ideas move through history can take place.

By way of conclusion, I can affirm that in its essence, the evolutionary impulse is the desire for the transcendent itself. This impulse includes a kind of perfection hunger whose satisfaction seeks an ultimate reality. Satisfying this hunger involves cultivating a life of spiritual experience—a life of beauty, truth, and goodness—which inevitably involves the ongoing work of creating relative degrees of perfection within our midst.

Bibliography

Blackstone, Judith, et al. "Dialogues on Nonduality." *Inner Explorations* (website). http://www.innerexplorations.com/ewtext/dialogue.htm/.

Dodge, Shyam. "Thich Nhat Hanh's Imaginary Soul." http://speculativenonbuddhism.com/2012/10/12/thich-nhat-hanhs-imaginary-soul/.

Ferrer, Jorge N. "Participation, Metaphysics, and Enlightenment: Reflections on Ken Wilber's Recent Work." In *Transpersonal Psychology Review* 14.2 (2011) 3–24.

Godman, David. *The Power of Presence: Part One.* Lithia Springs, GA: New Leaf, 2000.

Holmes, Urban T., III. *A History of Christian Spirituality: An Analytical Introduction.* La Vergne, TN: Church Publishing, 2002.

Ives, Christopher, ed. *Divine Emptiness and Historical Fullness.* Harrisburg, PA: Trinity, 1995.

Küng, Hans, et al. *Christianity and World Religions.* Translated by Peter Heinegg. Garden City, NY: Doubleday, 1986.

Loy, David. *Nonduality: A Study in Comparative Philosophy.* 1988. Reprint, Atlantic Highlands, NJ: Humanities, 1997.

McIntosh, Steve. *Developmental Politics: How America Can Grow into a Better Version of Itself.* Saint Paul, MN: Paragon House, 2020.

———. *The Presence of the Infinite: The Spiritual Experience of Beauty, Truth, and Goodness.* Wheaton, IL: Quest, 2015.

The University Record, vol. 1. Chicago: University of Chicago Press, 1897.

Wikipedia, s.v. "Lai Zhide." http://en.wikipedia.org/wiki/Lai_Zhide.

Wilber, Ken. *Integral Spirituality: A Startling New Role for Religion in the Modern and Postmodern World.* Boston: Shambhala, 2007.

9

The One and the Many in Spirituality and Religion

A Participatory Vision

Jorge N. Ferrer

The problem of the One and the Many—or universalism and pluralism—
is not only the focus of this anthology but has also plagued philosophical
and religious thinking for centuries.[1] In this chapter, I focus on a particular
iteration of the problem: the relationship between unity and multiplicity
in contemporary spirituality and religion.[2] Critical questions about this
relationship include these: Is there an underlying unity behind the multiplicity of religious experiences, teachings, world views, and ultimates? Or
should one rather understand such a plurality of creative spiritual expressions without reference to any essential unity? Are religions stemming from
a primordial unity, heading toward a final unification, both, or neither? Is

1. E.g., Bracken, *One in the Many*; Rushdooney, *One and the Many*; Schuon,
Transcendent.

2. For a participatory understanding of the term *spirituality*, see Ferrer, *Revisioning*.
As for "religion," I deliberately offer no definition of this term in this chapter. I take
the position that although definitions can be helpful as springboards for open-ended
inquiry—when offered in a heuristic, provisional, and culturally situated fashion—they
can also blind researchers and scholars to crucial elements of the studied phenomenon.
This is especially so with a phenomenon as diverse and multifaceted as religion. A major
problem is that any definition of religion will inevitably emphasize some religious phenomena, marginalizing one or another religious tradition, feature, or element—or, even
worse, leaving them out. Thus, instead of offering an a priori definition of such a protean
concept, I opt to allow its meaning to gradually emerge in the text's discussion. For key
discussions of the problems inherent in generic, universal, and essentialist definitions of
religion, see W. C. Smith, *Meaning and the End*; J. Z. Smith, *Imagining Religion*; Asad,
Genealogies; McCutcheon, *Manufacturing*; and King, "*Philosophia perennis*."

it legitimate to privilege the One over the Many or the Many over the One in religious thinking? Or should one rather contemplate the relationship between the One and the Many in more dialectical, complementary, and creative ways? And so forth.

Before I offer some tentative responses to these questions, the first part of this chapter introduces a participatory perspective of human spirituality from which such answers are derived. In the second part, I uncover the spiritual narcissism characteristic of the prevalent historical approach to religious diversity, as well as briefly discuss the shortcomings of the main forms of religious pluralism that have been proposed as its antidote. In the third part, I introduce a participatory approach to religious pluralism, showing how it can provide a fresh appreciation of religious diversity that avoids the dogmatism and competitiveness involved in privileging any particular tradition over the rest without falling into culturallinguistic or naturalistic reductionisms. The Conclusion outlines a more relaxed spiritual universalism that dialectically embraces both the One and the Many.

An Outline of Participatory Spirituality

The participatory approach holds that human spirituality essentially emerges from human cocreative participation in an undetermined mystery or generative power of life, the cosmos, or reality.[3] More specifically, I argue that spiritual participatory events can engage the entire range of human epistemic faculties (e.g., rational, imaginal, somatic, vital, aesthetic) with both the creative unfolding of the mystery and the possible agency of subtle entities or energies in the enactment—or "bringing forth"—of ontologically rich religious worlds.[4] In other words, the participatory approach presents

---

3. Ferrer, *Participation*; Ferrer and Sherman, "Introduction." In addition to the influence of many spiritual, psychological, and philosophical schools and my own lived spiritual inquiry, my participatory perspective is particularly indebted to Tarnas's participatory epistemology (see Tarnas, *Passion*), Maturana and Varela's enactive paradigm of cognition (Maturana and Varela, *Tree*; Varela et al., *Embodied Mind*), Albareda and Romero's Holistic Transformation (Romero and Albareda, "Born on Earth"; see also Ferrer, *Participation*), and Panikkar's pluralistic account of religion (see Panikkar, "Religious Pluralism"; Panikkar, "Invisible Harmony"; and Panikkar, *Mysticism*). Exchanges with the pioneer participatory thinker and practitioner John Heron (see Heron, *Feeling*; Heron, *Sacred Science*; and Heron, *Participatory*) helped me to develop and refine my perspective in significant ways. Important aspects of my work also emerged in contradistinction to Wilber's integral theory (see Wilber, *Sex, Ecology, Spirituality*) and other classical transpersonal models.

4. My use of the term *enactive* is inspired by Varela et al.'s innovative articulation of a nonrepresentational paradigm of cognition (see Varela et al., *Embodied Mind*;

an enactive understanding of the sacred that conceives spiritual phenomena, experiences, and insights as *cocreated events*. By locating the emergence of spiritual knowing at the interface of human multidimensional cognition, cultural context, subtle worlds, and the deep generativity of life or the cosmos, this account avoids both the secular post/modernist reduction of religion to cultural-linguistic artifact and, as discussed below, the religionist dogmatic privileging of a single tradition as superior or paradigmatic. The rest of this section introduces five distinctive features of the participatory approach: spiritual cocreation, creative spirituality, spiritual individuation, participatory epistemology, and the integral *Bodhisattva* vow.

Dimensions of Spiritual Cocreation

Spiritual cocreation has three interrelated dimensions—intrapersonal, interpersonal, and transpersonal. These dimensions respectively establish participatory spirituality as embodied (spirit within), relational (spirit in-between), and enactive (spirit beyond).

Intrapersonal cocreation consists of the collaborative participation of all human attributes—body, vital energy, heart, mind, and consciousness—in the enactment of spiritual phenomena. This dimension is grounded in the *principle of equiprimacy*, according to which no human attribute is intrinsically superior or more evolved than any other. As Romero and Albareda[5] pointed out, the cognicentric (i.e., mind-centered) character of Western culture hinders the maturation of nonmental attributes, making it normally necessary to engage in intentional practices to bring these attributes up to the same developmental level that the mind achieves through mainstream education.[6] In principle, however, all human attributes can participate as equal partners in the creative unfolding of the spiritual path, are equally capable of sharing freely in the life of the mystery here on Earth, and can also be equally alienated from it. The main challenges to intrapersonal

---

see also Thompson, *Mind in Life*). The participatory formulation adapts and extends the enactive paradigm—originally limited to the perceptual cognition of the natural world—to account for the emergence of ontologically rich religious realms, which are cocreated by human multidimensional cognition and the mystery or generative force of life or the cosmos. By including the epistemic role of all human ways of knowing (e.g., somatic, emotional, imaginal, archetypal) in the enactive process, participatory theory also extends the perceptual-cognitivist focus of the original enactive paradigm. For an important synthesis of biocognitive, phenomenological, and transpersonal participatory accounts of enaction, see Malkemus, "Toward a General Theory."

5. Romero and Albareda, "Born on Earth."
6. See Ferrer, *Participation*; Ferrer et al., "Embodied Participation."

cocreation are cognicentrism, lopsided development, mental pride, and disembodied attitudes to spiritual growth. Possible antidotes to those challenges are integral practices, the cultivation of mental humility, the integral Bodhisattva vow (see below), and embodied approaches to spiritual growth. Intrapersonal cocreation affirms the importance of being rooted in *spirit within* (i.e., the immanent dimension of the mystery) and renders participatory spirituality essentially *embodied.*[7]

Interpersonal cocreation emerges from cooperative relationships among human beings growing as peers in the spirit of solidarity, mutual respect, and constructive confrontation.[8] It is grounded in the *principle of equipotentiality*, according to which "we are all teachers and students" insofar as we are superior and inferior to others in different regards.[9] This principle does not entail that there is no value in working with spiritual teachers or mentors; it simply means that human beings cannot be ranked in their totality or according to a single developmental criterion, such as brainpower, emotional intelligence, or contemplative realization. Although peer-to-peer human relationships are vital for spiritual growth, interpersonal cocreation can include contact with perceived nonhuman intelligences, such as subtle entities, natural powers, or archetypal forces that might be embedded in psyche, nature, or the cosmos.[10] The main challenges to interpersonal cocreation are spiritual pride, psychospiritual inflation, circumstantial or self-imposed isolation, and adherence to rigidly hierarchical spiritualities. Antidotes to those challenges include collaborative spiritual practice and inquiry, intellectual and spiritual humility, deep dialogue, and relational and pluralistic approaches to spiritual growth. Interpersonal cocreation affirms the importance of communion with *spirit in-between* (i.e., the situational dimension of the mystery) and makes participatory spirituality intrinsically *relational.*[11]

Transpersonal cocreation refers to dynamic interaction between embodied human beings and the mystery in the bringing forth of spiritual insights, practices, states, and worlds.[12] This dimension is grounded in the *principle of equiplurality*, according to which there can potentially

7. Ferrer, *Participation*; Heron, *Participatory*; Lanzetta, "Wound of Love."

8. Ferrer, "Integral Transformative Practice"; Ferrer, *Participation*; Heron, *Sacred Science*; Heron, *Participatory.*

9. Bauwens, "Next Buddha"; Ferrer et al., "Embodied Participation."

10. E.g., Heron, *Sacred Science*; Heron, *Participatory*; Jung, *Red Book*; Rachel, "Daimonic Ecologies."

11. See, e.g., Heron, *Sacred Science*; Heron, *Participatory*; Heron and Lahood, "Charismatic Inquiry."

12. Ferrer, *Revisioning*; Ferrer, *Participation.*

be multiple spiritual enactions that are nonetheless equally holistic and emancipatory. This principle frees participatory spirituality from allegiance to any single spiritual system and paves the way for a genuine, ontologically and pragmatically grounded, spiritual pluralism. The main challenges to transpersonal cocreation are spiritual disempowerment, indoctrination, spiritual narcissism, and adherence to naive objectivist or universalist spiritualities. Antidotes include the development of one's inner spiritual authority and the affirmation of the right to inquire,[13] heretical courage, and enactive and creative spiritualities.[14] Transpersonal cocreation affirms the importance of being open to *spirit beyond* (i.e., the subtle dimensions of the mystery) and makes participatory spirituality fundamentally inquiry-driven[15] and *enactive.*[16]

Although all three dimensions interact in multifaceted ways in the enactment of spiritual events, the creative link between intrapersonal and transpersonal cocreation deserves special mention. Whereas the mind and consciousness arguably serve as a natural bridge to subtle spiritual forms already enacted in history that display more fixed forms and dynamics (e.g., cosmological motifs, archetypal configurations, mystical visions and states), attention to the body and its vital energies may grant greater access to the more generative immanent power of life or the mystery.[17] From this approach, it follows, the greater the participation of embodied dimensions in religious inquiry, the more creative one's spiritual life may become and a larger number of creative spiritual developments may emerge.

A Creative Spirituality

In the infancy of participatory spirituality, spiritual inquiry operated within certain constraints arguably inherited from traditional religion. As Eliade[18] argued, many established religious practices and rituals are "reenactive" in their attempt to replicate cosmogonic actions and events. Expanding this account, I have suggested that most religious traditions can be seen as "reproductive" insofar as their practices aim to not only ritually reenact mythical

13. Heron, *Sacred Science*; Heron, *Participatory.*

14. Ferrer and Sherman, "Introduction"; Ferrer and Sherman, eds., *Participatory Turn.*

15. Heron, *Sacred Science*; Heron, *Participatory.*

16. Ferrer, *Revisioning*; Ferrer, "Spiritual Knowing"; Ferrer, *Participation*; Ferrer and Sherman, eds., *Participatory Turn.*

17. Ferrer, *Revisioning*; Ferrer, *Participation.*

18. Eliade, *Sacred and Profane*; Eliade, *Cosmos and History.*

motives but also to replicate the enlightenment of their founder or to attain the state of salvation or freedom described in allegedly revealed scriptures.[19] Although disagreements about the exact nature of such states and the most effective methods to attain them abound in the historical development of religious ideas and practices—naturally leading to rich creative developments within the traditions—spiritual inquiry was regulated (and arguably constrained) by such pregiven unequivocal goals.

Participatory enaction entails a model of spiritual engagement that does not simply reproduce certain tropes according to a given historical a priori, but rather embarks upon the adventure of openness to the novelty and creativity of nature or the mystery.[20] Grounded on current moral intuitions and cognitive competences, for instance, participatory spiritual inquiry can undertake not only the critical revision and actualization of prior religious forms but also the cocreation of novel spiritual understandings, practices, and even expanded states of freedom.[21]

Spiritual Individuation

This emphasis on creativity is central to *spiritual individuation,* that is, the process through which a person gradually develops and embodies her unique spiritual identity and wholeness. Religious traditions tend to promote the homogenization of central features of the inner and outer lives of their practitioners—for example, encouraging them to seek the same spiritual states and liberation, to become like Christ or the Buddha, or to wear the same clothes (in the case of monks). These aspirations may have been historically legitimate, but after the emergence of the modern self,[22] our current predicament (at least in the West) arguably calls for an integration of spiritual maturation and psychological individuation that will likely lead to a richer diversity of spiritual expressions.[23] In other words, the participatory approach aims at the emergence of a human community formed by spiritually differentiated individuals.

It is important to sharply distinguish between the modern hyperindividualistic mental ego and the participatory selfhood forged in the sacred fire of spiritual individuation. Whereas the disembodied modern self is

19. Ferrer, *Participation*; Ferrer and Sherman, eds., *Participatory Turn.*

20. Ferrer, *Revisioning*; Ferrer and Sherman, *Participatory Turn*; Heron, "Spiritual Inquiry"; Heron, *Participatory.*

21. See Ferrer, *Participation.*

22. Taylor, *Sources of the Self.*

23. See Ferrer, *Participation.*

plagued by alienation, dissociation, and narcissism, a spiritually individuated person has an embodied, integrated, connected, and permeable identity whose high degree of differentiation, far from being isolating, actually allows him or her to enter into a deeply conscious communion with others, nature, and the multidimensional cosmos. A key difference between modern individualism and spiritual individuation is thus the integration of radical relatedness in the latter.

Integral Bodhisattvas

Since the conscious mind is the seat of most individuals' sense of identity, an exclusive liberation of consciousness can be deceptive insofar as one can believe that one is fully free when, in fact, essential dimensions of the self are underdeveloped, alienated, or in bondage—as the dysfunctional sexual behavior of numerous modern spiritual teachers attests.[24] As discussed above, participatory spirituality seeks to foster the harmonious engagement of all human attributes in the spiritual path without tensions or dissociations. Despite his downplaying the spiritual import of sexuality and the vital world, Sri Aurobindo[25] was correct when he wrote that the liberation of consciousness cannot be equated to an integral transformation entailing the spiritual alignment of all human dimensions.

With this in mind, I have proposed an integral Bodhisattva vow in which the conscious mind renounces its own full liberation until the body, the heart, and the primary world can be free as well from alienating tendencies that prevent them from sharing freely in the unfolding life of the mystery here on Earth.[26] Needless to say, to embrace an integral *Bodhisattva* vow is not a return to the individualistic spiritual aspirations of early Buddhism because it entails a commitment to the *integral* liberation of all sentient beings, rather than only of their conscious minds or conventional sense of identity. Likewise, as the above description reflects, my use of the term *Bodhisattva* does not suggest a commitment to early Buddhist accounts of liberation as extinction of bodily senses and desires and release from the cycle of transmigratory experience (*samsara*).[27]

24. E.g., Edelstein, *Sex and the Spiritual Teacher*; Kripal, "Debating."

25. Aurobindo, *Life Divine*, 942–44.

26. Ferrer, "Spirituality and Intimate Relationships"; Ferrer, *Participation*.

27. On this issue, see Collins, *Nirvana*; Harvey, *Selfless Mind*.

Participatory Epistemology and Critical Theory

It cannot be stressed strongly enough that participatory pluralism (discussed below) does not entail the uncritical or relativistic endorsement of past or present religious understandings or forms of life. Put differently, the participatory rejection of an objectifiable pregiven spiritual ultimate referent does not prevent qualitative distinctions in spiritual matters. To be sure, like beautiful porcelains made out of amorphous clay, traditions cannot be qualitatively ranked according to their accuracy in representing some imagined (accessible or inaccessible) original template. However, this account does not mean discernment cannot be cultivated regarding more (or less) evocative, skillful, or sophisticated artifacts.

In addition, whereas the participatory turn renders meaningless the postulation of qualitative distinctions among traditions according to a priori doctrines or a prearranged hierarchy of spiritual insights, these comparative grounds can be sought in a variety of practical fruits (e.g., existential, cognitive, emotional, interpersonal). Specifically, I have suggested three basic guidelines: (a) the *egocentrism test,* which assesses the extent to which spiritual traditions, teachings, and practices free practitioners from gross and subtle forms of narcissism and self-centeredness; (b) the *dissociation test,* which evaluates the extent to which the same foster the integrated blossoming of all dimensions of the person; and (c) the *eco-socio-political test,* which assesses the extent to which spiritual systems foster ecological balance, social and economic justice, religious and political freedom, class and gender equality, and other fundamental human rights.[28]

Two important qualifications must be made regarding these guidelines: First, some spiritual paths and liberations may be more adequate for different psychological and cultural dispositions (as well as for the same individual at distinct developmental junctures), but this does not make them universally superior or inferior. The well-known four yogas of Hinduism (reflection, devotion, action, and experimentation) come quickly to mind in this regard, as do other spiritual typologies that can be found in other traditions.[29] Second, the participatory emphasis on overcoming narcissism and selfcenteredness, although arguably central to most spiritual traditions, may not be shared by all. Even more poignantly, most religious traditions would likely not rank too highly in terms of the dissociation or the eco-socio-political tests; for example, gross or subtle forms of repression, control, or strict regulation of the human body and its vital/sexual

---

28. Ferrer, *Revisioning*; Ferrer, *Participation.*
29. Beena, *Personal Typologies*; H. Smith, "Spiritual Personality Types."

energies (versus the promotion of their autonomous maturation, integration, and participation in spiritual knowing) are rather the norm in most past and present contemplative endeavors.[30] Likewise, many religions have had a demonstrably negative environmental impact;[31] supported violence, militarism, and authoritarian regimes;[32] and brought about serious violations of human rights[33] even though they have also provided vital resources to secure them.[34] Thus, the integrative and socially engaged thrust of the participatory turn is foundational for the development of a participatory critical theory of religion.

More positively, these tests normatively point toward the universal ideal of a *socially responsible integrated selflessness,* which (although the attainability of a fully integrated selflessness is open to question) can act as a regulative principle à la Habermas's "ideal speech situation."[35] The idea of integrated selflessness is thus capable of providing procedural criteria for critical discernment in spiritual matters, that is, concerning how qualitative distinctions in spiritual discourse might be made. From this evaluative principle, applicable standards, rules, or tests to assess spiritual choices and practices can be derived. In addition to self- and peer assessment,[36] one might consider the use of standardized tests such as the Narcissistic Personality Inventory or NPI.[37] In addition, the thoughtful combination of other tests may indicate the degree of psychosomatic integration of spiritual states, for example measures of transcendence used with measures of body intelligence and awareness.[38]

To sum up, the emancipatory epistemology of the participatory approach assesses spiritual paths according to the degree to which they foster both an overcoming of selfcenteredness and a fully embodied integration. With this outline of participatory spirituality established, the discussion now turns to the question of religious pluralism and its participatory response.

30. Ferrer, *Participation.*

31. E.g., Nelson, ed., *Purifying.*

32. Juergensmeyer, *Terror;* Victoria, *Zen at War.*

33. Ghanea-Hercock, ed., *Religion and Human Rights.*

34. Banchoff and Wuthnow, eds., *Religion and the Global Politics.*

35. Habermas, *Theory.*

36. E.g., Heron, *Co-operative Inquiry;* Heron, *Sacred Science.*

37. Raskin and Terry, "Principal Components Analysis."

38. E.g., Anderson, "Body Intelligence."

Religious Pluralism and Spiritual Narcissism

Religious globalization, new religious movements, transnational religions, global proselytism, old and new fundamentalisms, religious violence, multiple religious identities, ecumenical services, religious syncretism, secular and postsecular spiritualities—all these are among the many remarkable trends that shape the religious landscape of the beginning of the twenty-first century. Despite the rampant materialism still dominant in an increasingly technocratic world, it is clear that these are times of rich spiritual diversity, proliferation, and innovation. For instance, when David B. Barrett, the main editor of the massive *World Christian Encyclopedia*,[39] was asked what he had learned about religious change in the world after several decades of research, he responded with the following: "We have identified nine thousand and nine hundred distinct and separate religions in the world, increasing by two or three religions every day."[40] Although there may be something to celebrate in this spiritual cornucopia, it is also clear that the many conflicting religious visions of reality and human nature are a major cause of the prevailing skepticism toward religious and spiritual truth claims. Against the background of modernist assumptions about a singular objective reality, it is understandable that the presence of a plurality of mutually exclusive accounts leads to the confident dismissal of religious explanations. It is as if contemporary culture has succumbed to the Cartesian anxiety behind what W. E. Hocking called the "scandal of plurality,"[41] the worry that "if there are so many divergent claims to ultimate truth, then perhaps none is right."[42]

This competitive predicament among religious beliefs is not only a philosophical or existential problem; it has also has profoundly affected how people from different credos engage one another and, even today, plays an important role in many interreligious conflicts, quarrels, and even holy wars. Although it would be naive to claim that these conflicts are mostly driven by competitive religious sentiments (economic, political, ethnic, and social

39. Barrett et al., *World Christian Encyclopedia*.

40. Quoted in Lester, "Oh Gods!," 28.

41. Hocking, *Coming World Civilization*.

42. Clarke, *Oriental Enlightenment*, 134; Bernstein, in *Beyond Objectivism and Relativism*, coined the term *Cartesian anxiety* to refer to the relativistic worries (e.g., about intellectual and moral chaos) derived from the failure to find secure foundations for human knowledge and morality. These worries, for Bernstein, are ultimately specious and need "to be questioned, exposed, and overcome" (19). Here, I give the term a different twist to refer to the Cartesian (i.e., objectivist) roots of the disconcertment produced by the existence of a multiplicity of conflicting religious accounts supposedly referring to a single pregiven reality, however naturalistically or supernaturalistically such a reality is conceived.

issues are often primary), the rhetoric of religious exclusivism or superiority is widely used to fuel fundamentalist attitudes and justify interreligious violence across the globe. As Amartya Sen compellingly argued,[43] exclusive religious identities are often exploited to perpetuate violence and religion-based terrorism—after all, it is much easier to kill your neighbor when you believe that God is on your side. The theologian Hans Küng famously said that there can be "no world peace without peace among religions,"[44] to which I would add, "There might not be complete peace among religions without ending the competition among religions."

Typical responses to the scandal of religious plurality tend to fall along a continuum between two drastically opposite positions. At one end of the spectrum, materialistic, scientifically minded, and "nonreligionist" scholars retort to the plurality of religious worldviews to downplay or dismiss altogether the cognitive value of religious knowledge claims, regarding religions as cultural fabrications that, like art pieces or culinary dishes, can be extremely diverse and even personally edifying but never the bearers of any "objective" truth whatsoever.[45] At the other end, spiritual practitioners, theologians, and "religionist" scholars vigorously defend the cognitive value of religion, addressing the problem of religious pluralism by either endorsing the exclusive (or ultimately superior) truth of their preferred tradition or developing universalist understandings that seek to reconcile the conflicting spiritual truths within one or another encompassing system. Despite their professed integrative stance, most universalist visions of human spirituality tend to distort the essential message of the various religious traditions, hierarchically favoring certain spiritual truths over others and raising serious obstacles for interreligious harmony, open-ended spiritual inquiry, and social harmony.[46]

Uncovering Spiritual Narcissism

A few marginal voices notwithstanding,[47] the search for a common core, universal essence, or single metaphysical world behind the multiplicity of religious experiences and cosmologies can be regarded as over. Whether guided by the exclusivist intuitionism of traditionalism or the fideism of

43. Sen, *Identity and Violence.*
44. Küng, "Christianity," 194.
45. E.g., Rorty, "Pragmatism."
46. Ferrer, *Revisioning.*
47. Lings and Minnaar, eds., *Underlying Religion*; Oldmeadow, *Journeys East*; Stoddart, *Remembering.*

theological agendas, the outcome—and too often the intended goal—of such universalist projects was unambiguous: the privileging of one particular spiritual or religious system over all others. In addition to universalism, the other attempts to explain religious divergences have typically taken one of the three following routes: exclusivism ("my religion is the only true one, the rest are false"), inclusivism ("my religion is the most accurate or complete, the rest are lower or partial"), and ecumenical pluralism ("there may be real differences between our religions, but all lead ultimately to the same end").

The many problems of religious exclusivism are well-known. It easily fosters religious intolerance and fundamentalist tendencies, and prevents a reciprocal and symmetrical encounter with the other where divergent spiritual viewpoints may be regarded as enriching options or genuine alternatives. In the wake of the scope of contemporary religious diversity, the defense of the absolute cognitive superiority of one single tradition over all others is more dubious than ever. Inclusivist and ecumenically pluralist approaches suffer from similar difficulties in that they tend to conceal claims for the supremacy of one or another religious tradition, ultimately collapsing into the dogmatism of exclusivist stances.[48] Consider, for example, the Dalai Lama's defense of the need of a plurality of religions. While celebrating the existence of different religions to accommodate the diversity of human karmic dispositions, he contends that final spiritual liberation can only be achieved through the emptiness practices of his own Gelukpa school of Tibetan Buddhism, implicitly situating all other spiritual choices as lower— a view that he believes all other Buddhists and religious people will eventually accept.[49] Other examples of inclusivist approaches include such diverse proposals as Kukai's ranking of Confucian, Taoist, and Buddhist systems as progressive stages toward his own Shingon Buddhism; Swami Vivekananda's proclamation of (Neo-)Vedanta as the universal "eternal religion" (sanatana dharma) that uniquely encompasses all others; the Baha'i belief in its representing the last and highest, although not final, revelation of a succession of religions; and Wilber's arrangement of all religious goals as hierarchical stages of spiritual development culminating in his own articulation of a nondual realization.

I propose that the various approaches to religious diversity—exclusivism, inclusivism, and ecumenical pluralism (more about the latter in a moment)—can be situated along a continuum ranging from more gross to more subtle forms of *spiritual narcissism*, which ultimately elevate one's favored tradition or spiritual choice as superior. That the Dalai Lama himself,

---

48. Ferrer, *Revisioning*; Halbfass, *India and Europe*.
49. D'Costa, "Near Triumph."

arguably a paragon of spiritual humility and open-mindedness, holds this view strongly suggests that spiritual narcissism is not necessarily associated with a narcissistic personality but rather is a deeply seated tendency buried in the collective realms of the human unconscious. In any event, the bottom line is that, explicitly or implicitly, religious traditions and schools have persistently looked down upon one another, each believing that their truth is more complete or final, and that their path is the only or most effective one to achieve full salvation or enlightenment. The next section examines several types of religious pluralism that have been proposed in response to this disconcerting situation.

The Varieties of Religious Pluralism

Religious pluralism comes in many guises and fashions. Before suggesting a participatory remedy to the prevalent spiritual narcissism in dealing with religious difference, I critically review here four major types of religious pluralism: ecumenical, soteriological, postmodern, and metaphysical.

Ecumenical pluralism admits genuine differences among religious beliefs and practices, but maintains that they all ultimately lead to the same end.[50] The problem with this apparently tolerant stance is that whenever its proponents describe such a religious goal, they invariably do it in terms that favor one or another specific tradition (e.g., God, the transcendently Real, or emptiness). This is why ecumenical pluralism not only degenerates into exclusivist or inclusivist stances but also trivializes the encounter with "the other"[51]—after all, what is really the point of engaging in interfaith exchange if practitioners already know that they are all heading toward the same goal? A classic example of this stance is Karl Rahner's famous proposal that devoted practitioners of other religions could attain salvation by walking different paths because, although they do not know it, they are "anonymous Christians" who are delivered through God's grace.[52] Students of religion have for decades pointed out the contradictions of pluralistic approaches that postulate an equivalent end point for all traditions.[53] A genuine religious pluralism, it is today widely accepted, needs to acknowledge the existence of alternative religious aims, and putting all religions on a single scale will not do it.

50. E.g., Hick, *Interpretation of Religion*; Hick and Knitter, eds., *Myth of Christian Uniqueness*.

51. Cf. McGrane, *Beyond Anthropology*.

52. Rahner, "Christianity."

53. Cobb, *Christ*; Cobb, *Transforming*; D'Costa, *Christian Uniqueness*; Nah, *Religious Pluralism*; Panikkar, "Jordan"; Panikkar, *Invisible Harmony*.

In response to these concerns, some scholars have proposed a *soteriological pluralism* that envisions a multiplicity of irreducible transformative or experiential goals associated with the various religious traditions.[54] Due to their diverse ultimate visions of reality and personhood, religious traditions stress the cultivation of particular human potentials or competences (e.g., access to visionary worlds, mind/body integration, expansion of consciousness, overcoming of suffering), which naturally leads to distinct human transformations and states of freedom or fulfillment. A variant of this approach is the postulation of a limited number of independent but equiprimordial religious goals and conceptually possible ultimate realities, for example, theism (in its various forms), monistic nondualism (à la Advaita Vedanta), and process nondualism (as in Yogacara Buddhism).[55] The soteriological approach to religious difference, however, remains agnostic about the ontological status of spiritual realities, being therefore pluralistic only at a phenomenological level (i.e., admitting different human spiritual fulfillments) but not at an ontological or metaphysical one (i.e., at the level of spiritual realities). For example, although discussing several possibilities, Heim is uncertain about the metaphysical vision behind his "more pluralistic hypothesis"[56] and ultimately slips back to an objectivist and representational account of spiritual truth as universal and pregiven: "Among the various religions," he stated, "one or several or none may provide the best approximate representation of the character of that cosmos, explaining and ordering these various human possibilities within it."[57] This relapse is also evident when, after comparing the different religious ends to different cities, he writes, "I regard these cities as sites within a single world, whose global mapping has a determinate character."[58]

The combination of pluralism and metaphysical agnosticism is also a chief feature of the *postmodern* solution to the problem of conflicting truth claims in religion. The translation of religious realities into culturallinguistic fabrications allows postmodern scholars to explain interreligious differences as the predictable upshot of the world's various religious beliefs, practices, and language games.[59] In other words, the various gods and goddesses, spirits and ancestors, archetypes and visionary worlds, are

54. E.g., Heim, *Salvations*; LaFargue, "Radically Pluralist."

55. Kaplan, *Different Paths*.

56. Heim, *Salvations*, 146.

57. Heim, *Salvations*, 215.

58. Heim, *Salvations*, 220.

59. Cupitt, *Mysticism*; Flood, *Beyond Phenomenology*.

nothing but discursive entities.[60] Postmodern pluralism denies or brackets the ontological status of the referents of religious language, which are usually seen as meaningless, obscure, or parasitic upon the despotic dogmatism of traditional religious metaphysics. Further, even if such spiritual realities were to exist, the human cognitive apparatus would only allow knowing the culturally and linguistically mediated experience of them.[61] Postmodern pluralism recognizes a genuine plurality of religious goals, but at the cost of either stripping religious claims of any extralinguistic veridicality or denying that such truths can be known even if they exist.

A notable exception to this trend is the *metaphysical* or *deep pluralism* advocated by a number of process theologians.[62] Relying on Whitehead's distinction between "God's unchanging Being" and "God's changing Becoming," this proposal defends the existence of two ontological or metaphysical religious ultimates to which the various traditions are geared: God, which corresponds to the biblical Yahweh, the Buddhist Sambhogakaya, and Advaita Vedanta's Saguna Brahman; and Creativity, which corresponds to Meister Eckhart's Godhead, the Buddhist emptiness and Dharmakaya, and Advaita Vedanta's Nirguna Brahman. A third possible ultimate, the cosmos itself, is at times added in connection to Taoism and Indigenous spiritualities that venerate the sacredness of the natural world. In addition to operating within a theistic framework adverse to many traditions, however, deep pluralism not only establishes highly dubious equivalencies among religious goals (e.g., Buddhist emptiness and Advaita's Nirguna Brahman) but also forces the rich diversity of religious ultimates into the arguably Procrustean theistic molds of God's "unchanging Being" and "changing Becoming."

Participatory Spiritual Pluralism

The participatory approach embraces a pluralistic vision of spirituality that accepts the formative role of contextual and linguistic factors in religious phenomena, while simultaneously recognizing the importance of nonlinguistic variables (e.g., somatic, imaginal, energetic, subtle, archetypal) in shaping religious experiences and meanings, and affirming the ontological value and creative impact of spiritual worlds.

Participatory pluralism allows the conception of a multiplicity of not only spiritual paths but also spiritual liberations, worlds, and even ultimates. On the one hand, besides affirming the historical existence of multiple

60. Braun, "Religion."
61. E.g., Katz, "On Mysticism."
62. Cobb, *Transforming*; Griffin, ed., *Deep Religious Pluralism*.

spiritual goals or "salvations,"[63] the increased embodied openness to immanent spiritual life and the spirit in between fostered by the participatory approach may naturally engender a number of novel holistic spiritual realizations that cannot be reduced to traditional states of enlightenment or liberation. If human beings were regarded as *unique* embodiments of the mystery, would it not be plausible to consider that as they spiritually individuate, their spiritual realizations might also be distinct even if potentially overlapping and aligned with each other?

On the other hand, participatory pluralism proposes that different spiritual ultimates can be enacted through intentional or spontaneous participation in an undetermined mystery, spiritual power, or generative force of life or reality. Whereas I take these enactions to be ultimate in their respective spiritual universes, this consideration in no way relativizes the various traditions' ultimates—nor does it posit a supraultimate spiritual referent beyond them. In contrast, as discussed below, I hold that participatory enaction allows one to not only move away from representational and objectivist accounts of spiritual cognition, but also avoid the problematic *dualism of the mystery and its enactions.* Hence, the participatory perspective does not contend that there are two, three, or any limited quantity of pregiven spiritual ultimates, but rather that the radical openness, interrelatedness, and creativity of the mystery or the cosmos allows for the participatory cocreation of an indefinite number of ultimate self-disclosures of reality and corresponding religious worlds.

In this context, the question of religious pluralism can be satisfactorily answered by affirming the undetermined, generative power of life or the mystery, as well as the human participatory role in its creative unfolding. It is time to overcome spiritual narcissism and hold spiritual convictions in a more modest, discriminating, and perhaps spiritually seasoned manner— one that recognizes the plausibility of a multiplicity of spiritual truths and religious worlds while offering grounds for the critical appraisal of dissociative, repressive, and oppressive religious expressions, beliefs, and practices. To envision religious manifestations as the outcome of human cocreative communion with an undetermined mystery—or creative power of life or reality—allows affirming a plurality of ontologically rich religious worlds without falling into any of today's fashionable reductionisms. The many challenges raised by the plurality of religions can only be met by embracing the spirit of a critical pluralism.

In addition, a participatory approach envisions the long searched for spiritual unity of humankind, not in any global spiritual megasystem

---

63. Ferrer, *Revisioning*; Heim, *Salvations.*

or integrative conceptual framework, but in the shared lived experience of communion with the generative dimension of the mystery. In other words, the spiritual unity of humankind may not be found in the heavens (i.e., in mental, visionary, or even mystical visions) but deep down into the earth (i.e., in the embodied connection with a common creative root). As the saying attributed to the thirteenth-century Persian poet and mystic Rumi describes, "Maybe you are searching among the branches for what only appears in the roots." The recognition of these creative roots may allow for firmly growing by branching out in countless creative directions without losing a sense of deep communion across differences. Such a recognition may also engender a sense of belonging to a common spiritual family committed to fostering the spiritual individuation of its members and the eco-socio-politically responsible transformation of the world.

The pluralistic spirit of the participatory approach should not eclipse its "more relaxed" spiritual universalism—although eschewing dubious equations among spiritual ultimates (e.g., the Tao is God, emptiness is structurally equivalent to Brahman, and similar, quite empty I believe, equations), the participatory approach affirms an underlying undetermined mystery or creative spiritual power as the generative source of all spiritual enactions.[64] The shared spiritual dynamism of the participatory approach should be distinguished from any Kantian-like noumenon or "thing-in-itself" endowed with inscrutable qualities and compared with which all spiritual ultimates are always incomplete, culturally conditioned, or cognitively constrained phenomenal manifestations.[65] In contrast, the enactive epistemology of the participatory approach does away with the Kantian two-worlds dualism by refusing to conceive of the mystery as having objectifiable pregiven attributes (such as personal, impersonal, dual, or nondual) and by affirming the radical identity of the manifold spiritual ultimates and the mystery, even if the former do not exhaust the ontological possibilities of the latter. Put simply, the mystery cocreatively unfolds in multiple ontological directions.

Crucially, the avoidance of the *dualism of the mystery and its enactions*[66] substantially minimizes the problem of sectarianism. Building on

64. Ferrer, *Revisioning*; Ferrer, *Participation*.

65. E.g., Hick, *Interpretation of Religion*.

66. This formulation also distances my position from the traditionalist dualism between various "relative absolutes" (i.e., of the different religious worlds) and the Absolute in itself, which is posited to exist behind the religions' absolutes as "the Godhead in Its Infinitude and Oneness [. . .] above all relativity" (Nasr, *Knowledge and the Sacred*, 294). Thus, when Abramson, in "Emperor's New Clothes," charged the participatory approach with conflating "the 'Absolute that is beyond all religious Absolutes' with the multiple Absolutes of the different traditions" (42), he misunderstood that such a move is not a conflation but a deliberate overcoming of an arguably pernicious spiritual

both the enactive paradigm's account of cognition as embodied action and its rejection of representational theories of knowledge,[67] I maintain that in the same way an individual is her actions (whether perceptual, cognitive, emotional, or subtle), the mystery is its enactions. In this understanding, *emptiness (shunyata), the Tao, and the Christian God (in their many inflexions) can be seen as creative gestures of the mystery enacted through participating human (and perhaps nonhuman) individuals and collectives.*

Not positing a supraultimate spiritual referent beyond its specific enactions has two very important consequences. First, it preserves the ontological ultimacy of those enactions (e.g., God, emptiness, Tao, Brahman) in their respective spiritual universes, avoiding the traditionalist and neo-Kantian demotion of those ultimates to penultimate stations.[68] Second, it short-circuits the feasibility of promoting one tradition as objectively superior (i.e., holding the most accurate picture of the mystery), excising ontological competitiveness at its root and arguably settling one of the main challenges of religious pluralism.[69]

The problem of doctrinal ranking is further minimized by both the participatory grounding of qualitative distinctions on pragmatic values (e.g., integrated selflessness, embodiment, eco-socio-political justice), and its equiplurality principle, according to which there can potentially be multiple spiritual enactions that are nonetheless equally holistic, emancipatory, and ethically just.[70] I stand by these values—not because I think they are universal, objective, or ahistorical (they are not), but because I firmly believe that their cultivation can effectively reduce today's personal, relational, social, and planetary suffering.

To be sure, the specificities of the various spiritual, transformational goals often derive from ontological views about the nature of reality or the divine. Likewise—and even more so in participatory, enactive context—transformational goals impact ontological matters, thus possibly slipping

---

dualism. This dualism of the mystery and its enactions is pernicious: It not only binds scholars and practitioners alike to objectivist and hierarchical frameworks, but also paves the way for interreligious exclusivism and spiritual narcissism (i.e., once a supraultimate Absolute is posited, practitioners can—and often do—claim their own religion's Absolute to be the closer, better, or more accurate account of the supraultimate Absolute). In addition, as King observed in "The *Philosophia perennis* and the Religions of the World," no religious practitioner would accept her professed spiritual ultimate to merely be a "relative absolute."

67. E.g., Chemero, *Radical Embodied*; Thompson, *Mind In Life*; Varela et al., *Embodied Mind.*

68. King, "*Philosophia perennis*"; Nah, *Religious Pluralism.*

69. Ferrer, "Spiritual Knowing"; Ferrer, *Participation.*

70. Ferrer, *Participation.*

back into doctrinal rankings (e.g., the goal of the embodied integration of consciousness arguably demotes traditional Shamkya Yoga's dualistic metaphysics and its attendant spiritual aspiration of isolation—*kaivalyam*). As the equiplurality principle maintains, however, the participatory ranking is not itself precipitated by the privileging of a single spiritual goal, but rather explodes into a plurality of potentially holistic spiritual realizations that can occur within and outside traditions. This principle is founded on the double rejection of an objectivist account of the mystery and a representational paradigm of cognition, according to which there can be only one most accurate representation[71] of an original template with supposedly pregiven features. Taken together, these features release participatory spirituality from the dogmatic commitment to any single spiritual system and pave the way for an ontologically and pragmatically grounded spiritual pluralism.

Summing up the discussion so far, the participatory approach provides a framework that minimizes problematic hierarchies based on doctrinal ontological beliefs about the mystery (e.g., as being ultimately personal, impersonal, monistic, dual, or nondual), while conserving grounds for the criticism of dissociated, disembodied, narcissistic, and oppressive visions and practices. This proposal offers pragmatic standards for qualitative distinctions among spiritual insights and practices while avoiding the "holistic fallacy"—that is, the spurious belief that cultures (or religious traditions) can be assessed to be superior or inferior to each other as wholes, ignoring how internally multilayered and diverse they actually are.[72]

While the participatory proposal might not entirely settle the question of ontological ranking, I maintain that the question is significantly relaxed through the qualification of the mystery as undetermined, the affirmation of a potential plurality of equally holistic visions unfolding through different enactions of the mystery, and the focus on transformational outcomes to make spiritual qualitative distinctions. Sectarianism cannot be fully overcome conceptually (i.e., through any theoretical framework, whether participatory or not), but I propose that it can be transcended in the realm of human experience. This transcendence comes through an attitude of intellectual humility and genuine openness to the other, as well as to the world's mysteries—particularly those mysteries that surpass the conceptual mind and can paradoxically (for the human mind, that is) house incompatible spiritual enactions, orientations, and values.

71. For nonrepresentational epistemologies, see Frisina, *Unity*.
72. Benhabib, *Claims of Culture*.

Conclusion: Back to the One and the Many

In a participatory context, the relationship between the One and the Many cannot be consistently characterized in a hierarchical fashion. Although my work emphasizes the plurality of spiritual worlds, I should stress here that I do not believe that either pluralism or universalism per se is ontologically superior or spiritually more evolved. There is a way, I believe, in which one can legitimately talk about a shared spiritual or cosmic creative power, one reality, one world, or one truth. On the one hand, the discussion about whether there is one world or a multiplicity of different worlds is ultimately a semantic one—and therefore metaphysically a pseudoproblem. In other words, one can understand the various spiritual worlds as dimensions of a single multidimensional cosmos or multiverse, which, as even some modern cosmologists hold, may not be just *expanding outward but also inward*.[73] On the other hand, a shared spiritual ground needs to be presupposed to make interreligious inquiry and dialogue possible and intelligible. After all, traditions do understand each other and frequently developed and transformed themselves through rich and varied interreligious interactions. The strict incommensurability of traditions needs to be rejected on logical, pragmatic, and historical grounds.

The spiritual universalism of the participatory vision, however, does not establish any hierarchy of positive attributes of the ultimate mystery: Nondual insights are not higher than dual, nor are dual higher than nondual. Personal enactions are not higher than impersonal, nor are impersonal higher than personal. And so forth. Since the nature of the mystery is undetermined, spiritual qualitative distinctions cannot be made by matching our insights and conceptualizations with any pregiven features. In contrast, qualitative distinctions need to be made on the basis of the emancipatory power of spiritual enactions for self, relationships, and world. Moreover, because of their unique psychospiritual dispositions, individuals and cultures may emancipate themselves better through different enactions of the spiritual power. This approach not only paves the way for a more constructive and enriching interreligious dialogue but also opens up the creative range of valid spiritual choices potentially available to us as individuals. In sum, *this vision brings forth a more relaxed and permissive spiritual universalism that passionately embraces (rather than reduces, conflates, or subordinates) the variety of ways in which the sacred can be cultivated and embodied, without falling into spiritual anarchy or vulgar relativism.*

73. Gould, *Universe in Creation*.

The relationship between the One and the Many cannot be then consistently characterized in a hierarchical fashion—and even less in terms of spiritual evolution. While there surely are "lower" and "higher" forms of both universalism and pluralism (i.e., more or less rigid, sophisticated, encompassing, or explanatory), my sense is that *the dialectic between universalism and pluralism, between the One and the Many, displays what may well be the deepest dynamics of the self-disclosing of the mystery*. From the rigid universalism of rational consciousness to the pluralistic relativism of some postmodern approaches, from integral types of universalism to the emerging spiritual pluralism of interfaith dialogue, the mystery (or at least its human understanding) seems to swing from one to the other pole, from the One to the Many and from the Many to the One, endlessly striving to more fully manifest, embody, and embrace love and wisdom in all its forms. Newer, more nuanced, and more embracing universalist and pluralistic visions will very likely continue to emerge, but the everlasting dialectical movement between the One and the Many in the self-disclosing of the mystery renders misleading any abstract or absolute hierarchical arrangement between them. If I am right about the generative power of the dialectical relationship between the One and the Many, then to get stuck in or freeze either of the two poles as *the* Truth cannot but hinder the natural unfolding of the mystery's creative urges. This is why, although originally offered in a different context, the following remark by Habermas seems pertinent to bring this chapter to a close: "The metaphysical priority of unity above plurality and the contextualist priority of pluralism above unity are secret accomplices."[74]

Bibliography

Abramson, John. "'The Emperor's New Clothes: Ferrer Isn't Wearing Any—Participatory Is Perennial. A Reply to Hartelius." *Transpersonal Psychology Review* 17.1 (2015) 38–48.

Akyalcin, Errol, et al. "Measuring Transcendence: Extracting Core Constructs." *Journal of Transpersonal Psychology* 40 (2008) 41–59.

Anderson, Rosemarie. "Body Intelligence Scale: Defining and Measuring the Intelligence of the Body." *Humanistic Psychologist* 34 (2006) 357–67.

Asad, Talal. *Genealogies of Religion: Discipline and Reasons of Power in Christianity and Islam*. Baltimore: Johns Hopkins University Press, 1993.

Aurobindo, Sri. *The Life Divine*. 6th ed. Pondicherry, India: Sri Aurobindo Ashram, 2001.

Banchoff, Thomas, and Robert Wuthnow, eds. *Religion and the Global Politics of Human Rights*. New York: Oxford University Press, 2011.

74. Habermas, *Postmetaphysical*, 116–17.

Barnard, G. William, and Jeffrey J. Kripal, eds. *Crossing Boundaries: Essays on the Ethical Status of Mysticism.* New York: Seven Bridges, 2002.

Barrett, David B., et al. *World Christian Encyclopedia: A Comparative Survey of Churches and Religions in the Modern World.* 2 vols. 2nd ed. Oxford: Oxford University Press, 2001.

Bauwens, Michel. "The Next Buddha Will Be a Collective: Spiritual Expression in the Peer-to-Peer Era." *ReVision* 29.4 (2007) 34–46.

Beena, Chintalapuri. *Personality Typologies: A Comparison of Western and Ancient Indian Approaches.* New Delhi: Commonwealth, 1990.

Benhabib, Seyla. *The Claims of Culture: Equality and Diversity in the Global Era.* Princeton: Princeton University Press, 2002.

Bernstein, Richard J. *Beyond Objectivism and Relativism: Science, Hermeneutics, and Praxis.* Philadelphia: University of Pennsylvania Press, 1985.

Bracken, Joseph A. *The One in the Many: A Contemporary Reconstruction of the God-World Relationship.* Grand Rapids: Eerdmans, 2001.

Braun, Willi. "Religion." In *Guide to the Study of Religion*, edited by Willi Braun and Russell T. McCutcheon, 3–18. London: Cassell, 2000.

Chemero, Anthony. *Radical Embodied Cognitive Science.* A Bradford Book. Cambridge: MIT Press, 2009.

Clarke, J. J. *Oriental Enlightenment: The Encounter between Asian and Western Thought.* London: Routledge, 1997.

Cobb, John B. Jr. *Christ in a Pluralistic Age.* Philadelphia: Westminster, 1975.

———. *Transforming Christianity and the World: A Way beyond Absolutism and Relativism.* Edited by Paul F. Knitter. Faith meets Faith Series. Maryknoll, NY: Orbis, 1999.

Collins, Steven. *Nirvana and other Buddhist Felicities.* Cambridge Studies in Religious Traditions 12. Cambridge: Cambridge University Press, 1998.

Coward, Harold G. *Pluralism in World Religions: A Short Introduction.* Oxford: Oneworld, 2000.

Cupitt, Don. *Mysticism after Modernity.* Religion and Modernity. Malden, MA: Blackwell, 1998.

D'Costa, Gavin, ed. *Christian Uniqueness Reconsidered: The Myth of a Pluralistic Theology of Religions.* Faith Meets Faith Series. Maryknoll, NY: Orbis, 1990.

———. *The Meeting of Religions and the Trinity.* Faith Meets Faith Series. Maryknoll: Orbis, 2000.

———. The Near Triumph of Tibetan Buddhist Pluralist-Exclusivism. In *The Meeting of Religions and the Trinity*, 72–95. Faith Meets Faith Series. Maryknoll, NY: Orbis, 2000.

Duckworth, Douglas. "How Nonsectarian is 'Nonsectarian'? Jorge Ferrer's Religious Pluralist Alternative to Tibetan Buddhist Inclusivism." *Sophia* 53 (2014) 339–48.

Edelstein, Scott. *Sex and the Spiritual Teacher: Why it Happens, When It's a Problem, and What We All Can Do.* Boston: Wisdom, 2011.

Eliade, Mircea. *Cosmos and History: The Myth of the Eternal Return.* Translated by Willard. R. Trask. 1959. Reprint, London: Arkana, 1989.

———. *The Sacred and the Profane.* Translated by Willard R. Trask. New York: Harcourt Brace Jovanovich, 1959.

Ferrer, Jorge N. "Integral Transformative Practice: A Participatory Perspective." *Journal of Transpersonal Psychology* 35.1 (2003) 21–42.

————. "Spirituality and Intimate Relationships: Monogamy, Polyamory, and Beyond." *Tikkun: Culture, Spirituality, Politics* 22 (2007) 37–43, 60–62.

————. "Neo-Piagetian Transpersonal Psychology: Dancing in-between Pluralism and Perennialism. Essay review of Edward J. Dale's *Completing Piaget's Project: Transpersonal Philosophy and the Future of Psychology.*" *Journal of Transpersonal Psychology* 47 (2015) 124–38.

————. *Participation and the Mystery: Transpersonal Essays in Psychology, Education, and Religion.* Albany: State University of New York Press, 2017.

————. "Spiritual Knowing as Participatory Enaction: An Answer to the Question of Religious Pluralism." In *The Participatory Turn: Spirituality, Mysticism, Religious Studies,* edited by Jorge N. Ferrer and Jacob H. Sherman, 135–69. Albany: State University of New York Press, 2008.

Ferrer, Jorge N., and Jacob H. Sherman. "Introduction: The Participatory Turn in Spirituality, Mysticism, and Religious Studies." In *The Participatory Turn: Spirituality, Mysticism, Religious Studies,* edited by Jorge N. Ferrer and Jacob H. Sherman, 1–78. Albany: State University of New York Press, 2008.

————, eds. *The Participatory Turn: Spirituality, Mysticism, Religious Studies.* Albany: State University of New York Press, 2008.

————. *Revisioning Transpersonal Theory: A Participatory Vision of Human Spirituality.* State University of New York Press, 2002.

Ferrer, Jorge N., et al. "Embodied Participation in the mystery: Implications for the Individual, Interpersonal Relationships, and Society." *ReVision,* 27.1 (2004) 10–18.

Ferrer, Jorge N., et al. "Integral Transformative Education: A Participatory Proposal." *Journal of Transformative Education* 3 (2005) 306–30.

Flood, Gavin. *Beyond Phenomenology: Rethinking the Study of Religion.* London: Cassell, 1999.

Friedman, Harris L. "The Self-Expansiveness Level Form: A Conceptualization and Measurement of a Transpersonal Construct." *Journal of Transpersonal Psychology* 15 (1983) 37–50.

Frisina, Warren G. *The Unity of Knowledge and Action: Toward a Non-Representational Theory of Knowledge.* SUNY Series in Philosophy. Albany: State University of New York Press, 2002.

Ghanea-Hercock, Nazila, ed. *Religion and Human Rights.* Critical Concepts in Religious Studies. London: Routledge, 2010.

Gould, Roy R. *Universe in Creation: A New Understanding of the Big Bang and the Emergence of Life.* Cambridge: Harvard University Press, 2018.

Griffin, David Ray, ed. *Deep Religious Pluralism.* Louisville: Westminster John Knox, 2005.

Habermas, Jürgen. *Postmetaphysical Thinking: Philosophical Essays.* Translated by William Mark Hohengarten. Cambridge: MIT Press, 1992.

————. *The Theory of Communicative Action.* Vol. 1, *Reason and the Rationalization of Society.* Translated by Thomas McCarthy. 2 vols. Boston: Beacon, 1984.

Hakeda, Yoshito S., trans. *Kūkai: Major Works.* With an account of his life and a study of his thought. UNESCO Collection of Representative Works: Japanese Series Records of Civilization: Sources and Studies 87. New York: Columbia University Press, 1972.

Halbfass, Wilhelm. *India and Europe: An Essay in Understanding.* Albany: State University of New York Press, 1988.

—————. *Tradition and Reflection: Explorations in Indian Thought.* Albany: State University of New York Press, 1991.

Harvey, Peter. *The Selfless Mind: Personality, Consciousness and Nirvana in Early Buddhism.* Richmond, UK: Curzon, 1995.

Heim, S. Mark. *Salvations: Truth and Difference in Religion.* Maryknoll: Orbis, 1995.

Heron, John. *Co-operative Inquiry: Research into the Human Condition.* London: Sage, 1996.

—————. *Feeling and Personhood: Psychology in Another Key.* London: Sage, 1992.

—————. *Sacred Science: Person-Centered Inquiry into the Spiritual and the Subtle.* Rosson-on-Wye, UK: PCCS Books, 1998.

—————. *Participatory Spirituality: A Farewell to Authoritarian Religion.* Morrisville, NC: Lulu, 2006.

—————. "Spiritual Inquiry as Divine Becoming." *ReVision* 24.2 (2001) 32–42.

Heron, John, and Gregg Lahood. "Charismatic Inquiry in Concert: Action Research in the Realm of 'the Between.'" In *The Sage Handbook of Action Research: Participative Inquiry and Practice*, edited by Peter Reason and Hilary Bradbury, 439–62. 2nd ed. London: Sage, 2008.

Hick, John. *An Interpretation of Religion: Human Responses to the Transcendent.* New Haven: Yale University Press, 1989.

Hick, John, and Paul F. Knitter, eds. *The Myth of Christian Uniqueness: Toward a Pluralistic Theology of Religions.* Faith Meets Faith Series. Maryknoll, NY: Orbis, 1987.

—————, eds. *The Myth of Christian Uniqueness: Toward a Pluralistic Theology of Religions.* 1987. Reprint, Eugene, OR: Wipf & Stock, 2005.

Hocking, William Ernest. *The Coming World Civilization.* New York: Harper, 1956.

Ingram, Paul O., and Frederick J. Streng, eds. *Buddhist-Christian Dialogue: Mutual Renewal and Transformation.* 1986. Reprint, Eugene, OR: Wipf & Stock, 2007.

Jung, Carl Gustav. *The Red Book = Liber Novus.* Edited by Sonu Shamdanasi. Translated by Mark Kyburz et al. Philemon Series. New York: Norton, 2009.

Juergensmeyer, Mark. *Terror in the Mind of God: The Global Rise of Religious Violence.* Comparative Studies in Religion and Society 13. Berkeley: University of California Press, 2000.

Juergensmeyer, Mark, et al., eds. *The Oxford Handbook of Religion and Violence.* Oxford Handbooks in Politics & International Relations. New York: Oxford University Press, 2012.

Kaplan, Stephen. *Different Paths, Different Summits: A Model for Religious Pluralism.* Lanham, MD: Rowman and Littlefield, 2002.

Katz, Steven T. "On Mysticism." *Journal of the American Academy of Religion* 56 (1988) 751–61.

King, Sallie B. "The *Philosophia perennis* and the Religions of the World." In *The Philosophy of Seyyed Hassein Nasr*, edited by Lewis Edwin et al., 203–20. The Library of Living Philosophers 28. Chicago: Open Court, 2001.

Kripal, Jeffrey J. "Debating the Mystical as Ethical: An Indological Map." In *Crossing Boundaries: Essays on the Ethical Status of Mysticism*, edited by G. William Barnard and Jeffrey J. Kripal, 15–69. New York: Seven Bridges, 2002.

Küng, Hans. "Christianity and World Religions: Dialogue with Islam." In *Toward a Universal Theology of Religion*, edited by Leonard J. Swidler, 192–209. 2nd printing. Faith Meets Faith Series. Maryknoll, NY: Orbis, 1988.

LaFargue, Michael. "Radically Pluralist, Thoroughly Critical: A New Theory of Religions." *Journal of the American Academy of Religion* 60 (1992) 693–716.

Lanzetta, Beverly. "Wound of Love: Feminine Theosis and Embodied Mysticism in Teresa de Avila." In *The Participatory Turn: Spirituality, Mysticism, Religious Studies*, edited by Jorge N. Ferrer and Jacob H. Sherman, 225–44. Albany: State University of New York Press, 2008.

Lester, Toby. "Oh Gods! An Explosion of New Religions Will Shake the 21st Century." *Atlantic Monthly*, February 2002, 37–45.

Lings, Martin, and Clinton Minnaar, eds. *The Underlying Religion: An Introduction to the Perennial Philosophy*. The Library of Perennial Philosophy. The Perennial Philosophy Series. Bloomington, IN: World Wisdom, 2007.

Malkemus, Samuel A. "Toward a General Theory of Enaction: Biological, Transpersonal, and Phenomenological Dimensions." *Journal of Transpersonal Psychology* 44.2 (2012) 201–23.

Maturana, Humberto R., and Francisco J. Varela. *The Tree of Knowledge: The Biological Roots of Human Understanding*. Boston: New Science Library, 1987.

McCutcheon, Russell T. *Manufacturing Religion: The Discourse of Sui Generis Religion and the Politics of Nostalgia*. New York: Oxford University Press, 1997.

McGrane, Bernard. *Beyond Anthropology: Society and the Other*. New York: Columbia University Press, 1989.

Nah, David S. *Religious Pluralism and Christian Theology: A Critical Evaluation of John Hick*. Eugene, OR: Pickwick Publications, 2012.

Nasr, Seyyed Hossein. *Knowledge and the Sacred*. Gifford Lectures. Albany: State University of New York Press, 1989.

Nelson, Lance E., ed. *Purifying the Earthly Body of God: Religion and Ecology in Hindu India*. SUNY Series in Religious Studies. Albany: State University of New York Press, 1988.

Ogilvy, Jay. "The New Polytheism: Updating the Dialogue between East and West." *East-West Affairs* 1.2 (2013) 29–48.

Oldmeadow, Harry. *Journeys East: 20th Century Western Encounters with Eastern Religious Traditions*. The Library of Perennial Philosophy. The Perennial Philosophy Series. Bloomington, IN: World Wisdom, 2004.

Panikkar, Raimon. *Invisible Harmony: Essays on Contemplation and Responsibility*. Edited by Harry James Cargas. Minneapolis: Fortress, 1995.

———. "The Invisible Harmony: A Universal Theory of Religion or a Cosmic Confidence in Reality?" In *Toward a Universal Theology of Religion*, edited by Leonard J. Swidler, 118–53. 2nd printing. Faith Meets Faith Series. Maryknoll, NY: Orbis, 1988.

———. "The Jordan, the Tiber, and the Ganges; Three Kairological Moments of Christic Self-Consciousness." In *The Myth of Christian Uniqueness: Toward a Pluralistic Theology of Religions*, edited by John Hick and Paul F. Knitter, 89–116. Faith Meets Faith Series. Maryknoll, NY: Orbis, 1987.

———. *Mysticism and Spirituality*. Edited by Milena Carrara Pavan. Opera Omnia Series 1. Maryknoll, NY: Orbis, 2014.

———. "Religious Pluralism: The Metaphysical Challenge." In *Religious Pluralism*, edited by Leroy S. Rouner, 97–115. Boston University Studies in Philosophy and Religion 5. Notre Dame, IN: University of Notre Dame Press, 1984.

Rachel, Alex. "Daimonic Ecologies: An Inquiry into the Relationships between the Human and Nonphysical Species." In *Daimonic Imagination: Uncanny Intelligence*, edited by Angela Voss and William Rowlandson, 321–39. Newcastle upon Tyne, UK: Cambridge Scholars, 2013.

Rahner, Karl. "Christianity and the Non-Christian Religions." In *Christianity and Other Religions: Selected Readings*, edited by John Hick and Brian Hebblethwaite, 19–38. Oxford: Oneworld, 2001.

Raskin, Robert, and Harry Terry. "A Principal-Components Analysis of the Narcissistic Personality Inventory and Further Evidence of Its Construct Validity." *Journal of Personality and Social Psychology* 54 (1988) 890–902.

Romero, Marina T., and Ramón V. Albareda. "Born on Earth: Sexuality, Spirituality, and Human Evolution." *ReVision* 24.2 (2001) 5–15.

Rorty, Richard. "Pragmatism as Romantic Polytheism." In *The Revival of Pragmatism: New Essays on Social Thought, Law, and Culture*, edited by Morris Dickstein, 21–36. Durham: Duke University Press, 1998.

Rothberg, Donald. "How Straight is the Spiritual Path?: Conversations with Buddhist Teachers Joseph Goldstein, Jack Kornfield, and Michelle McDonald-Smith." *ReVision* 19 (1996) 25–29.

Rushdooney, Rousas John. *The One and the Many: Studies in the Philosophy of Order and Ultimacy*. 1971. Reprint, Vallecito, CA: Ross House, 2007.

Schuon, Frithjof. *The Transcendent Unity of Religions*. Wheaton, IL: Theosophical Publishing House, 1984.

Sen, Amartya. *Identity and Violence: The Illusion of Destiny*. New York: Norton, 2006.

Smart, Ninian. "The Global Future of Religion." In *Global Religions: An Introduction*, edited by Mark Juergensmeyer, 124–31. New York: Oxford University Press, 2003.

Smith, Huston. "Spiritual Personality Types: The Sacred Spectrum." In *In Quest of the Sacred: The Modern World in the Light of Tradition*, edited by Seyyed H. Nasr and Katherine O'Brien, 45–57. Oakton, VA: Foundation for Traditional Studies, 1994.

Smith, Jonathan Z. *Imagining Religion: From Babylon to Jonestown*. Chicago Studies in the History of Judaism. Chicago: University of Chicago Press, 1982.

Smith, Wilfred Cantwell. *The Meaning and End of Religion: A Revolutionary Approach to the Great Religious Traditions*. London: SPCK, 1978.

Stoddart, William. *Remembering in a World of Forgetting: Thoughts on Tradition and Postmodernism*. The Library of Perennial Philosophy. Perennial Philosophy Series. Bloomington, IN: World Wisdom, 2008.

Stoeber, Michael. *Theo-monistic Mysticism: A Hindu-Christian Comparison*. Basingstoke, UK: St. Martin's, 1994.

Tarnas, Richard. *Passion of the Mind: Understanding the Ideas That Have Shaped Our World View*. New York: Ballantine, 1993.

Taylor, Charles. *Sources of the Self: The Making of the Modern Identity*. Cambridge: Harvard University Press, 1989.

Tenzin Gyatso (H. H. the XIVth Dalai Lama). *The Bodhgaya Interviews: His Holiness the Dalai Lama*. Edited by José Ignacio Cabezón. Ithaca: Snow Lion, 1988.

Thompson, Evan. *Mind in Life: Biology, Phenomenology, and the Sciences of Mind*. Cambridge: Belknap, 2007.

Varela Francisco J., and Natalie Depraz. "Imagining: Embodiment, Phenomenology, and Transformation." In *Buddhism & Science: Breaking New Ground*, edited by

B. Alan Wallace, 195–230. Columbia Series in Science and Religion. New York: Columbia University Press, 2003.

Varela Francisco J., et al. *The Embodied Mind: Cognitive Science and Human Experience.* Cambridge: MIT Press, 1991.

Victoria, B. Daizen. *Zen at War.* War and Peace Library. Lanham, MD: Rowman & Littlefield, 2006.

Wilber, Ken. *Integral Spirituality: A Startling New Role for Religion in the Modern and Postmodern World.* Boston: Integral Books, 2006.

———. *Sex, Ecology, Spirituality: The Spirit of Evolution.* Boston: Shambhala, 1995.

——— 10 ———

emergent dialogue

The Intersection of the HigherWe and Dialogue Practice

THOMAS STEININGER AND ELIZABETH DEBOLD

"COGITO, ERGO SUM" wrote René Descartes in *Discourse on the Method*, published in 1637.[1] That simple statement, quoted in every introductory philosophy class, represents the culmination of a process in human development that began around 800 BC, which some historians call the Axial Age.[2] This period marked a new axis in human and cultural development across the globe, from China to India to Greece. What began to emerge then is something that we take so for granted today, a "sense of individual identity, as distinct from the tribe and from nature."[3] Nearly a thousand years later, Descartes's "I think, therefore I am," represents the culmination of this development in the West. The achievement of the self-reflective, self-contained, separate, rational "I" eventually made the scientific revolution, the Kantian Enlightenment, and liberal democracy possible.

Today, argues theologian Ewert Cousins,[4] we are at the beginning of another, equally significant time of transition that he calls the Second Axial Period. Noting that consciousness evolution proceeds by recapitulation, Cousins argues that this next great current in cultural evolution will incorporate the ground of unity that pre-Axial tribal cultures had access to, but on a deeper and larger scale. As he notes, "having developed self-reflective, analytic, critical consciousness in the First Axial Period, we must now, while retaining these values, reappropriate and integrate into that

1. Descartes, *Discourse*, 159.
2. Jaspers, *Origin and Goal*, 1.
3. Cousins, "World Religions," section 2, para. 6.
4. See Cousins, "World Religions."

consciousness the collective and cosmic dimensions of . . . consciousness."[5] Cousins recognized the urgency for such an integration to happen in order to respond to the crises we are facing as a globalized human community.

We agree with Cousins that the emergence of a new capacity for collective consciousness would have implications as profound as the emergence of individuated consciousness. If the "I think, therefore I am" consciousness brought about the scientific revolution, what revolution, or evolution, could such an integrated, collective awareness bring about? We are witnessing today, in various community contexts around the world, whether through serendipity or intention, extensive experiments in intersubjective consciousness. These new forms of collective awareness are often called "We Spaces" among those engaged in integral philosophy and practice. The two of us writing this chapter were engaged for over twenty years within the EnlightenNext spiritual community founded by Andrew Cohen. A central aspect of our work together during those years was an experiment with new we-spaces, which we even then called HigherWe.

Since 2001, we two have explored and further developed this practice of HigherWe. After the failure of the EnlightenNext experiment, we in Germany independently developed this work further as a dialogue practice that we call *emergent dialogue*.[6] Just as the "I" of Descartes's *cogito, ergo sum* made new realms of human innovation possible, our belief is that the "we" in the HigherWe will bring about new capacities of creativity that can better address the complexity and conflicts we face in a highly networked, globalized world. Our hope is that *emergent dialogue* is and can be a small contribution to this new We-Space culture.

emergent dialogue and the HigherWe

Before one can understand *emergent dialogue*, one needs to understand what we mean by the "HigherWe." While it may sound almost self-explanatory, it's actually somewhat counterintuitive. Imagine a group of individuals sitting in a circle, engaging in a deep dialogue. The HigherWe is not the group, nor about individuals in a group; nor is it about an experience that they are

5. Cousins, "World Religions," section 2, para. 6.

6. *emergent dialogue* has been developed by us during the last fifteen-plus years. The impetus for this dialogue work was twofold: to create a "lower threshold" of our collective-consciousness work and to find a new way of bringing different perspectives together, mainly at the Herbstakademie, a partnership between the Integral Academy and Info3 (a progressive anthroposophical magazine) and us. We would like to thank our partners from the Herbstakademie, Sonja Student and Jens Heisterkamp, as well as our colleagues from *emerge bewusstseinskultur* e.V.

having together. While the starting point is a specific "we" in a conversation setting, what we mean by the HigherWe is not constrained by any kind of limited "we space" that is defined by the people present. Its meaning and reality are not reduced to any particular individuals. The group is a gateway for an awareness of consciousness as process within the shared internal or intersubjective space. The HigherWe opens up when a sufficient number of individuals within a group are awake to this intersubjective dimension as a living, creative reality. The HigherWe is an awakened intersubjective field that is consciousness aware, process aware, and content conscious. The human heart experiences the HigherWe as something sacred that one feels humbled by, and compelled to protect and nourish. At the same time, it is simply and most profoundly who we are.

The HigherWe emergence depends on a deep, ongoing experiential awareness of the reality and living presence of consciousness between human beings in a committed conversation. Many contemporary spiritual practitioners have had meditation experiences of consciousness as the timeless formless Absolute. The HigherWe is the experience of consciousness *in* time and space. Just as sitting on a meditation cushion is a limited setting in which one can experience limitlessness, a group conversation setting is a similarly limited setting in which one can become aware of an unlimited potential that is part of a much bigger process. They are, needless to say, related. Deep, sustained realization of that One-without-a-second in meditation leads to an ongoing, sensed recognition of a "prior unity" in the present moment, a sense of nonseparation within a field of undivided interrelatedness.[7] The human experience of depth in both meditation and HigherWe practice is freedom or ecstasy—which literally means "unfixed," referring in this case to a release from the bounded sense of self. As the sense of limitation drops, it gives rise to a living current between individuals that then "un-fixes" our creative capacities, making it possible to realize, understand, and make connections that weren't available before. In fact, being aware of consciousness in motion in time and space, together within the circle of individuals engaged in dialogue, always has a slight upward pull, a lift, toward the horizon of potential. Inherent to it is an alertness, curiosity, and interest about the not-yet. Placing attention on the shared field within the dialogue circle, the possibility and potential of the next moment, unknown, pulls. "The unknown is born in the dialogue between us and through us, out of a creative nothingness and a 'not-yet-thought' that arises when this intuition of the whole arises in our experience," says Maria Zacherl, a dialogue facilitator of *emergent dialogue.* "When we open ourselves to it, it comes alive in

7. Adi Da, *Prior Unity.*

our expression." So, the more each participant gives to the whole and leans in to the field with genuine curiosity, the more the whole awakens to itself and a shared intelligence begins to be expressed through the group. This is the HigherWe.

The HigherWe is a decisive shift from individual consciousness; it creates a new identity of "self-as-process" within a larger, cosmic process. Something completely undivided opens up between the collective in the intersubjective that is self in a much deeper sense than one's usual identity. Unlike individuated, personal subjectivity, the inner space of the intersubjective has no limits: the inner is the outer; the outer is the inner. In other words, when the individuals in the group have the repeated, almost uncanny experience of having their own thoughts and insights expressed by others in the group, the recognition of a shared interior experience develops. Participants experience themselves as a fractal focal points of a field of consciousness unfolding between them. This experience is fundamentally different from being just a part of a circle or a point in a circle. One begins to identify more with the process, relaxing into a deeper sense of self as limitless, nonseparate, undivided unfolding. Simultaneously, because the HigherWe concerns collectives of human beings, the process is always dialogical: it is an unfolding of human culture and, ultimately, of the cosmos that has no end because there is always more to include and integrate. Through us and as us, in the emergence of the HigherWe, the Whole wakes up to the Whole.

While the HigherWe is a profound spiritual practice and experience, *emergent dialogue* is more its pragmatic application in the form of an easier to implement dialogue practice. We have used this practice as a process facilitation method for conferences, as a means to think better together in business or board meetings, as a way to deepen community and support individual realization and transformation, and as a practice to engage in complex problem solving in business. *emergent dialogues* do not demand that participants, or a critical mass of them, expand their identity. Nor are they about consciousness in the deep sense of the word. In fact, this process has been used successfully in business contexts where participants had no understanding of meditation, consciousness, or spirituality. Facilitators of *emergent dialogue*, who have deeply experienced that they are not separate from this larger process, can hold an awareness and space that liberates the creativity between a group of human beings. It's not identity changing but when there is enough gravity, or weight, given to the field to open up space for the creative process as such, something new is possible.

Thus, *emergent dialogue* is a practical application of the HigherWe that can be used in any context where real dialogue is called for. By "dialogue," we mean a group conversation in which perspectives are shared with the aim of coming to a deeper understanding or resolution. This process catalyzes creative momentum within a group by asking participants to take certain inner postures under the direction of a facilitator who is skilled in holding a HigherWe context. These inner postures (which we will explain later in this chapter) ask participants to behave in ways similar to the ways that individuals who are awake to the HigherWe consciousness would respond. Thus, they begin to function as a whole, and through the facilitator's awareness of the field of alive nonseparate intersubjectivity, they can catalyze creative emergence. As Mike Kauschke, an *emergent dialogue* facilitator, clarifies, "we often experience how a field of higher consciousness is not simply preexisting between us. It gets born in its own aliveness to the degree that we start to be open for it."[8] Truly *emergent dialogue* requires participation, and participation in such a dialogue often leads to the recognition that we can work deeply and creatively together with our differences, and that the creative flow is more important than one's self-importance. If a significant number of the individuals in the group have the interest and capacity to care about the project that the group is engaging with, beyond their own beliefs about what "should be" or their status in the group, it is possible to facilitate emergence in a dialogue. Thus, it can be productively used and understood by people with a more secular understanding of consciousness. Particularly given the fact that the awareness is growing that we, on this planet, are in a process together and have to find ways to really interact that do not start from the presumption of primary differences and our individuated self-sense but on being together in a living society on a living globe—or even just in a living organization. We see *emergent dialogue* as a potentially key cultural practice for developing a transindividuated culture that includes and transcends our personal focus. One of the unintended consequences of our "I" (or "me") focused culture has been an unsustainable consumerism that now threatens the biosphere. Cultivating a holistic, collective intelligence would make it easier for us to directly recognize our interconnectedness and interdependence with all life on Earth. Moreover, the complexity of the "wicked" problems that we now face as a human species call for more than individual genius and call us to bring together a wide range of human knowledge and experience to find new solutions. Perhaps *emergent dialogue* could be one method to assist in our transition from the First Axial Period where the individual was the focal point into a Second Axial Period in which the "collective and cosmic" dimensions of consciousness become

8. The quotations and descriptions from our colleagues that appear across this chapter were generated in training seminars and dialogues. These individuals have contributed to the development of *emergent dialogue* through their committed participation. In a sense, we consider them our cocontributors.

incorporated into our ongoing, daily awareness.[9] The present crisis of our planet has here also quite a positive side. Through its urgency it becomes itself a catalyst to accelerate this necessary development of consciousness.

The I, the We, and the It of Potentiality

To bring a Wilberian Integral frame to *emergent dialogue*, working in this way brings into awareness three different perspectives of "potentiality space"; the I, the We, and the It.[10] This potentiality space refers to the previously unknown capacities and awareness that arise in a collective context, both in its pragmatic form in *emergent dialogue* and in an intentional HigherWe practice. First, there is the potentiality space for the individual to discover that there is room to grow both horizontally and vertically. Horizontally, the individual expands her or his understanding related to the topic under discussion. Vertically, the individual can realize that there is a depth of Being and capacity for shared creative consciousness that lead to a more inclusive, transpersonal experience of self. Participants often experience aspects of self within the dialogue that at least loosen their fixed ideas about their psychological selves while at the same time deepening individual autonomy. One caveat, however, is that these vertical I-shifts are initially dependent on the HigherWe context: when one leaves the context, the habitual patterns of self reassert themselves. This can be confusing. Also, one can become consistently able to lean in, as it were, and *respond to* the collective field of a HigherWe yet not be *responsible for* holding this consciousness.[11] However, by becoming increasingly sensitive and responsive to the HigherWe context through practice, one gradually develops the capacity to be responsible for it. To develop the sensitivity and awareness to maintain contact with these more transpersonal dimensions, outside of a context in which the HigherWe is evoked, takes a great deal of effort, sensing capacity, and awareness.

From the We, there is a similar horizontal and vertical potentiality space. In a more "functional" or pragmatic *emergent dialogue*, the horizontal We creates a greater sense of interpersonal connection and possibility to work well as individuals together. Yet in a dialogue that evokes the HigherWe, what participants describe as a sacred dimension opens as a collective awareness of unity beyond the apparent diversity of the individuals present.

9. Cousins, "World Religions," section 2, para. 6.

10. Thank you to Sonja Student for giving us this integral perspective on the "Möglichkeitsraum" in the context of our dialogue work.

11. The distinction between being "responsive to" and "responsible for" the HigherWe was made by Andrew Cohen in a meeting with his core students.

This perception does not stop at the boundaries of the dialogue group. Rather, it is an experience of comprehensive presence. There is a realization that there is someplace new to go *together,* and that only we can do this—there is no other higher power that will intervene to take the next steps forward. This vertical recognition of the potentiality space of the We can be loosely thought of as a fourth face of God, extending into the collective or lower left quadrant. Wilber has recognized the different faces of Spirit[12] as the I, the Divinity in each human being; the You, the ultimate Other; and the Its, the cosmic process itself.[13] The HigherWe as a fourth face of God would be the sacred intersubjective space, the space of a comprehensive presence not separate from ourselves.

The potentiality space of the It within an *emergent dialogue* relates to the content or subject matter of the conversation itself. Because this dialogue work is expressly concerned with content through generating solutions or developing new ideas, the It has more significance here than in HigherWe practice. The It in *emergent dialogue* also has a horizontal and vertical dimension. Horizontally, this dialogue process can organize existing information and bring the various participants and their perspectives into a more unified understanding of the issues at hand. Vertically, a really alive and synergistic dialogue can produce breakthrough ideas that often come from "left field," which the participants often experience as an emergence. The sense in the group is that "everything falls into place" and a new creative coherence with a new potential comes to life. From the point of view of this new perspective, the problems or concerns at the beginning of the dialogue seem almost to disappear, as the solution or right response simply becomes evident. Developing the It as content in this way is the key purpose of *emergent dialogue.*

Prerequisites for HigherWe Emergence

The HigherWe asks for more from participants than *emergent dialogue* does. The HigherWe needs highly individuated, autonomous individuals who freely choose to surrender to a process larger than themselves. It is a transindividuated We-space that transcends individuality and also builds on it.

12. Wilber, *Integral Spirituality*, 159.

13. Thomas Steininger observes that there are seven Faces of God: the I, the Divine within the individual self; the You, the Absolute Other to which one bows down; the It, the Divinity expressed in a particular thing; the We, the enlightened intersubjective; the plural You, the many faces of the Divine in the diverse Deities humans worship; the Its, the panentheistic Divine Cosmic Unfolding; and the aperspectival Absolute that reveals itself in deep meditation.

This is distinguished from a preindividuated, tribal We based on custom and conformity. For this space to unfold, those present must direct their attention to a non-separate reality between them. There, a holistic, shared process of consciousness emerges that underlies the HigherWe. Coercion and subordination prevent this process. The participants must decide, each for him- or herself, not to participate from an attitude of separation. This process needs not a passive but an active letting go of our self-centered and separative motives. It is not will as one typically understands it; it is will in the form of surrender. Here, both merge into a common motive. In this conscious surrender, the HigherWe reveals itself as a joint, cocreative, and integrative process. In other words, the independence of the individual is expressed here in surrender to a freely recognized, communal, and universal process.

Through this willing, agentic surrender to this process, a new form of identity is also revealed, which has its own and different motivation. Personal motives lose their importance. In a deep calmness of the heart, a willingness to surrender to the cocreative process emerges. This requires mature people with self-confidence and an ability for self-reflection. At the same time, the HigherWe needs the willingness to leave behind the self-focus of the ego. By a mature individuality we mean the ability to separate oneself—to recognize thoughts, feelings, motivations, and behavior as one's own—in order to be able to take responsibility. The HigherWe needs this individual responsibility so that a larger process can unfold in freedom.

This development of the personal ego was an evolutionary breakthrough that Jaspers[14] recognized by naming the Axial Period as a fundamental shift in history, and it is foundational to HigherWe emergence. With the development of the "I" or ego, human consciousness became individuated and could stand against what one could call the "Primary We," the more undifferentiated tribal and collective consciousness. Individuated moral agency thus became possible. In the two and a half thousand years since the Axial Period, human consciousness has developed so that now, as postmodern individuals, our attention is habitually focused on the self-absorbing and mesmerizing stream of thoughts, feelings, and sense impressions occurring within us. *And* this structure of individuated experience, and the sensitivity and awareness that it has given rise to, are necessary for the recognition, holding, and understanding of the universal process of consciousness, so that a HigherWe can develop.

For the individual participant, the HigherWe entails a shift of identification from the personal ego to the emerging, intersubjective process itself as self, accessed through the HigherWe. "Identification" is a tricky concept

14. See Jaspers, *Origin and Goal.*

in psychology that is related to "shadow," or the elements of our experience that have been intentionally placed outside of our conscious awareness. However, while shadow is something we consider to be negative, identification is not. At least not until and unless one wants to change it. We tend to expect, or assume, that we each have an identity that relates to our gender, race, class, religion, and cultural backgrounds. In addition, our identity is related to our special gifts, habitual fears, and coping strategies developed through our personal history. Identity, then, is how we construct ourselves as different and separate from others. For many of us, our adult identities have been hard-won and are fiercely defended even though much of what we are identified with is not conscious. What we identify with as self is truly the skin we are in, the eyes we see with. It is "me." Our identifications are not our ideas or feelings, but the actual values that structure what we think, feel, and do. While our unique identities are the gifts we bring to the intersubjective space, we have to loosen our grip on our separate identity to make room in ourselves for deeper dimensions of who we are. To become a portal for the HigherWe, one works to expand one's identity so that, before thought, one's reference point is on the ever-changing process that is unfolding within and around us within the larger process of cosmic evolution. It's a tall order. Such a change brings one in touch with a depth of nonseparation that holds all of life. Simultaneously, in this experience, one becomes aware of the evolutionary impulse that incessantly strives within us for higher forms of integration. It shows itself as a living whole, not a homogenized, undifferentiated whole, but a living, ever-differentiating unity. Ever new voices and experiences emerge within it without splitting off from the process. Our own self emerges as a fractal focal point of this holistic dynamic. The experiences of an "inside" and "outside" remain distinct in this perception but they are not separate. And our personal knowledge, our life experience, all weave themselves into this great universal dialogue, which is itself the expression of the human striving for wholeness and integration.

The HigherWe only becomes apparent when enough people present experience this shift in the focus of their identity. Then intention and attention shift away from the individual to an integrated and integrating whole. How many people or what proportion this is, we don't know (this could obviously be consciously explored). Returning to the distinction between being responsive to the HigherWe context and responsible for it, that people are open to the HigherWe does not yet mean that they are able themselves to hold in an active and creative way this perspective and depth of this consciousness, or to initiate independently the emergence of the HigherWe. The shift of identity at first is situational—a willing suspension of self-focus. Even the willingness to make this shift temporarily is significant.

The Practice of emergent dialogue

emergent dialogue provides a way that the power of HigherWe work can be brought to the service of human creativity without demanding so much of the individuals participating. Only the facilitator needs to have an authentic connection to and understanding of the HigherWe space, lessening the demand on individuals. Participants can be complete novices or have little experience with the practice themselves. They do not need to shift their identity, only the willingness to engage in the process and the concern that brings them together. The authentic willingness to come together for something in common already changes our attitude away from ourselves, towards a shared concern. The HigherWe perspective allows *emergent dialogue* to break through the usual groupthink. They consciously use the creative friction of different perspectives for a collective, cocreative process.

The focus on the HigherWe within a dialogue context where individuals meet to create solutions or explore some particular pragmatic or intellectual terrain is *emergent dialogue*. It catalyzes a freedom from old, stuck patterns of response to release a creative momentum in a group. The intelligence of the whole becomes far more than the sum of its parts. The focus on what is happening between dialogue participants in the intersubjective space, rather than on individual contributions or psychological dynamics, gives rise to a synergistic dynamic. However, a dialogue with a strong content focus also brings its own unique challenges: content is hypnotic, particularly when feelings run high in any direction, whether positive or negative, and lose touch with the potentiality of the intersubjective space. While there are inner postures for engaging in the practice, in order for this type of dialogue to be most successful, the skill of a facilitator who has an authentic alignment with the HigherWe context is most often necessary.

What we call the "Six Inner Postures" for *emergent dialogue* offer a way to approach the dialogue. They aren't rules or instructions to be handed out. They are clues that a facilitator can use for the dialogue. In our experience, a formal introduction of a dialogue with these six items to be mindful of sometimes becomes a distraction itself. Participants then often lose sight of the actual dialogue "under the spell" of the "Six Inner Postures" that one wants to do justice to. However, a dialogue can only unfold its full power if one immerses oneself completely in it. For the facilitator as well as the participants, this means staying "inside" the dialogue rather than observing or commenting on it from a distance.

These inner postures come from observing how group participants in a HigherWe context actually behave when their attention and intention is focused on the living intersubjective process unfolding between them.

This creates a context that looks, from the outside, "as if" the members of the collective have made a shift of identity and are consciously awake to the HigherWe—which can happen spontaneously—but they only need to shift their attitude. In other words, while a full shift of identification is not necessary, participants need to set aside their self-importance, the sense that "I'm right," superiority/inferiority and other ways of insisting on being separate for the sake of the dialogue process. The less any one person acts out of the habit that one's individual perspective is more important than the intersubjective engagement, the more successful, joyous, and surprising the dialogue will be.

These six inner postures are not injunctions addressed to the individuals who are part of the conversation, but attitudes that express certain productive ways to contribute to creating the open field of a HigherWe together. Intentionally, the statements primarily reflect the "we," not the separate "I's" who are participating.

1. *Real dialogue arises when we are more interested in what we do not yet know rather than in what we already know.* The position of not knowing and wanting to know creates a space that helps undercut the fixed positions that individuals hold, particularly when the dialogue is about matters that are emotionally significant or have critical implications for the participants. Moreover, listening for what isn't known places the attention of the group on the living moment and the creative potential within it.

2. *It is easy to be too intellectual or too personal. Dialogue comes alive through our shared interest in what emerges, between us, in content and in the field of consciousness.* Being too intellectual means speaking in a way that is separate from one's own living experiences. We can engage in highly philosophical matters when each statement arises from a reckoning with what is being said. Being too personal means being caught in one's story, which pulls the attention of the group away from creating a shared "we" space, perceiving how a larger truth resonating in dialogical space shines through one's specific, own experience. Allowing for such authenticity triggers a current of shared aliveness, and with it, a deeper understanding and increasingly perceptible field of consciousness emerges between one another.

3. *Really listening to each other enables us to develop a conversation that builds on each others' contributions. Really listening allows us to come together in an ever-opening comprehension. Really listening allows us to come together in an ever-opening comprehension.* "Really listening"

means turning inward to the field of consciousness from which the contribution arises, while withholding one's own usual reactions and judgments. To truly listen, one must not force another's statements into the framework of one's own ideas or prejudices. In this way, responses emerge in shared consciousness that are often unexpected and vivid. As Daniela Bomatter, a facilitator of *emergent dialogue*, explains, "this process can catalyze a HigherWe when enough people in the group are willing to completely let go of their conditioned minds and listen deeply into the field of consciousness between them."

4. *Authentic interest in the other is one of the sources of creativity. Through our attentiveness to the shared dialogic field, creative solutions arise precisely at the points of friction that otherwise often turn into conflict, solutions that are not available to any of us alone.* When there are conflicting perspectives in a dialogue, this easily leads to an inner division between those present. However, such fragmentation prevents the HigherWe from arising. Of course, one does not have to agree with every point of view. What is needed is an attitude of respect and an authentic curiosity towards the other. If we succeed in keeping the field between us from fragmenting, this often becomes the seed of an unforeseen integration of perspectives in which a new whole becomes visible.

5. *We are always connected to the whole. In listening and in speaking, the potential of dialogue thrives on our being actively present in the dialogue. Bring yourself fully in.* This is the most directive of the foundations: true dialogue thrives on participation. This does not mean that every participant must speak; however, each needs to pay attention and give oneself energetically to the whole. Otherwise, the circle can have "dark" spots that affect the creative momentum itself and prevent valuable information and perspectives from entering the dialogue.

6. *Each dialogue finds its true meaning in recognizing itself as part of a larger dialogue.* When a group begins to access the HigherWe consciousness field reliably, there is often an exhilaration that can very quickly turn into a group narcissism and a more or less subtle form of arrogance. The need for new holistic, dialogic forms and their integration is an evolutionary movement that is happening across the globe. All dialogues are elements of larger historical, dialogic fields, ultimately including all humanity and beyond. Directly perceiving how each field of dialogue is embedded in larger contexts and releasing it from its isolation fundamentally transforms the dialogue.

Depending on the context, these inner postures can be adapted or revised to meet the needs or level of the participants. The facilitator can use much simpler, directive language in situations where *emergent dialogue* process is being used in a business/work context for the purpose of facilitating collective work, rather than really seeking creative breakthrough or emergence (e.g., "Be more interested in what you don't know rather than in the ideas and beliefs that you have brought to the meeting"). For example, in Caritas, a large nonprofit organization, Marlene Potthoff used the process in a hundred-person all-day planning meeting. She trained some of the members of her staff to be "facilitators" so that they could understand and work with several aspects of the guidelines (being interested in what you don't know, listening, and building on prior contributions) so that they could lead the process at a table of eight to ten people. She introduced the dialogue process to the whole group, giving them confidence in her competence while maintaining her own awareness of the whole consciousness field, thus "holding the space" for the group. Afterwards, Potthoff noticed that there was a qualitative difference in the consciousness field compared to previous planning meetings: there was greater focus at the tables and a greater intention held by the whole group. However, none of the participants were aware of the difference. Within the context, they responded in new ways, but as individuals, they did not notice that their behavior had changed. More importantly, and pragmatically, many of the teams at the tables came up with creative ideas that had not been considered before. They also worked with much greater cooperation. At the end of the meetings, when a representative of each group was asked to present, the representatives spoke with a simplicity, directness, and clarity that was unusual. Even more interesting was the composure that they expressed when, toward the end of the presentations, the director decided unexpectedly to shorten the meeting to give himself a longer time to speak. In a situation that usually would have created anxiety and chaos, the group as a whole and the representatives making the final presentations kept their cool and clarity.

Facilitating an *emergent dialogue*

While the Six Inner Postures provide a strong foundation for engaging in creative dialogue, we find that the facilitator's connection to the HigherWe space liberates the dialogue from the usual grind of meetings or problem-solving. Yet facilitation is an art, and the art of facilitation in an *emergent dialogue* is quite demanding because it requires more than mastering a skill set or technique. The facilitator needs to have the subtlety and capacity to awaken the participants to the potentiality space in the collective—often without using terms like "consciousness" or anything that seems esoteric. There isn't a one, two, three process that works every time. The dialogue facilitator holds the complexity and tension between the group's points of view, and intervenes and supports the dialogue through a sensitive process of discovery, building resonance, and a constant search for new creative openings. A skilled facilitator will succeed in finding a precise transition to what is new and alive in the dialogue. But this requires the courage to speak without knowing. One has to allow the words to come "out of HigherWe-space," so to speak, rather than from one's own preconceived ideas. This is a special form of "presencing," to use Otto Scharmer's[15] term: the facilitator senses into the potentiality space of the field in which the dialogue is happening and brings into presence the intelligence that becomes apparent through such transrational sensing. Ultimately, the facilitator focuses the consciousness for the group and tunes in to the HigherWe, which is not simply a passive stance but an active, sensing attunement, while being fully in the dialogue.

We have found that facilitators need a solid base in meditation in order to trust enough to let go of the mind's reactions and to stay present in the face of confusion and complexity. The essence of meditation practice, as we understand it, is an open and detached presentness. Regular meditation practice allows us to loosen our pervasive attachments. The consistent practice of meditation enables a letting go of attachment so that in dialogue something can arise and come into awareness beyond what we hold in our minds. We break the habit of grasping onto our thoughts and feelings. Through this deep letting go in meditation, Through deep letting go in meditation, one discovers a deep foundation, a power, a thus-ness. Some experience it as the "source of everything." Trusting in this self-perceiving awareness makes it easier to remain open, even within strong conflicts, without losing balance. In meditation, for example, a regular silent sitting practice, this detached self-awareness of consciousness develops, through ongoing experience of pure presence, in the presence of the subtle movements and changes of consciousness, and also when thoughts and feelings "rage" with their full force.

Good dialogue facilitators, we find, need to have some experience with the HigherWe. This is for several reasons. First, most obviously, without experiencing the HigherWe, the facilitator will not be clear about the intersubjective potentiality space and cannot facilitate from it. Yet, equally importantly, explicit HigherWe practice helps to purify one's motivation. In a sensitive HigherWe field, increasingly subtle self-oriented motives—rather

---

15. Scharmer, "Presencing."

than giving to the whole—become apparent. One can see and feel the places that inhibit us from being able to engage in the potentialities of the inter-subjective space. One becomes familiar with one's blind spots and reactive tendencies that make it difficult to be a conduit for a different intelligence. Within the HigherWe context, as a collective, these different habits of separation are seen, not as the exclusive problem of the individual, but as a reflection of where we are as human beings. They represent the evolutionary conundrums that we all face. This impersonal view on the most personal human defenses and habits that subtly divide us from each other provides a larger and more liberating perspective on one's self. Both meditation and HigherWe practice, taken together, give the facilitator a basis for more easily intuiting these evolutionary stress points within a dialogue. However, the dialogue facilitators' own trust in a conscious, living presence is one of the most important supports for *emergent dialogue.*

How does an *emergent dialogue* go? After the facilitator introduces him- or herself, s/he explains the purpose for the conversation and introduces whichever inner postures are appropriate for the context. The details of the introduction (Do the participants know each other? What are their expectations?) are typically arranged in advance. After these basics, the facilitator can invite the group to sit for a few minutes quietly in order to ground the group and open the participants to a wider sense of being present. In this way, the facilitator's depth begins to bring a subliminal coherence to the group as a whole. If this isn't possible because the participants would find it too uncomfortable, reading an inspiring quote about collective dialogue or emergence can also cohere the group in a larger perspective.

With this grounding, the facilitator then opens the dialogue by focusing attention on the potentiality space that exists in intersubjective engagement—the interpersonal We of the group held within the facilitator's deeper awareness of the HigherWe that goes beyond those present. The focus of attention is twofold: first, the facilitator invites the participants to sense the potential of the group; and second, s/he holds an awareness of the prior unity underlying and interpenetrating the diversity in the group. Maintaining this deeper awareness is crucial. Particularly as conflicting perspectives come to light and the tensions in the group become apparent, holding an awareness of this whole enables the facilitator to stay alert to opportunities to make unifying distinctions and clarifying integrations within the conversation. Rather than getting trapped in a problem-oriented mindset in which one is trying to come up with solutions, by holding the whole in awareness the facilitator stays with "possibility consciousness"—an attitude in which one realizes that there is always the potential for a surprising resolution or creative emergence that no one can foresee. To hold this attitude means that the facilitator has to be *in* the conversation that s/he is *actually in*. In other words, holding "possibility consciousness" doesn't mean having an idea about the way the process should go or the outcome should be. If one has these ideas, they will destroy the potential of the dialogue because the facilitator will be responding to something that is not the reality in front of him or her. The potential and possibilities for the dialogue cannot come from what one thinks should happen but only from what is actually happening. This is so obviously true that it seems strange to mention it, but time and again, as a facilitator, one feels a creeping dissatisfaction or frustration and interprets this to mean that the "right" things aren't happening. But it is the conclusion—that the dialogue is somehow going wrong—that means that one has stopped engaging "in" the dialogue. Frustration, impatience, irritation have to be born by the facilitator without drawing conclusions about what this means about the dialogue or the participants. Only when one is tuned in to the dialogue happening in the intersubjective can one intervene in ways that can catalyze new understanding in the collective.

emergent dialogue, as we have said, is consciousness aware, process aware, and content conscious. Consciousness awareness refers to the space, or dimension, in which *everything* is happening now. To be process aware means to be attentive to the dynamic unfolding happening in time and space. Content-consciousness refers to the topic of the dialogue. In a dialogue, the facilitator holds this three-fold focus. Throughout the conversation, the facilitator keeps his or her focus on the Whole and on the living edge of the dialogue rather than becoming engrossed in the content. This takes practice and skill. The facilitator has to respond in the language of the content, but needs to anchor his or her attention in consciousness and unfolding process. In many ways, it's like simultaneously listening to and conducting music, except the "notes" of the music relate to the different shades of space in between. When does it feel shut down, heavy? Where does the heaviness come from? What has weight and gravitas in the conversation? What leaves a hole, a sense that no sense was made? Where are the sharp edges? When is an opening made? What is the rhythm? Following this music, the facilitator supports the dialogue by inviting individuals to move on when an energetic opening appears or by pointing out resonances between speakers or by allowing silences just to be there. Often, but only depending on the capacity of the group, the facilitator can make conscious to the group these different musical strains, which heightens and deepens the awareness in the group itself: did you sense the shift that just happened? Can you feel that there's a heaviness in the room—is there something that needs to be said but hasn't been said? And so on.

Since the facilitator holds the consciousness field for, and hopefully with, the collective, he or she can be particularly challenged to maintain this focus when there is conflict in the group. One has to develop a sense of how much tension the group can hold and stay together. When it becomes too much, the group will almost instantly fragment. Staying calm and not personalizing the tension is really important in order to look for ways to intervene by calling the group's attention to some authentic means of integration, and thus model how the participants can respond to these tensions themselves. Not personalizing the conflict also can be freeing for the participants who are experiencing the contrary perspective. This often means making room for emotions—anger, fear, or tears—but not making them the focus of the conversation. In postmodern interpersonal contexts, we tend to focus on the pain or hurt, giving the individual time and space to process their feelings in ways that, while they may create an emphatic connection, also tend to reinforce separation. In an *emergent dialogue*, we don't stop or stigmatize the feelings, but we focus on the meaning and intention of the feelings that the individual is bringing into the dialogue and room. When the facilitator responds in this way, by pulling out key points and ensuring that they are part of the mix, the individual integrates into the group and the group, then, as a whole can consider the contributions, work with them, and find a creative way forward. Sometimes, it may be useful and necessary to bring dialogue groups into dialogue with each other—such as across divisions of gender, culture, or race—so that the collective blind spots in one group can be made visible by the other and vice versa.

While sometimes even the best facilitator can be stymied by a participant who does not want to engage in collective inquiry, when these dialogues do catalyze emergence, they are often illuminating and surprising to everyone involved—including the facilitator. The collective feels uplifted, connected in a fresh and light way that they experience as compelling and unusual. Often participants note that they "saw" each other differently, in a new light, as it were. Solutions to stuck points in the organization, between people, and relating to work arise throughout the dialogue process in ways that seem almost too simple. Afterwards, many participants speak of a sense of liberation. And, once a creative momentum develops within the dialogue, the sense that one person "owns" an insight or solution drops away because new ideas seem to emerge from the whole, through individuals certainly, but different participants often say with astonishment that they were thinking the same thing. The solutions are sourced by the field, which is the potentiality space of the We.

Differences with Other Dialogue Practices

While this may already be evident, *emergent dialogue* differs from other contemporary dialogue practices in several crucial ways. First, it is *transpersonal*. We tend to speak of the *transindividual*. The term "transpersonal" has a specific meaning in psychology, which generally refers to individual development into higher states and stages of conscious awareness.[16] Yet we are using "transpersonal" to mean that which includes and goes beyond individuality. We use the term *transindividual*—in which our individuality is maintained, built on, and transcended. Regardless, the focus, anchored by the facilitator, is on the intersubjective, both as a field of consciousness and as an unfolding creative process—the We potentiality space. In other words, attention is *not* on the disparate individuals who make up the group and their subjective experiences. While individual experiences remain important, what is happening in the whole is the priority.

In other words, *emergent dialogue* starts from a "We" space, not with an "I-Thou" or an "I-You" space. Many important practices for personal development create a sense of "We" through a focus on the feelings and emotional responses of an individual "I" in relation to another or others, the "You." These practices generate an intimacy and catalyze a sense of togetherness that breaks the isolation of the postmodern separate self.[17] These methods look into the feelings and emotional responses of the participants as a primary driver of insight and dialogue. Some also focus on achieving an interpersonal transparency between the participants—through doing pairing exercises or small groups where individuals speak about their thoughts and feelings as they arise, such as Thomas Hübl's Transparent Communication. Others, in the collective intelligence field, look to gather ideas and insights from as many individuals as possible to see the themes and "shared wisdom" held in the group.[18] In distinction, *emergent dialogue* considers individual experiences primarily in the context of a collective process, and the creative emergence inherent therein. Carried by an alertness for the nonseparateness that underlies all of us, the dialogue facilitator's attention is focused on this special potential of the we-space. In this way, such a dialogue becomes *consciousness aware*.

Second, *emergent dialogue* holds *diversity within unity*. This is something different from unity or Oneness. Some dialogue or creative group methods call on the spiritual insight of nonseparation that is experienced

16. See, e.g., Walsh and Vaughan, *Paths*.

17. See, for example, Patricia Albere's *Evolutionary Collective* website (https://evolutionarycollective.com/).

18. See Brown and Isaacs, *World Café*.

in meditation as the foundation for their work. One particularly notable example of such a practice comes from the Adi Da community. We have great resonance with their practice of discussion from a position of prior unity. The shared realization, or even assumption, of prior unity enables groups to engage with the creative friction of diversity without falling into factions around identity, thus it is an essential starting point. In our work, though, we have come to realize that a source of creative potential also lies precisely in co-emphasizing a diversity that cannot be resolved, in order to bring it in dialogically. Unity without diversity often creates homogenization or groupthink. Diversity without unity creates relativism and division that can fragment into nihilism. *emergent dialogue* thrives on the diversity of perspectives that emerge in lively dialogical processes. They need this diversity in order to create—in a deep field of unity—a lively, ever-advancing integration.

This leads to the third point: *emergent dialogue* is *process-conscious*. The process that we are referring to is the process of the evolution of consciousness itself. While many dialogues or group process methods explore the dynamics arising between individuals,[19] this isn't our focus. We are not referring to an interpersonal process, as important as that can be. The process that the facilitator attends to is based on the movement in consciousness toward integration through differentiation. When one is awake to the unfolding process in the whole at the level of consciousness, the dynamics of integration and differentiation become more transparent—visible as a creative momentum. Awareness of process provides both directionality and multiplicity of perspectives because, just as the deepest level of Being is undivided, so the process itself is and can only ever be one entire evolving cosmic whole. *emergent dialogue* is an invitation to consciously engage in this cosmic process even in very specific pragmatic contexts. The result, for many participants, is a glimpse at a new possibility of being human together. "In the praxis of catalyzing *emergent dialogue*," notes facilitator Nadja Rosmann, "we transcend the division between the spiritual and the profane. There is only one life and we try to find out how to express the one, and how to live it."

Conclusion

Our hope for our HigherWe and *emergent dialogue* work is that it can become an instrument for a vibrant coexistence of the many different perspectives on this globe. Our perspectives are so fragmented today. This alone is causing immeasurable damage. We need a new creative togetherness at all levels of society. Our inability to simply come together in a creative way at

19. Such as Tavistock or the work of the A. K. Rice Institute.

work, in our organizations, or even in our private lives is one of the main reasons why so many good ideas and ethical concerns that already exist are not coming to fruition. Beyond these all-too-ordinary difficulties that we humans have in working together, there are far bigger divisions that we have yet to figure out how to work with holistically and creatively. The historical rifts and fractures between nations, cultures, and social groups, if we are to find common creative responses, must be addressed from many sides simultaneously. To return to Ewert Cousins again, we need to develop a "complexified global consciousness" that would "not [be] a mere universal, undifferentiated, abstract consciousness. It will be global through the global convergence of cultures and religions and complexified by the dynamics of dialogic dialogue."[20] We see new human capacities emerging in the intersubjective potentiality space that give us great inspiration and hope that humanity can develop such a global consciousness and find a way forward together, even in the face of collapse. Our survival depends on realizing that we share one human project on this planet, and our humanness depends on the deeply knowing that we are One and that our differences are essential to the full expression of that One. As the West begins to realize the limitations of modernist instrumental reasoning and exploitation and postmodern individualism and consumerism, there are stirrings of a need for a postpersonal culture that honors the individual yet holds a larger unifying depth and context. The often desperate search among postmodern Westerners for meaning and purpose is an almost instinctive recognition that we need deeper rooting, real connection, and a higher aspiration than can be found in a materialistic, self-focused life.

Even as hundreds of thousands of people are risking their lives to reach the West, we who have had the privileges that the West affords are, more and more, intuitively reacting against the juggernaut of a one-sided modernity because it threatens to turn every aspect of human life and all of nature into a commodity for sale. The HigherWe emergence has the potential to deepen our humanity and reweave the web of our relationships. It is impetus for a new, complex, communal creativity. We consider ourselves, along with the other contributors to this book, to be extremely fortunate to be part of that movement that is awakening We, us, to the urgency and potential of such a transformation. The achievement of individuated identity has been so significant and, as we can see, has now become a threat to the world. The emergence of collective thinking, sensing, caring, creating, and knowing offers, as Cousins says, a Second Axial shift in the direction of a more humane life on this planet. This shift or transition comes none too soon.

20. Cousins, "World Religions," section 4, para. 5.

Our work and wish is that *emergent dialogue* can be used to further develop these shared creative capacities. The potential for a new HigherWe is now emerging, and with it a new possibility for being human together.

Bibliography

Brown, Juanita, with David Isaacs. *The World Café: Shaping Our Futures through Conversations That Matter.* San Francisco: Berrett-Koehler, 2005.

Cohen, Andrew, and Ken Wilber. "The Guru & the Pandit: Dialogue XIV—A Living Experiment in Conscious Evolution." *What Is Enlightenment?* 35 (January-March 2007) 46–58. https://s3.eu-central-1.amazonaws.com/wieoldissues/wie_en_weboptimized/EN_issue_35.pdf/.

Cousins, Ewert. "The World Religions: Facing Modernity Together," 1997. https://static1.squarespace.com/static/5464adeoe4b055bfb204446e/t/572119ca55598627640bea88/1461787082702/The+World+Religions+-+Facing+Modernity+Together/.pdf .

Adi Da. *Prior Unity: The Basis for a New Human Civilization.* Bethesda, MD: Is Peace 723, 2015.

Albere, Patricia. *Evolutionary Collective* (website). https://evolutionarycollective.com/.

Debold, Elizabeth. "Epistemology, Fourth Order Consciousness, and the Subject-Object relationship . . . or How the Self Evolves with Robert Kegan." In *What Is Enlightenment?* 22 (Fall-Winter 2002) 143–54. https://s3.eu-central-1.amazonaws.com/wieoldissues/wie_en_weboptimized/EN_issue_22.pdf/

Descartes, René. *Discourse on the Method of Rightly Conducting the Reason, and Seeking Truth in the Sciences.* 1637. Gutenberg Project E-Text 59: http://www.gutenberg.org/etext/59/ (release date July 1, 2008).

Jaspers, Karl. *The Origin and Goal of History.* Translated by Michael Bullock. New Haven: Yale University Press, 1953.

Patten, Terry. "Enacting an integral revolution: How can we have truly radical conversations in a time of global crisis?" Paper presented at the Integral Theory Conference, San Francisco, 2013.

Phipps, Carter. "A Matter of Integrity." *What Is Enlightenment?* Special Tenth-Anniversary Edition 20 (Fall-Winter 2001) 25–27. https://s3.eu-central-1.amazonaws.com/wieoldissues/wie_en_weboptimized/EN_issue_20.pdf/.

Scharmer, Otto. "Presencing: Learning from the Future as It Emerges; On the Tacit Dimension of Leading Revolutionary Change." Presented at the Conference On Knowledge and Innovation May 25–26, 2000, Helsinki, Finland; and at the MIT Sloan School of Management, October 20, 2000. http://www.welchco.com/02/14/01/60/00/05/2501.HTM/.

Stein, Zak. "On Spiritual Teachers and Teachings." *Journal of Integral Theory and Practice* 6.1 (2011) 57–77. http://www.zakstein.org/wp-content/uploads/2014/10/Stein_SpiritTeachersFINAL-copy.pdf/.

Venezia, A. "I, we, all: Intersubjectivity and We Space, post-metaphysics, and human becoming: An integral research project." Master's thesis, John F. Kennedy University, 2013.

Walsh, Roger, and Frances Vaughan, eds. *Paths beyond Ego: The Transpersonal Vision.* New York: Tarcher, 1993.

Wilber, Ken. *Sex, Ecology, Spirituality. The Spirit of Evolution.* Boston: Shambhala, 1995.

———. *Integral Spirituality: A Startling New Role for Religion in the Modern and Postmodern World.* Boston: Shambhala, 2007.

11

Closing Remarks by the Editor[1]

Oliver Griebel

The Many-One Tree of Cultures

I will not draw a conclusion here; I will merely try and round off this volume, giving you a bit of further context about what can be meant by *unity in diversity*, or respectively, *the Many-One*. Mark that I permit myself to take up on a number of points I already touched on in my "Human Beings on This Planet" essay, because not everyone will be able to work their way through that chapter with its natural-philosophy issues that demand quite some science-related educational background, people who therefore would miss points that I think are key. Therefore the present chapter has some (but not much), say, redundancy relative to the "Human Beings on This Planet" chapter. On the other hand, it puts many-one thinking much more into what I think is its sociocultural-historical context: its roots in a postmodern subculture/counterculture whose phase of defiance, as it were, many-one thinking tries to grow out of.

While usually the editor of an anthology has to keep his particular ideas out of a general introduction, or in the present case, "outroduction," the many-one approach is so novel, and the special approaches so diverse, that I permit myself to risk some framing which is quite novel in itself. Indeed, it matters to me to avoid misunderstandings due to accepted paths whereas many-one thinking tries new ways relative to markedly postmodernist approaches.

Of course, it tries to preserve the best of postmodern and green thinking, so not nearly everything is novel, many-one thinking also sharing a great deal with related *post*-postmodern approaches that lack the explicit many-one approach. I already mentioned the idea of a cosmic evolution

1. Translated and revised by the author.

throughout which matter, life, culture, and persons do not just follow each other, but build upon one another and belong together. What isn't new either is the hope that the civilizational and intellectual and humane and spiritual development on this planet doesn't have to run out with the current enmity and logjam between traditional culture, modernist culture, and what for convenience I will call *green, postmodernist* or *alternative* culture. If this culture-war blockade *à l'américaine* persists, it's not hard to predict a disoriented and disintegrating late modernity stumbling into ecological collapse. Many-one thinking tries to find ways towards a new level of civilization comprising many essential and precious things from each of the cultures now at war.

The variety and distinctiveness and interplay of life-forms, cultures, and persons is crucial. The many-one idea of evolution or development or progress is a bit like the growing branches and twigs of a tree. More, by the way, than it resembles the confluence of ditches and rivers into the one sea, since we are talking about evolution on this planet, where persons live in a great variety of cultures, nations, and economies, embedded in a physical environment of landscapes and "cityscapes," climate zones and economic areas. Given all the entities and phenomena, the complex coherence and balance, but also the instability and the "maze" we experience on Earth, can we even imagine all of it somehow flowing together?

Since this book is not only about spirituality but also about our civilizational-ecological prospects, one has to observe the facts of the history of humankind, of planet Earth, and of the universe. Again and again, geological catastrophes like earthquakes, floods, volcanic eruptions, or ice ages, have led to mass extinctions, leading in turn to new boosts of evolution of species and ecosystems. Has this dynamic ever stopped, and is there a chance it will, with the ecological and even geological impact we humans have made and are making on our planet? Today, some seem to talk quite relaxedly about the "overuse of natural resources" or "climate change." But what is ahead of us is not a steady, tranquil stream, let alone a flowing together, dissolving in the one sea. Even though for many subsystems and details we can't tell what we are currently doing to this planet, it is clear that there will be a major mass extinctions of species (major even in the billions of years of Earth's history) and more frequent and violent calamities; there will be growing general weather stress for big parts of humanity, with great problems for agriculture and for supplying the basic needs of billions of people. And there will have to be a huge, strenuous effort to swiftly transform our working, building and consuming from modern sprawl and overrun of nature toward a ripening, sustainable economy, which is carefully tending our place inside the biosphere, trying to slow and heal some of the damage already done. If this is not supposed to be mere wishful thinking, we will need to start re-thinking and rebuilding at once, and for the rest of this century and beyond, this will absorb a bulk of our work and technology and exchanges and use of goods and services, of our political, social, and intellectual energies.

The cultural and worldview development we are talking about here can only spring from such a strain on all our forces, from a permanent crisis management, and from fighting against decay and conflict and violence and selfishness. Maybe it's only under such severe circumstances that the ecological, social, and political companionship of everyone on Earth can form—at least in the minds of many. For them, this will also mean a growing awareness of what we are in this world, as living, mental, and spiritual beings. Yet, many-one thinking is also practical; in fact it is more practical and also in a large sense more political than the many worldviews with a more idealistic or transcendent or psychological emphasis. To be practical means, among other things, learning to accept one another as being different, to take each other as we are, to get it together as best we can, with all the inevitable differences and tensions.

Among the civilizations of human history, the post–World War II Western world, mainly informed by modern and to a lesser extent by green-postmodern life realities and mindsets, has developed furthest beyond thinking in terms of Us and Them, beyond the terms of clan, of shared tradition, of fellow citizens or insiders—a thinking that often keeps us from cultivating the awareness of our common human fate, which the escalating eco-crisis forces upon us so clearly. Thus the Western world has the best starting point to make something of the whole-system crisis while other parts of the world are affected by the crisis in much worse ways. The Western world therefore has the best opportunity and at the same time the main responsibility, having caused and let slide and finally let escalate, in its blind craving for more and more, a crisis which since the 1970s was perfectly foreseeable. Now we hit physical and biological and technical frontiers. The saying *After us, the flood!* (*Après nous, le déluge!*), with climate change has received a literal meaning in addition to the figurative one.

And, by the way, it is also the Western world which has the most to lose, not only in terms of comfort and abundance, but also in terms of humane standards; in terms of healthcare, housing, and the workplace; in terms of social security and safety from violence. The crisis is tangible, existential: not only because it brings the threat of natural disaster and social disruption right into the well-to-do quarters of European and North American cities, but also because it causes migrations that will destroy the Western middle-class market democracies unless they forgo much of their deceptively favorable consumption and convenience, unless they simply give for free much of their work and knowhow to peoples who are poorer and more affected by the ecological crisis. Mentalities will have to change a lot and quickly indeed, but swift changes in mentalities and resolute politics are possible, at least thinkable—as soon as the less idealistic and solidary are no longer able to hide from the fact that their own life quality, those of their people and nation, and the very future of their children are at stake. This would be a very concrete unity in diversity indeed, an evolution and integration concerning the *ways* we live on this planet.

Another emphasis of this book is the unity-in-diversity of our *views* about the world, the idea of ultimate reality itself being many-one in essence, as the spirit or stuff or Divinity or wholeness which spirituality and religion on the one hand and metaphysics on the other are both about (that is, the philosophy of "the most basic basics"). There are, I think, several core many-one ideas quite novel in the history of philosophy and theology. One of them is the refusal of reductionism. In many-one thinking, unlike in most worldviews present and past, the cosmos in all its variety and complexity is not and cannot be reduced to some ultimate unity without ultimate diversity, a unity which typically has been thought of as the one material or spiritual "stuff," the one transcendent God, or the one world formula. Nor is the cosmos reduced to some form of dualism, for example spirit versus matter. And it is not reduced to some plurality lacking an underlying ultimate unity either: be it strictly individual physical objects or life-forms or cultural enactions or consumer-citizens or whatever. Only once we give up trying to reduce diversity to unity or unity to diversity will we get the many-one cosmos, the coherence-in-complexity of unique things and beings and persons, and only then do we get what many call "emergence," the perpetual branching out of our cosmic tree into limbs and blooms of ever-new kinds and individuals.

Raving like this, it is a great temptation to paint an all-too-lyrical picture of the social, spiritual, ecological, and personal maturation for all humankind on this planet: the divine tree with all its branches, the unique ecosystems and cultures and personalities, which go on reaching toward the divine sun and enrooting themselves deeper and deeper into the divine ground.

The Tension between Our Transience and our Hopes of Deliverance

Yet our Earth is not the whole cosmos; it's only one finite celestial body, one among many. It would be a reduction too if we thought that this planet and the community of cultures and societies and persons on it can, just like

that, evolve or be transformed into a state of maturity, healing, or perfection. While the emergence and development of life and consciousness and
personhood "here below" in my view unveils a great deal of the spirit and
meaning and Divine which the whole cosmos is, it is also true that Earth
and the biosphere with our lifeworld and us individuals in it are bearing
a host of not-so-blissful system constraints, inertias, fragilities, handicaps,
and injuries—all kinds of limitations that won't let the shared tree of humankind on our planet "grow into the sky." In this growing "tree" there are
countless dead ends, detours, and difficult birthings. I can't imagine how
the life-threatening crisis of modernity we just now are experiencing can
be seen as part of a straight or steady or guided history of salvation in a
traditional way.

   This need not keep us from speculating about how humans may one
day spiritually "touch" or "reach" the One, be it in the future (on something
like the Christian Last Day), in little spiritual circles, upon our death, on the
meditation cushion, in philosophical visions of wholeness, or in an afterlife.
There are traditional religious ideas that don't fit well with our tree of living
beings and persons on this planet, whose branches in many respects are
messy, scrubby, struggling for light, withering and dying back. Still there
also may be quite diverse visions of care, not neglect, coming from God,
visions which respect the frame a natural universe sets to our hopes. My intuition is that one of the real big questions arising in this context will remain
open, indeed *is meant to remain open*, namely if human civilization on this
planet is somehow being protected from geological and cosmic and biological and autodestructive catastrophes cutting short to our humane and moral
and spiritual progress. Can humankind one day perish incidentally, for no
reason, just like that? Why should we matter to a natural universe after all;
but then again, how could a spiritual cosmos not bother? This uncertainty
and a consciousness of being so fragile is something we must live with, I
believe, and maybe is just meant to be this way. In any event, nothing in
humankind's history suggests that we are somehow nursed or protected or
spared or saved by (or from!) nature on Earth. Consider the last Ice Age,
during which we as a species developed in the last million years roughly,
with a brutal glacial maximum not even twenty thousand years ago,[2] and
with an equally dire melting and flood about ten thousand years ago.[3] The
mere hope that in the future this kind of geological event will not reappear
because of our civilization, for the sake of our further humane and spiritual
evolution, is pure speculation. Why, indeed, and then again, why not? Both

2. Wikipedia, s.v. "Last Glacial Maximum,"
3. Wikipedia, s.v. "Holocene Glacial Retreat."

is speculation, and that's why everyone is entitled to hope and have faith in the cosmos being a home and place of healing and flourishing.

Because of the modern, rational, scientific side of any serious many-one thinking this has to be a main matter of discussion—in order *to merely face* the awesome puzzle because we cannot ignore the facts of evolution and history, not in order *to settle* it. If our cosmos has a spirit of its own, how caring can "it" possibly be? That is, might it not only be caring about us, but caring for us? Sober, factual, scientific thinking has to be part of many-one thinking, as I see it. It can't be otherwise if we want to achieve a true synthesis of traditional, modern, and green-alternative mindsets. If we manage to make progress here, this will transform each of these mentalities fundamentally. Not least for green thinking, devised as alternative to traditional-modernist thinking almost by definition, this will mean a painful process of self-critique and rethinking. Indeed, mainly in the 1960s, this culture and mindset emerged as a countermovement and demarcation vis-à-vis modern exploitation and traditional bondage. Only in recent years have philosophical movements like participatory thinking, evolutionary thinking, process thinking, and integral thinking begun to move beyond this excessively black-and-white confrontation.

Elites with a Many-One Consciousness, Spiritual Leaders, Worldview Forerunners

Painful rethinking inside green-postmodern culture means acknowledging that all of a sudden quite a few things about traditional as well as modern thinking should be right in important respects, while some contrary green commonplaces appear to be one-sided and exaggerated. Most of all it will have to be accepted that large parts of humankind are "wired" traditionally and modernly, and many, likely most of them won't and can't become different kinds of persons, since their backgrounds, biographies, and life conditions are the way they are. I am sure that even in my home country of Germany, where the impacts of alternative culture can strongly be felt across all classes and milieus, large parts of the people will never become green-postmodern-minded in a strong sense.

This means there is a transcultural kind of unity in diversity which we are not just to honor, but which we must learn to welcome as a fate and responsibility. Not nearly every woman and man is markedly ambitious, gifted, or interested in social, ecological, or spiritual concerns. It is a major challenge for many-one-minded people to take the countless traditionalists and modernists around the world, take them as they are, to fight with them and for them, not in order to convert them, but instead to perform the unlikely feat of letting them be who they are, while winning them over for an economic, political, social, and ecological development which all groups, cultures, nations, and civilizations together urgently, almost desperately need.

However, this cannot come about unless larger parts of the elites in all parts of the world (that is, those who have influence, no matter where or how) evolve culturally, intellectually, and spiritually. Assuming that these kind of many-one elites will ever form, they will be a colorful bunch of people who as persons live by their values and convictions: they will be mentors and multiplicators, catalysts and activists, decision-makers and donors too—not supergurus, illuminati, or philosopher-kings. They certainly will not fit the old categories of eco-freaks or squares or yuppies; they rather will be a new generation adopting and adapting from each culture what is valuable and livable, for the sake of a humane future, human growth, and becoming more conscious about our place as human beings in the cosmos.

I would like to mention what I see as yet another field of rethinking if a many-one synthesis is meant to grow out of its origin: green ideas about personal and spiritual growth conceived as an antithesis to the traditional and modern images of how a person ought and ought not to be. *Since the spiritual outburst of the late 1960s it has been difficult for many people who see themselves as spiritual rather than traditionally religious to distinguish the view of the Divine which Southern and Eastern Asian traditions held and hold, from what the Western spiritual folk pick for themselves recombining and reinterpreting views to fit with their antitraditional and antimodernist values and convictions.* Green-postmodern culture felt the need to distance itself, in terms of religion, from traditional, theological, square, church religion, and "converted" to (mostly) Asian religion; yet it couldn't help Western-postmodernizing it in the process (for better or worse by the way). And this "Weastern" spirituality—if I may call it that—really is not good at carefully distinguishing itself from Eastern religion. The reception of the Buddhist idea of *shunyata* (ultimate reality lacking any essence of its own, often translated by *emptiness*) and of the Hindu idea of *advaita* (ultimate reality lacking any duality, often translated by *nonduality*) in postmodern spirituality is typical in this respect. In recent decades, Weastern spirituality has merged these teachings into an emptiness-nonduality kind of theology most popular within the spiritual crowd.

I already broached this religion/spirituality issue in the "Opening Remarks" chapter, and I would like to put this in a context of cultural evolution, and its strained dialectics and hopefully integration perspectives now. Who cares that Buddhism and Hinduism in the Asian countries where they are at home still are fiercely opposed about what ultimate reality is? For Buddhists and Hindus in Asia, *advaita* does not equal *shunyata*. Who cares that *advaita* thinker Shankara is in no way uncontroversial in Hindu theology, and that neither is *shunyata* thinker Nagarjuna in Buddhism? Who cares that both Buddhism and Hinduism have always been deeply traditionalist, that is, patriarchal, world-withdrawal, and pre-science religions?

John Heron, in his 1998 book *Sacred Science*, had the courage (considering the often East-glorifying psychospiritual scenes in which he was teaching and working) to point out not only Hinduism's and Buddhism's merits and attractions for theism-and-savior-weary Westerners, but also their downsides:

> The problem with both traditions is that, however much they are up-dated and brought into relation with the idiom of contemporary life, they carry the blight of world-denial from their ancient and problematic cultures. Their monism and pantheism is of the acosmic variety [. . .] They flee the Many, via meditative dissociation, to find the One [. . .] They have no adequate concept of repression, of its effects and what to do about it. They have an entirely underdeveloped relation to the social and natural worlds, having no autonomous ethics, politics, human and natural sciences. [. . .] They have no affirmative notion of the person as a spiritual presence in the world, but reduce the embodied person, without remainder, to an illusory separated self-sense composed of fear, attachment and misplaced desire. [. . .] They have an entirely authoritarian, patriarchal approach to the development of the spiritual life.[4]

There has been emancipatory progress made in West-Eastern spiritual circles since the abuses of the wild 1960s and early 1970s, yet I think it is safe to say that the often uncritical, nay, surrendering attitude towards patriarchal Eastern religions and religious figures still shows deep ambivalences in the souls of the Western spiritual folk, not few of them hiding from themselves what they can't admit: (more or less) spiritual trips of ego, domination, and submission.

We really should take this kind of problem with postmodern spirituality seriously. As many-one views, post-postmodern ones in general are evolving out of green culture and milieus; they have to become aware that the glorification of Eastern *shunyata-advaita* mysticism has to be seen in the context of this genuinely Western counterculture, which is aimed against Western-style oppression, social control, alienation, exploitation, rampant growth, which is

4. Heron, *Sacred Science*, 26.

demonizing the West—and here's the spiritual side of it: which is identifying bad Western traditionalism-modernism with the Western personal God, and therefore sanctifying Eastern traditions with an impersonal Divine. The unity-in-diversity idea of integrating green values with traditional and modern ones no longer permits for this kind of prejudice. Of course, there is a rather non-dual (in the sense of advaita-shunyata-based) option in many-one thinking, where the One, and therefore the divine Spirit, is void. Yet this nondual option can't be a many-one *posit*. There is also—and this is essential—a panentheistic option with a "not less than personal" One, this option being many-one too, possibly even better suited to reconcile spirituality and religion.

This being said, we can now get to the crucial question about how growth or development or evolution of the human person should be ap-proached in a many-one manner. Indeed, when green-postmodernist counterculture designed its anti-authoritarian spirituality as opposed to authoritarian religion, not only has it opted for an ultimately nonpersonal Divine but also for an ultimately nonpersonal person, as it were, all persons being ultimately reduced to the Not-Even-One Void Spirit. I think it is fair to say that alternative spirituality, right from the start, has been strongly influenced by the Eastern idea of overcoming one's own personhood (often called the "self" or the "ego") by becoming aware of oneself as void spirit, not as a person of her/his own. Another formative view in Western green spiri-tuality has been the idea that this nonpersonal awareness can be achieved by letting oneself be taught and guided by gurus and monks and writers who have already gotten there, who are said to be "enlightened," "realized," already "awakened" to void spirit, and who therefore live it and reveal it. In many-one thinking, however, with its complementarity of the many minds and the one spirit, spiritual growth of a person cannot mean "overcoming oneself."

Spiritual evolution, the growing care about and participation with humankind, Earth, and cosmos, in many-one thinking cannot mean glori-fying sages and saints and spiritual teachers, and in the process neglecting or abandoning one's ordinary personality. Instead, spiritual *participation* should rime with personal *individuation*. If there is some future or aim or destiny beyond ordinary life and death for us tiny beings on this huge planet, can it really be wise today to believe this would not start with ordi-nary persons becoming more and more themselves in their body and their social life and their political and ecological engagement in this late-modern world? A salvation coming from above or inside cannot just be lightly pre-supposed any more in the way theists and mystics have most often done even recently. We have to take part and therefore better feel and understand our part in the big and important and often dangerous things we are doing or at least causing collectively in the modern world, for all their mixed blessings. There is no spiritual glory or fame involved with this, most of the time.

While the One reflects itself in each of us, this reflection is never nearly complete, just because the parts are not nearly the whole. Even the spiritually or philosophically quite rare and special persons who are able to look way beyond the "early" family and personality they start with, as well as beyond their inherited culture and the horizon of their epoch, even these persons in many respects remain bounded by just these roots. It is something relatively rare during the evolution of culture and civilization that persons are so aware of open roads of development, ready for progress in terms of the political-social, in art, in spirituality, in human relationships or in philosophy, persons who are also dedicated to fostering others through their actions and talk and making and writing. These people are *creating* something out of themselves, but they are also *being created* by the evolving civilization and social background in which they grew up.

The cultural and intellectual and spiritual evolution of humankind is partly being prepared and accompanied by such persons—in so many different and related ways. Many-one thinking should have learned its lessons from modern and postmodern thought. What a spiritual teacher or writer or a philosopher produces remains the work of this special person, one work among others. It is not the immediate word, gesture, or act of the whole divine or cosmic spirit. The One expresses itself only through the many, and therefore not through any one of them, purely and encompassingly. No single worldview is independent of the character which expresses itself through it, independent of the conceptual influences which flow together in it, or independent of the special life conditions of the thinker living in the civilization which brought her or him forth. Even the very greatest among them have their limitations, even a Laozi, a Buddha, a Socrates, or a Jesus.

How to appreciate the greatness of these—in a way immortal—teachers of humankind while putting them in the historical, social, cultural, and intellectual context they belong? Many-one thought goes beyond the relativism of postmodern philosophy. Recognizing the inevitable limitations of even the rightly most influential spiritual teachers still doesn't make their role in the big evolution of humankind arbitrary or negligible. The awareness which we can reach about our place inside the One is enhanced by the creations and insights of many worldview pioneers of humanity, if only in long and difficult searching movements. Each thinker (just like each member of a thinker's audience) is only one among the twigs and branches in the tree of cosmic-cultural evolution. And as the saying goes, "not everything grows on one branch."

The *Many* Contexts, Justifications, Authorities, and Ambitions—inside the *One* Truth

The questions as to how much of the one cosmos, spirit, or God can manifest itself in one person and its worldview of course touch the divine importance billions of people attribute especially to Jesus and Buddha. It is clear that Jesus of Nazareth was way ahead of his culture and era, in many respects. However, looking critically at what John the Evangelist and Paul of Tarsus and the early Christian thinkers known as "the Church Fathers" contributed to the Bible and the basic tenets of Christian theology, it is hard to deny that they have added some views of their own to the person of Jesus, and to who he himself thought he was—especially regarding his status as *the* God-and-Man-in-one savior of humankind. Something similar is true of Buddha as well, to whose teachings notably Nagarjuna and Zen have added some of their own views, quite drastically changing the meaning of salvation as compared with the views attributed to the historical person Siddhartha Gautama aka "Buddha" himself. In any case, Jesus and Buddha cannot both at once have the unique importance for humankind which their respective believers think they have; this much seems obvious. Many-one thinking is polar and complementary, which likely is incompatible with a complete manifestation of the One in any of the Many, and even more the manifestation of the One in *just one* of the Many.

One of the concerns of this book is to incite holders of postmodern-spiritual ideas inspired by Madhyamaka Buddhism and Vedanta Hinduism ("emptiness" or "nonduality"), to incite holders of traditional Christian ideas ("the personal God" or "souls"), and to incite holders of naturalistic-modern ideas to deal with one another, instead of at best ignoring the ideas of others or at worst trying to reduce these ideas in light of one's own ideas. The extent to which one does or doesn't play this reduction game is a pretty good test for which worldviews in practice stand in the way of unity-in-diversity, notwithstanding routinely used unity rhetoric. The decisive questions are of the following kind: Do you present your own views as obvious, and other views as absurd, meaningless, unnatural, confused, or illusory? Do you omit or discount views which speak against yours? Do you discuss ideas different from yours in a simplistic or distorted or downright false way—that is, not the way they were set out and justified in the first place?

Inside green-postmodern spirituality, the vice of the pseudo-obvious and the pseudo-absurd is ever present—for example in the Zen worldview which goes so far as to deny it is a worldview, and doesn't understand that it can't help being one. Or the already mentioned emptiness-nondual assumption according to which the Divine can only be beyond any quality, even beyond being aware of itself, or caring about beings. What makes the situation even more difficult is a widespread confusion due to the ambiguity of the notion of "nonduality." By this notion some mean *no ultimate dualisms*—that is, no ultimate splits or antagonisms, which I think is a consensus among evolutionary approaches; while others mean *no ultimate dualities*— that is, not even polarities and complementarities! If taken in this latter sense, nondual thinking would be the very opposite of many-one thinking, the Many-One being polar and complementing *by definition*. What's more, this many-one duality is precisely not a dualism, and is nondual(istic) in that sense. As in all philosophical pseudodissensions about what some notion "obviously means," when really it is a matter of definition, we should just be clear with one another. Do I see the One, the cosmic Spirit, Life, or God rather as "void" and unpersonal, rather as "full" and personal, or maybe as something in between? Let us try to get the differences and commonalities right, instead of doing foolish things like accusing others that they "just don't get nonduality." Indeed, let us try and get at the nuances, the interplay, to get beyond the pseudo-absurd and the pseudo-obvious.

What do you mean? This was one of the two inquiry maxims that one of my philosophy teachers, back in the '90s at Munich University, asked us students to heed. The other one was: *How do you know?* Everyone of us co-authors, I think, is aware that it needs explaining why some spiritual teacher from any ancient or medieval or modern civilization should have such an overwhelming meaning for all humans of all epochs and civilizations, as Christians and Buddhists believe their respective founders have. Correspondingly, if a group of thinkers loosely tied together by their common "many-one" concern, like the ones in this anthology, claims to explain more fully than the ancient teachers and masters what our mixed traditional-modern-postmodern civilization is and how it might evolve into something more promising, then they too will have to justify this kind of ambition. What seems clear to me is that it's precisely today's mixture of traditional values, modern reason, and alternative humanism which opens insights which Jesus or Buddha or any spiritual teacher of premodern times could not possibly have had. Furthermore, we are trying to make an evolutionary step beyond broken and helpless modernity, beyond a war of cultures and a nature crisis which seems in many respects to be beyond any wisdom from the past. How, indeed, can the enormous authority attributed to Buddha and Jesus do justice to the sheer mass and diversity of humankind today, to the complexity of modern civilization, and to the dimensions of the changes it needs in order to survive?

We won't be able to address nearly all the assumptions especially of green spirituality and/or traditional religion, which have to be reconsidered and rediscussed. None of them, however, are meant to be devalued: neither the importance of revelation scriptures, traditions, or confessions; nor the importance of their founding figures; nor the importance of meditation. Yet if all of this is to be seen in the context of its time and culture and personnel, then we must finally begin to put it in the context of the whole history and complexity of humankind—a staggering challenge that has to live up to its own cautiously encompassing ambition in the first place.

In philosophy a claim to absoluteness, whether explicit or implied, is to a certain extent inevitable. Even relativism, for instance, can't avoid setting itself up as absolute. If relativists were consequential enough to say that their relativism holds only for themselves and like-minded persons, then why should other people bother or feel concerned? And whoever claims to set everything other people say in its appropriate limited context obviously needs a larger context to justify why and how they think they are entitled to do so. However, such an absoluteness in philosophy should confine itself to very careful and broad claims. That's how I see many-one thought anyway. It only can yield the broadest framework, and a style and ethos of philosophizing.

Philosophers or spiritual teachers who believe they can build a strict, full-blown, self-contained theory will have to justify why they think they can tell so precisely (or how the persons they got their teachings from knew so precisely). We know so little, and with so little precision and certainty and comprehensiveness, about death or matter or our own human mind for instance, and that's just why philosophers are entitled to make "educated guesses," that is, to speculate within reasonable limits. Yet if we do, we have to explain and discuss properly. And this is something prevented by the ego- and groupthink-driven splits, ironically even inside the evolutionary-integral worldview scene itself for example, whose spokespersons often are *not willing* to speak with one another—if they take notice and bother about each other at all.

These philosophical splits, which usually are mutual disregard, are made even worse by the splits that divide the Western world into language areas and nations whose elites are unable even to properly talk about deep worldview issues. The present anthology makes only one hesitating early step towards a unity-in-diversity also across language gaps. It was published in German in 2019, and may be published in French in the not too distant future. However, this group of coauthors comprises not only one Austrian, one Canadian, one Englishman, one Spaniard, and two Germans . . . but four American men and women. That's why I would like to make some remarks about the dominance of US thinkers in worldviews related to many-one thinking, which is to do with the emergence and history of this kind of thought mostly in the United States.

The Recent History of Transpersonal Psychology, Integral Philosophy, and Cosmic-Evolutionary Thought

In order to better understand our many-one planet we need to bear in mind and accept the limits of languages and culture regions, like the "Anglosphere." The USA is a cultural area closely related to the Europe but is also politically, culturally, and intellectually very different from European civilization. Europeans—and I can speak of Germans firsthand—often naively receive and adopt spiritual literature from across the Atlantic like some kind of pure, unmediated revelation, degrading themselves to something like a spiritual province, almost a colony, yet without understanding much about the limitations and downsides of American language and culture and mentalities. Two huge problems for and with Americans are the lack of self-critical judgment, and too much focus on self-assertion and sales.

I would not have invited so many Americans to this project if this nation of extremes had not also some of the best, standing for the very opposite of its vices. However, "Asian-American" spiritual literature pretending to be able to single-handedly explain the mystic traditions, the Divine, and the order of things has become a problem in Western nations, not least in Germany where the US is often demonized as the "bad" America and sometimes also glorified as the "good" America. There is an enormous naiveté about the philosophical-spiritual USA, which is also often oblivious to the great European intellectual and critical tradition. We ought to start balancing better the strengths of American thinking, the European history of humanities and intellectual tradition, and ancient Asian mysticism and the philosophies associated with it.

Many-one thought (especially its evolutionary part) was pioneered by Western and Eastern thinkers like Gotthold Ephraim Lessing,[5] Georg Wilhelm Friedrich Hegel, and Jean Gebser.[6] Later on, in two big boosts, the first one around 1970, and a second since the mid-1990s, it has been advanced by for the most part US thinkers: most prominently by Abraham Maslow, Clare Graves, Ken Wilber, and the team of Don Beck and Christopher Cowan. The influence of transpersonal psychology has been most important in this process, a movement which Maslow (together with Stanislav Grof, Michael Washburn, and others) had evolved from humanistic psychology since the

5. Lessing, *Education.*
6. Wikipedia, s.v. "Jean Gebser."

end of the 1960s.[7] Sociologist Clare Graves's ideas, which he developed in the 1970s,[8] and upon which Beck's and Cowan's mid-1990s theory called *Spiral Dynamics*[9] is based, were greatly influenced by Maslow too. And Ken Wilber had been the "rising star" of transpersonal psychology for many years, since the mid-1970s,[10] before he broke the mold in the mid-1990s—after transpersonal psychology had resisted[11] letting itself be integrated in Wilber's (then new) Integral Theory.[12]

7. For a *Brief History of Transpersonal Psychology* see Grof, *Brief.*

8. For a very good introduction into Graves's so-called ECLET model, see "Graves's Levels," Wikipedia Foundation; the prices for even used copies of the rare book *The Never Ending Quest,* with Graves's key writings around his model, edited by one of Graves's disciples, late Christopher Cowan, and his wife Natasha Todorovic, probably are prohibitive for most people.

9. This was not only to become the name of the movement emerging out of Graves's model, but also was the title of the book by Graves's disciples Don Beck and Christopher Cowan that started this movement in 1996. For more about Spiral Dynamics, as well as its delicate relations with Wilber's Integral Theory, see for instance Wikipedia, s.v. "Spiral Dynamics."

10. Starting around 1975 with *The Spectrum of Consciousness,* originally a paper published in Journal of Transpersonal Psychology, 1975, Vol. 7, No.2 (retrievable at https://www.atpweb.org/jtparchive/trps-07-75-02-105.pdf), a paper which subsequently became a bestselling and long-selling book.

11. See Ferrer, *Revisioning,* Heron, *Way Out,* and Heron, *Way Out Further.* Heron's first essay initiated a crossing of swords with Ken Wilber, who replied with the essay Wilber, *Response to Heron,* upon which Heron responded with *Way out Further . . .* whereupon Ken Wilber offered kind of a draw, that Heron accepted.

12. Integral Theory (Wilber) proper began with his 1995 bestseller *Sex, Ecology, Spirituality.* While Wilber came from the peer-to-peer transpersonal community, the Integral community turned out to be much more of a master-and-chosen-disciples-and-gratefully-receptive-audience endeavor, much of it ambitious and inspired and interesting, albeit in no way a (self-)critical peer-scholars community any more. There have been serious and impressive attempts to lift the Integral community to such a peer-academics status, for instance by Bruce Alderman, Sean Esbjörn-Hargens and others with their project of a "Complex Integral Realism," trying to treat the teachings of Wilber, Roy Bhaskar and Edgar Morin on par, as co-including approaches (documented in Alderman, *In-Dwelling,* and in Bhaskar et al., *Metatheory*), but in my opinion they have changed too little about Wilberian Integral. Why? To be sure, it would be an illusion to require that in a peer-to-peer community there must be no *spiritus rector*; in fact, in most of them, there are even several strong *spiritus rectores . . .* indeed it seems that there *have to be* several such leaders, and that these must have a strong peer ethos, preventing them from abusing their influence. And in both process thought and transpersonal psychology this seems to have worked. By contrast, right from the start, Ken Wilber had problems suffering any genuine peers besides him in "his" Integral community, and the way he tried to control the conditions for him to be criticized is a disconcerting example indeed for almost anti-peer-to-peer behavior: see Ferrer, *Reflections on Ken Wilber,* Wilber, *Suggestion for Readings the Criticisms of my Work,* Edwards, *Some Comments to Ken's Message,* or Wilber, *Reply to Edwards.* The

Jorge Ferrer and John Heron, who have contributed to the present volume, have both played a role in the self-preserving of genuine transpersonal ideas of an out-branching participation-individuation throughout history, as opposed to Wilber's idea of a cosmic-spiritual convergence toward nonduality,[13] as he interprets it, which is *no ultimate dualities*:

> But the Ultimate is different, precisely because it is not different from anything. It is the only "referent" that has that quality (although that quality, too, is formally denied to it). The reason is that any mental concept makes sense only in terms of its opposite (spirit versus matter, form vs. formless, light versus dark, infinite versus finite, conscious versus unconscious, etc.). But

---

power dynamics of one "strongman" defining and founding and trying to control the debate in a community just seems to make it hard if not impossible to do science and humanities proper. There are serious problems of scientific and personal ethos here. I also see a problem of distorting-misleading inclusivism with Ken Wilber's Integral. Indeed I feel that he has done a disservice to the potential of his ideas as *one among several* post-postmodern spiritual-philosophical approaches, by the unsubtle, inadequate way he tried to include *any* approach into his own. The place he concedes to the God of theistic and post-theistic religion in his system of spiritual evolution, which in short is a premodern, *mythic-traditional* place, shows that Wilber didn't know or bother enough about Western philosophy and theology in order to do them justice. The Western philosophical concepts of mind and personhood (comprising intentionality, reflexivity, agency, responsibility as basics) and the theological concepts around a not-less-than-personal Divine are little to do with mythology proper (Jehovah and the Christ, the Buddha and the Buddha Nature, and Brahma-Shiva-Vishnu arguably are all partly myth-narrative, partly theology); in fact, the Western intuitions and speculations around qualities of Ultimate Reality to do with the mind and personhood are just as serious and respectable as Wilber's emptiness/nonduality conception of the Ultimate, and his pretty broad-brush views about stages of civilizational-cultural evolution, which is conceived as an evolution of God-views too. If however the complexity of the ways people imagine, feel, and understand Ultimate Reality are forced into simplistic schemes, they can only be distorted and reduced to something different.

13. Trying not to go beyond the scope of this volume here, let me just mention that Wilber combines his Emptiness/Nonduality view of the Divine with an ontology-epistemology which I will call *holonism*, positing a hierarchy of *holons*, that is, whole-parts of all kinds, each embedded in superior holons as well as embedding inferior ones, a "holarchy" (holonic hierarchy) infinite both upwards and downwards, with all the holons being perspectives of Wilber's ultimate Emptiness/Nonduality looking at its other perspectives (for details see Wilber, *Sex, Ecology, Spirituality*). This holonism is not the same as a many-one *cosmic holism*. To be sure, cosmic holism too has the idea of major stages of emergence in cosmic evolution, but it tries to keeps things down to earth, quite literally, settling for living beings emerging from insensate matter, persons from sentient beings, for their lives inside planetary ecologies and mental-spiritual relation(ship)s with a cosmic wholeness not separate but of course hugely different from the systems and beings it encompasses, in its dimensions and complexity as well as all-presence. Different approaches . . .

ultimate Nonduality has no opposite, and thus no concept can accurately represent it *in principle* (including that one).[14]

Heron and Ferrer didn't believe in a predestined spiritual aim and end for any genuine spiritual development. They were not prepared to abandon the ramifying tree of individuation-participation, with an *ultimately real* distinction-nonseparation between the individuating Many, and the One they are all participating in. Moreover, they could not find[15] this idea consistently shared by all major mystical traditions, as Ken Wilber believes it is, suggestively talking about *the Great Traditions*.[16]

Many-one thinking goes beyond standard transpersonal psychology in several respects, and John Heron was a pioneer, maybe *the* pioneer of this still novel way of thought. Not only was he a transpersonal teacher and facilitator for decades, but as I already pointed out, with his book *Feeling and Personhood*, way back in the early 1990s, he managed to sketch, almost in passing, a metaphysics which then he called "one-many" thinking.

As I said before, I prefer using the notion "many-one," so I can better refer not just to John Heron's seminal ideas but also to independent if related approaches. "Many-one" allows an embrace of quite different approaches like the ones gathered in this book, ranging from cosmic holism through evolutionary spirituality and integral philosophy to transpersonal/participatory thinking and panentheism. And there are certainly more—actually process thought, for instance. Yet, the many-one framework is so very broad because it doesn't start from a markedly religious premise about the Divine, not even a panentheistic one. Ferrer's view for instance clearly is many-one, but not panentheistic, his *Mystery* certainly not being a God in any usual religious or spiritual sense. Many-one thinking just assumes *some kind of* ultimate Unity-Duality-Plurality. No more, no less. Being holistic, polar, and plural at once, it precludes one-sided reductions, that is, the many monisms, dualisms, or pluralisms (in the strict sense of *ultimately just plurality*) which make up most philosophies, ancient and modern.

14. Wilber, *Integral Semiotics*, 32–33. This essay is excellent as a short introduction into Wilber's "neo-Nagarjunian" Emptiness . . . and it shows the serious risk of self-defeat that this approach runs.

15. See Ferrer, *Revisioning*, 103–5.

16. He proclaims it in the very title and subtitle of his 2017 book *Religion of Tomorrow: A Vision for the Future of the Great Traditions*.

Many-One Exchange between the US and Europe

This book, let me emphasize it once more, is also about the unity-in-diversity in the Western world. US psychologists, philosophers, sociologists, theologians, and "freelance" spiritual writers have made important steps for the West as a whole, in terms of a worldview of cosmic-cultural evolution. At the same time, the United States has recently set new standards in terms of profiteering, warring cultures, the decay of democracy, and war against nature. May Old Europe, which owes much to America, help it change its ways and views, setting an example of how to defend and evolve values which, as yet, are stronger in Europe, less corrupted by the rule of money and ambition for power and fame.

Why should this matter on both sides of the Atlantic? There is no doubt that the prospects of our common civilization are grim unless the two major cores of the West, which are the US and the European Union (and here again it won't work without France and Germany working together) join to initiate a fundamental system change. Of course, without or against China, the ecological rebuild of world economy won't be possible, but if the old middle-class, consumer, nature-exploiter, and technology superpowers Europe and the USA won't instigate it . . . it won't come from China alone. The whole-system change we need will fail without a rethinking (what is often called a paradigm shift) which must begin in the Western world.

We are still far from a true exchange about culture-evolutionary, participatory, panentheistic, integral, and related worldviews inside the West, not just a one-way flow coming from America, but also streaming back from Europe, which is divided not least due to language barriers. Not only would thinkers all over the Western world have to be willing and able to talk; the still tiny circles aware of these new ideas also would have to learn to read and write English well enough so that exchange of ideas could flow back and forth between Western nations, say, more or less effortlessly. English has already become, irrevocably I believe, the only possible lingua franca for future global philosophical and spiritual calls for unity in diversity. Unless Europeans and others adapt, philosophy and spiritual writing with worldwide resonance will more and more become a US-American monopoly, with the few exceptions in philosophy at large, such as Jürgen Habermas, Bruno Latour, Edgar Morin, or Peter Sloterdijk—exceptions confirming what is the rule.

To date, concerning many-one-related approaches, not much has come from the major nations of thinkers and intellectuals that France and Germany used to be; although some has come from Scandinavia, notably an approach called metamodern.[17] Just imagine an anthology like the present one, but with contributions also by French-writing or Swedish-writing authors, appearing in English-, French-, German-, and Swedish-language editions, finding an audience in all of these language spheres. This would only be a tiny first step, yet as things stand, this would be a sensation. That is to say how much many-one thinking as a common Western endeavor still is in its most tender fledgling age.

Bibliography

Alderman, Bruce. "Integral In-Dwelling: A Prepositional Theology of Religions." *CONSCIOUSNESS: Ideas and Research for the Twenty-First Century* 4.4 (2016). https://digitalcommons.ciis.edu/conscjournal/vol4/iss4/2/.

Bhaskar, Roy, et al., eds. *Metatheory for the Twenty-First Century: Critical Realism and Integral Theory in Dialogue*. Ontological Explorations. Abingdon, UK: Routledge, 2015.

Beck, Don Edward, and Christopher C. Cowan. *Spiral Dynamics: Mastering Values, Leadership, and Change*. Business Book Summary. Hoboken, NJ: Wiley-Blackwell, 1996.

Cowan, Christopher C., and Natasha Todorovic, eds. *The Never Ending Quest: Dr. Clare W. Graves Explores Human Nature*. Santa Barbara: ECLECT, 2005.

Edwards, Mark. "Some Comments on Ken's Message to the Readers of Critical Essays on the 'World of Ken Wilber' Site." *Integral World* (website). https://www.integralworld.net/edwards20.html/.

Ferrer, Jorge N. "Reflections on Wilber from a Participatory Perspective." *Integral World: Exploring Theories of Everything* (website). https://www.integralworld.net/ferrer4.html/.

———. *Revisioning Transpersonal Theory: A Participatory Vision of Human Spirituality*. SUNY Series in Transpersonal and Humanistic Psychology. Albany: State University of New York Press, 2002.

Freinacht, Hanzi. *The Listening Society*. Metamodern Guide to Politics 1. Lund: Metamoderna, 2017.

Grof, Stanislav. "A Brief History of Transpersonal Psychology." *International Journal of Transpersonal Studies* 27 (2008) 46–54. https://citeseerx.ist.psu.edu/document?repid=rep1&type=pdf&doi=61a4145050aa834da4a92710818e4b447689d124#page=51/.

Heron, John. *Feeling and Personhood: Psychology in Another Key*. London: Sage, 1992.

———. *Sacred Science: Person-Centred Inquiry into the Spiritual and the Subtle*. Ross-on-Wye, UK: PCCS, 1998.

———. "A Way Out for Wilberians." *Integral World: Exploring Theories of Everything* (website). https://www.integralworld.net/WilbErrs.htm/.

———. "Way Out Further." *Integral World: Exploring Theories of Everything* (website). https://www.integralworld.net/further.html/.

---

17. See Freinacht, *Listening Society*.

Lessing, Gotthold E. *The Education of the Human Race*. Internet Modern History Sourcebook (series of websites). https://sourcebooks.fordham.edu/mod/1778lessing-education.asp/. •

Wilber, Ken. "Ken Wilber's Response to John Heron." *Integral World: Exploring Theories of Everything* (website). https://www.integralworld.net/heron.html/.

———. "Integral Semiotics." http://integral-life-home.s3.amazonaws.com/Ken%20Wilber%20-%20Integral%20Semiotics.pdf?fbclid=IwAR1asaCS3YiPpa8LgAuCBjZfXrRZ9FwqatV1LNTJtUzRLhlLWpolFJEW7h4/.

———. *Religion of Tomorrow: A Vision for the Future of the Great Traditions—More Inclusive, More Comprehensive, More Complete*. Boulder, CO: Shambhala, 2017.

———. "Reply to Edwards." *Integral World: Exploring Theories of Everything* (website). https://www.integralworld.net/wilber.html/.

———. *Sex, Ecology, Spirituality: The Spirit of Evolution*. Boston: Shambhala, 1995.

———. "A Suggestion for Reading the Criticisms of my Work on Frank Visser's 'World of Ken Wilber' Site." https://www.integralworld.net/wilber_wokw.html/.

———. *The Spectrum of Consciousness*. Wheaton, IL: Quest, 1977.

Wikipedia, s.v. "Graves's emergent cyclical levels of existence." https://en.wikipedia.org/wiki/Graves%27s_emergent_cyclical_levels_of_existence/.

———, s.v. "Holocene Glacial Retreat." Wikipedia Foundation, last modified 3 Jan 2023. https://en.wikipedia.org/wiki/Holocene_glacial_retreat/.

———, s.v. "Jean Gebser." https://en.wikipedia.org/wiki/Jean_Gebser/.

———, s.v. "Last Glacial Maximum." https://en.wikipedia.org/wiki/Last_Glacial_Maximum/.

———, s.v. "Spiral Dynamics" https://en.wikipedia.org/wiki/Spiral_Dynamics#Beck's_%22Spiral_Dynamics_integral%22_(SDi)/.